Interpreting Musical Ges

MUSICAL MEANING AND INTERPRETATION
Robert S. Hatten, editor

ROBERT S. HATTEN

Interpreting Musical Gestures, Topics, and Tropes

Mozart, Beethoven, Schubert

INDIANA UNIVERSITY PRESS
Bloomington and Indianapolis

This book is a publication of

Indiana University Press
Office of Scholarly Publishing
Herman B Wells Library 350
1320 East 10th Street
Bloomington, Indiana 47405 USA

iupress.indiana.edu

First paperback edition 2017
© 2004 by Robert S. Hatten

The paper used in this publication meets the minimum requirements of
the American National Standard for Information Sciences—Permanence
of Paper for Printed Library Materials, ANSI Z39.48-1992.

Manufactured in the United States of America

The Library of Congress has cataloged the original edition as follows:

Hatten, Robert S.
Interpreting musical gestures, topics, and tropes : Mozart, Beethoven, Schubert / Robert S. Hatten.
p. cm. — (Musical meaning and interpretation)
Includes bibliographical references and index.
ISBN 0-253-34459-X (cloth : alk. paper)
1. Music—Semiotics. 2. Mozart, Wolfgang Amadeus, 1756–1791—
    Criticism and interpretation. 3. Beethoven,
Ludwig van, 1770–1827—Criticism and interpretation. 4. Schubert,
    Franz, 1797–1828—Criticism and interpretation.
I. Title. II. Series.
ML3845.H35 2004
781'.1—dc22

2004008468

ISBN 978-0-253-03007-8 (pbk)
ISBN 978-0-253-03027-6 (ebook)

1 2 3 4 5 22 21 20 19 18 17

Contents

Acknowledgments   vii
Introduction   1

PART ONE: MARKEDNESS, TOPICS, AND TROPES

1. Semiotic Grounding in Markedness and Style: Interpreting a Style Type in the Opening of Beethoven's *Ghost* Trio, Op. 70, no. 1   21

2. Expressive Doubling, Topics, Tropes, and Shifts in Level of Discourse: Interpreting the Third Movement of Beethoven's String Quartet in B♭ Major, Op. 130   35

3. From Topic to Premise and Mode: The Pastoral in Schubert's Piano Sonata in G Major, D. 894   53

4. The Troping of Topics, Genres, and Forms: Bach, Mozart, Beethoven, Schubert, Schumann, Brahms, Bruckner, Mahler   68

PART TWO: MUSICAL GESTURE

Introduction to Part Two   93

5. Foundational Principles of Human Gesture   97

6. Toward a Theory of Musical Gesture   111

7. Stylistic Types and Strategic Functions of Gestures   133

8. Thematic Gesture in Schubert: The Piano Sonatas in A Major, D. 959, and A Minor, D. 784   177

9. Thematic Gesture in Beethoven: The Sonata for Piano and Cello in C Major, Op. 102, no. 1   201

10. Gestural Troping and Agency   217

Conclusion to Part Two   233

PART THREE: CONTINUITY AND DISCONTINUITY

Introduction to Part Three   237

11. From Gestural Continuity to Continuity as Premise   239

12. Discontinuity and Beyond   267

Conclusion   287
Notes   291
Bibliography   323
Index of Names and Works   339
Index of Concepts   347

Acknowledgments

I must begin by thanking Gayle Sherwood, music editor at Indiana University Press, for her help in launching the series "Musical Meaning and Interpretation." Her wisdom and encouragement have been instrumental in shaping the series. I am also grateful for her constant support during work on my own manuscript.

For the inspiration to write about musical gesture I am indebted to two dear friends, Alexandra Pierce and David Lidov, whose pedagogical and theoretical work on gesture has been pathbreaking and personally revelatory. Besides their contributions as music theorists, Alexandra and David are also composers and pianists, and their compositions and performances reveal deep insight into the expressive and structural significance of musical gesture. Leonard Ratner's introduction to Classical topics and Wendy Allanbrook's analysis of the rhythmic gestures of those topics in Mozart were early and profound influences. More recently, my friend Raymond Monelle has brought greater historical and cultural awareness to the conceptualization and interpretation of topics. I regret not having more opportunity to exchange ideas on gesture and subjectivity with the late Naomi Cumming, a friend who graced this world too briefly. She left a body of work filled with her durable spirit and philosophical discernment. For the countless others whose work I found relevant to this study, I must defer acknowledgment to the notes. Gesture is everyone's concern, and in sketching a prolegomenon to a theory of gesture, I must also acknowledge that it was not possible to credit every inflection this common word has acquired from music scholars and performers past and present.

I am deeply grateful for close readings of the complete manuscript by both Patrick McCreless (chair of the Yale University Department of Music) and William Kinderman (chair of the Division of Musicology at the University of Illinois at Urbana-Champaign). Tamara Balter, my doctoral student at Indiana University, read the complete manuscript and offered valuable insights. Al Frantz, concert pianist and former student of mine at Penn State University, read and suggested improvements to Chapter 7. I am grateful to the faculty and students at the many universities and international conferences where I have presented portions of the book. Their reactions and comments have kept my mind and ears open.

Progress on the book was facilitated by two sabbaticals, one at Penn State University (fall 1995–spring 1996) and the other at Indiana University (fall 2002), and faculty research grants at both institutions. In addition, a generous publication subvention from the Society for Music Theory supported the setting of musical examples. I am deeply appreciative of these many forms of support.

Ken Froelich, doctoral student in composition at Indiana University, set the majority of the musical examples, and beautifully so. It was a pleasure to work with him.

I would like to dedicate this book to the memory of Erkalene McCormack Ousley, inspiring piano teacher and dearest of family friends for over thirty years. She taught me throughout my high school years to love classical music in all its forms, and her positive influence transformed my life.

Earlier versions of portions of this book have appeared in the following journals and collections, to which I am most grateful:

Part of the Introduction and part of Chapter 9: "The Expressiveness of Structure and the Structuring of Expression: Gesture, Style, and Form in Later Beethoven," in *Beethoven: Studien und Interpretationen,* ed. Mieczysław Tomaszewski and Magdalena Chrenkoff (Kraków: Akademia Muzyczna, 2000), 43–51 (invited paper, international symposium, "Beethoven: Structure and Expression," Akademia Muzyczna, Kraków, 1998).

Chapter 1: "The Opening Theme of Beethoven's 'Ghost' Trio: A Discourse in Semiotic Method," *Applied Semiotics/Sémiotique appliquée* 4 (1997), 191–200. URL: http://www.chass.utoronto.ca:8080/french/as-sa/ASSA-No4/index.htm. (invited paper, special issue on "The Semiotics of Music: From Stylistics to Semantics," guest-edited by Eero Tarasti).

Chapter 2: "Plenitude as Fulfillment: The Third Movement of Beethoven's Quartet in B♭, Op. 130," to appear in *The String Quartets of Beethoven,* ed. William Kinderman (Urbana: University of Illinois Press) (invited paper, international symposium on the Beethoven String Quartets, University of Victoria, Canada, 2000).

Chapter 3: "Schubert's *Pastoral:* The Piano Sonata in G Major, D894," in *Schubert the Progressive: History, Performance Practice & Analysis,* ed. Brian Newbould (Aldershot, U.K.: Ashgate, 2003), 151–68 (invited paper, Leeds International Schubert Conference, 2000).

Chapter 4: "The Troping of Topics in the Symphony," in *Beethoven 2: Studien und Interpretationen,* ed. M. Tomaszewski and M. Chrenkoff (Kraków: Akademia Muzyczna, 2003), 87–110 (invited paper, international symposium, "Von Beethoven zu Mahler: Im Kreis der Grossen Sinfonik," Kraków, 2000).

Part of Chapter 8: "Schubert the Progressive: The Role of Resonance and Gesture in the Piano Sonata in A, D. 959," *Intégral* 7 (1993), 38–81. Reprinted in French in *Cahiers F. Schubert* 9 (October 1996), 9–48.

Part of Chapter 8: "Thematic Gesture, Topics, and Tropes: Grounding Expressive Interpretation in Schubert," in *Musical Semiotics Revisited,* ed. Eero Tarasti (Imatra and Helsinki: International Semiotics Institute, 2003) (*Acta Semiotica Fennica XV;* Approaches to Musical Semiotics 4), 80–91.

Parts of Chapters 6, 8, and 10: "Musical Gesture," eight lectures, Cybersemiotic Institute (ed. Paul Bouissac, University of Toronto), 1997–99. URL: http:/www.chass.utoronto.ca/epc/srb/cyber/hatout.html.

First half of Chapter 10: "Gestural Troping in Music and Its Consequences for Semiotic Theory," in *Musical Signification: Between Rhetoric and Pragmatics* (Proceedings of the Fifth International Congress on Musical Signification, Bologna,

1996), ed. Gino Stefani, Luca Marconi, and Eero Tarasti (Bologna: Clueb, 1998), 193–99.

First half of Chapter 12: "Interpreting the First Movement of Beethoven's Op. 132: The Limits of Modernist and Postmodernist Analogies," in *Beethoven 2: Studien und Interpretationen,* ed. M. Tomaszewski and M. Chrenkoff (Kraków: Akademia Muzyczna, 2003), 145–60 (invited paper, international symposium, "Beethoven und die Musik des 20. Jahrhunderts: Zeit der Apokalypse und Hoffnung," Kraków, 2001).

Second half of Chapter 12: "Beyond Topics: Interpreting the Last Movement of Beethoven's Op. 132," in *Muzyka w kontekście kultury* (Festschrift honoring Prof. Mieczysław Tomaszewski), ed. Małgorzata Janicka-Słysz, Teresa Malecka, and Krzysztof Szwajgier (Kraków: Akademia Muzyczna, 2001), 361–68. Also to appear in *Proceedings of the 7th International Congress on Musical Signification,* Imatra, Finland, June 2001.

Interpreting Musical Gestures, Topics, and Tropes

Introduction

The book you are about to read complements my first book, *Musical Meaning in Beethoven* (1994), as part of a larger inquiry into musical meaning. Those who have not read the first volume, however, will find this one self-sufficient in its explanation and application of several key concepts: markedness, style types, strategic tokens, topics, expressive genres, and tropes. The latter part of the Introduction reviews some of these ideas in a fresh context, applying them to works of Mozart and Schubert. Those more familiar with my theoretical approach may wish to skip these basic illustrations and begin with Chapter 1, a more nuanced case study that integrates interpretation (the expressive significance of a passage) and theory (the reconstruction of a style type) in a close reading of the opening of Beethoven's *Ghost* Trio, Op. 70, no. 1. Chapter 2 features a new style topic, *plenitude,* generalized from a close interpretation of the Andante of Beethoven's String Quartet, Op. 130. Another topic, the pastoral, is reconceived in Chapter 3 as a *mode* with affiliations to the literary pastoral; I demonstrate how its expressive meaning expands in Romantic works such as Schubert's Piano Sonata in G Major, D. 894. Part One concludes with Chapter 4, in which I examine the troping of topics and genres, here in a wider context ranging from Bach to Mahler.

Part Two is the core of the book, six chapters devoted to a new theory of musical gesture. Gesture is introduced from an interdisciplinary perspective in Chapter 5, developed for music in Chapters 6 and 7, applied to works of Beethoven and Schubert in Chapters 8 and 9, and related to agency and troping in Chapter 10. The approach to musical gesture addresses its synthesis of elements, its emergent expressive potential, and its role in both immediate and extended musical discourse. My interest in this area owes much to the groundbreaking work of Alexandra Pierce (1994) on movement as a means of analyzing gesture, structure, and meaning in music, and to David Lidov (1987, 1993) on the semiotic status of gesture and its importance for embodied meaning in music. The late Naomi Cumming (2000) shared my interest in gesture's synthetic and emergent aspects (including those qualitative dimensions of musical experience that are often relegated to the field of performance) and the emergence of an embodied subject in music. My approach is not that of philosophical aesthetics, as in Cumming; rather, I begin by surveying a variety of scientific studies to help ground the extraordinary role of gesture as one manifestation of an evolutionarily refined capacity to interpret significant energetic shaping through time. Human gesture may be understood as a fundamental and inescapable mode of understanding that links us directly to music's potential expressive meaning.

Having established a set of principles for human gesture, I then propose a speculative theory for musical gesture, exploring composers' negotiation of human gestures within the constraints of a musical style (including its notational and performance practices). My primary focus is on the Viennese Classical tradition, from Mozart to Beethoven and Schubert. The emergence of Romantic subjectivity is reflected in Mozart, and even more prominently in Beethoven and Schubert, but it must be emphasized that each was trained in the gestural practices of a more Classical tradition which forms the substrate for their individual gestural explorations.

I should note that my theoretical treatment of musical gesture is not limited to what one might term the "default" level of phenomenal perception of nuances and cognition of their affective import, although initial perceptual synthesis and cognition of emergent expressive meaning are profoundly significant parts of our encounter with musical gestures. Beyond such practiced interpretive immediacy, a competent listener will grasp the thematic and rhetorical functions of certain gestures within a given musical style. Furthermore, although musical gestures are often made distinctive through specific articulations, dynamics, and pacing or timing—and given unique shape by the systematic potential of rhythm and meter, texture, and timbre—they cannot be fully described without reference to the more "syntactic" levels of musical structure and process.[1] These syntactic levels are shaped by the overlapping disciplines of counterpoint, harmony and voice-leading, phrase structure and form, and in many cases, motivic developing variation. Chapters 8 and 9 addresses complete works by Beethoven and Schubert in order to demonstrate how a larger dramatic trajectory may be generated by an expressively motivated discourse of thematic gestures.

Gesture challenges us not only in its negotiation with higher structuring, but in its internal synthesis and integration of elements. These elements are typically treated separately, not only in historical theories of music but also in treatises or manuals devoted to performance practice. Separation—characteristic of an *analytical* approach to musical understanding and often inadequate even to the explanation of structure and process—may be fruitfully complemented by a more *synthetic* approach. In my earlier book (1994), I linked a more structuralist account (oppositions, their marked asymmetries, and their expressive correlations) to a more hermeneutic interpretation—one that goes beyond general types of meanings to address their particularity as encountered in the unique contexts of individual works. The stylistic growth of *correlational* meaning may reflect the further articulation of general types, but this more logical process is counterbalanced by *troping*—the often unpredictable and even extra-logical process by which new meaning emerges from atypical or even contradictory associations between more established meanings. There is yet a further mode of meaning that was only implicitly addressed in my earlier book, most notably in the treatment of reversals or undercuttings. This more synthetic mode of understanding is best exemplified by the *gestural*, with reversals and undercuttings understood as a subcategory of *rhetorical* gestures.

The work of synthesis through which various musical elements combine into an *emergent* entity (not predictable as merely the sum of its parts) applies not only to gesture but also to *topics* (patches of music that trigger clear associations with styles, genres, and expressive meanings) and *tropes* (the interpretive synthesis of, for example, otherwise contradictory topics that are juxtaposed in a single functional location or rhetorical moment). Thus, the larger project uniting the three parts of this book is a pursuit of a neglected synthetic (or at least fully integrative) approach to music. Gestures, topics, and tropes involve syntheses whose emergent interpretation cannot be merely after the fact, as a mere summing up of analytical detail. Nor, on the other hand, can critical interpretation ignore these processes by presupposing that listeners somehow "put it all together in their minds." Rather, the modes of synthesis and emergence can and must be woven into the very fabric of musical explanation. Interpretation—whether at the level of perception or cognition, and whether evaluative in its judgment of form or creative in its participation in the emergence of meaning—relies on synthetic categories such as gesture from the start.

A strictly analytical approach cannot easily convey this aspect of an interpretive competency. While analysis plays a necessary role in discovering discrete building blocks as systematically encoded by a musical style (pitch inventories, scales, chords, rhythmic units, etc.), it must be complemented by a cognitively richer account of how listeners so successfully, and at times so transparently, combine these discrete elements into meaningful elements of musical discourse—indeed, how they serve the more flexible and malleable ends of expressive shaping at all levels of structure. Tree hierarchies (as developed by Lerdahl and Jackendoff 1983) imply modes of cognitive processing that demand constant evaluations (yes/no, more/less) at every node—hardly an efficient model to explain the mind's constant leaps to coherent structures and meanings. It would be like trying to claim that the tongue needed to complete a detailed analysis of ingredients before concluding that something tasted good—whereas the senses synthesize on a routine basis.

Nevertheless, synthetic entities such as thematic gestures can and do engage levels for which current analytical models are adequate. In analyzing the developing variation of a gesture, one need not reinvent Schoenberg's insights into the developing variation of a motive. But one must distinguish the gestural from typical assumptions about motives and *Grundgestalten,* which are often defined in terms of pitch structure (generative cells) and rhythmic patterns, to the neglect of articulation, dynamics, and temporal pacing. When one works from a gestural perspective, these neglected elements may move to the foreground as essential constituents of a characteristic energetic shaping through time. A gestural perspective can thus lend significance to elements that are often overlooked by theorists or relegated to surface expressive nuance by performers. Ideally, a gestural approach can bring theorists and performers closer together as they share perspectives on various stylistic traditions. To put it simply, theorists can learn to appreciate the structural role of performers' expressive nuances, and performers can learn to recognize the expressive significance of the structures analyzed by theorists.

One of the most interesting properties of gesture is its continuity, even across rests or articulated silence. This property has led me to consider the expressive effects of continuity and discontinuity in other dimensions of musical structure, notably texture and form. Chapter 11 addresses continuous texture and perpetual motion as marked features with respect to the more typical, articulated textures of the Classical period. The second half of the chapter returns to the notion of plenitude as a possible expressive premise for three of Beethoven's late fugues. Chapter 12 explores discontinuity as a marked feature in the first movement of Beethoven's String Quartet in A Minor, Op. 132, and weighs the evidence for an underlying dramatic continuity. By contrast, the second half of the chapter grapples with the last movement's relatively continuous textures, noting how the lack of obvious topics provides yet another challenge for interpretation. Together, Chapters 11 and 12 raise some of the larger implications of my approach to synthetic categories involving continuity through time—specifically, how our capacity to synthesize and interpret emergent meaning affects our processing of stylistic innovation at all levels of musical organization.

Recent Orientations toward Musical Meaning

The past two decades have witnessed a growing interest among musicologists and theorists in defining and interpreting musical meaning. Musicology has been affected by two fundamental reorientations, which I will broadly characterize as the *critical* and the *ideological*.[2] The first significant new path for musical meaning was charted by Joseph Kerman (1985), who issued an impassioned plea for *criticism* as a broader interpretive endeavor. This important proposal, stemming from an even earlier "position paper" (Kerman 1965), was complemented by pleas for more historically informed criticism (Treitler 1989) and more stylistically informed critical analysis (Meyer 1973, 1989). Kerman urged musicologists and theorists to move beyond positivist historical and formalist analytical approaches in order to fully *interpret* (not merely classify, quantify, or describe) a far wider *range* of piece-specific and cultural evidence, with the goal of reconstructing a *historically contextualized* account of musical meaning.

The second, more *ideological* reorientation came hard on the heels of the first and was given a controversial feminist spark by Susan McClary (1991).[3] A broader ideological agenda is programmatically set out in Lawrence Kramer's (1990, 1995, 2002) trilogy of books on musical meaning, a series of approximations toward, and appropriations of, a *postmodern* cultural critique. Kramer seeks to *deconstruct* the entire enterprise of musicology along postmodern lines, moving away from traditional conceptions of the work and the composer to consider musical *texts* as *situated* at the intersections of *cultural practices*.[4] Meanings are then viewed as *mobile* and *contingent*, not governed by a single perspective (such as one might reconstruct as the composer's intent) but participating in the multiple exchanges of their use. In his interpretive forays Kramer often practices a freely associational approach in posing the discourses that might be occasioned by a musical text. These discourses are often launched by peculiar or unusual structural features that demand to be interpreted, opening up *hermeneutic windows* that lead to *cultural tropes*. Kramer's tropes are then diagnosed for their *ideological* content (constructions involving gender and sexuality, institutionalized power, and the like), and the interpretation often leads from the musical text to a cultural critique or even a radical *deconstruction* of a composer's ideological commitments as reflected in one or more musical works.

Kerman, McClary, and Kramer often situate their interpretive preferences in opposition to a favorite straw figure, the systematic musicologist (or theorist) who labors under the illusion of scientific objectivity in an exhaustive pursuit of verifiable *facts*, avoiding problematic issues of interpretation in reconstructing, from *"safe" evidence*, a *chronicle* of music history, *definitive editions* of musical works in proper chronological sequence, and *systematic analysis* of their structures, with the latter leading to *taxonomies* and *comparative analyses of stylistic features*. But the grand generalizations, or *master narratives*, presupposed by this naive musicologist are shown to have undermined the pseudo-scientific enterprise from the start. For McClary, the pathetic straw figure is typically a man speaking with an authoritative, patriarchal voice and defending a position of cultural hegemony. Critical examination and deconstruction of these scholars' ideological biases (whether involving gender, race, nationality, or institution) inevitably reveals a sadly misguided and rigid *Musikwissenschaft* that ignores the very life substance of what it would attempt to explain.

Of course, historically this is something of a fiction, since hermeneutic strands constantly enlivened the discourse and artistic commitment of past generations of musicologists, even as these scholars worked on the necessary foundational tasks of the discipline. Ironically, there was a healthy tradition of hermeneutics in German musicology—to mention only the studies of Eggebrecht and Floros and the philosophical writings of Dahlhaus—that was often ignored when tying positivistic research to its roots in German musicology. Not everything earlier musicologists had achieved would have to be redone, even if new interpretive approaches suggested helpful alternatives, either by reframing earlier claims or by presenting new ones.

Enough of the negative stereotype of "scientific" musicology (as practiced in the United States) was on target, however, to foster an equal and opposite reaction. First, criticism could provide a means of penetrating closer to the *significance* of music, and second, postmodern cultural critiques could counteract the problem of meaning as *essentialized* (whether as inherent in a musical work, as intentionally controlled by a composer, as exclusively claimed by a listener, or as reconstructed too determinately by a scholar). Instead, meaning would be conceived as freely circulating among communities of interpreters. And those interpreters would be seen as inextricably part of an ongoing exchange of cultural meanings, of which music could be understood as one of many equal contributors (Kramer 1990).

This vision was anthropologically rich in its promotion of local knowledge and "thick description" (Geertz 1973) over grand systems. But ironically, at the same time criticism sought to bring scholars closer to the work's individual or particular meaning, a postmodernist cultural critique was encouraging other scholars to back away from the work's inaccessible, essentialist core and orbit more safely about its sphere of influences—those discourses, ideologies, and cultural practices claimed as crucial to the contextualization of its meanings (plural).

It is not surprising that such contextualization might lead away from the individuality of a work as carrier of distinctive meanings—indeed, concepts such as the individual work as carrier of distinct meaning were themselves suspect. But I would argue that an adequate explanation of style growth and change must include an account of internal generative processes, even if the initial impetus for change is an external motivation. An individual composer's choices within the constraints of a style—or extending beyond those constraints in purposeful ways—may well lead to growth or change from within.[5] Viewed from these two perspectives (the importance of a work's individual meanings, and the need to account for growth and change), the postmodern approach may be seen as lacking a consistent grounding in the most important of cultural practices embracing a work as text: the *musical style* (or styles) from which it draws established cultural meanings, and against which it creates new meanings (Meyer 1989; Hatten 1982, 1994). In my own work I have defined style as "that competency in symbolic functioning presupposed by the work of art" (Hatten 1982) and argued for its reconstruction in tandem with historical reconstruction of a given work's meanings. In this sense neither close interpretation of the work nor historical reconstruction of the style warrants censure as "essentialist."

The postmodern tilt toward ideological cultural contextualization suggests not only that the musical work is always vulnerable to such discourses in its interpretation, but also that its composer is equally vulnerable. As an alternative model, consider the following image: a musical work is surrounded in its compositional gestation by the placenta of a *musical style* that filters out those aspects of culture that are extraneous to its growth, while taking in all that is essential nourishment from that culture. But to extend the analogy, style is not a perfect filter—just as alcohol or caffeine can have a deleterious impact on the fetus, so pernicious ideological contents can be imposed on a work from the surrounding culture—whether directly influencing the composer's compositional choices, or indirectly influencing the listener's interpretive biases. In such cases of imposed ideological content, the work of McClary and Kramer can be brilliantly illuminating. Nevertheless each musical work (after granting its problematic status *as* a work, rather than merely an elusive intertext) is inescapably more (or other) than the sum of the cultural practices it sets into motion. How we reconstruct the stylistic context and interpret the work's negotiation within that context are the crucial issues.

In the face of postmodernism, I maintain that the "aesthetic" is no illusion. Within a realm of scholarly discourse that is increasingly aware of contingency and relativity, I maintain that we still have access to *relatively objective* (by which I mean *intersubjectively defensible*) historical meanings—both at the general level of style (which can be *reconstructed* to a degree that the evidence will allow) and at the more detailed level of a work (which must be interpreted not only from stylistic knowledge but also through hermeneutic inquiry). The latter requires a mixture of deep empathy for the potential expressive significance of a musical work, and careful argumentation that can justify unusual structures as the plausible outcomes of work-centered expressive motivations.

With a theory of musical gesture, I address our *embodied* access to musical meaning—ironically, an arena highly favored by New Musicologists, who apparently do not sense any contradiction between essentialized meaning in the body and essentialist meaning in a musical work. I am not primarily concerned with my own, subjective bodily responses as they pertain to the embodied experience and pleasures of listening or performing, as artistically evoked by Suzanne G. Cusick (1994), although I will inevitably reveal my own "kinesthetic empathy" with the physiological aspects of musical performance, as Andrew Mead (1999) has defined them. In my heuristic suggestions for getting closer to gestural meaning through performance, I have been profoundly influenced by Alexandra Pierce's (1994) interpretive pedagogy of movement and gesture for performers, which I summarize briefly in Chapter 6. My primary goal, however, is to sketch out a comprehensive theory of musical gesture, ranging from the biological and cultural to the music-stylistic and strategic, and from the thematic and dialogical to the rhetorical and tropological—all of which are relevant to the historical reconstruction and interpretation of embodied meanings *as they are configured within* musical works—and as they are revealed in performance.

In applying the theory to the interpretation of musical gestures in Mozart, Beethoven, and Schubert, I presuppose the situated subjectivity of an empowered composer, able to work not just *in* but also *beyond* the cultural practices of the time. This conception of intentionality, as revealed in the work, is critical to reconstructing the aesthetic core of the work's possible meanings—a core not equivalent to the diffuse history of critical reception that often biases interpretation in light of later cultural needs and practices. I do not claim there must be one and only one musical meaning in my interpretive quest, but rather that we can propose plausible, contemporaneous meanings, at an appropriate level of generality, while recognizing that language is inadequate to specify the particular synthesis of associations and correlations triggered by a musical event. Nevertheless, even if a late work of Beethoven's might have been fully understood in its time only by Beethoven himself, it is possible to demonstrate ways in which one could have understood what Beethoven so carefully achieved—the signposts are plentiful. On the other hand, I would not deny that we value (or critique) historical works for more than might have been intended by their composers. I simply contend that we should have a better idea of how such works could have been interpreted at the time of their creation, and that this is a necessary complement to the kinds of meanings they might have for us today, when we factor in the perspectives of all the styles, interpretive approaches, and ideological stances that have emerged or been reconstructed since their time.

While I freely admit that semiosis of all kinds—from the aesthetic to the ideological—has its place in a healthier, expanded field of musical studies, I am also concerned that some of the ideologically based interpretations fostered by the New Musicology may offer suggestive webs of association insufficiently grounded in a style or its analytical evidence.[6] As I argued over twenty years ago (Hatten 1982), style does not exhaust semiotics; rather, it selects among possible meanings based on their relevance to an ongoing—and central—music-stylistic practice. I will attempt to ground my interpretations of musical gestures, topics, and tropes within the constraints of a style, considered as that cultural context most relevant to a work. I have found that the deeper I go into the interpretation of a work, the broader my conception of the stylistic competency implied by its creation. But the reverse is equally true—the richer my understanding of a musical stylistic competency, the deeper my interpretation of its creative manifestations. This "methodological dialectic" (Hatten 1982: 100; 1994: 29–30) provides a series of "checks and balances" for those choices we make when reconstructing a style (as a plausible generalization from the evidence of several works) and when interpreting a work (as a plausible manifestation of a given stylistic competency). If an ad hoc interpretive claim leads us to propose an expanded stylistic competency, we must then accommodate the claim within a larger contextual interpretation of the given work, find examples in other works by the same composer, and explain the expanded competency as part of a plausible growth process in the style.

Chapter 1 offers an example of how one might proceed in "grounding" such an interpretive claim for a striking event in a Beethoven piano trio by contextualizing a larger interpretation and proposing a systematic growth process in the style. It also offers a model of the endless gathering of evidence, and the multiple perspectives of analytical and interpretive approaches, that can guide and sharpen our expressive claims. I do not pursue this exhaustive degree of rigor in subsequent chapters that deal with more than one significant musical event, for obvious reasons. My examples throughout have been chosen to provide a degree of cross-referencing that not only lends further support to my interpretive claims, but also helps clarify and strengthen my theoretical arguments for the importance of gestural, topical, and tropological interpretation.

Oppositions, Markedness, Topics, and Tropes

Those readers not familiar with my approach to musical meaning as developed in my work on Beethoven (Hatten 1994) may find the following three sections helpful, since they review the role of marked oppositions, topics, and tropes in interpretation. I have chosen my examples from Mozart and Schubert in order to demonstrate the wider applicability of these concepts.[7] I first examine the problematic critical/aesthetic opposition between musical structure and musical expression, and then explain how markedness theory can help us interpret the correlations between oppositions in structure and oppositions in expression. The last section explores an opposition of topics that invites tropological interpretation.

Although Part Two of the book, devoted to a theory of musical gesture, forgoes an exhaustive analysis of oppositions in order to focus more on the synthetic interpretation of distinctive shapes in all their particularity, I do not mean to diminish the functional role that oppositions can play in grounding a systematic typology of gestures. For an early demonstration of this principle, see Allanbrook's (1983: 67) oppositional modeling of the typical meters and rhythmic gestures of dances used as topics and styles in the operas of Mozart.

Rethinking a Problematic Opposition

One of the interesting aspects of the New Musicology is its embrace of Derrida's deconstruction of binary oppositions in culture, an approach that has also found its way into semiotic theory through the work of Raymond Monelle (1992, 2000). As an acknowledgment of the usefulness of a deconstructive approach, I offer my own critique of a binary opposition in the critical language I have inherited, a difficult opposition that has hampered efforts to explain expressive meaning in music.[8] The terms "structure" and "expression" are often conceived in dichotomous fashion as though they were separate (if complementary) aspects of a musical work. Consider the following ways that relationship has been conceived:

1. Structure as the shell and expression as the filling (or structure as the cake and expression as that which is added, like icing).
2. Structure as static, background form (or coherence), and expression as dynamic, foregrounded process.
3. Structure as syntax, and expression as semantics.

These familiar oppositions reflect the alignment of several terms: form, background, and static state are associated with structure; and meaning, foreground, and process are associated with expression. As I have cautioned (Hatten 1994: 278), one of the dangers of this perspective on expression is the confusion of what is focally *expressive* (foregrounded, hence "brought out" in performance) with *expression* in its entirety. Clearly we need a definition that captures the contributions of all levels of structure to the expressive meaning of a work. Consider another characterization of the opposition:

4. Structure refers to relationships inherent in the score and expression to those relationships as made manifest and embodied in sound (performance).

With this definition we come closer to the notion that expression is a *translation* of structure (or structural relationships) at all levels. But as Nicholas Cook (1999: 243) astutely observes, if the structures and processes revealed by Schenkerian analysis are "expressed" in performance as a literal sonic manifestation of the hierarchy of relationships among levels of voice-leading, this merely gives "a psychological interpretation to Hanslick's metaphysical model of musical autonomy." I would also observe that this definition overlooks the possibility that expression may itself be structured. Consider the following formulation:

5. Structure is the generative code for which expression is the structured result.

The analogy here is to genetic structure and expression. The DNA code provides the structure, and it is transcribed to the RNA on the way to being translated into, or "expressed as," the amino acids of proteins. The problem with this analogy is that it assumes structure exists a priori, "in the genes." It also risks confusing the structure of the *work* with the implied structures of a *style*. Consider an alternative construction:

6. The work is an expression of the potential structures of a generative style.

This formulation captures an essential distinction between work and style, but fails to account for the performer's creative, not merely re-creative, role in the chain of "expressions"—or might we now say: *interpretations?*[9] For, clearly, an expression of a structure, or expression that results in structure, depends on an array of interpretive choices that lend human distinctiveness and character to an otherwise disembodied realization of relationships (compare Meyer 1989).

Figure I.1 illustrates what would appear to be a complementary chain of expressive ideas leading to structures, and structures being in turn expressed, or *realized,* as structures in new realms. Its interlinked interpretations suggest Charles Sanders Peirce's chain of interpretants.[10] The last part of this chain captures the ambiguity in our use of the terms "expression" and "structure." We could as easily state that we "structure an expression" as that we "express a structure" (see Figure I.2). Note also how these two verbs relate the processes of composing, performing, listening, and criticizing or analyzing, in terms of their shared functions.

Ausdruck and *Struktur,* the two concepts that have so often been put into opposition, now appear in an interpenetrating, *yin-yang* relationship, with balancing claims as both processive verbs and end-state nouns: we "expressively structure" (or "structurally express") the "*Ausdrucktur*" of our creative interpretations. It is this constant fusing or *troping* of structure and expression that I will explore in my interpretation of topics, tropes, and gesture in the chapters to come.

Expression may indeed be richly structured, and *Ausdruck* need not be narrowly conceived as *Ausbruch*—the expressive outburst, or that which is most salient, foregrounded, or strategically *marked* in the work. An expressive point of intensity, or *crux,* is indeed "crucial" in the structuring of an expressive interpretation, but the expressive whole is more than the sum of its climaxes or marked moments. As we strive to realize the beauties of a processive *and* hierarchical (Meyer 1973) structure in its entirety, our goal is not, as I have cautioned earlier, "to pluck the fruits of expressivity off the branches of structural trees" (Hatten 1994: 278), but rather to achieve an appropriately balanced (structural and expressive) manifestation of foreground *and* background, melody *and* accompaniment, yearning *and* fulfillment.

With the theory of gesture to be introduced in Part Two, I will argue that gestural syntheses can complement and provide a corrective for overly analytical approaches to structure, helping bridge the gap in the unnecessary opposition "musical structure *or* expression," and easing us past the conceptual logjam of their simplistic opposition. But this problematic binary opposition in our critical theory must not be confused with the irreducible (cognitively necessary) oppositions that play a crucial role in the development of musical systems—or any semiotic system that features complex syntactic organization. It is here that markedness theory can

Style → Expressed **(composer)** → Structured (notated score) → Expressed **(performer)** → Structured (performance) →

→ Interpreted as expressive **(listener)** → Structured (experience) → Expressed **(critic)** **(theorist)** → Structured (review) (analysis/ interpretation)

Figure I.1. Chain of expressed structures and structured expressions.

Composer Performer Listener	EXPRESSES	Structures implied by a style Structures implied by a work Structures implied by realization of a work in sound
	OR	
Composer Performer Listener	STRUCTURES	Expressions implied by a style Expressions implied by a work Expressions implied by a realization of a work in sound

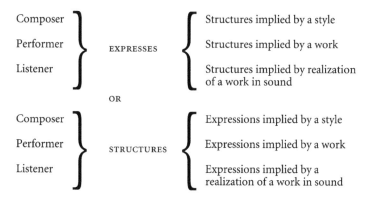

Figure I.2. "Expression" and "structure" as verb or noun.

play an important role, since systematic, stylistic oppositions have an asymmetrical structure that can be quite productive.

Markedness Theory and the Interpretation of Musical Oppositions

Markedness deals with one dimension of musical meaning, that which arises from difference, in the Saussurean sense that meaning is difference. Difference implies opposition, but the oppositions that are characterized by markedness are typically *asymmetrical:* one term is marked (with respect to some value or feature), and the opposing term (or field) is unmarked. The marked term is more narrowly defined and distributed, and, significantly, it has a correspondingly narrower realm of meaning than the unmarked term. For example, in some still current uses, the lexemes /woman/ and /man/ are in a marked relationship, with /woman/ more narrowly specifying /human female/, whereas /man/ is used to mean both /human male/ and, more generally, /human being/, when sex is not relevant to the context. Feminists rightly argue that power relationships lurk in such language, but the marked/unmarked coordination of opposition is at its base merely a fact of cognitive organization, and the marked term for sex can tilt in either direction. In the animal kingdom, for example, the female is typically the unmarked term; "duck" and "goose" are used either to specify the female or generically to refer to any of the species when sex is not relevant, whereas if one wants to refer specifically to the male, one must use the appropriately marked terms—"drake" and "gander," respectively.

There are three important consequences of this typical structuring of meaning for music. First, an opposition in musical structure (minor versus major mode) can correlate with an opposition in meaning (tragic versus nontragic, for the Classical style), which provides a systematic motivation for association that is stronger than association by mere properties or contiguities. This diagrammatic relationship, as C. S. Peirce would term it, enables a musical style to move beyond the most immediate or obvious of motivations for meaning, such as the straightforward iconicity of material similarity, or the immediate indexicality of contiguity and simple cause-and-effect relationships.[11] The symbolic level, based on habit or convention, is kept coherent by marked oppositions that support relatively stable types and their expressive correlations in a style. Musical works in that style can then develop strikingly creative tokens of those types—and provoke more challenging interpretations—while working from a coherent base of stable correlations. Thus, the systematic coherence of type identification and correlation *coexists* with the compositional flexibility of individualized tokens and the creative interpretation they foster. Of course, meaning as supported by marked oppositions can only be as specific as the given opposition affords, which is an advantage in reconstructing a style's core of meanings in this way. One is not tempted to overinterpret when reconstructing a general type correlation for a style; instead, a hermeneutic approach is more appropriate to interpreting a given work's variable tokens of a type.

Another advantage of markedness stems from the dynamic asymmetry of oppositions, which suggests a natural *growth* process by means of which styles carve out new niches of meaning by marking new features in creative tokens to form subtypes of the parent type.[12] Type generation results in further articulation of the oppositional network by introducing further oppositions within the semantic field of a marked term. Thus, meaning (the niche) and growth (its novelty) are inextricably linked in the model of markedness, since that which is new is marked, and the niche is more narrowly constrained in its meaning relative to the meaning of the parent type. And whereas the parent type may have originally been marked, it is now unmarked with respect to the new subtype.

To review: although systematic oppositions in a style may help guarantee underlying coherence and shared general meanings (*correlations*), a Classical composer such as Mozart will adapt the general to more specific ends, creating new meanings (*interpretations*) that go beyond the generic. On the other hand, in the case of a composer creating a new style, oppositions may appear to lie at the heart of a compositional poetics, as Danuta Mirka (1997) has demonstrated through her systematic analysis of Penderecki's approach to composition during his sonoristic period.

Simplistic notions of binarism are often treated with disdain by those New Musicologists who propose more subtle interpretations through associations of musical and cultural practices, as Lawrence Kramer (1990) has termed them. These looser associations among the ideologies of a culture, with its endless constructions of gender, social hierarchy, religion, disease, or national identity—to say nothing of the further deconstruction of a culture's inevitably repressed "other" or "supplement"—provide a rich field of cultural intertextuality and readymade cultural units to serve any interpretive end. Furthermore, the aesthetic intentions of the composer, as they might be reconstructed from a semiotic model of musical style and a hermeneutic approach to the expressive strategies of a work, are often displaced by consideration of the work as a cultural artifact. Ideological interpretation (at times ideological critique of a composer's presumed failure to avoid negative stereotypes, even if unwitting) tries a work on the basis of standards that may be quite different from those motivating its creation and expressive purport.

For example (to choose another musicologist whose work I admire), Richard Taruskin (1997: 378–88) moves smoothly in his account of Stravinsky's *Rite of Spring* from the ostinato structures and nonprogressive harmonies of the music, to the biologism inherent in primitivism, with its loss of subjectivity and individuality, hence loss of compassion for the victim (a species of antihumanism), to the pronounced similarities with Nazi ideology, and by extension, "its roots in European history and ideas" (387), and ultimately, in the following essay, to an examination of Stravinsky's anti-Semitism and self-interested concern to distance himself from Jewish musicians in a futile quest to preserve performances of his music in pre-war Nazi Germany (458). Whether or not this was Taruskin's intention, how can our interpretation of the *Rite of Spring* not be tainted when we are left to presume a causal link in this infamous chain of associations? And should we then reject the music of Stravinsky? If the ideological is now irrevocably wedded with the structural and aesthetic, how can we be sure we have not obscured the latter by adopting an ideological slant too hastily?

If, on the other hand, binary oppositions seem too mechanistic, how might they be construed in a way that respects the ongoing evolution of musical meaning? How, in other words, might one go beyond the major versus minor, happy versus sad correlation, when there are more complex expressive meanings at work? In the following brief consideration of the Queen of the Night's arias from *The Magic Flute,* I demonstrate how a marked oppositional analysis reveals consistent use of stylistic correlations, but also how these correlations are adapted to support different kinds of musical expressive meaning, as appropriate to the given dramatic situation. With the text and the dramatic scenario to guide us, the expressive import of each example appears fairly transparent.[13]

To begin with the text, there is a very clear binary opposition at work in the libretto of *The Magic Flute,* that between night and day. We need no better evidence of the way a Classical composer would map that distinction tonally than the act 2 finale, where the Queen of the Night (in C minor) is "vanquished" by Sarastro's "speech act" (Austin 1962; Searle 1970), which wills into existence the sun's bright rays (in E♭ major). When presented with any such negative-positive opposition, a composer in this style who chooses to underline it tonally will likely assign the minor key or mode to the negatively valued and the major to the positively valued term. Thus, without necessarily claiming that every case of minor "means" sadness, or badness, or any particular thing, we could perhaps agree that oppositions in cultural meaning will map onto oppositions in musical structure in a consistent fashion. After hearing enough instances of such mapping, we may begin to associate minor more literally with particular properties. But the subtlety of markedness theory is that it applies to oppositions of meaning and their mappings in analogous music structural oppositions, rather than to the isolation of a single structure and the specification of its meaning. This principle corresponds well with Peirce's diagrammatic conception of meaning, in that we represent the structure of the opposition, rather than imposing arbitrary reference on a given musical event.

Why might major have taken the positive pole versus minor? We can, of course, speculate on the raised versus lowered third, or on the greater number of dissonant intervals that occur in minor due to the options of raised $\hat{6}$ and $\hat{7}$, or on the "chord of nature" as being major. But as important as these motivations are to that elusive, "complete" explanation, with markedness one need not explain "why" in order to substantiate the *consistency* with which, in a given style, the opposition major/minor correlates with positively/negatively valued oppositions in meaning.

Compare what might seem to be contradictory uses of major and minor mode, to see how this approach makes "binarism" more flexible. In her first appearance the Queen of the Night sings a dramatic recitative in regal B♭ major as she reassures Tamino. The regal character, of course, is not a correlation of major mode, but of the ceremonial march figures and dotted rhythms that allude topically to the French Overture style. After a positive B♭ major introduction, the Queen's aria begins in G minor. If we assumed minor were simply "negative," we might conclude that Mozart is warning us about the Queen's true (evil) character. But, of course, this is not the case here. Instead, the operative word is *Leiden,* or "sorrows," in m. 2 of the Larghetto, fitting a general correlation of sadness. Thus, in singing a minor-mode lament for her lost daughter, the Queen appears highly sympathetic (regardless of the selfish reasons that may lurk behind her "grief"). And since suffering is "dysphoric," it must be mapped onto a minor mode.[14]

Analogous to the opposition between E♭ major and C minor in act 2, the tonal mapping here seems fitting and leads to further interpretation: B♭ major for regal power and authority, G minor for the Queen's suffering and presumed weakness in not being able to prevent the abduction, and a return to B♭ major in the concluding section for the Queen's attempt to embolden Tamino to rescue her daughter. Interestingly, both sides of the opposition between major and relative minor are employed by the Queen to enlist Tamino's aid: the minor mode supports what we will later recognize as a manipulative attempt to generate sympathy. Thus, when the Queen's true character is revealed, we can further interpret these apparently sincere meanings as somewhat hypocritical or manipulative.

In the Queen's second aria, the D-minor, *Sturm und Drang* setting of "Der Hölle Rache kocht in meinem Herzen" ("hellish revenge steeps in my heart") is undercut by a sudden shift to F major in m. 11 for the Queen's warning to Pamina. The Queen wants her daughter to kill Sarastro and steal his powerful sun-cross medallion, and she alludes in macabre fashion to his death ("if you don't thoroughly feel Sarastro's death pains . . . "). Why would Mozart choose the major mode for this image of death or murder? Simply because it is an outcome *positively* desired by the Queen—she sings it with power and pride (an ascending arpeggiation suggesting the heroic topic in mm. 11–12, capped by an exultant cascade on "Sarastro Todesschmerzen" in mm. 13–14 and 15–16). Furthermore, her positive attitude toward something so evil is guaranteed to produce a much more chilling effect on an audience (like the high, staccato figuration that suggests an evil witch's laughter later in the aria). The threat, were Pamina not to share in the Queen's plans and emotions, is indicated by the completion of the phrase "then you'll no longer be my daughter." Since losing her daughter would not be pleasing to the Queen, despite her threat, this passage features vii^{o7}/V moving to V in mm. 19–20. The use of a dissonant diminished-seventh chord is conventionally associated with anguish or grief; it appears here as a result of mixture within a prevailing major mode.

One may draw from these examples a clear moral in applying markedness to music: one term of an opposition does not necessarily have a fixed meaning. As in Peircean theory, any general correlation stemming from a marked opposition must be further interpreted according to the context of its use. Nevertheless, with consistent use, terms of an opposition begin to take on what appears to be independent correlations (typical connotations, if you will), and it becomes easy to assume that X literally means (or stands for) Y. Indeed, this is one way correlational meaning congeals over time, producing the illusion of fixity at a later stage of presumed arbitrariness, when we no longer remember original motivations or attend to the underlying oppositions that contribute to the coherence of meaning in a style. It is because of this growth process that it is possible to assume (after the fact) a degree of "arbitrariness" in language—an emergent illusion deriving from the systematicity inherent in complex semiotic codes, enabling them to support coherent interpretation.

Does expressive meaning arise solely from markedness that is foregrounded for attention? It may be the case that only those marked moments in life cause us to question the unmarked continuities of existence, the repetitive, diurnal rhythms of life. And we may grant that investigations are often sparked by feelings of incompleteness in our understanding of a musical passage (compare Kramer's rationale for his proposed "hermeneutic windows"; 1990: 5–6). We may even be led beyond our unmarked stylistic understanding by marked aspects of the work's "surface," such as an unusual combination of stylistic elements. But the surface is only part of the *strategic* markedness a composer brings to bear at all levels of a work's structure; the use of unmarked stylistic material may also be expressive at some level (recall my critique of the opposition between structure and expression in the previous section). When typical material is combined in atypical ways, however, it may engender a *trope*. Like a metaphor in literary language, a trope is sparked from the collision or fusion of two already established meanings, and its interpretation is emergent.[15] The unpredictability of creative troping, as opposed to the more logical articulation of types into subtypes, makes it much harder to defend theoretically. Nevertheless, troping is an essential component of a theory of musical meaning; artistic creativity, after all, is often surprising and unpredictable.

Topical Opposition and Troping

The striking alternation of dance themes and sonata development is a marked aspect of Schubert's late Piano Sonata in E♭ Major, D. 567.[16] Sonata implies drama and the consistent pursuit of a dramatic discourse, whereas dance revels in local figuration and climax within global alternation and repetitive schemes. Given the concatenation of dance and dramatic development as topical foci in this sonata, one is forced to look further.

I will claim that the "drama" of this movement is *tropologically* conceived as a working out of the opposition between the relaxed realms of dance, represented by the principal and secondary themes (Examples I.1a and I.1c), and the charged progressiveness of development in sonata, represented by the elaborations and transitions (Example I.1b) in the exposition and the development section. Marked moments of dissonance and turns to the minor (as in the transition, Example I.1b) can delineate stages in a drama by increasing agitation and leading to a crisis. The recapitulation's variation of the opening theme is self-consciously embellished by syncopation and diminution, as if reflecting the agitation of the development section. The closing theme of the exposition also develops the idea from m. 16, climaxing on a "crisis" diminished-seventh chord that is an established marker of dramatic tension.

Does the dance suggest the dialogic—the pairing of two dancers? Or is it already a metaphor for a single agent's internal states? I suspect the latter. Beethoven's Piano Sonata in E♭ Major, Op. 31, no. 3, also features internal contrasts and "drama" in its opening theme (see Example 7.20), with four different kinds of gestures but only one implied agent.[17] Schubert's sonata thematizes the tension between two states, as implied by dance (nonconflicted, diatonic, idealized space) and drama (conflict-driven temporality, with injected hints of suffering in the use of modal mixture and chromatic harmony). The oscillation between states, or play of genres, becomes for sophisticated listeners an important *emergent* meaning for the work.

With Schubert we have prior understanding of the correlations inherent in each "type" of music, and these are clues toward the interpretation of the emergent trope. Indeed, the hybridization of style types is a phenomenon of style growth that can be predicted systematically. Elsewhere (Hatten 1994: 121) I constructed a matrix that showed the possible cross-referencing of thematic, developmental, and closural *materials* with their functional *locations*. In puzzling over the apparent contradiction between closural material in a developmental location, I realized that Beethoven had achieved just such a trope in the development section of the first movement of his String Quartet in B♭ Major, Op. 130. But it is one thing to systematically explore all possible combinations as displayed by such a matrix, and

Example I.1. Schubert, Piano Sonata in E♭ Major, D. 567, first movement.
a. First theme.
b. Transition.
c. Second theme.

another to interpret the expressive meaning that emerges from their unusual combination. To map the disposition of each "type" in the ongoing drama of their alternation, as in the case of dance themes and sonata material in the Schubert movement, is but one step toward interpreting the significance that emerges from their dialectical encounter—a significance for which verbal precision may indeed be too limiting.

I have said nothing thus far about musical gesture, which traditionally has been relegated to the field of expression, although the gestural character of the opening theme of the Schubert sonata is clearly relevant to its interpretation. Can gesture be conceived by the composer as one of the elements of structure? Is gesture sufficiently generative or thematic such that its "expression" can affect the resulting structure of the work, as well as its meaning? I will defer answers to Part Two, which introduces a theory of musical gesture. Having illustrated some of my approaches to musical meaning, I bring this extended introduction to a close. Chapter 1 will serve to demonstrate how an integration of these approaches might respond to the demands of critical interpretation and historical contextualization, as so eloquently urged by Kerman, Meyer, and Treitler.

Part One: *Markedness, Topics, and Tropes*

1 Semiotic Grounding in Markedness and Style: Interpreting a Style Type in the Opening of Beethoven's *Ghost* Trio, Op. 70, no. 1

Beethoven's Piano Trio in D Major (*Ghost*), Op. 70, no. 1, was composed in 1809. Its minor-mode slow movement, Largo assai ed espressivo, is filled with such chromaticism and tremolos that Czerny (1970: 97) associated it with the scene from Shakespeare where Hamlet encounters the ghost of his father. William Kinderman (1995: 134) notes that the uncanny attribution is literally warranted; however, the connection is not with *Hamlet* but with *Macbeth*. In 1808 Beethoven was sketching ideas for an opera based on a *Macbeth* libretto by Heinrich von Collin, and sketches for the abandoned opera project are found interspersed with ideas for the slow movement of the trio.

If a semiotic approach to musical meaning depended on such programmatic suggestions, I might well have chosen the slow movement for investigation. But it is to the decidedly less gloomy first movement that I wish to direct attention, specifically to the opening theme complex. I plan to demonstrate how we can come to a deeper understanding of the expressive meaning of this opening by pursuing evidence from a variety of perspectives. My semiotic approach is both *structuralist,* in reconstructing the stylistic types that correlate with general expressive meanings, and *hermeneutic,* in interpreting the strategic designs through which a composer individualizes and particularizes the tokens of those types, thereby achieving unique expressive meanings. And my approach is directed toward understanding *how* music has meaning, not merely *what* it might mean, from the perspective of a historically informed reconstruction of the style. In the course of teasing out the subtleties of the opening of the trio, I will demonstrate the breadth of my semiotic approach, not as a substitute for other kinds of analysis, but as a means of interpreting their results and revealing further aspects of the work's expressive design.

A characterization of the first theme complex (Example 1.1), from the opening up to the counterstatement launching the transition at m. 21, might read like this: "With an energetic burst akin to the opening of the Piano Sonata, Op. 10, no. 3, the unison opening motive, x, sequences upward before breaking off with a surprise shift to F♮. Sustained in the cello like a written-out fermata, this F♮ is then supported by a consonant B♭ in the piano, before moving to an F♯ above a cadential $^6_4$ and the elided beginning in the cello of a more lyrical first theme, y." This description blends structural terminology (motive, sequence, cadential $^6_4$, elision)

Example 1.1. Beethoven, Piano Trio in D Major (*Ghost*), Op. 70, no. 1, first movement, opening themes.

with expressive characterizations ("energetic," "surprise shift"), and even draws intertextually on a similar piano sonata opening. A closer analysis, perhaps inspired by Schenkerian voice-leading and an intuition about elliptical structures, might claim that the Bb–F consonant fifth in m. 6 implies an unstable German augmented sixth, which resolves in contrary motion by half steps to a cadential $^6_4$, and thus the whole opening may be understood as a briefly interrupted expansion of a key-defining progression.[1] Students of Leonard B. Meyer (1973) might emphasize the delayed realization of an implied F# (deferred by F♮), or point out that the thematic arrival in m. 7 is not *congruent* with the proper arrival of the tonic in the bass, which is delayed until m. 11. And disciples of Rudoph Réti (1951) would delight in discovering that the cello idea, "y," is an augmented inversion of the opening "x" motive, suggesting the presence of a unifying *Grundgestalt*, Schoenberg's term for a generative thematic contour or cell.

More historically oriented interpreters would cite E. T. A. Hoffmann's instructive review of 1813 (in Charlton 1989: 300–24), observing that what I have labeled as motives x and y are, interestingly, identified as first and second themes by Hoffmann, although he apparently is unaware of their inversional relationship. Based on his review of the Op. 70 piano trios and his better-known review of Beethoven's Fifth Symphony, Hoffmann is recognized as being the first music critic to demonstrate the organic, motivic, and generational process through which Beethoven develops his larger heroic-period forms. Hoffmann concentrates on the "ingenious, contrapuntal texture" of the development, which he presents in full score, not otherwise available for study in this form at the time of his article. He describes crucial modulations and provides a figured bass reduction of the rewritten transition in the recapitulation, foreshadowing the advent of Schenkerian reductions. Hoffmann is also credited as one of the earliest critics (but see Momigny) to combine structural and expressive insights in his analyses. In this review he comments on the character of the "second theme" (beginning with my motive "y"), noting that it "expresses a genial serenity, a cheerful, confident awareness of its own strength and substance." I think we might be in general agreement with his assessment, although he offers us no particular reasoning to support it.

After this series of observations, both obvious and subtle, what more is there left to say? We have historical warrant for both theoretical analysis and expressive interpretation of the passage. We have revealed its secrets with respect to the implied German augmented sixth in m. 6, the noncongruence of thematic and tonal arrivals in mm. 7 and 11, respectively, and even the organic derivation of "y" from "x." Indeed, what more could a semiotic approach offer, assuming we have applied such a range of productive analytical and historical approaches?

A great deal more! For what I have presented thus far is merely analogous to parsing a poem, analyzing its syntax, and offering a subjective impression of one of its moods. We need not blithely accept Schenker's insistence that pitch structure, with a little metric interpretation thrown in, reveals the "true content" of music (as Schenker implies in the title to one of his *Meisterwerk* [1930] essays: "Beethovens 3. Sinfonie zum erstenmal in ihren *wahren Inhalt* dargestellt" [my italics]). Nor should we stop at what sensitive ears such as Hoffmann's may have heard. Instead, we can further explore how the structures we have discovered might be based on typical meanings in the style, and how they might be creating unique kinds of meanings within the constraints of that style. I call the first kind of meaning a *stylistic correlation*, based upon the generalization of *types;* the second kind of meaning is a *strategic interpretation*, and it is based upon the creation of *tokens*. A helpful way to explore the meanings of stylistic types is to investigate the structural oppositions that enable us to identify them, and that keep them systematically coherent. Oppositions in a style are asymmetrically structured as marked versus unmarked (see the Introduction), and their markedness values map onto similarly marked-unmarked oppositions in musical meaning. An example will illustrate.

I earlier analyzed the implied augmented-sixth chord in mm. 6–7 as resolving to a cadential $^6_4$. But this $^6_4$ chord does not sound cadential; rather, it evokes a very strong sense of arrival, hence, my coining of the term "arrival $^6_4$" (Hatten 1994: 15, 97). Other examples may be found in the slow movement of the *Hammerklavier* (m. 14), as well as the coda to the first movement of Op. 101 (m. 90). Notice that the rhetorical effect of resolution of dissonance, as a kind of "breakthrough" arrival, is more telling at the moment the $^6_4$ occurs than at the actual cadence. Here the $^6_4$ is not only an arrival but an *initiation*—it launches an important theme and thus functions, however poetically, as a structural downbeat for the "y" theme (while deferring a more powerful, root tonic structural downbeat for the cadence in m. 21 that launches the transition). The lyrical "y" theme unfolds above what at first suggests an ongoing dominant pedal, but harmonically the theme does not sound unstable—unlike the agitated dominant pedal points enhancing the (tragic) obsessiveness of the second themes in the first movements of Op. 2, no. 1 (in the relative major, A♭, but with mixtural ♭6̂) and Op. 31, no. 2 (in A minor, the dominant of D minor). The stability of the "y" theme is evidence of a semiotic (and contextual) reinterpretation of dissonance; although the $^6_4$ eventually resolves, it does not do so with a traditional 5̂–1̂ cadential bass, but rather slips up by step to tonic (mm. 10–11). Thus, the $^6_4$ is no longer as dependent on its resolution to a dominant, but stands on its own, as a poetically enhanced tonic. There are several motivations for this consonant effect. The theme sounds presentational, as though elevated, and on a pedestal. The dominant pedal provides this pedestal effect, and thus it can be heard as a separate "strand" independent of the stable tonic with which we assume a theme would begin. But the pedal 5̂ also resolves the instability and rhetorical questioning of the implied German augmented sixth. Just as poignant lowered 6̂ resolves to 5̂ in the bass, the questioning lowered 3̂ is pulled up to raised 3̂ in the upper voice. The positive, Picardy-third effect of this resolution also enhances the relative stability of the subsequent measures, and the glowing consonance of the major triad offers perceptual affordance to this interpretation. Finally, when we hear the augmented inversion in "y" as a (noble, expansive) transformation of the (hectic) opening motive "x," its glowing harmonic presentation (as an arrival $^6_4$ supporting a tonic over pedestal dominant) sounds truly fitting.

These are but a few of the contextual reasons for semiotically reinterpreting a $^6_4$ that in traditional theory would be interpreted merely as a dissonant sixth and fourth above the dominant chord's root, waiting to resolve to the fifth and third.

How might markedness contribute to the explanation of this instance of style growth? To begin, the opposition between minor and major (exemplified between mm. 5–6 on the one hand, and mm. 1–4 and 7 on the other) can be quite powerful. In m. 5 the turn to minor clouds an otherwise positive emotional state with an uncertainty that is potentially poignant—perhaps a forewarning of the tragic. In m. 7 suspended uncertainty is resolved rather gloriously into the arrival $^6_4$, thus encapsulating the potentially negative within the larger embrace of the positive.

In stylistic terms minor is marked within major, and thus m. 5 marks the first expressive crux of a movement that begins with a rather general positive energy. Topically Beethoven's opening suggests a mix of the heroic and hunt-based pastoral, but with such helter-skelter energy that it appears to be setting up a *comic* reversal. The marked term of an opposition, in this case "minor," correlates with a narrower realm of meaning. Here the mutated third scale degree (F♮) disrupts with its strong stylistic correlation, interpretable as dysphoric: poignant, or potentially tragic. Major, on the other hand, is typically unmarked in the Classical style and correlates with a much broader realm of meaning—generally, the nontragic, which includes heroic, pastoral, and *buffa* modes. But when major mode in turn reverses (and resolves) the minor, as in m. 7, it can draw on the marked status of the Picardy third within the realm of minor (Hatten 1994: 42). Thus, m. 7 may be heard as the second expressive crux of the movement. The almost premature, positive resolution of poignant uncertainty also puts its stamp on the *expressive genre* of the movement as a whole. We can be fairly certain that this movement will have a nontragic outcome (though the issue of F♮ and B♭ will have its own consequences thematically and tonally).

It would be a misunderstanding to assume that a particular musical event is either simply marked or unmarked; rather, it may entail a number of oppositional relationships, each of which contributes something to the overall interpretation of the event. Thus, the minor mode in mm. 5–6 is both marked with respect to the previous major, and unmarked with respect to the following major. Furthermore, markedness values may actually reverse as styles grow or change. For example, the cadential $^6_4$ is marked as unstable relative to its syntactical role in a cadence. As an arrival $^6_4$, however, it may be marked as stable relative to its resolution of a German augmented sixth (or other dissonant chord), especially when in conjunction with a strong thematic arrival. The pedal point on a dominant is marked as unstable in most environments, but it may be marked as stable when arising from an arrival $^6_4$. This historical style change—which might be described more neutrally as the contextual migration of a cadential $^6_4$—is exemplified by many works of Franz Liszt, in what has been dubbed the "salvation $^6_4$." Richard Cohn (personal communication) brought to my attention a written account by Gustav Jenner of his composition lessons with Brahms (Frisch 1990: 185–204) in which Brahms cautioned against overuse of this kind of $^6_4$: "As excellent as the effect of this chord can be— naturally I am referring only to cadential six-four chords—it is often nothing but the symptom and in its flabbiness the true reflection of a completely lame and exhausted imagination" (198). The first movement of the FAE Sonata for Violin and Piano, written by Schumann's student Dietrich, provides ample illustration of the rhetorical abuse of arrival $^6_4$'s through overuse. Liszt also uses the arrival $^6_4$ to launch a contrasting lyrical theme in major, entirely over a pedestal dominant pedal.

For an example of the noble use of a pedestal dominant in Beethoven, consider the second theme from the first movement of Beethoven's last piano sonata, Op. 111 (Example 1.2a). Here an arrival $^6_4$ (m. 50) links resolution of the thematized diminished-seventh chord (m. 49) with the initiation of a positive theme, whose nobility is further cued by dotted rhythms (associated with the ceremonial). The theme would be unstable only to a Schenkerian; phenomenologically it is exquisitely stable—again, as though presented on a pedestal—and only its brevity and parenthetical appearance between diminished-seventh chords attest to its still-illusory status in the expressive drama of the movement. The tragedy of the first movement manages only to hint at this more positive realm. In the coda a resignational emphasis on the minor subdominant leads to a final resolution of the thematized diminished seventh as vii^{o7} to Picardy-third tonic. But this unsettled coda leads us to expect a more profound transformation, which Beethoven will provide with the transcendent final movement, an expanded set of variations in glowing C major.

The next three examples illustrate an interesting growth process with respect to the arrival $^6_4$ as a type in Beethoven's style, and as appropriated by Schubert. In the coda to the finale of Beethoven's Sonata for Piano and Cello in A Major, Op. 69, a *subito piano* marks a rhetorical arrival $^6_4$ on the *subdominant* in the piano (Example 1.2b, m. 195). Note, however, that the pedal fifth of the IV chord is already present, and thus the pedestal effect is already in place in the piano part. Instead of the lowered third (F♮) which would occur with the German augmented sixth (not appropriate as an elaboration of the subdominant), Beethoven employs an augmented dominant of IV, written with an E♯. Note also that the cello has the bass, emphasizing the resolution of E♯ to F♯, and producing, in effect, an "arrival $^6_3$" on the subdominant.

In Beethoven's Sonata for Piano and Cello in D Major, Op. 102, no. 2, the coda to the first movement features the arrival $^6_3$ on the tonic chord (Example 1.2c, m. 143), logically appearing in this inversion because of its proper voice-leading resolution of an inverted German augmented-sixth chord (m. 142) with lowered $\hat{3}$ in the bass. The sense of a "breakthrough" arrival (or return, in this case) is perhaps even stronger because of the unusual inversion. Clearly Beethoven is expanding his use of this effect; an arrival $^6_3$ illustrates style growth in this rhetorical and poetic treatment of harmony.

Finally, in Schubert's Piano Sonata in A Major, D. 959, the last statement of the rondo theme in the finale is broken by rhetorical pauses and a reinterpretation over a German augmented sixth (Example 1.2d, m. 342). Rather than resolve "properly" with an arrival $^6_4$, Schubert instead continues the theme where he left off, which happens to be on I$^6_3$ (m. 344). The resolution is atypical, but the effect is rhetorically familiar, if we understand the arrival $^6_3$ as a variant of the arrival $^6_4$. The warmth of the return to an unambiguous A major is gesturally enhanced by the turn figure in the melody, a "sweetening" ornament that provides an appropriate sense of reassurance at this point. Here rhetorical or poetic resolution takes priority over nor-

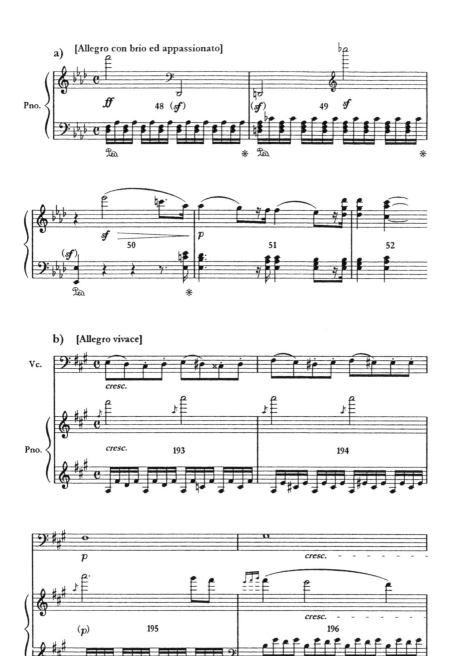

Example 1.2. Examples of tonic arrival $^6_4$ and arrival $^6_3$.
a. Beethoven, Piano Sonata in C Minor, Op. 111, first movement, arrival of second theme on dominant "pedestal" (mm. 50–52).
b. Beethoven, Sonata for Piano and Cello in A Major, Op. 69, last movement, arrival $^6_3$ in the coda (m. 195).

Example 1.2. Examples of tonic arrival $^6_4$ and arrival $^6_3$.
c. Beethoven, Sonata for Piano and Cello in D Major, Op. 102, no. 2, first movement, arrival $^6_3$ in the coda (m. 143).
d. Schubert, Piano Sonata in A Major, D. 959, arrival $^6_3$ in the coda (m. 344).

mative voice-leading resolution. Not only is this an instance of style growth in Schubert, but it offers more evidence that expressive motivations, as opposed to formalist ones, are generating that growth.

Returning to the *Ghost* Trio (Example 1.1), the further interpretation of the "y" theme's arrival $^6_4$ as positive would also take into account the lyrical character of the cello line and the hint of pastoral in the parallel thirds of the piano accompaniment. These have familiar stylistic correlations which contribute to the total effect. Another, more strategic mode of interpretation involves the thematic opposition between motives "x" and "y," a compositional premise that Beethoven works out through the movement. For example, the transition section uses a rhythmically ironed-out diminution of the "y" theme for its liquidation of the counterstatement, bringing "y" in closer relation to the eighth notes of "x." The development section juxtaposes and mixes the two motives in contrapuntally complex arguments that also touch on the tonal implications of the B♭. And the recapitulation further juxtaposes the two themes, with the "x" motive in D minor interrupting the return of "y." We have no comparably significant (thematically marked) motive for the second key group of the rather compact exposition, and the closing motives lead to a motivic melodic cadence that recalls the "y" motive. Thus, the "discourse" of the movement, its enacted drama, concerns the relationship of the two motives introduced at the outset—the same motives pursued in E. T. A. Hoffmann's analysis as first and second themes.

In terms of phrase construction, the "x" motive is introductory. While clearly grouping in two beat units, it is metrically ambiguous as to which beat is the downbeat. Furthermore, the sequencing of the motive evades clear periodicity (a stylistic expectation for thematic material); the rhythmic irregularity and modal interruption of "x" forces us to wait for "y" in order for a *Satz,* or sentence, to begin. The periodic *Satz* from mm. 7–21 is nevertheless built mosaically out of the two-bar motive "y," compressed to one-bar sequential extensions (mm. 14–16), with a more brilliant, almost cadenza-like flourish in the piano to expand the cadence (mm. 17–21). Its structure is not 4 + 4 but 4 + 11 bars, due to the additive and developmental extensions. The theme is a single sentence in terms of overall harmonic progression, however, since the first four bars are dedicated to the arrival $^6_4$'s becoming dominant and then stepping up to tonic.

Thus, both motives are parts of something larger to which they contribute; "y" is not merely a resolution of the phrase-structural instabilities of "x." I noted earlier that "y" shares its contour with "x." Beethoven brings about an integration of the dual perspectives of "x" and "y," both contrapuntally (in the development) and with rhetorical juxtapositions (in the recapitulation). Where does this lead us? First, to the question of agency. Often a dramatic contrast at the opening of a movement is used dialectically (McClary 1986; Eckelmeyer 1986). With this movement I experience a single agency, and I think that the above analysis indicates why. Motives "x" and "y," while direct contrasts on the surface, are dual perspectives from a single vantage point, that of the implied agency of the work. Notice that what I mean by agency goes beyond the triple agency of three performers, or three contrapuntal lines, as in the familiar metaphor of a chamber work being a conversation among equals. Granted, this concept of singular agency embracing different instruments, voices, and thematic contrasts may appear a bit vague. Carolyn Abbate (1991) and Scott Burnham (1995) have developed the concepts of "voice" and "presence" to more closely characterize these effects of agency. Although he does not address the trios, Burnham notes that in Beethoven's works from the second period we hear the agency of heroic struggle, and we tend to project ourselves as enactors of that struggle. Even within such a model, I would claim, a sudden loud chord might suggest an external agency, threatening the "pilgrim's progress" of the central, or internal, agency with which we might identify. Here the sudden shift to minor in m. 5, suspended rhetorically in m. 6, is in my interpretation an internal shift, as the protagonist-agent is caught up short, pauses to ponder, and then is reengaged in m. 7 with a transformed kind of energy that bespeaks not necessarily heroic effort, but assured insight.

Does this appear to be a big interpretive jump on my part? Recall E. T. A. Hoffmann's characterization of this theme: "genial serenity, confident awareness of its own strength and substance." We typically read and accept such descriptions without any real qualms—or else ignore them as mere sentimentality. But notice how Hoffmann's words take on fresh significance, given a more exhaustive semiotic interpretation. Hoffmann was hearing sensitively and musically (despite his incomplete formal analysis). He simply had no theory that would rigorously support the more poetic side of his interpretation.

The literary Hoffmann often emphasized the poetic and the romantic aspects of music. In his short story "Ritter Gluck" (1972 [1809]: 8) he refers to the tonic and dominant (scale degrees) as giant colossi, and the *Tierce* (the third scale degree) as a soft youth with a sweet voice, evidence that supports my own characterization of stark open fifth versus sweet third in a discussion of unusual tonic triad doublings in Beethoven (Hatten 1994: 50–56).

There is another reason to argue for agency that goes beyond a theme's "self-awareness"—and in this case to argue for a single agency in these opening bars. It has to do with performance, and with the gestural interpretations to which performers must commit themselves. Listen to the opening eight bars, perhaps comparing more than one performance.

In some performances there is a noticeable break, due to bowing, between mm. 6 and 7 in the cello. Unfortunately the tension of gestural continuity is thereby broken, and we hear an interpretation in which the F♮ dies away, only to be displaced by the F♯. But if the move from F♮ to F♯ is both motivic and part of a larger dramatic scheme, as outlined above, then we must hear instead a kind of transformation: as though F♮ melted (and hence was "transformed") into F♯, without losing the gestural tension that, if properly executed, could carry us over the suspended time of mm. 5 and 6.[2]

That F to F♯ is indeed motivic may be argued from more evidence than its clear use here as part of a structural juncture, or expressive crux, that marks the beginning of the lyric y motive with such unforgettable magic. The end of the exposition has a curious overlapping of harmonies that also blurs the final cadence in A, such that we focus more on the plagal close, IV–(vii°$_3^4$)–I (Example 1.3, mm. 64–67). The potential perfect authentic cadence in mm. 62–63 is clouded by the move from V^{m9} to V^7/IV, an undercutting often employed to cue a codetta (Hatten 1994: 41). The conflict between F♮ in the V^{m9} and F♯ in the IV, anticipated by the trill, involves a similar transformation from tension (the diminished-seventh and dominant-ninth sonorities) to extremely relaxed consonance (via the dominant seventh of IV to the subdominant itself). While F to F♯ is pursued twice in the piano trills, and is ech-

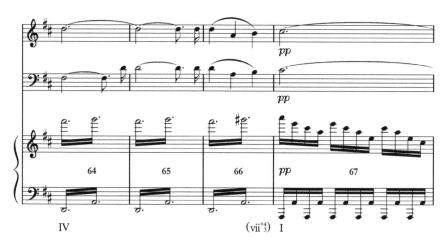

Example 1.3. Beethoven, *Ghost* Trio, first movement, close of the exposition.

oed by G to G♯ to A for the elaborated plagal cadence, the cello has an equally telling move from G♯ to G♮, undercutting a potential authentic cadence in mm. 62–63. This yielding reversal, in which a resignational pulling-down is more than compensated by the positive arrival on the subdominant, results in the trope of abnegation, or spiritual acceptance, that gives such appropriate expressive significance to this exquisitely subtle closural strategy.[3] The piano trills allow an otherwise syntactically impossible concatenation of F–F♯ and G♯–G to occur right at the point of negated syntactic closure, m. 63, and this expressive crux sums up the more transcendent goal of the expressive genre. When the tritone C♯–G in violin and cello resolves in m. 64 to the subdominant, the effect is further enhanced, and prolonged, by the analogous contrary motion by half step. Expressive fulfillment is achieved with the strings' reengagement in m. 66 of a melodic gesture derived from "y," closing the exposition in the proper key of A major. Finally, the sublime character of extreme registers on the piano adds to the benediction of this substitutional plagal cadence, which has taken on an expressive role analogous to the Picardy-third cadence in a minor-mode work.

Returning to Example 1.1, note that in m. 6 the B♭–F analyzed as an incomplete German augmented sixth has its own implications, stemming from the other plausible interpretation of the chord as a root position B♭ triad, or ♭VI in D major. Beethoven cannot resist playing with this potential, both glancingly in the development, and more decisively after the intrusion of the "x" motive in minor just after the start of the recapitulation. This time, F♮ appears in the piano as well as the cello and resolves to the "y" theme in (of course) B♭ major.

Having contextualized the meaning of the theme in m. 7, both with respect to the opening dramatic gesture and with regard to the consequences of the thematized resolution of m. 6, how might one characterize its inherent expressiveness as a *gesture*? Its contour is similar to one used in m. 6 of the Cavatina of Beethoven's String Quartet in B♭ Major, Op. 130, which I interpreted as a "tragic reversal" (1994: 213). But the context is quite different, and the result is affectively worlds apart. In the trio the hopeful ascent is indeed reversed, but not negated, since the drop is enfolded within the harmony of V^7 and is further resolved by step to complete a safely consonant, triadic outline that could be reduced as $\hat{3}$–$\hat{5}$–$\hat{1}$. Yet the descending interval from $\hat{5}$ to $\hat{7}$ does have a certain yielding quality, like a graceful acceptance of boundaries, in its reversal of the initial ascent from $\hat{3}$ to $\hat{5}$. In turn, that tucked-in drop could be heard, in conjunction with the positive arrival $^6_4$ and pedestal dominant pedal, as somehow reassuring in its balanced motion. By comparison, nothing seems likely to stop the unbalanced additive sequencing of the "x" motive in the very beginning, until it encounters the silence that anticipates a surprising and parenthetical F♮.[4]

What is interesting about the "y" theme is that both its stability and instability can be interpreted positively in terms of affective meaning.[5] This would appear impossible if the binarism I espoused were the kind that Lawrence Kramer condemns in *Classical Music and Postmodern Knowledge* (1995: 34–51). In the so-called "logic of alterity," which his postmodernist New Musicology would deconstruct, the oppositions are between self and other, and that which is personally valued versus that which is excluded or defined by negation. Such oppositions are ideologically loaded, as we all know. I trust that the kinds of oppositions I have discussed here can be viewed in a different light, and it is from this standpoint that I would preserve the structuralist component, alongside the hermeneutic, in my model of music semiotics. While it is true that any opposition can be freighted with ideological baggage, we should nevertheless recognize that the mechanism of asymmetrical opposition is simply one of the fundamental ways in which cognition works. It is not an evil that must be rooted out, but rather a useful tool for helping us make those kinds of discriminations that move from perceptual categories to cognitive concepts.

In fairness to Kramer, I share his regard for pluralism, if not complete eclecticism, in my theoretical approach. Our goals are quite different, however, despite what may appear on the surface to be a similar quest: to demonstrate how so-called "extramusical" meaning is intrinsic to our musical understanding. As Kramer explains it,

> What postmodern knowledge offers classical music is the chance to acknowledge and explore, to de- and reconstruct, its relationship to modern subjectivity, and in so doing to form a different relationship to the postmodern subjectivities that may now be in the making. (1995: 34)

My goal, on the other hand, is to reconstruct the stylistic competency—cultural practice in the historical sense—that is presupposed by the musical work in its historical context. While recognizing that I can only do so from a present subjectivity, I nevertheless find that this kind of history is no more or less problematic than the kinds of history we have pursued in other arenas. We can never know with certainty, but we can come closer to stylistic understanding as a goal by pursuing a more rigorous course than Kramer might deem possible. His model of musical meaning is that of a communicative "economy" in which our own ideas have equal weight with the composer's as we fill out the missing elements in music's only "partly determinate subjectivity" (23). Under that regime associations can float rather freely in unconstrained cultural contexts. In my approach, on the other hand, there is continual refinement of a model of style that works to constrain interpretive claims, or subject them to more compelling modes of argument and standards of evidence. Progressively one can build the groundwork (by reconstructing style and style growth) that will support, or lead one to refine, or even reject, earlier interpretations. At the same time, through the hermeneutic component of interpretation, one can access and evaluate those personal and cultural exchanges that Kramer prizes as the goal of a more equal "dialogue" with music's potential meanings.

Thus, in seeking to establish a basis for musical meaning in a given composer's output (style types, their expressive correlations, and their further interpretation in musical works—within the contexts of strategic events) one's role is analogous to that of a trial lawyer who must make a case, by creating plausible generalizations or narratives, that accounts for all the available evidence. Postmodernist approaches may consider this to be a flawed enterprise, impossible from the start, but I have found the results to reward the effort. It is less a leap of faith for me to attempt to approach Beethoven's meanings in this way than it is for me to accept some of the associative leaps of a facile New Musicology, especially when they go beyond plausible intentions by historical individuals, to the unwitting psychological and cultural biases in which cultural subjects are inevitably trapped. I want to understand what Beethoven might have wanted to mean, not to psychoanalyze his efforts or to reduce him to a pawn of cultural forces beyond his control. Though my approach recognizes the stylistic and intertextual relationships that guarantee coherence of types and strategies from one work to the next, it also acknowledges the ways in which a composer can create works whose individuality lead to growth (or even change) of cultural values or meanings. Thus, I would not dissolve the "autonomous" work into a mere node at the intersection of cultural practice, viewed through the peephole of present-day subjectivity, but rather reconceive the individual work as emerging from a dialectic of stylistic and strategic motivations as grounded in an historical context.

Thus, in pursuing my semiotic approach, I part company from at least this strain of the New Musicology. I believe that one needs not only a plurality of evidence and method, but a unifying rigor that comes from a stylistically and historically grounded model of musical meaning. That model should help explain how meaning is coherent and consistent, and help lead us to reconstruct deeper levels of meaning that might not have passed through our untrained cultural filters. In turn, it will lead us to a consistency in our reconstruction, from which we can move more confidently toward further interpretations—continuing in dialectical fashion the productive interaction between a growing stylistic competency and an expanding sensitivity to interpretive nuance, between the generalization of the type and the subtleties of the token.

2 Expressive Doubling, Topics, Tropes, and Shifts in Level of Discourse: Interpreting the Third Movement of Beethoven's String Quartet in B♭ Major, Op. 130

The Andante con moto ma non troppo of Beethoven's Op. 130 is an unusual movement in an unusual quartet of six movements with an alternate finale.[1] I will argue that its unique expressive meaning can best be understood in terms of four aspects: its relationship to the other movements of the quartet, its treatment of an original topic as premise, its tropological exploitation of a hybrid form and genre, and its many rhetorical shifts in level of discourse. Together, these four arenas of creative innovation support a coherent expressive argument for the movement. They also reveal the way Beethoven extends the Classical style to embody an immediacy of expression akin to the unfolding of conscious experience. My expressive interpretation of the movement will also help explain the motivation behind atypical structural and formal events, and why Beethoven might have departed from sonata form so radically in this movement.

The evidence for expressive relationships between movements begins with the creative process itself. There are two extensive (and competing) accounts of the lengthy and fascinating compositional history of Beethoven's String Quartet in B♭, Op. 130. Each has something to contribute to my interpretation of the Andante movement, with respect to Beethoven's decision to include four inner movements before the finale. It will be helpful to begin with a brief summary of Barry Cooper's account (1990: 197–214). After completing the weighty first movement in B♭ major and the short Presto in B♭ minor, Beethoven abandoned several sketches for a slow movement in D♭ that would eventually become the Cavatina and quickly wrote the Andante, also in D♭, in its place. The finale, originally conceived as a much lighter and shorter movement, gradually evolved into a fugue, and then expanded into the monumental Grosse Fuge. The mammoth proportions of this finale led Beethoven to reconsider the middle of the cycle, adding another dance–slow movement pair to help balance the design. For the dance movement Beethoven chose the Alla danza tedesca he had originally considered using as the fourth movement of Op. 132 and transposed it from A to G major. And the slow movement evolved from earlier sketches into the Cavatina, now in E♭ major. Later, at the urging of Karl Holz and with a "financial inducement" from his publisher, Matthias Artaria, Beethoven composed the substitute finale that—according to Cooper—may have been closer to his original conception before the fugue called forth two more inner movements.

Klaus Kropfinger (1987: 305) offers a different version of the compositional genesis of Op. 130, emphasizing the crucial evidence in the sketches that Beethoven conceived of a fugal finale from the beginning. In the de Roda sketchbook, fol. 14^r (May–September 1825), the words "le[t]ztes Stück des Quartetts in B-Dur" (last movement of the quartet in B♭ major) precede a sketch of a theme that at one point is labeled "Fugha." Already on fol. 6^r Beethoven had sketched the opening of the first movement, appending the words, "Le[t]ztes Quartett [of the Galitzin set] mit einer ernsthaften und schwergängigen Einleitung" (Last quartet, with a serious and weighty introduction). Together, these bits of evidence suggest that Beethoven conceived of the work from the start as framed by two potentially weighty movements. Kropfinger (1987: 316) makes a strong case for the cumulative integration of a conceptual cycle, an integration that the original finale completes. He notes (1987: 301–303) that the financial incentive from Artaria that led Beethoven to decide on composing a new finale after only one day's consideration was actually offered several months after the initial performance of the work, and that Beethoven's decision in no way negates his initial conception, but in part reflects realities associated with Artaria's marketing strategies for the quartet (he had already decided to publish the fugue separately in a piano transcription of the entire quartet). In a later article (1994: 315) Kropfinger finds further reason to appreciate, if not prefer, the second finale, including a motivic/rhythmic resemblance between mm. 2–3 of the Cavatina and 5–6 of the second finale, which suggests that the second finale may be ironically reversing the seriousness of the Cavatina. The idea is suggestive, and I will explore possible rhetorical associations between inner movements as part of a larger expressive strategy in the quartet.

If Beethoven originally conceived of Op. 130 in terms of a typical four-movement cycle, one might suppose that in expanding to six movements he was moving toward a more relaxed organization akin to a suite. However, his design for the inner movements clearly suggests two *pairs* of contrasting movements, corresponding to the traditional model of scherzo–slow movement, but doubled. This logical inner expansion of the traditional four-movement cycle would have served not only to balance the weightier outer movements but also to project the first movement's dialectic of contrasting affects across the cycle as a whole. Consider the analogous movements of each pair. The "scherzo-like" movements feature a contrast between the relaxed Alla danza tedesca (IV), marked Allegro assai but heard in a leisurely one to the bar, and the highly intense Presto (II). The "slow" movements feature a contrast between the profound Adagio of the Cavatina (V) and the genial Andante of the third movement. Within each "scherzo-slow" pair Beethoven also foregrounds oppositions: the Andante third movement "responds" rhetorically and expressively to the Presto second movement, and tellingly, this pair of movements is sharply separated from the following pair by the highly disjunctive tonal shift from D♭ major to G major for the Alla danza tedesca fourth movement.

In his choice of tempo for the third movement, Andante con moto ma non

Example 2.1. Comparison of themes with staccato bass line.
a. Beethoven, Piano Sonata in A Major, Op. 2, no. 2, second movement.
b. Beethoven, Piano Sonata in E♭ Major, Op. 31, no. 3, second movement.

troppo, and his expressive indication of Poco scherzoso for the potentially tragic opening (itself a reference to the lament that opens the first movement), Beethoven signals an unusual, and perhaps hybrid, movement. Indeed, the Andante is soon inflected by the rhythmic energy of a lighter, easy-going scherzo. The sixteenth-note walking bass with which the leisurely first theme gets underway in m. 3 (Example 2.7, mm. 3–4) may be compared to similar textures in two middle movements from the piano sonatas (Examples 2.1a and b). The Andante tempo of the quartet movement falls midway between the Largo appassionato of Op. 2, no. 2 (clearly a slow movement in three) and the Scherzo: Allegretto vivace of Op. 31, no. 3 (clearly a scherzo in spirit, but with an overlaid lyric line and duple meter). Interestingly, Op. 31, no. 3 pairs a Scherzo with a Menuetto, but the Menuetto alludes to the missing slow movement by means of its lyrical opening strain. The Andante third movement of Op. 130, on the other hand, might be viewed as a *trope* at the level of genre, in that it creatively fuses the playfulness and rhythmic drive of a scherzo with the tunefulness of an Andante.

What further evidence might support an interpretation of paired movements? With its initial gesture in the first violin, not only does the Andante allude to the

Example 2.2. Derivation of the Andante's opening sigh (a) and link with the Presto (b) in Beethoven, String Quartet in B♭ Major, Op. 130.
a. First movement, opening theme.
b. Second movement, closing measures.

lament opening of the first movement (Example 2.2a), but it also appears to respond, speculatively, to the B♭ minor of the Presto (Example 2.2b) before shifting
gears tonally and rhythmically into D♭ for a first theme group. The play of B♭♭ versus A♮ in mm. 1 and 2 (Example 2.7) is notated to imply vii°⁷/D♭ in m. 1 and vii°⁶₅/B♭
minor in m. 2, but the listener who is not also performing the work would probably
hear both B♭♭ and A as leading tones in B♭ minor, thereby prolonging the key of the
Presto. When the A♮ in m. 2 is expressively reversed to A♭ (*dolce*) at the end of the

measure, the sigh relaxes into a contented D♭ major (note the "collapsing" parallel tenths in the viola and cello that respond to the A♭'s "yielding" effect).

Lawrence Kramer (1990: 22) introduces a trope he calls "expressive doubling" to help interpret a relationship between movements in four Beethoven piano sonatas that have only two movements (Opp. 54, 78, 90, and 111). According to Kramer, in these sonatas the second movement not only provides contrast but significantly *responds* to the first movement as well, dialectically interpreting its problematic issues by transposing them to "a higher or deeper plane, a more brilliant or profound register" (30). How might one adapt Kramer's concept to interpret the relationship between the paired inner movements of Op. 130? The Andante expressively doubles the Presto's obsessive drive by counterposing a leisurely pace suggestive of the workaday world. An interpretation at this stage might claim that the Andante comments on the abnormal intensity of the Presto by proposing a more humane alternative. There is more to the expressive doubling, however, than a speculative opposition of expressive states based on contrasting tempi. Following Kramer, "whatever conflicts or instabilities appear in the lower term of the doubling tend to be carried over into the higher term" (31). Indeed, the Presto experiences a series of dramatic reversals in its transition from the trio back to the scherzo proper (Example 2.3), and the Andante expressively doubles this idea with its own series of reversals and deferrals, distractions and interruptions, that affect the otherwise contented forward progress of its texture. These various disruptions demand closer analysis and interpretation.

But first consider the following pair of movements. The Cavatina is already linked with the subsequent fugal finale by means of the common tone G.[2] Can it also be construed as an expressive doubling of the previous Alla danza tedesca? Perhaps not as obviously as the Presto and Andante pair, since there is no linking transition. Nevertheless, there are indicators that support an explicitly framed opposition. Each movement is based on an imported topical genre; the *Ländler*-like *deutscher Tanz*, a low-style peasant dance, contrasts with the high-style vocal genre of the Cavatina (Examples 2.4a and b). Both genres draw on simplicity as a means of achieving their expressive effects. Like the previous pair, these two movements each have disruptive episodes, but they relate more closely to each other in that the disruptions are both fragmentary and to some degree dissociative.

The coda of the German dance features a disorienting permutation of isolated solo measures (Example 2.5a), turning what might initially have suggested an echo of the cadence into a complete retrograde of the four isolated motives of the second phrase (one in each instrument), followed by a normal ordering of the first phrase of the theme, also parceled out in solo motives. The Cavatina features the parenthetical *Beklemmt* (oppressed, *Angst*-laden) recitative, in which the first violin as soloist projects an emotional collapse in a rhythm suitably dissociated from the accompanying strings (Example 2.5b). Finally, the opening themes of each movement feature "sighing" and broken-off articulations, whereas the Presto and Andante themes feature textural continuity within their main themes. The striking gestural character of the Alla danza tedesca, in which the articulations of the odd measures suggest wistful sighs, is complemented by traces of *empfindsamer* broken

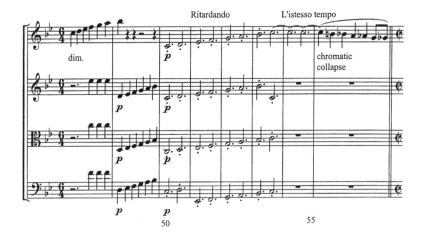

Example 2.3. Dramatic reversals in the transition to the return of the Presto of Beethoven, Op. 130.

declamation in the Cavatina (the literal sigh figure in m. 3 is "choked" off and the second violin fills the emotion-laden gap). In terms of expressive doubling, the Cavatina might thus be understood as responding to the dance's relatively surface expression with a greater depth of emotional intimacy; but the dance is touching in its own way, with gentle yet undeniable yearnings that also suggest a deeper purport.

As for the Presto and Andante movements, there is further compelling evidence for their expressive pairing. The Andante alludes to the Presto theme—somewhat skeletally, to be sure—in mm. 81 and 83 (compare Examples 2.6a and b). The sig-

(a)

(b)

Example 2.4. Framed opposition between the fourth and fifth movements of Beethoven, Op. 130.
a. Opening theme, Alla danza tedesca.
b. Opening theme, Cavatina.

nificance of this spectral echo will emerge from a closer analysis of the Andante's other disruptions and their implied shifts in level of discourse. The main themes of the two movements (Examples 2.6a and 2.7) also support an interpretation of expressive doubling. The Presto features a motivic third emerging from a sequential stepwise descent. The Andante sequences its thirds in a stepwise ascent. This opposition may be interpreted dialectically as a pessimistic descent (in the Presto)

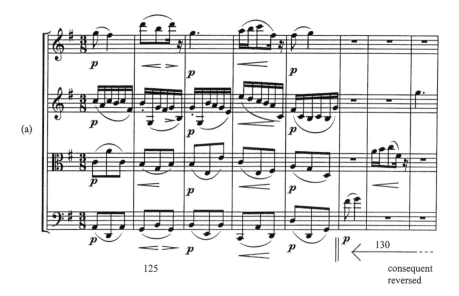

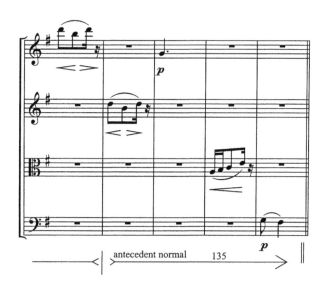

Example 2.5. Dissociative events in the fourth and fifth movements of Beethoven, Op. 130.
a. Permutation of measures of the theme near the end of the Alla danza tedesca.

(b)

Example 2.5. Dissociative events in the fourth and fifth movements of Beethoven, Op. 130.
b. *Beklemmt* episode in the Cavatina.

countered by an optimistic ascent (in the Andante). Furthermore, the contrasting tempi support an expressive opposition between obsessive irritation in the more dynamic Presto and naive, good-hearted optimism in the Andante proper.

Textural evidence for expressive doubling arises from both movements' density of activity, suggestive of the clockwork topic proposed by Leonard Ratner. Ratner (1980: 391) cites three examples from the third movement of Op. 130 as topical representations of a clocklike mechanism in which "the wheels appear to have a highly eccentric motion, at times running completely wild." I think the function of such textures in this movement is part of a larger textural strategy, motivated by a concern for what I will call *plenitude,* conceived as both premise and topic for each movement. Expressively, plenitude implies saturation or repleteness, and as such, the prototypical state of plenitude would be one of suffused, contented fulfillment. An exemplary treatment of plenitude as premise is found in the Adagio of the Ninth Symphony, and, indeed, the transcendent effect of diminutions in Beethoven's late variation sets is based on a progressive strategy of textural saturation. But plenitude need not be tied to a particular affective state; the obsessive Presto in Op. 130 conveys a dysphoric plenitude, expressively doubled by the euphoric plenitude of the Andante. As part of a compositional *premise,* plenitude may be understood as a desired goal achieved by processes that lead to the ultimate saturation of texture, and fulfillment—perhaps even apotheosis—in the case of a theme. As a *topic,* the relative textural, registral, and activity-level saturation characteristic of plenitude is present in the opening themes of both Presto and Andante, Examples 2.6a and 2.7 (mm. 3–10), and is supported as well by the hint of perpetual motion in each theme's consistency of rhythmic texture.

The processes that contribute to plenitude include the following, most of which appear in the opening eight measures of the Andante (see Example 2.7):

Expressive Doubling, Topics, Tropes, and Shifts in Level of Discourse 43

Example 2.6. A thematic link between the second and third movements of Beethoven, Op. 130.
a. Opening theme of the Presto.
b. Spectral echo in the Andante.

a. Phrase and motivic construction by (varied) repetition of thematic/ textural units, often featuring textural inversion. Measures 1–2 are constructed as 1 + 1, mm. 3–6 as 2 + 2, and mm. 7–8 as ½ + ½ + ½.
b. Diminutional variation procedures (occurring later in the movement). Diminutions add rhythmic complexity and density to the texture; compare the extra activity when the theme returns in m. 38 (see Example 2.7).
c. An expressive crux (m. 7) characterized by "fulfillment" and tending to-

Example 2.7. Beethoven, Op. 130, third movement (Andante con moto ma non troppo), mm. 1–26. (*Continued on the next page.*)

Example 2.7. *Continued*

ward stasis; varied repetition of a marked motivic/textural idea as if for pure enjoyment (compare the Andante moderato sections from the Adagio of the Ninth Symphony).
d. A sense of "timelessness" as extended continuities override sharp formal articulations (e.g., the evaded cadence in m. 8).

To create a more dramatic expressive genre from this premise, Beethoven counters the timeless suffusion of textural and temporal plenitude by means of a wide range of disruptive strategies. As with other topical premises— for instance, the heroic struggle to achieve victory—this progress toward ultimate fulfillment is impeded and deflected to create a dynamic trajectory. But some of the disruptions also imply what I have called *shifts in level of discourse* (Hatten 1994: 174–88) in that the sudden reversal suggests a self-reflexive response or shift in consciousness on the part of a single agent, rather than an external agency antagonistic to the progress of a protagonist. Such shifts may also imply a Romantic ironic comment on the prevailing musical discourse, subverting or dismissing that which is seen as too self-indulgent, or too naive, or simply in need of a midcourse correction.

Interestingly, some of these disruptive strategies are motivated by the very temporal extensions and irregularities that result from working out the premise of desired plenitude. When continuities overly prolong states of fulfillment, they may begin to imply states of distraction, diffusion, wandering, or winding down from euphoria into a state of depression. Other, more confrontational strategies highlight *discontinuity* by means of reversals, deferrals, sudden recognitions, redirections, and projections that may in turn be positive rechargings of expressive energy that has become diffused, as well as negative displacements of euphoric states that cannot hold. Whatever the disruptive strategy, the fulfillments of plenitude are thereby made to appear fragile, and hence more valuable, since they are subject to eventual decay or displacement.

Beethoven breaks new ground stylistically in his treatment of disruptions and shifts in levels of discourse. The temporal/textural premise of plenitude itself—so different from the more directed, progressive energies and forceful breakthroughs of his heroic style—also opens a new expressive field. Euphoric fulfillments are disrupted at the very point we might begin to believe they would go on forever, or they are allowed to stutter and decline as their energies dissipate. The result can be seen to represent, or enact, something akin to a reflective stream of consciousness or desire.

The following analysis examines in detail the remarkable sequence of disruptions and digressions, noting their role in undercutting or deflecting the blissful experience of plenitude (see Example 2.7 for the first part of the analysis).

1. (Mm. 1–10) The first theme gets fully underway in m. 3, reaches an expressive crux in m. 7, and luxuriates in its *subito piano* yet expansive arrival in the dominant, A♭ major, by treating a half-bar idea to two varied repetitions. This is the first expressive crux in the movement. An expected cadence in A♭ in m. 8 is bypassed harmonically, and the rhythmic sequencing extends until a quiet cadence regains the tonic.

2. (Mm. 10–13) The cadence figure is then subject to clocklike pizzicato imitation and remodulation to A♭, only to be displaced by a theme that, although clearly in A♭, does little more than cadence. After variations on its cadential melodic descent, the discourse becomes diffuse, and a sudden V^7/IV serves to inject new energy.

3. (Mm. 13–17) Another cadentially oriented theme ventures forth in the cello. It is echoed in increasingly thicker textural variation (plenitude without expressive fulfillment) until its diffused stasis is more forcefully disrupted in m. 17 by an unexpected V^6 of F, what I have elsewhere analyzed as a "recitative chord" (Hatten 1994: 15)—a dislocating major $^6_3$ that suggests the "paragraph break" of a recitative. Beethoven imported these $^6_3$ recitative chords into nonoperatic music to cue a sudden shift in discourse, often entailing a more intimate or direct expression by the implied agent.

4. (Mm. 17–19) But instead of spawning a new theme, as had the previous interruption, this sudden seizing of the dramatic reins engenders a rhythmic figure that is distracted by reiterated cadential gesturing. But tonic never solidifies, and the reactive passage merely prolongs the disruptive V of F. Wedgelike intensification in m. 19 is sharply displaced by an isolated D♭ (as expressive ♭6̂), posed like a question or a warning ("nicht diese Töne"?) and functioning as a pivot for the return to an idealized state, as represented by the main theme.

5. (Mm. 20–25) Resolving to C, the D♭ has indeed triggered a return to the main theme, but in brighter C major, not F, which complements the greater saturation of texture (a canonic imitation at the fifth begins on the second beat) and enhances its sense of plenitude. This reprise of the main theme, the only idea thus far with sufficiently marked expressive character to qualify as a central focus for the discourse, then embarks on a journey through a series of keys. The theme is both developed (fragmentation and sequence in mm. 21 and 23) and characteristically varied (new textural setting in mm. 22–23) in what appears to be a development section, but this leads, progressively and texturally intensified, to a new expressive crux (again in the dominant, A♭ major) marked *Cantabile*, beginning in m. 26 (perhaps also suggesting a fulfilled closing theme for an exposition moving from D♭ to confirmed A♭).

6. (Mm. 26–38) Plenitude is fulfilled with this thematic arrival. The descending melodic second is reminiscent of the expressive crux in m. 7, made more thrilling here by acceleration or diminution and more replete by its elaboration into a fully achieved melodic phrase. Texturally and registrally the passage is saturated, and the decorative grace-note turns unmistakably mark the euphoric character of the arrival. A varied repetition hints at return with its modulation to D♭ in m. 30, but the melodic cadential trill is again disrupted, in m. 31, by V^4_2 of ii. This disruption, *subito pp*, merely serves as a cutback to enhance the ongoing fulfillment of the theme and its plenitude. Continuous sixteenths lead to an even more decorative version of the second expressive crux; the exquisite scalar ascents and their sequential treatment (mm. 32–35) extract still more pleasure from this thematic fulfillment. Just when it might appear that the euphoric might be prolonged indefinitely, a premonitory ♭6̂–5̂ in A♭, recalling the sighs of mm. 1–2, falsely prepares the tonal return of the main theme in D♭.

7. (Mm. 38–63) The main theme returns with further diminution in the accompaniment, as though replete with the pleasures of the previous section, and the literal return of material (with appropriate tonal resolution) marks a sonata recapitulation. After the extended cadence back to D♭, the pizzicato imitative echoes are transposed down a fifth, and the subsidiary, "cadential" themes are resolved to D♭. The interruptive recitative chord is now V^6/B♭, ♭$\hat6$ leads to F instead of C, but surprisingly, what appeared to be the beginning of a development section is faithfully recapitulated as well. The second expressive crux returns in D♭, but this time it is truncated to make room for a truly transcendent elaboration.

8. (Mm. 64–67) Just as before, the varied repetition of the second crux moves down a fifth, here from D♭ to the subdominant G♭. But the melodic cadential trill in m. 65 is suspended by a fermata, and instead of an interruption by V/ii, a cadenza-like treatment of the ascending scale returns us to the *first* expressive crux (from m. 7), now in the subdominant, and with a sense of transcendent return to what had already been the expressive goal of the first theme. But this time the first expressive crux cadences on schedule (last beat of m. 67), normalizing the previous two phrase extensions and saving cadential evasion for a later surprise.

9. (Mm. 68–73) The pizzicato imitative echoes of the original transition do not herald a new theme here; instead, they get "stuck" in a clockwork stasis and then appear to suffer a "slippage" (mm. 71–73) as a partly chromatic sequential descent slides to a diminished-seventh reference to the ambiguous opening bars of the movement. The enharmonically conceived diminished seventh at first resolves to the black hole of V/d, emblematic of the depths to which depression has wound down from transcendent bliss. Another attempt is made, but the progression to V/D♭ is not secured by a subsequent tonic chord. When a third try replicates the A♮ of m. 2 without the softening reversal to A♭, it signals a further treatment of the dysphoric.

10. (Mm. 74–76) The main theme returns, but it is subjected to a circle-of-fifths sequence that allows the poignancy of the introductory sighs to infect the optimistic cast of the theme, which is now reversed by a continuously chromatic melodic descent.

11. (Mm. 77–79) The less-disruptive passage used to evade cadences in mm. 28 and 31 is used here in an attempt to regain positive orientation—almost willfully, as if one were trying to convince oneself—but the gambit is not successful.

12. (Mm. 80–84) A sudden cadential evasion, again to V/ii as in m. 31, sets up a state of suspended animation and the most spectacular shift in level of discourse thus far. The circle-of-fifths sequence with which Beethoven created the chromatic slippage in the return of the main theme at mm. 74–75 may have suggested a parallel with the sequential Scherzo theme. Here the clockwork effect returns in slow motion with a bass line that echoes the previous movement's theme, both in mm. 81 and 83, and the spectral recollection suggests a consciousness haunted by its less-euphoric past.

13. (Mm. 84–88) The extreme displacement of mm. 80–84) is ultimately resolved by a brief transition in m. 84 that regains the positive and energetic realm of the second expressive crux for an even more fully saturated closing four bars

(mm. 85–88). Plenitude has the last word; despite the motivic liquidation in m. 86, the texture continues to increase in density, and by m. 87 all the voices are in thirty-second notes. Even the elegant arpeggiation of the final tonic (m. 88) features registral saturation in a last reverberation of the idealized state of plenitude.

This account of strategies of plenitude and counterstrategies of disruption has made reference to sonata form as referential frame and point of departure. The recapitulation involves resolution down a fifth of material heard earlier in the movement, and the music from the fermata in m. 65 to the end could be analyzed as an extensive coda. More problematic for a sonata form analysis are the following:

1. The move to the dominant occurs too soon, and the crux of the main theme in m. 7 is in A♭. The dominant key is cadentially evaded in m. 8 and then regained in m. 10 without any dominant prolongation that would strongly articulate a second-theme arrival.
2. The lack of clear articulation at the presumed end of the exposition. However, both the recitative chord (m. 17) and the premonitory ♭$\hat{6}$ (m. 19) are disruptive cues indicating that the forward progress of an exposition has been thwarted, and the return of the main theme in a new key (m. 20) suggests the fresh momentum of a development section.
3. The placement in the pseudo-development section of a second expressive crux in A♭ expressing fulfillment (m. 26 ff.), and its appearances in D♭ not long after—the modulation to D♭ occurs within the varied repetition of the theme in mm. 29–30, and its sequential treatment begins in D♭ (m. 32 ff.). This euphoric expressive crux may thus be recapitulated down a fifth without any threat to the resolutional status of the return section, which would not be the case if the material were more dissonant (as in a typical development section).

The form of this movement may reflect certain sonata organizing principles, but these unusual features suggest that an expressive interpretation may be more to the point in capturing the relevant dramatic trajectory of its form. The following summarizes the expressive argument of the movement.

The main theme (m. 3) embodies the premise of the movement with its sturdy, optimistic, stepwise ascent from the doldrums of the initial sigh gesture, enfolded in a textural plenitude that reaches fulfillment with the first expressive crux in m. 7. The enjoyment of that arrival is not really earned; rather, it appears as a moment of spiritual insight, and its reiterated half-bar idea is akin to a reverberation in consciousness. The attempt to maintain this idealized state is ultimately frustrated, and even the attempt to pin it down with a definite cadence is undercut. Much of the remainder of the movement may be read as a series of attempts to regain what has been briefly experienced, and the "development" does indeed "will" itself toward an ecstatic opening-out that becomes its climax of plenitude (m. 26 ff.). The "recapitulation" also replicates much of the development down a fifth, allowing us to reexperience that ecstatic opening, and trumping it expressively by means of a cadenza-like fermata and transcendent return to the original expressive crux (mm. 65–67). A series of slippages create drama in the coda, where depression threatens to displace transcendence. But even the spectral recall of the Presto—in a melancholic frame that suggests not only the suspension of time but also its omnipresence as clockwork—cannot derail the final peroration of the second expressive crux in its glorious plenitude.

Traditional formal articulations have a properly dramatic function in sonata form conceived as a dramatic scheme. What Beethoven explores in his late style, as I have demonstrated elsewhere (Hatten 1994: 24), are alternative sites of drama, often overriding or subverting the traditional structural sites of a conventional form. In this movement the play of continuity versus discontinuity (see Chapters 11 and 12) takes center stage, and sonata form recedes to the background. As formal schema is negotiated by expressive genre, and lyricism is troped by scherzo-like playfulness, the unique expressive synthesis of the movement begins to emerge.

At a larger formal level, the expressive doubling of Andante and Presto movements reflects the troping in the first movement between Adagio/slow-introduction sighs and Allegro fanfares. The dialectical engagement and intercutting of themes based on contrasting gestures is the central premise of a dissociative opening movement that strives to achieve integration, as Kerman (1966: 305–13) observes in his perceptive analysis.[3] The first movement's disruptions are principally due to the action of intercutting between these two seemingly incompatible ideas, each contending for control of the discourse in the opening of the movement and at the junctures of development and coda. The coda achieves thematic closure with what Kerman (312) calls the "forced wedding of the *adagio* and *allegro* themes," as Beethoven attempts to synthesize, and through voice-leading connections, stitch together a kind of resolution to the conflict between these two ideas, despite their ultimately irreconcilable tempi and meters. It is in the coda that a masterful, if elusive, trope is achieved.

Disruptions in the Andante, however, are understood more as shifts *away* from the perceived dissolutions of fulfillment, as first realized by the expressive crux in mm. 7–8 and its liquidation in m. 9. As shifts in *level* of discourse, these various discontinuities imply a self-conscious subjectivity or agency—musing upon loss, reacting with determined energy, or spiraling down into depressive obsession. The shifts of discourse in the Andante suggest a sequence of emotional states that are not only experienced but subsequently engaged by self-reflection and reactive feelings—in other words, the mixing of thought and emotion characteristic of fully human consciousness. Irony at times emerges from the play of self-consciousness and its dismissals: either simultaneously (the *poco scherzoso* undercutting of self-pitying sighs) or successively (the recitative-chord disruption that brings wandering distraction up short). There is an intriguing tension in the movement between two possible ways of losing one's path—either by extended euphoria that may lose its sense of directed motion and dissolve in thematic liquidation, or by various modes of distraction that may lead to depression or melancholy. And, ironically, continuity may be marked either as euphoric fulfillment or dysphoric obsession.

In forging his musical language Beethoven often relies more on the expressive associations available from key relationships in the tonal system, rather than the generative tonal schema of sonata form as currently theorized. In the Andante we have seen how sonata form yields to the idiosyncratic development of a new thematic *topic* (plenitude), conceived within the *trope* of slow movement and scherzo styles, and broken up by self-reflexive *shifts in level of discourse.* Beethoven's speculative treatment of plenitude as premise, however, goes far beyond a surface play with clockwork textures. The various disruptions of that surface reveal a deeper quest in which plenitude as contentment or fulfillment soon begins to represent an elusive state of spiritual bliss—that which emerges without being earned, is experienced without being consumed, and dissolves simply because it cannot be sustained. The poignancy of this movement is not that of typical tragedy, but—as in the Alla danza tedesca, and even more devastatingly in the Cavatina—the evanescence of that which is most deeply felt and cherished.

3   From Topic to Premise and Mode: The Pastoral in Schubert's Piano Sonata in G Major, D. 894

Beethoven's Sixth Symphony (1808) is the last great model of the characteristic pastoral symphony from the Classical era. Although many other works of the late eighteenth and early nineteenth centuries include topical pastoral allusions—for contrasting themes in sonata form movements, for episodes in rondos, or for the trios of minuets or scherzos—they do not feature the programmatic series of scenes from nature typical of the characteristic pastoral as a genre.[1] In the emerging Romantic era, however, a new pastoral *mode* begins to shape the main thematic lines and overall dramatic trajectory of works that at the same time may embrace a wider range of topics than strictly pastoral ones. As I have argued elsewhere (Hatten 1994: 67–111), Beethoven's Piano Sonata in A Major, Op. 101 (1816), may be understood as expressively shaped by the pastoral in this sense.[2] The pastoral elements in Schubert's Piano Sonata in G Major also extend beyond mere topical allusion, while resulting in something other than a conventional, characteristic pastoral genre. I will argue that this four-movement work is one manifestation of a Romantic evolution of the pastoral, understood as an overarching mode that coordinates the dramatic trajectory and expressive significance of the work on the basis of pastoral principles and outcomes. The motivations behind this development may be understood in relation to the pastoral as it evolves in the other arts. I will thus begin with a brief overview of the pastoral in literature, and continue with the evolution of the pastoral in Romantic consciousness. These generalizations will ground the more specific expressive interpretations I will propose for the Schubert sonata.

Literary scholars attempting to define the pastoral in all its many manifestations, from shepherds in Arcadia to *Alice in Wonderland,* tend to agree on certain fundamental elements. William Empson summarizes one of these elements concisely as "the pastoral process of putting the complex into the simple" (1960 [1935]: 23). Peter Marinelli (1971: 11) elaborates this theme along Empson's lines:

> The dominant idea of pastoral is a search for simplicity away from a complexity represented either by a specific location, . . . from which the refuge is in a rural retreat to Arcadia; or from a specific period of individual human existence (adulthood), from which the refuge is in the visions of childhood.

Here simplicity is also associated with a separate, idealized space or time. That Nature can fill the role of such an idealized world implies the presence of its opposite, the more complex urban world of a present reality that already forms the dialectic background for the earliest pastoral poetry. As W. W. Greg (1984 [1906]) notes, the *Idylls* of Theocritus were "directly born of the contrast between the recollections of a childhood spent among the Sicilian uplands and the crowded social and intellectual city-life of Alexandria" (80). It is the turn from the complexities of urban existence toward what Renato Poggioli (1975 [1957]) identifies as either lost happiness or lost innocence that underlies much of the attraction of pastoral literature.

Poggioli (1969 [1959]: 47–48) also documents the shift toward what he calls the "pastoral of the self" in Shakespeare and Cervantes (proto-Romantics for Friedrich Schlegel) with the move away from the bucolic Italian concern with passion and sex to a more philosophical development of the themes of melancholy and solitude. Here the pastoral retreat can also be "a retreat from both the reality and the dream of love" (50), as exemplified by the character of Marcela in one of the episodes from *Don Quixote*. Marcela takes on the role of shepherdess and denies all suitors, preferring instead "the silent company of nature" and "the soul's intercourse with itself" (53).

The importance of the individual is echoed by Paul Robinson (1985), who notes that the Romantics "conceived of nature in a particular relation to the self." As he argues, Nature "became for them the medium through which the self achieved an essential wholeness . . . the means through which the self realized itself" (80). Robinson treats Schubert's song cycles and Berlioz's opera *Les Troyens* as complementary extremes in Romanticism's concern for "nuances of individual emotion" on the one hand and the epic panorama of universal history on the other (60). But the song cycle "releases the composer from the need to portray a social order" (81) and thus features a single individual, for whom Nature provides analogues of personal emotions.

David E. Wellbery (1996) emphasizes similar points in his study of the emergence of Goethe's lyric poetry from a stylistic tradition of idyllic prose.[3] For Wellbery, the lyric privileges subjectivity and "compensatory access to a bliss forever lost" (13) over the social roles and generic social norms of the idyll. Temporality in the lyric is discontinuous, foregrounded, and phenomenological for the experiencing subject, as opposed to the continuously unfolding and untroubled natural rhythms of the idyll. This gives the lyric a more ecstatic character, at times akin to "mystic rapture" (15). In the lyric, Nature is conceived as a productive force, not a backdrop or scene, as in the idyll. And the lyric features an inner intimacy marked by the "phantasms, yearnings, memories, and wishes" of the imaginary (17).

Schubert's lyricism may be seen as highly compatible with the pastoral as mode in its subjectivity, inner temporality, and intimate reflection. Viewed from this perspective, Schubert's implementation of the lyrical pastoral in an otherwise dramatic genre, sonata form, may be understood as an effective trope. The shifts among extended moments of lyric reverie enable dramatic discontinuity to coexist with pastoral continuity in a realm of subjectivity, intimacy, and phenomenological temporality. Although Wellbery's subject is "the birth of lyric song out of the spirit of idyllic prose" (18) in the lyric poetry of the young Goethe, we can find a similar impulse in Schubert's intimate approach to the pastoral.

Charles Rosen (1995) delineates another major change in the Romantic conception of Nature, now conceived in terms of landscape instead of idealized Arcadia. Rosen parallels the developments in landscape painting and, more importantly, descriptive writing about landscapes as perceptively analyzed by Friedrich Schiller in a 1794 review of Friedrich Matthisson's landscape poems. Schiller draws the connection to music as that art form by which feelings can be represented through their form, not their content, and he observes that "insofar as landscape painting or landscape poetry works musically, it is a representation of the power of feeling, and consequently an imitation of human nature" (127). This new interpretive perspective had consequences both for pastoral as an expanded mode and for music as an appropriate medium of that expansion, beyond the limited programmatic basis of pastoral as literary or musical genre. As Rosen explains,

> The charms of landscape painting and poetry are no longer simply the evocation of the beauties and the delights of a pastoral existence, nor the virtuosity of the artist's imitation of the objects of Nature. What Schiller demands is that the poet and the artist show us the correspondence between the sensuous experience of Nature and the spiritual and intellectual working of the mind. Only this can give landscape the dignity of epic poetry and religious and historical painting. (1995: 129)

The song cycle, in Rosen's view, is elevated by this correlation of inner emotional and outer physical landscape to "a vehicle of the sublime," possessing "epic status, a genuine monumentality, without losing the apparent simplicity of a personal expression" (124, 125). Schubert's Piano Sonata in G is, of course, a textless work without obvious program, for which Rosen's summary of Schumann's *Davids-bündlertänze* appears especially relevant:

> A work of pure instrumental music with no visible program recreates the sense of time and memory of Romantic landscape. This work no more needs a program than the great Romantic representations of landscape needed historical reference, an intrigue, or a plot. (236)

Tonal music has an independent capacity to cue various temporal realms by means of sharp musical oppositions, not only in mode, but in key, theme, topic, texture, meter, tempo, and style as well. These shifts, if extreme or sudden, may also suggest alternative physical spaces, and hence, by analogy, a range of disjunctive psychological states. Schubert's opposition of minor and major to represent the opposition between present, tragic reality and a more euphoric past—either real or imagined—has been noted by many scholars, including William Kinderman (1986). The opposition may be achieved not only by the turn from minor to major, or by the striking modulations and marked thematic contrasts noted by Kinderman, but also by a corresponding simplification in various musical elements that lends a pastoral character to these oases, conceived as idealized visions of lost happiness or innocence.

To summarize the above discussion, for the early Romantic period I am presupposing the cultural availability of a pastoral mode that may include various aspects of the following scenario: (1) an individual retreating from a complex and less-euphoric reality (2) in an attempt to regain lost simplicity, innocence, happiness, or the sublime—or to imagine a similarly euphoric present or future idealized state[4] (3) by inhabiting an idealized space of reflection or serenity that emulates those envisioned qualities, (4) and that may also evoke the monumentality of a landscape, with its poignant juxtapositions of geological time, historical time, and individual memory.

To create these associations, Schubert must draw upon the tradition and conventions of pastoral expression in music, both characteristic and topical. Without claiming that any of the following in isolation would necessarily cue the pastoral, it is possible to argue (Hatten 1994: 97–98) that these musical features are at least consistent with a pastoral interpretation: pedal point, slow harmonic rhythm, simple melodic contour with gentle climax, compound meter, major mode, parallel thirds, and subdominant inflection.[5] Many of these features suggest an underlying principle, by analogy to pastoral literature: *simplicity as opposed to complexity*. Other, more specifically pastoral figures range from imitations of birdcalls to the conventional horn fifth, the latter suggesting the *distance* of a landscape or forest as well as its pastoral character. Charles Rosen (1995: 117) interprets horn calls as symbols of distance and hence expressive of "absence and regret," the classic examples being Beethoven's *Les Adieux* sonata, Op. 81a, and Schubert's "Der Lindenbaum." Other conventional cues increasingly favored by Romantics include the *siciliano* rhythmic gesture, musette or *Ländler* allusions, and modal inflections (especially Lydian, Dorian, and Mixolydian). I will also claim that the sonority of subdominant harmonies such as the ii^6_5 may acquire a pastoral connotation, since the mm^7 is a "gentler" harmonic complex. As the opening harmony of Beethoven's Piano Sonata in E♭ Major, op. 31, no. 3 (Example 7.20), a ii^6_5 is coupled with an evocative melodic motive that suggests both inward resignation (the falling fifth) and a gentle calling forth (the dotted-rhythmic setting). Although the resulting movement is best considered in the comic mode, it is a comedy that is inflected by the pastoral in the direction of gentler chiding and self-mockery, as signaled by the genial comic dismissal of the noble/heroic "arrival $^6_4$" in the opening theme. A "pastoralizing" of sonority persists into the twentieth century, as exemplified by the arpeggiated mm^7 chord that sets the scene for Debussy's piano prelude "La fille aux cheveux de lin" (The Maid with the Flaxen Hair).

Emphasis on subdominant harmony as well as modulation to the flat side is consistent with what might be considered a second fundamental principle of pastoral expression in music: *mollified tension and intensity*. This category may be expanded to include the undercutting of expressive climaxes, the employment of consonant appoggiaturas and other less dissonant figuration, and a more immediate amelioration of any dissonant irruptions or other disruptions that may occur.

Many of these features are found in Beethoven's expansion of the pastoral mode in Op. 101. In Schubert still others suggest the monumental and the timeless, two further markers of an ideal, and hence pastoral, space and temporality.[6] The opening of Schubert's G major sonata (Example 3.1) recalls Beethoven's similarly spaced and doubled G major tonic with which the piano opens the Fourth Piano Concerto,

Example 3.1. Schubert, Piano Sonata in G Major, D. 894, first movement, opening theme.

as William Kinderman has noted (1997: 160). Schubert's initial tonal shift is not, like Beethoven's, to the serene, chromatic-third-related B major, but to a marked B minor (m. 10). The passage features both a *ppp* dynamic level and one of Schubert's few indications for pedal; together, these markings imply additional use of the moderator pedal to create an otherworldly effect. Schubert quickly ameliorates the eerie and potentially tragic disruption of B minor by reinterpreting it as B major (m. 13), then merely shifting back to the dominant of G major (m. 16) for the counterstatement (m. 17).

The opening theme, however, is quite striking even before this little drama, and it displays both familiar and unfamiliar pastoral features. Major mode, compound meter, slow harmonic rhythm with implied pedal, parallel thirds, and a sequential move to the subdominant in m. 3 are familiar markers. The monumental character of the sustained tonic (with only a brief ripple of animation in m. 1, a hint of "pastoral fanfare," if you will) suggests a more profound vision of the pastoral as *troped* (Hatten 1994) or creatively merged, with the hymnlike dignity of a sustained sonority. The hymn is inflected by the rhythm of a dance in m. 2, which foreshadows the second theme's troping of waltz and pastoral topics.

Before examining that theme, however, it will prove useful to explore other possibilities for pastoral tropes, since these extend the topical range of musical materials that may be embraced by the pastoral mode. If we consider the quintessential pastoral to be idyllic, untroubled music in major mode with pedal, slow harmonic rhythm, subdominant emphasis, parallel thirds, and simple lyricism in a slow tempo, then what of other, more mixed kinds of pastoral? In which directions might the pastoral plausibly trope with other topics? Dances such as the *siciliano* (as in one of Brahms's variations on a theme of Haydn) or slow gigue with yodel (as in the finale of Beethoven's Piano Sonata in D Major, Op. 28) are already quintessentially pastoral. A more tropological example may be found in the opening of Schubert's Piano Sonata in A Minor, D. 537, which features a *siciliano* rhythm in $\frac{6}{8}$, pedals on tonic and dominant, slow harmonic rhythm, and parallel thirds—but in the context of minor mode and a faster tempo (Example 3.2a). The *forte* opening suggests the realm of the epic, modified by pastoral features to what might be termed the balladic. Compare, in this respect, the first of Brahms's "Edward" Ballades, Op. 10, no. 1 (Example 3.2b).

A clear example of the troping of pastoral with hymn is found in the second theme of the first movement of Schubert's Piano Sonata in A Minor, D. 784, with its four-voice texture and male choir registration combined with pastoral pedal, slow harmonic rhythm, subdominant emphasis, and simple texture (see Example 8.6, m. 61 ff.). The troping of the pastoral with imitative or canonic textures is found most strikingly in the trio of the third movement of Beethoven's String Quartet, Op. 59, no. 2, with its simple Russian folk tune, and the trio of the second movement of Op. 101, with its bizarre, rustic canon announced by a pastoral "fanfare" (another trope) on a dominant pedal (see Example 10.1c).

Finally, the pastoral can be expanded in the direction of a more fully elaborated singing style, as in the rondo finale of Beethoven's Op. 90, which features in its opening measures not only a serene melody centered on the "sweet" scale-degree $\hat{3}$

Allegro ma non troppo.

a. Schubert, Piano Sonata in A Minor, D. 537, first movement.

Andante.

b. Brahms, *Edward* Ballade, Op. 10, no. 1.
Example 3.2. Tropings of the pastoral in Schubert and Brahms.

in major, but also a reiterated inner pedal, parallel thirds, and a simple harmonic rhythm (compare the opening of Op. 101).

Returning to the first movement of the Schubert G major, consider how the second theme (Example 3.3a) both resonates with the pastoral and transcends the trope of pastoral and waltz topics.[7] Each $\frac{12}{8}$ measure begins to sound like a hyper-measure of four dance measures, due to the persistent *siciliano* rhythmic figure on the first two beats of each large measure. The slow harmonic rhythm, simple step-wise and sequential melodic gestures, and long-range pedal point are clear pastoral cues, but the enormous temporal expansion of the passage belies its rather typical overall phrase structure—an eight-bar *Satz* with a two-bar extension at the end. Ten bars of $\frac{12}{8}$ sound like forty bars of $\frac{3}{8}$, given the leisurely tempo (*molto Moderato*), and it is easy to lose track of the hierarchical structure as the additive process becomes more and more mesmerizing. The troping of pastoral is original here with Schubert, although something similar occurs in Beethoven's Sixth and Seventh Symphonies, with their hypnotic reiterations of motivic and rhythmic figures. Schubert's theme is characterized by relative harmonic stasis with a slow move to a melodic climax. The climactic resolution to tonic in m. 36 is undercut by the decrescendo that begins one measure earlier (recalling the typically pastoral softening of climaxes). In m. 37 Schubert substitutes variation of the theme for a more Classical development or continuation, contributing still further to the sense of an idealized and visionary pastoral space. The second theme moves into a higher register and achieves a complete saturation of texture by means of constant sixteenth-

Example 3.3. Schubert, D. 894, first movement.
a. Second theme.

note diminution. Plenitude (see Chapter 2) of textural repleteness is the expressive goal. Even the undercut climax suggests a luxuriance that needs no sharper point of expressive focus, since the entire passage already revels in the fulfillment that a typical climax would have achieved. The wavelike textural effect suggests a kind of spilling over of sheer pleasure, which I would interpret as a timeless pastoral fulfillment of perhaps both lost innocence *and* lost happiness.

The development section shifts mode in both senses, from major to minor, and from the timeless pastoral to the epic/balladic, with a sense of engaged struggle in a present reality. Now the first and second themes are pitted dialectically against each other, and the second theme provides pastoral oases as relief from the increasingly monumental conflict implied by the *fff* climaxes of the first theme in Bb minor (Example 3.3b). The second theme "ameliorates" this tension, after a pedal dominant introduction (m. 76), by shifting to Bb major, and the pastoral is troped this

Example 3.3. Schubert, D. 894, first movement.
b. Excerpt from the development section.

time by means of a topical allusion to imitation that further suffuses the texture. Fragmentation into two two-bar units is not conceived in a typical developmental sense; instead, the two-bar units achieve cadential closures (to B♭ in m. 78 and V/E♭ in m. 81) that serve as premature resolutions of what had been endlessly postponed in the exposition. These abbreviated appearances lack the textural and temporal fulfillment of the exposition's second theme group, and they seem more vulnerable as brief encapsulated visions of a lost pastoral. The treatment of the second theme is thus expressively developmental with respect to the pastoral trajectory of the work, but somewhat nondevelopmental in a Classical syntactic sense.[8]

In the recapitulation Schubert eliminates the B minor disruption of the exposition's first theme group, but the dark key will return in the middle movements. The remainder of the recapitulation is a rather predictable transposition of the events of the exposition, which has unfortunate consequences for the second theme group. Down a fifth, it loses some of the sparkling registral contrast that created such magic in the exposition, and thus it seems less fulfilling.[9]

The codetta's return to the first theme features the typical V⁷/IV harmonization that marks closure, but Schubert adds a brief coda that merely grounds the tonic by reiteration of the initial thematic gesture. This emphasis on tonic as sonority, with a final V⁷ over tonic pedal resolving to I, is a strategically appropriate resolution of the pastoral monumentality with which the movement began. It also features a reverberant effect by which repeated notes sustain a sonority, a technique I have discussed with reference to the late A major piano sonata as well (Hatten 1993). Reverberation as a means of sonic decay, and the use of sounded overtones (found in later movements), are evidence of Schubert's remarkable ear for the acoustical properties of sound. As an exploitation of the "natural" overtone series, these effects may also be allied to a more broadly conceived pastoral mode.[10]

The second movement features a simple air that prolongs each downbeat with a consonant melodic pitch, structurally outlining the tonic triad (Example 3.4a). The use of mere consonance as expressive substitute for an appoggiatura or other dissonance is a primitive but effective device that is easily affiliated with pastoral simplicity. This simplicity is further reflected in the bald accompaniment and occasional octave doubling of the melodic line. At the double bar (m. 9), Schubert adds an intertextual allusion to the pastoral opening of Beethoven's Op. 31, no. 3 (see Example 7.20), and then echoes the phrase with a *pianissimo* passage featuring parallel thirds.

The pastorally inflected theme, set off in rounded binary form, is immediately countered in the first episode by a stormy passage in B minor, a key area already marked as tragic by its dissonant intrusion at the beginning of the first movement. After moving to a forceful cadence in F# minor, Schubert begins a more immediate process of amelioration, as conditioned by the pastoral mode (Example 3.4b). A Neapolitan-inflected pleading motive (mm. 40–44), a chameleon-like shift to F# major (mm. 45–47), and a *ppp* cadential echo over dominant pedal featuring parallel tenths and an overtone effect (mm. 47–49) comprise the progressive stages of this gradual, pastoral transformation. The return of the opening theme further ameliorates the rude shock of the episode with thirty-second-note diminutions, an effect of euphoric plenitude within the context of a *galant* sensibility that inflects the simple pastoral from the personal toward the social.

The third-movement Menuetto reengages B minor as a tragic key, opening with an impassioned eight-bar theme. Once again, the continuation features contrastive amelioration. The consequent phrase is suddenly soft, with a hint of pleading, and it modulates to the relative major. The same strategy is employed in the second strain, where stormy D minor is gradually mollified by a mixtural transformation to D major before a rounded-binary return of the first strain.

The trio is unmistakably pastoral, troping a music-box musette with a *Ländler*-like rhythmic gesture (Example 3.5). Pastoral elements include the triple-pedal dominant drones and the modal transformation to B major. This pastoral oasis is extremely static in its first strain, recalling the pastoral stasis of the first movement. Instead of balancing the four-bar opening with a typical consequent phrase, Schubert simply allows the first idea to fade away, with a reverberating echo of the opening anacrusis over a prolonged tonic (mm. 59–62). It is the second strain (m. 63 ff.) that contrastively develops the implied dance gesture, by troping the pastoral with the emerging sophistication of a waltz (note the dynamics and the articulation of the left hand).

The merging of pastoral with waltz poses some interesting questions for interpretation, since there might appear to be a contradiction between the solitude of

a. Opening theme.

b. Excerpt from the B section.
Example 3.4. Schubert, D. 894, second movement.

pastoral and the social element of a more urban dance. Whereas dances such as the *siciliano, Ländler,* and gigue are transparent tropes because of their long association with the pastoral, the waltz (or the urbanized *Ländler*) is a topical allusion to the intimate music-making Schubert shared at the piano with his friends during his evening *Schubertiades.* These social gatherings of dancing, singing, and games promoted an idealized community as a kind of artistic Arcadia and offered a pastoral oasis from the stresses or alienating effects of urban society.[11] The troping of pastoral and waltz may also have been suggested by Schubert's own experience in mixing topics in his waltzes.[12]

Example 3.5. Schubert, D. 894, third movement, trio.

The *ppp* dynamics in the trio further support the analogy of an intimate acoustic space with an inner psychological state. When the second strain prepares the dominant (mm. 68–72) for a thematic return in vi, but the normative G♯ minor is displaced by a glowing G♯ major (m. 73 ff.), the mystically remote key is a further marker of an intimate tonal/psychological space. Regardless of whether one interprets that space as evoking an idealized present, a future vision, or a reminiscence of the past, it is quintessentially pastoral in character.

The finale is an expanded rondo that begins with several clearly pastoral markers: ♯$\hat{4}$ suggesting a Lydian inflection, pedal on G, slow harmonic rhythm, musette-like melodic circling, and parallel tenths instead of a more complex counterpoint—all within the first three bars (Example 3.6a). Pastoral drumbeats echo the melodic cadence with a plagal I–IV–I over a pedal V in mm. 3–4, and parallel thirds are involved in the harmonic oscillation. The drumbeat echo suggests a rustic accompaniment to the melody that begins in m. 9. If this rhythmic gesture is intended as an allusion to the repeated-chord motif from the B minor Menuetto, or the repeated chords in the B minor contrasting theme from the Andante, the previously tragic connotation is appropriately mollified by soft dynamics and a major-mode setting. Further pastoral features in the finale include the plagal cadencing of phrases in mm. 12–13 and 17–18 and the simple doubling of the melodic line in parallel thirds. Although the D♯ (♯$\hat{5}$) inflection in m. 12 is a typical galant feature (an embellishing incomplete lower neighbor to the third of the subdominant), in this context, and as doubled in thirds with the B, it recalls the modal flavoring of the opening ♯$\hat{4}$, adding a piquant, folklike effect.

The repeated-chord motif is echoed fragmentarily in the contrasting dance epi-sodes in C major and E♭ major. Understood as a variant of the first episode's theme in C major, the E♭ episode can support its own, parenthetical episode, a contrasting theme in C minor. This theme recalls the pleading responses to B minor in the Andante and the Menuetto, and its doleful minor mode is appropriately amelio-rated by subsequent mutation to C major for a thematic transformation.

The extensive coda to the rondo is launched by a shift from G to B♭ major and a "trumping" of the main theme in a higher register. An appropriately pastoral coda then features an extensive play, quasi-musette, above syncopated dominant and tonic drone pedals (Example 3.6b). This playing out of register is familiar from the pastoral coda with horn fifths that closes the first movement of Beethoven's *Les Adieux*, Op. 81a. A similar leave-taking in the Schubert sets up a last, motto-like statement of the theme in a high register, closing to a root-position tonic and met-ric resolution of the repeated-chord motif.

I have argued that the Schubert G major sonata displays the expressive coordi-nation of an emerging pastoral mode, as Romantically conceived. If the pastoral provides an idyllic retreat from the complexities of urban life, might its use in mu-sic imply a corresponding retreat from the complexities of sonata form? The first movement satisfies the Romantic conception of sonata form in terms of basic sec-tions, themes, and tonal areas, although it may depart from Classical "sonata style." Interestingly, as Andreas Krause (1996: 16) observes, either the publisher (Tobias Haslinger, in 1827) or perhaps Schubert himself changed the title from the auto-graph's "Sonate" to "Fantasie oder Sonate," and the *Wiener Zeitung* advertised the work as "Fantasie, Andante und Allegretto," referring to the first, second, and fourth movements, with the Menuetto omitted in an apparent oversight. The ad-dition of *Fantasie* as title for the first movement gives evidence of a conflict be-tween style and form. Perhaps the timeless, reflective character of the exposition suggested *Phantasie* in the more Romantic sense of a work of the imagination that transcends the principled rhetoric of sonata. Indeed, the exposition, while remark-ably regular in tonal and thematic construction, sounds anything but normal, since the expressive treatment of thematic ideas eludes the structural rhythms and de-velopmental rhetoric of sonata. The development section, on the other hand, is per-haps weakened by an overly forced dramatic rhetoric, burdening themes that had previously escaped such generic treatment.

Despite this possible weakness, there is a remarkable subtlety in the entire work's cyclic integration by means of both the overarching pastoral mode and the cross-movement thematic and tonal allusions and resolutions I have noted. Krause (1996: 103) finds thematic cross-reference and pastoral character in all four of the sonatas written from 1825 to 1826, beginning with the unfinished *Reliquie* sonata in C ma-jor, D. 840, continuing with the A minor, D. 845, and D major, D. 850, and conclud-ing with the G major, D. 894, which Krause considers a "Nachspiel" (93). Krause analyzes a shared family of motives to support his thesis of a work group (84–97), and he interprets the keys of movements according to C. F. D. Schubart's (1972 [1806]) taxonomy, in which G major is characterized as "Alles Ländliche, Idyllen-

a. Opening theme.

b. Excerpt from the coda.
Example 3.6. Schubert, D. 894, fourth movement.

und Eklogenmässige, jede sanfte und ruhige Bewegung des Herzens" (All rustic, idyllic, and eclogue-moderate, every gentle and calm emotion) (103). Each of the earlier three sonatas clearly has its pastoral moments, especially portions of the first movement of the *Reliquie* and the second movements of the A minor and D major sonatas. But the G major is, in my view, more thoroughly imbued with the pastoral. In this sense the work parallels Beethoven's Op. 101, which is coordinated by an overriding pastoral impulse despite the troping of pastoral with contrasting topics. In Op. 101 the march, hymn, triumphant/heroic fanfare, and learned style each make their claim on the expressive character of the work, but all within the context of the pastoral as expressive genre.

Elsewhere (Hatten 1994) I have defined a pastoral expressive genre as an organizing principle ensuring that any dissonances and disruptions will not overly threaten a serene outcome. But that is hardly a prescription for a dramatic trajectory, as found more clearly in expressive genres such as the tragic-to-triumphant or tragic-to-transcendent. Indeed, the pastoral in both literature and music may appear episodic as opposed to projecting a clear dramatic line. Paul Alpers (1996: 70), in writing on the pastoral in literature, reinforces this point: "Like pastoral romances, pastoral dramas are episodic, characterized by set pieces, relatively unmarked by the shapings and energies of plot." My attempts to draw together the various pastoral "markers" in Schubert's G major sonata may not add up to a completely coherent genre, even with the excuse of episodic construction, but certainly a "mode" of interpretation is implied by the pastoral in its overarching influence on the work. If that interpretation, for Schubert, implies a pastoral retreat, it is not as escape from the world, but as penetration to the sublime by means of the fulfillment of plenitude and the timelessness of mystic oneness. From a landscape of contemplative solo reflection, occasionally disrupted by reminders of less-euphoric realities, we are led to a finale that celebrates the social pastoral as implied by rustic folk dance. And the finale implies a redemptive outcome by reintegrating the individual into an idealized, communal world. This, in loose outline, might be considered the pastoral trajectory of Schubert's G major sonata.

4   The Troping of Topics, Genres, and Forms: Bach, Mozart, Beethoven, Schubert, Schumann, Brahms, Bruckner, Mahler

Troping in music may be defined as the bringing together of two otherwise incompatible style types in a single location to produce a unique expressive meaning from their collision or fusion (Hatten 1994).[1] Troping constitutes one of the more spectacular ways that composers can create new meanings, and thematic tropes may have consequences for the interpretation of an entire multimovement work. Topics are style types that possess strong correlations or associations with expressive meaning; thus, they are natural candidates for tropological treatment.

As Raymond Monelle (2000: 198–206) has shown in his insightful analysis of the tropological relationship between the topics of subject and countersubject in Bach's Fugue in A♭ (WTC II), such tropes need not be limited to later styles. In Example 4.1 the subject is a *galant* theme that "comes from the world of the trio sonata" (199), while the countersubject is a typical lament, with its descending chromatic line exemplifying the *passus duriusculus,* a typical figure from the middle of the sixteenth century (Williams 1997) that signified the "pathetic, painful, distressed, tender, sorrowful, anxious" (Monelle 2000: 198). The tropological significance of this combination of a cheerful, positive subject and a lament-based countersubject is interpreted by Monelle in terms of a positive subject that "dispels" the "obscurity and neurasthenia of the countersubject" (200), at least at first. But the interesting aspect of tropes is their multivalence, and one could also interpret the countersubject as inflecting the subject, perhaps lending a seriousness or learned gravity to the otherwise sturdily optimistic subject.[2]

While two voices may feature contrasting topics whose connotations merge in a tropological interpretation, it is also possible to find the merger at the level of genre, where all voices are participating in the fusion. The Gigue from Bach's first French Suite in D Minor (Example 4.2) is a clear example of the use of French overture and fugue as topical treatments of a gigue. The dotted rhythms and flourishes of the ceremonial French style, and the fugal treatment associated with the faster section of the French overture, so completely characterize the opening that one might ask in what sense the gigue is still present in the trope. But if one plays the dotted rhythms with the "swing" of a gigue, as opposed to the double-dotted

Example 4.1. Bach, Fugue in A♭ Major, WTC II, opening entries of subject and countersubject with tonal answer.

French overture, and in a tempo that is faster than a ponderous overture but slower than a quick gigue, then the blend between the topics begins to emerge—energetic, yet serious. Minor mode and learned-style imitation are not new to the genre. Bach's gigues typically feature imitation (and melodic or textural inversion at the double bar), and the next two minor-mode gigues in the French Suites, in C minor and B minor, are no exception. But their $\frac{3}{8}$ meters are typical for the gigue (as a subdivision of the compound meters generally associated with the genre), whereas the common time of the D minor gigue can only hint at a more typical $\frac{12}{8}$ by means of the relaxed treatment of the dotted rhythms mentioned earlier. The French overture features flourishes and directional reversals around heavily accentuated longer notes, and this heaviness tempers the jaunty fleetness of a typical gigue. Bach's trope is thus an ingenious way to enhance the expressive weight and closural force of the last dance, in keeping with the seriousness of the entire suite.

Topical troping can occur, as we have seen, at the thematic level and at the level of genre. One more example from Bach will demonstrate how troping can occur on several levels in a single work. Laurence Dreyfus (1996: 224–32) offers a fascinating and systematic analysis of a suite movement, the "Echo" that concludes the Overture in B Minor from Bach's *Clavier-Übung*, Part II. Although he does not use the term "trope," I would suggest that four tropes that emerge from his brilliant analysis of this movement—not all of which are specifically topical.

The first is a trope at the level of formal genre that merges a binary dance form with the *ritornello* structuring of a concerto. This superficially *galant* dance movement, as Dreyfus deems it, employs a more sophisticated use of *ritornelli* than the Italian Concerto that precedes it in the *Clavier-Übung*. Eight *ritornelli* of varying length are marked with R's above the score in Dreyfus's example. The second trope

Example 4.2. Bach, French Suite No. 1 in D Minor, Gigue, opening entries of the subject.

is in the treatment of texture, and it involves a play with expectations for *solo* versus *ritornello*. Bach orchestrates some *soli* sections as *tutti* (m. 22) and some *ritornelli* sections as *soli* (m. 13) through the use of both dynamics and texture. The third trope, similar to the second, is achieved by use of the *concertato* contrast within solo sections (the *forte* versus *piano* "echo" that gives the piece its name), as seen in mm. 5–6. Once again, solo sections are troped with *tutti* characteristics. The fourth trope involves a mixture of tonalities within what is typically a single-key statement of the *ritornello*. Bach subtly recombines *ritornello* segments in different keys, and in this case the rationale is not purely expressive. By pursuing what Dreyfus terms "research" in his inventory of inventions, Bach first realizes that a literal transposition into another mode, or a use of invertible counterpoint, may create undesirable intervals or parallelisms. He then "researches" a solution by shifting to another key in mm. 33–36 (from D major to E minor) and mm. 45–52 (from G major to E minor). Although Bach's original reason for connecting segments in new ways may have been to avoid contrapuntal weaknesses, his "research" is also creative in that it highlights relationships among hitherto nonadjacent ideas, which may in turn engender tropological interpretations.

The Classical Character Variation and Romantic Character Sets

One laboratory for experimentation with topical troping in the Classical style is the character variation, in which the topical character of a theme may be mixed with various contrasting topical types. Mozart's Piano Sonata in D Major, K. 284 (1775), preserves the theme's characteristic gavotte rhythm—a two-quarter-note upbeat (Example 4.3a) in subsequent variations that feature not only traditional diminution but also topical or characteristic treatment (including brilliant, learned, singing, *empfindsamer,* and *buffa* styles, as well as the ubiquitous march topic). Two instances of topical troping on the theme are found in Variation VI (Example 4.3b), which fuses the gavotte rhythmic gesture with a cross-hand dialogue reminiscent of the gigue from Bach's Partita in B♭, and Variation VIII (Example 4.3c), which treats the gavotte rhythm as a playful fanfare motto and offers a further trope with legato parallel thirds in a pastoral topical dialogue. How one might interpret the blend of fanfare, gavotte, and pastoral is anyone's guess; ironically, Mozart's topical play at times suggests the *ars combinatoria* in its speculative explorations. But from such abstract bricolage, Mozart developed an expressive flexibility capable of a great range of nuance. As Allanbrook (1983) notes, the play of topics can achieve richer operatic characterizations, and not merely by marking class distinctions. Cherubino, for example, exemplifies the troping of adult ardor (heartfelt, if extravagant) and adolescent immaturity (naive, and at times comical).

Topical troping does not depend on a prior, established theme; the troping of topics is also featured in sets and cycles of relatively independent dances or character pieces by Schubert and Schumann. Tropings of waltz and march may be found in Schubert's Waltzes, D. 145, and Schumann's *Carnaval* (Examples 4.4a and 4.4b). Schubert's set of waltzes concludes with fanfare/drum roll gestures, and Schumann's *Carnaval* is framed with waltz-metered "marches." Such tropes lend the waltz a more powerful, public, ceremonial, and even authoritative character (as in the case of the Schumann).

The troping of topics is featured by Beethoven in the finale to the Ninth, the locus classicus for integration of genres as well as topics, drawing from the realms of opera, oratorio, concerto, and symphony. But its "all embracing" trope (Hatten 1994) is also enhanced by the fusion of multiple topics, as in the high- and low-style march treatments of the "Freude" hymn theme, or the learned counterpointing of the gigue-transformed hymn theme with the "Seid umschlungen" cantus theme. In the latter example the trope of gigue/hymn is further troped by the double-fugal combination and a chorale-prelude-like textural treatment of the cantus theme.

Thematic Transformation and Troping in the Nineteenth-Century Symphony

The Lisztean appropriation of this technique need not feature troping. Thematic transformation preserves a theme's melodic contours without a genuine sharing of two topical characters; instead, the theme is reclothed in a contrasting and distinctive topical costume and thus treated more like a character in an unfolding, often programmatic plot. On the other hand, Bruckner's combining of polka and chorale in a passage from the finale of the Third Symphony demands tropological interpretation (the "stark dualism of this world," in Bruckner's formulation) in part because Bruckner does not attempt any further musical integration between two topics that are stratified in their simultaneous performance (Example 4.5).

The trope of polka and chorale is a striking musical event, but it is not as compositionally productive as, for instance, that of the "pilgrims' processional" topic

Example 4.3. Mozart, Piano Sonata in D Major, K. 284, variation finale.
a. Theme.
b. Variation VI.
c. Variation VIII.

Example 4.4. Trope of waltz with fanfare (a) or march (b) elements.
a. Schubert, Waltz in E Major, D. 145, no. 12.
b. Schumann, *Carnaval,* Op. 9, finale, opening theme.

Example 4.5. Bruckner, Symphony No. 3 in D Minor, finale, trope of polka and chorale.

in Bruckner's Fourth Symphony (Example 4.6a), a fusing of chorale-prelude and march topics that had already become, as Constantin Floros first noted (1980: 160–66, 178–79), a topos in its own right—an early example is the second movement of Berlioz's *Harold in Italy*. The pilgrims' processional topic supports the allegorical interpretation of the Fourth Symphony as a kind of pilgrim's progress, especially when the topic returns prominently in the finale (Example 4.6b). The finale of the Fifth Symphony, on the other hand, tropes on the juxtaposition of fugue and chorale prelude to underline its spiritually triumphant trope (for further interpretation of these symphonies, see Hatten 2001).

We have seen how march or fanfare topics have been used for tropological effect in waltzes that remain in triple meter. Mahler's Sixth Symphony features an unusual "march-scherzo" whose conflicting metrical expectations ($\frac{4}{8}$ for march versus $\frac{3}{8}$ for scherzo) are literally realized in the changing time signatures after R68 and in the "Altväterlich" trio at R73, with its troping of march and *Ländler* (Example 4.7). Mahler's comment to his wife that the trio represented the faltering

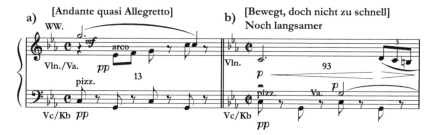

Example 4.6. Bruckner, Symphony No. 4 in E♭ Major, pilgrims' processional topic.
a. Second movement, main theme.
b. Finale, second theme (shifts to slower tempo and C minor).

Example 4.7. Mahler, Symphony No. 6 in A Minor, second movement, trope of march and *Ländler* topics.

steps of his children at play, staggering through the sand (Floros 1993 [1985]: 175), may be reconciled with an interpretation that finds fragile innocence in the trio, as opposed to the more demonic energies of the scherzo, a "dance of death" in Robert Samuels's interpretation of the movement (1995).

A precedent for Mahler's play with metric regrouping may be found in the minuet movement of Mozart's *Linz* Symphony, K. 425, where a brief march figure implies a metric rebarring of $\frac{4}{4}$ within the prevailing $\frac{3}{4}$ meter (Example 4.8), as supported by the harmony. Here the troping of minuet and march results from a successive rather than simultaneous fusion of topics.

I turn now to an extended analysis of topical troping and its significance for interpreting the Third Symphony of Johannes Brahms. After the opening motto (Example 4.9a, mm. 1–3) the first movement features a theme in hemiola ($\frac{3}{2}$), effectively troping march and triple time—a phenomenon with precedents, as we have observed in Mozart, Schubert, and Schumann. The march topic is enhanced by the sense of struggle with $\frac{6}{4}$, but the perception of $\frac{3}{2}$ gives way to $\frac{6}{4}$ only when the motto from the opening appears in diminution in the winds against a waltzlike figure in the strings (m. 7). The metric shift yields both a hypermetric $\frac{12}{4}$ (the four-pulse motto with bass in mm. 7–8) and a submetric interpretation of $\frac{3}{4}$ (each A measure interpreted as two $\frac{3}{4}$ measures—the typical waltz hypermeasure, as danced). Measures 11–12 feature the motto in $\frac{12}{4}$ metric displacement (off one quarter note)

Example 4.8. Mozart, Symphony No. 36 in C Major (*Linz*), K. 425, third movement, trope of minuet and march (interpolation).

against the $\frac{3}{4}$ liquidation of the march into waltz cadence figures. The $\frac{6}{4}$ ($\frac{3}{4}$ + $\frac{3}{4}$) division prevails throughout the transition beginning in m. 15, in which march-like repeated quarter notes are integrated with waltzlike eighth-note arabesques (mm. 18 and 26). When the musette-like second theme appears in A major (Example 4.9b, m. 36) the written meter changes to $\frac{9}{4}$ for a notated hemiola. Here the troping of topics is not as immediate, since the pizzicato bass and drone fifths are absorbed into the musette topic, and the march aspect recedes to a distant background. When this theme is featured in the development section (Example 4.9c), it is expanded by interpolation (sequencing the second $\frac{3}{4}$ unit) and thus made to fit the prevailing $\frac{6}{4}$ meter (as $\frac{12}{4}$, given the two-measure phrase length). Now the pizzicato occurs on every $\frac{3}{4}$ subunit, and the marchlike element adds tropological force to the minor-mode intensification of the musette theme.

Similarly, the waltzlike closing figure from mm. 11–12 is intensified in the coda to achieve a remarkable expressive effect (Example 4.9d, mm. 198–202), as a lament-bass descent from IV to iv⁶ to V⁷ continues by yielding through the seventh (B♭) to a I⁶, with the delayed resolution finally releasing the tension in a thematically motivated, gentle resolution. The march topic in this example is emphasized by the *sf* punctuations in the bass on D and D♭, and the fortissimo bass on C to B♭, with a *rf* on B♭, resolving to A. The resolution restores the easier waltzlike character, even while echoing the descending fourth with which the march theme began. That theme recurs in its $\frac{3}{2}$ hemiola for a final statement at the cadence, echoing gracefully in diminuendo and augmentation to a quiet close. The waltz gesture fades away, and Brahms avoids a triumphal march ending.

Example 4.9. Brahms, Symphony No. 3 in F Major, Op. 90, first movement.
a. First theme. (*Continued on the next page.*)

The second movement implements the march as a pilgrims' processional (Example 4.10a), with the solemn I–IV–I–IV progression from the end of m. 1 to the end of m. 2 providing the harmonic cue, and the chorale aspect suggested by orchestration and texture more than by melodic line. Interestingly, there are further tropological effects: the pastoral stasis in m. 1 (expanded tonic) and an echo of the first movement's motto in the first clarinet, with dotted rhythms, in m. 3; the "cor-

a. First theme. *Continued*

Example 4.9. Brahms, Symphony No. 3 in F Major, Op. 90, first movement.
b. *Musette*-like second theme.

Example 4.9. Brahms, Symphony No. 3 in F Major, Op. 90, first movement.
c. Expansion and mutation of the second theme in the development.

rect" intervallic form of the motto is reserved for the closing gesture, mm. 21–23.
The pilgrims' processional topic for this opening theme is fully realized topically
only upon its elaborated return (Example 4.10b); interestingly, the pizzicato quarter-
note bass line begins exactly with the defining plagal progression in the theme.
Ultimately, the plagal character of the theme will be foregrounded in the quiet
codetta to the movement.

   Another kind of march, one with a noble/ceremonial triplet that is often used
by Brahms for evocations of quiet strength or faith (compare, for example, the E♭
middle section of Brahms's Capriccio, Op. 116, no. 3), enters in m. 41 with a stepwise melodic line (Example 4.11a). The theme is accompanied by repeated pairs of
chords; these chords echo the initial iambic rhythm and support the continuous
quarter-note pulse reminiscent of a march. References to the first movement may
create the strongest cyclical effect for the symphony, but it is this theme, or its
rhythmic and topical character, that Brahms brings back in the finale (Example
4.11b).[3] It is a strategy that may have inspired Bruckner in the design of the finale
of his Fourth Symphony, briefly mentioned above. In Brahms's finale the theme is
orchestrated in chordal texture, and thus the second rhythmic value is reduced in
order to maintain the constant pulse of the march (here, a half-note tactus in cut
time).

   The third movement, Poco Allegretto, is in $\frac{3}{8}$, but its opening theme (Example

Example 4.9. Brahms, Symphony No. 3 in F Major, Op. 90, first movement.
d. Resolution of waltz/march intensification in the coda.

a. Opening theme.

b. Elaborated return of the opening theme.
Example 4.10. Brahms, Symphony No. 3, second movement.

Example 4.11. Brahms, Symphony No. 3.
a. Second movement, noble/ceremonial march theme (mm. 41ff.).

4.12) also alludes to the topical pilgrims' processional. The pizzicato bass and similar plagal progression recall the textural and harmonic treatment of the second movement's theme. The dotted-rhythmic anacrusis may also be heard as an inversion of the third beat of the first movement's march theme.

The unusual key scheme for the middle movements (C major followed by C minor) suggests that the Poco Allegretto is an "expressive doubling" (L. Kramer 1990: 22) or Derridean "supplement" (24) of the Andante. With its poignant yearnings, the third movement delivers a more personal, profound and passionate utterance than that offered by the Andante. The effect of yearning in the Poco Allegretto is intensified by the suspension of time in m. 1 that shifts the anacrucis figure to the downbeat of m. 2. This "stretching" gestural effect was anticipated in mm. 7–8 of the first movement (Example 4.9a), thematized with the expansion of the musette theme in the development (Example 4.9c), and foregrounded most effectively with the melodic resolution of G to F in mm. 201–202 of the coda (Example 4.9d). It was further developed as a gesture in the Andante by the expansion of the top note of the motto (Example 4.10a, mm. 3 and 4; and more expressively in mm. 21–23).

The finale also "stretches" its opening theme on its recurrence in mm. 9–13 by suspending time on the harmonized scale degree $\hat{6}$ of F minor (Example 4.13a). The effect strengthens the theme's family resemblance to the opening of the Andante, and the pizzicato bass at this point further links with previous topical inflections of the pilgrims' processional. The march's tragic undercurrent is countered by another kind of march, the noble/ceremonial (even *religioso*) chorale-type with

Example 4.11. Brahms, Symphony No. 3.
b. Recall of this theme in the finale (mm. 19–28).

Example 4.12. Brahms, Symphony No. 3, third movement, opening theme.

triplets (alluding to the second movement) that contrasts in A♭ major at m. 19 (Example 4.11b).

The first theme reacts to this noble/ceremonial march with an explosive gesture (Example 4.13b, mm. 30–31, and again in 36–37), effectively shifting from a foreboding undercurrent to an intense storm. The response in m. 52 (Example 4.13c) is a new version of the triplet-inflected noble march topic, now in C major, with pizzicato bass. Significantly, this tropological variant of the march features a heroic/triumphant theme in the horn and cello, suggesting an individualizing of the communal moral force implied by the noble/ceremonial march (Example 4.11b). The "stretching" idea plays a role in the development of this theme as well, and the triplets are made more personal than monumental by their gestural range (no longer stepwise).

In the development the more monumental and *religioso* triplet march from m. 19 is treated to a hocket/echo imitation, suggestive of the kind of spiritual "battle" that is being waged. The isolated triplet figure is eventually sequenced in a climactic passage that ends with stentorian duplets announcing an arrival $^6_4$ chord in F major. In a motto-like gesture anticipating Mahler's Sixth Symphony, the major $^6_4$ chord is mutated to minor (mm. 170–71). Triumph is emblematically reversed, and we are thrust back into the storm of the recapitulation at the point of its original outburst. The heroic theme returns triumphantly in F major, but the storms continue as in the exposition, and a climax in C minor is resolved to F minor before the coda is launched, at a point parallel to the development.

The opening theme appears transformed in the coda (Example 4.13d), but the transformation offers mixed messages. On the one hand, the theme is played in triplets, suggesting the ascendancy of the noble/heroic, and accompanied by *pizzi-*

84 *Markedness, Topics, and Tropes*

Example 4.13. Brahms, Symphony No. 3, finale.
a. Stretching of the first theme, mm. 9–13.

Example 4.13. Brahms, Symphony No. 3, finale.
b. Explosive gesture (mm. 30–31) and continuation of first theme (mm. 32–34).

Example 4.13. Brahms, Symphony No. 3, finale.
c. Heroic/triumphant third theme in C major, mm. 52ff.

Example 4.13. Brahms, Symphony No. 3, finale.
d. Transformed version of the first theme in the coda (mm. 252–57, viola; imitated in winds).

cati strings, suggestive of the pilgrims' processional. On the other hand, the melodic line is in the muted violas in the very distant key of B minor, and the *pizzicati* accompanying bits are fragmentary echoes of the theme in augmentation. This mysterious transformation is gradually resolved to F minor for a return of the "stretched" version of the opening theme. A transcendent shift to F major then permits tragic ♭$\hat{6}$ (D♭) to be reinterpreted as yearning ♯$\hat{5}$ (C♯ in m. 268), and the remainder of the coda serves to return and expressively integrate (1) the motto from the first movement, (2) the noble/ceremonial pilgrims' processional theme from m. 19, and ultimately (3) the march theme from the first movement, which winds down to a serene cadence.

To summarize, the penetration of the march topic in Brahms's Third Symphony goes much further than a straightforward, topical use of march themes. The atypical first movement meter supports heroic march gestures, not unlike the first movement of Beethoven's *Eroica*, with its unusual $\frac{3}{4}$ signature. Instead of a funeral march for the slow movement, however, Brahms offers the newer Romantic topic of a pilgrims' processional (with plagal progressions offering a distant echo of the solemnity of the funeral march), and contrasts it with a potentially heroic march idea. After the third movement's textural and plagal allusions to the march, the finale opposes *three* tropings of march-inflected ideas to create an overpowering drama of heroic struggle and ultimate redemption.

The troping of marches in various meters and with other topics or textures may be seen as providing a highly flexible expressive language that also guarantees a certain gestural coherence from one contrasting movement to the next. Just as much as key relationships and cyclic thematic returns, these topical and gestural cross-references (including the "stretching" idea) provide a basis for understanding the symphony in terms of a larger dramatic trajectory. Allegorically, the pilgrims' processional—itself a stylistically defined trope of chorale-like melody and march-like accompaniment—plays a role in delineating the progressive stages of a spiritual struggle. The monumental/*religioso* and noble/heroic marches, with their triplet authority, hint that the outcome will be positive, but the turn toward transformation at the end of the outer movements suggests an outcome that is more transcendent than triumphant. The march tropes lead inexorably to that outcome, lending a sense of spiritual weight and moral authority to an ultimately serene and visionary close.

In subsuming the triumphant within the transcendent, Brahms is in effect troping on the two expressive genres implied by those endings (Hatten 1994). This higher-level troping of expressive trajectory is supported by the lower-level troping of topics that has been the focus of my interpretation. Although tropes are creative means of achieving novel expressive ends, their very novelty makes them subject to the risk of misinterpretation. By troping upon already familiar topics, Brahms ensures that his distinctive themes will also be clearly interpretable in both their immediate expressive sense and their broader significance for the unfolding drama of his symphonic cycle.

Part Two: *Musical Gesture*

Introduction to Part Two

Perhaps no other term has been used in such a bewildering array of contexts as the term *gesture* in relation to music. What do we really mean by musical gesture? When we speak of a musical gesture, do we refer to physical action? Or motion abstracted from a human source? A sounding motive, or a notated one? Or a shaping of intensity, dynamics, and pacing? Is gesture something that must occur in the experiential present, or can a longer phrase be considered a gesture? Does a gesture have meaningful directed motion, describable in terms of voice-leading, such as a Schenkerian linear progression? Does a gesture have a direction? a goal? a point of culmination or climax? Can it be encompassed by a single musical event—a single note, or a rest?

Gesture is rich and complex phenomenon, and we may well cherish its suggestive if imprecise range of connotations, since we use the term interchangeably to stand for either a singular motive or the sweep of a climactic passage, a spontaneous individual movement or the conventionalized measure of a social dance. Yet these seemingly radically different meanings share a common source in what we intuit as being "gestural." It is that deeply musical intuition, held in various ways by every musician and avid listener, that I wish to clarify and refine, by developing a theory of musical gesture and—as a case study—demonstrating its relevance for interpreting works by Mozart, Beethoven, and Schubert.

When the central topic of this book has come up in conversation, I have often been asked exactly what I mean by "musical gesture." My first thought is, invariably, "How much time do you have?" The concept of gesture (like that of time itself) is endlessly fascinating, because it touches upon a competency that is fundamental to our existence as human beings—the ability to recognize the significance of energetic shaping through time. Yet that elemental observation cannot be expected to satisfy my interlocutor, who is generally seeking a more conventional definition with more direct relevance to musical experience. And although I can ask for more patience from my readers, I will nevertheless venture a preliminary list of perspectives on the concept of musical gesture, as a means of orienting the more detailed investigation to come. My goal is to construct a theoretically useful concept of musical gesture, and to demonstrate its importance for the analysis and interpretation of musical structure and expressive meaning.

1. Musical gestures are grounded in human affect and its communication—they are not merely the physical actions involved in producing a sound or series of sounds from a notated score, but the characteristic shaping that give those sounds expressive meaning. Machines have proven particularly inept at reproducing gestures from musical notation, since they lack that subtle variation in timing which practical notational systems cannot adequately convey. The same is true of per-

formances overly constrained by mechanical accuracy. The poet Peter Viereck, in his essay "Form in Poetry," put it best when he wrote, "Metronomes can't feel; the motion they tick is not gesture but tic" (1987: 215).

2. Musical gestures have meaning that is both complex and immediate, and often directly motivated by basic human expressive movements. They "go beyond" the score to embody the intricate shaping and character of movements that have direct biological and social significance for human beings. This is not to deny the further complexity of gestural meaning that emerges from symbolic motivations based on enculturation in a musical style, or the ritualized movements of its more traditional types (dances).

3. Gestures may be inferred from musical notation, given knowledge of the relevant musical style and culture. Indeed, even without access to relevant stylistic and cultural information, musical performers will seek to find a suitably expressive gestural embodiment of a musical score, perhaps by accommodating it to their own bodies' expressive styles.

4. Gestures may be inferred from a musical performance even when we do not have visual access to the motions of the performer. We have sufficient aural imagery to reconstruct as meaningful gestures those actual sounds that combine in smoothly nuanced ways.

5. Gestures may be comprised of any of the elements of music, although they are not reducible to them; they are perceptually *synthetic* gestalts with *emergent* meaning, not simply "rhythmic shapes." The elements synthesized in a musical gesture include specific timbres, articulations, dynamics, tempi, pacing, and their coordination with various syntactic levels (e.g., voice-leading, metric placement, phrase structure). In addition, cultural gestures, such as stylized dance or march rhythms (Allanbrook 1983), may contribute to higher-level syntheses such as topics (Ratner 1980).

6. The prototypical musical gesture is a unit in the perceptual present (typically within two seconds). It has initiation and closure, such that we can speak of a series of gestures, or gestural units. These units are analogous to prosodic units in speech, organized around nuclear points of emphasis, or beats.

7. When gestures encompass more than one musical event (a note, a chord, even a rest), they provide a nuanced continuity that binds together otherwise separate musical events into a continuous whole. Continuity in this sense is not equivalent to continuously sounding (as in *legato*); a discontinuous sequence of sounds (e.g., sounds separated by rests) may nonetheless be linked by a continuous thread of intentional and significant movement.

8. Gestures may also be hierarchically organized, in that larger gestures can be comprised of smaller gestures. Thus, we can speak of the larger (formal) gesture of a slow introduction as anacrusis to an Allegro, even though the slow introduction is comprised of many gestures. Phrase structure and melodic contour are two examples of the generalization of gesture to temporal dimensions greater than the perceptual present. Furthermore, composers may design levels of articulation or dynamics in conflict with the normative levels of metric accentuation and phrase structure (Beethoven offers striking examples).

9. Certain motive-length gestures may be marked as thematic for a movement, hence foregrounded and amenable to development, variation, or ongoing evolution by means of developing variation.

10. Gestures may encompass, and help express, rhetorical action, as in a sudden reversal, a collapse, an interruption, or a denial of implication. Rhetorical gestures disrupt or deflect the ongoing musical discourse, contributing to a contrasting dramatic trajectory.

11. Besides the correlative gestures a performer enacts in competently expressing a musical work on an instrument such as the piano, there may be higher-level gestures that a performer employs to help direct the listener's attention to the main structural outlines of a form, or an expressive genre. Such gestures play a narrative role at a higher level, not unlike the abstract pointing gestures that may accompany speech, as analyzed by the linguist and psychologist David McNeill (1992). They may also be inferred as part of the work, even in the absence of specific notational marking, given an understanding of the style.

12. Gestures provide a level of musical truth, in that they reveal intentions and modalities of emotion and action (Tarasti 1994) that make it difficult for music to "lie" (but not impossible—see Hatten 1992).

In the following chapters I will elaborate upon my conception of gesture as significant energetic shaping through time—a definition general enough to include all forms of meaningful human movement. For music, although my focus is on *aural* gesture—significant energetic shaping of *sound* through time—the interpretation of aural gesture entails a wide range of gestural competencies, including the interpretation of visual notation and the correlation of aural gesture with other sensory, motor, and affective realms of human experience. My primary field of investigation is music from the Viennese Classical performance tradition, as exhibited in the related though distinctive styles of Mozart, Beethoven, and Schubert. But the theoretical framing of gesture is clearly relevant to the interpretation of works in other musical styles, and I will occasionally make reference to a wider repertoire.

Chapter 5 launches a wide-ranging investigation of human gesture, drawing on a number of scientific disciplines to construct a plausible model of the basic competencies—from the biological to the social—that we bring to bear in interpreting gesture from every realm of human experience. Our competency in interpreting musical gesture is, as many have argued, grounded in more general perceptual and cognitive competencies, and these in turn support basic linkages between music and other human experience—connections that are essential for interpreting music's expressive meanings. I assume no scientific expertise on the part of the reader, nor do I claim to have specialized competency in these disciplines. What I offer is compelling evidence from a number of disciplines that supports the fundamental presuppositions of my theory of musical gesture and provides a foundation for further theoretical speculation and interpretation. I have provided a concise outline of those points at the end of Chapter 5, and those who wish to skip ahead are encouraged to read it before proceeding.

In Chapter 6 the investigation focuses on the foundations of a theory of musical gesture and explores some of the issues that attend an embodied and gestural interpretation of tonal and metric music from Western styles. Chapter 7 introduces a set of characteristic functions that musical gestures may serve in the formal and expressive structuring of a work, and interprets the various elements of Viennese Classical gestural types in light of the regulative conventions of performance practice and style. Individual and creative musical gestures are grounded in these conventions even as they extend or exceed them. Close interpretation of numerous shorter excerpts is complemented by extended examples from Mozart and Beethoven. Chapters 8 and 9 expand the interpretation of gesture to its role in the expressive structuring of multimovement works by Schubert and Beethoven, respectively. Chapter 10 returns to broader theoretical issues, exploring kinds of gestural agency and the possibility of gestural troping.

5 Foundational Principles of Human Gesture

The following competencies are crucial to the performance and interpretation of human gesture: (1) *functional coherence* (the subsuming of multiple actions toward a single goal or purport, conceived within a dynamic systems and event cognition framework), (2) *intermodality* (the capacity for analogous representation across all the senses and motor systems), and (3) *perceptual integration* (the ability to synthesize multiple sensations into objects and events that have continuity). I will also explore the expressive origins of gesture in (4) *intersubjectivity* (Trevarthen 1986a), a term applied to the early, interactive development of the communicative motivation, agency, and emotive character attributable to gesture. These interactive competencies will be shown to support the near-inevitability of meaningful gestural interpretation of music, even as the further symbolic organization of a musical style places higher demands on listeners' interpretive competencies than can be explained from biological, psychological, and developmental perspectives alone. It should be kept in mind that the competencies being investigated in this chapter are for the most part *prelinguistic* and thus *prior to the conceptual labels of language.* The conceptual categories explored by Lakoff and Johnson (1999), or Fauconnier and Turner (2002), and applied to music by Zbikowski (2002), have an important role to play once language enters the developmental picture, but (as these authors also emphasize) there are significant, prelinguistic, embodied categories in the brain, including dynamic event shapes with affectual associations that predate the more logical schemata elaborated by Johnson.

How might gesture be defined in a way that captures its prelinguistic, categorial status? I propose that human gesture be understood more generally as expressively significant, energetic, temporal shaping across all human modalities of perception, action, and cognition. Consider the remarkable range of integrative processes that animals and humans draw upon in their interactions with the world and each other, interpreting and enacting coherent movements with distinctive profiles. Our perceptions and actions are finely tuned to each other by means of an integrated *sensorimotor system* that enables us to (1) perceive—aurally, visually, and by touch, taste, and smell; (2) move to enhance perception and guide interpretation—shifting the eye or body, fingers or tongue to gain further perspective, and receiving feedback from the body's own states; (3) manipulate objects—using the hands to both interpret and shape, take apart and assemble, destroy and create; (4) articulate all parts of the body to communicate attitude, emotion, desire, power, and information of all kinds—wittingly or unwittingly moving facial muscles, or assuming bodily postures; and articulating the sounds, rhythms, and intonational curves of language; (5) move to interact with the environment—chasing, fleeing, catching, fighting, planting, harvesting—and so much else.[1] In order to work together so smoothly, the integrated sensorimotor system requires a *near-immediate representation* that corresponds to the dynamics of each element of the experienced environment, and that can provide an appropriate "fit" for each survival task required of the organism.

The *topographic* representations that the brain is able to achieve (Edelman 1992: 83–90; Tye 1995: 120, Damasio 1994: 102–103) enable animals to interpret potential predators from their "signatures" as creatures foregrounded by their movements and emissions (auditory, visual, olfactory), projecting distinctive temporal/energetic patterns as they interact with a variety of environmental resistances (a loud rustle of leaves implying a large animal).[2] Similar signs enable members of a community to "read" each other's emotional states from the signatures of muscular tension, or sexual states through complex signals that include everything from visual display (peacocks) to olfactory triggers (pheromones). With animals, the near-immediacy of recognition, and the reflexive responses required for survival, comprise what we unscientifically term "instinct"—either sophisticated *categorial perception* (the bloodhound's ability to precisely distinguish an enormous number of scents) or incredibly quick *perceptual-motor reactive loops* (reflexes such as the frog's tongue zapping anything that triggers its perceptual profile of a fly). Animals can achieve what appears to be the outcome of sophisticated decision-making processes, however "instinctually" motivated such activity may be (the coyote's evasion of human traps).

For humans, however, another level of conscious cognition emerges, and while its complexities result in a more creative response to problem solving, its self-critical consciousness can disrupt the smooth rhythms of sensorimotor responses. These precise interactions can often be restored by short-circuiting the critical faculties, as is fostered by Zen approaches to sports: "Let your body respond without interference, don't 'think' about it." Furthermore, humans trade higher cognitive processing, including generalization, conceptualization, and language, for the vast categorial inventories that animals such as the bloodhound possess, whether through neural networks (Churchland 1995: 27) or other perceptual mechanisms whose representations are not available for conscious inspection.[3] Our sensory memories are often stored with associative links to entire situational memories (or vice versa), including their attendant emotions (as in Proust's *Remembrance of Things Past,* where the tasting of a madeleine or the sound of a musical phrase evokes vivid emotional recall by association with the stored memory of a marked sensory experience).

What all these interlinked capacities depend upon is a representation that has functional and significant coherence, whether the task be interpreting a predator's presence from the sounds of rustling grass, or timing one's movements to meet the trajectory of a flying object in order to catch it. Our perceptual awareness of our own body in space and in motion, or *proprioception,* provides feedback for our actions no less than our perception of objects and events, or *exteroception* (Turvey and Carello 1995: 402). Our bodily movements in turn increase the information available to our perceptive organs, guided by what we have interpreted is out there, what needs we might have, and what goals we might want to achieve.

An action, according to Kugler and Turvey (1987: 407), is a relation that is "functionally specific, not anatomically specific." Thus, it is not the particular muscles employed, but the *function of an intentional action* that is central to the body's motor activity. Karl Pribram (1976: 307–308) cites scientific studies of cases in which motor-related portions of the cortex were damaged in soldiers with head wounds or experimentally removed from monkeys. Strikingly, the absence of the motor cortex "failed to paralyze any particular muscle or muscle groups," although "skill in certain tasks was impaired." Pribram concludes that "neither muscles nor movements were represented as such in the cortex," rather, "actions, as the specific environmental outcomes of movements, were represented."

The holistic representation of action in the brain is not static, however. Humans actively categorize according to the *dynamics* of an event rather than waiting to compare it with a schema stored in memory. The theory of rich "ecological perception" (Gibson 1966), a precursor to "event cognition" (McCabe and Balzano 1986), is a radical alternative to theories of pattern matching or categorization at higher levels.[4] The following principles of event cognition are extracted from McCabe's superb introduction (1986: 7–19), and they make a strong case for highly sophisticated perceptual capacities as they have evolved over time:

1. "When something moves or appears to change in any way (even by a change in the observer's perspective or through slow development over time), *it can be identified by the patterns produced by its own dynamic structure.*"

2. The presumed similarity of pattern "is not an arbitrary mental construction but is the result of physical law" and "a function of our own cognitive evolution under the same physical laws."

3. "Flow events characterize the necessary transformations of all material structures . . . that develop to conform to the everyday stresses inherent in the compression, tension, and shear of our gravitational atmosphere (Shuring 1978; Williams 1981)." "The flow patterns specify all the pertinent information about both the whole event and its parts without presenting the parts as separate (or abstractable)." Thus, "perceiving and abstracting separate attributes is unnecessary to acquiring and using flow pattern information."[5]

4. "The dynamic patterns that are produced by and specify both fast and slow events are the 'language' by which we know such phenomena. This gives us an *incarnate, specific, and efficient alternative to the mediated information of information processing, the matched patterns of pattern recognition, and the traditional schemas, categories, and concepts of cognition*" (my italics).

McCabe's claims are focused on perception, but as we have noted already, the human body integrates motor activity with perception. Dynamic systems theory goes further in exploring how we use our perceptions to fine-tune intentional movements. The theoretical approach emphasizes embodied, interactive, and evolving developmental processes:

> The cognitive system is not a computer, it is a **dynamical system.** It is not the brain, inner and encapsulated; rather, it is the whole system comprised of nervous system, body, and environment. The cognitive system is not a discrete sequential manipulator of static representational structures; rather, it is a structure of mutually and simultaneously influencing *change.* Its processes do not take place in the arbitrary, discrete time of computer steps; rather, they unfold in the real time of ongoing change in the environment, the body, and the nervous system. The cognitive system does not interact with other aspects of the world by passing messages or commands; rather it continuously coevolves with them. (van Gelder and Port 1995: 3)

These interactions with the dynamics of events in the world demand a coherent representation through each of the various sensory modalities involved. The generalization of gesture as "significant energetic shaping through time" depends upon the capacity of the senses to represent a "flow event" in this way and interactively to share their representations in order to integrate a barrage of perceptions into a singular event. The loosely interchangeable terms that describe this shared representation of events across the sensorimotor system are "intermodality" and "cross-modality." One also finds the term "amodal" used when the emphasis is on the invariance of representation as generalizable across any particular sensory modality, and thus not reducible to any specific sense (e.g., Donald 2001). Since the generalization implied by amodality may also suggest abstract representation as achieved by higher, symbolic levels of cognition, I will retain the terms intermodality and cross-modality for all instances of analogous representation or interaction among perceptual sources.

Intermodality

Thelen and Smith (1994: 192), working from a dynamic systems approach to the human development of purposeful movement, have coined the phrase "perception-action categories" to describe cases of intermodal integration in the human infant. They demonstrate that "cross-modal matching is intrinsic to infants in that the primary neural repertoire supports these linkages." In studying the development of the functional action of reaching in the infant, Thelen and Smith conclude that reaching is "an instance of an emergent perceptual-motor pattern [that] is acquired through the soft assembly of mutually interacting, equivalent, multiple-component structures and processes within a context" (249). Their work on the development of reaching examines not only multiple levels of intrinsic dynamics in the infant, but also how these change at various time scales (250). The obvious advantage of their perspective is that it begins to capture the flexibility humans enjoy in achieving goals of action by various combinations of means—and no two infants are exactly alike in the ways they incorporate muscles to achieve the same goal. (A similar flexibility may be seen to underlie the variety of competent realizations of musical gestures by different performers.)

Thelen and Smith (1994: 193) argue that "movement must itself be considered a perceptual system." Cross-modality is also found between different sensory modalities, as, for example, vision and hearing with respect to speech. Campbell (1999: 58) offers compelling evidence that "reading the face for speech . . . is pervasive in hearing people," not solely in nonhearing people who read lips. The McGurk illusion reveals this most strikingly: "when a face seen speaking an utterance such as 'aga' is dubbed to a synchronized voice saying 'aba', 'ada' is what is often 'heard'" (58). Massaro (1998: 443) notes that in such cases "the influence of one source increases as other sources become less influential, i.e., more ambiguous." Bruce and Young (1998: 209) offer supportive evidence that "the sounds that are easiest to lip-read tend to be those where the differences are the most difficult to hear, because they generally involve rapid acoustic changes of relatively low intensity." Massaro concludes that "at the information level, sources are evaluated independently" and "they are then integrated to achieve perception and interpretation." This "allows the combination of two imperfect sources of information to yield better performance than would be possible using either source by itself" (Massaro 1998: 443).[6]

Intermodality is a more useful underlying generalization than the "metaphors" that Johnson (1987) and Lakoff and Johnson (1979, 1999) attribute to any cross-domain mapping in their cognitive theory of embodied image schemata.[7] Their higher-level cross-domain mapping could, from this perspective, be understood as cognitively reifying the way lower-level perception works as it maps and coordinates representations from various sensory organs. Even at the level of linguistic expression, however, an observation such as "She's feeling down" may be understood not as metaphorical but as an aptly literal description of those bodily postures and facial gestures that naturally accompany feelings of sadness or grieving. Grieving postures and gestures are prior to verbalization; thus, they may motivate the direction of our subsequent verbal representations in a way that is more direct and less creative than the label, "metaphor" would imply. For my concept of musical troping (as developed in Chapters 4, 7, and 10) I reserve metaphor for those cases where conscious creativity is actively involved in the production or interpretation of meaning.

Perceptual Integration and Continuity

A prototypical gesture is a relatively short temporal gestalt that generally occurs within the temporal frame of the experiential present, or working memory (ca. 2 seconds). Typical gestures are thus advantageously positioned to take advantage of two major forms of representation in the brain: the immediate or imagistic, so crucial to identification of faces (and their emotive character),[8] and the sequential or temporal, so crucial to the identification of individuals through their movement. Oliver Sacks's (1985) famous case of the man who mistook his wife for a hat demonstrates graphically how, despite the loss of the first capacity, a musician was able to recognize his associates by means of the second capacity—the patterns of their bodies moving through space, or their walking "signatures."[9]

The prototypical temporal gestalt for music is melody, heard not as a succession of discrete events but as something that is "moved through" (interestingly, this formulation entails two of the basic assumptions about how we interpret an aural stream as music: observed movement and movement experienced by the listener who, by moving through a contour, traces a singular embodied movement).[10] There are case studies (Sacks 1974 [1973]) in which frozen or uncoordinated muscles, as in Parkinson's disease, can reengage in purposeful action if the patient sings an analogous contour of that action—thus suggesting that a temporal gestalt retrieved through prior *musical* encoding can help an individual bypass neurological motor blockage.

Prototypical gestures (those occurring within two seconds) are short enough to maximize imagistic input and yet long enough to trigger significant temporal input. In other words, these gestures are perceptually salient because they involve a fusion of both *immediate* (understood both as "instantaneous" and "issuing transparently") imagistic gestalts of complex individual events, and *temporally mediated* gestalts (understood as energetic shaping through time).

Immediacy is found in the "grain" or texture of an event in the perceptual present—in music this is typically applied to the timbre of a tone, but also to harmony—the "color" of a chord, and to orchestration—the timbral enrichment of a tone or chord. In Peircean terms the qualitative aspect of Firstness is relevant here. Temporal *mediacy* (invoking the dynamics of Peircean Secondness) is found in the coherence of sequential events heard as part of a continuous action, process, or agency—in music this is typically applied to progressions involving a sequence of durations, frequencies (pitch), and intensities, but also applicable to timbral sequences, as in cases of *Klangfarbenmelodie*. It is tempting to take my basic definition of the gestural and map it onto the four fundamental properties of sound: "the energetic [intensity] shaping [frequency, timbre] of a process through time [duration]." This simplistic mapping conveys something of the synthetic character of music at all levels, not merely the gestural. Indeed, the notion could be generalized as follows: Synthesis (or integration) is characteristic of perception in any modality, and of those actions that take on analogous forms.[11]

Continuity is that aspect of integration that pertains to the perception of events—the flow patterns described above in the discussion of functional coherence. An event leaves its trace on the perceiver, and its perceptual integration as an event reflects both continuity and patterning as an integrated temporal and imagistic gestalt. As McCabe (1986: 18) observes, the schemata of flow patterns can be conceived as "incarnate summary patterns of persistence and change that specify events as integral wholes." As both event cognition and dynamic systems approaches attest, we are highly competent in both perception and action with respect to unified, purposeful "events as integral wholes," and we use all the information available from the entire sensorimotor system.

Intersubjectivity and Affect Attunement

Thelen and Smith (1994: 193) cite evidence that "by 4 months, infants are very good at recognizing the match between heard speech and seen facial movements" (Kuhl and Meltzoff 1982). Daniel Stern (1985: 140–46) argues that what researchers have seen as imitation of the mother by the infant in the first weeks is actually "affect attunement" and thus "matching, but not faithful imitation." For Stern, "what is being matched is not the other person's behavior *per se*, but rather some aspect of the behavior that reflects the person's feeling state" (142). This nonetheless intermodal matching includes such variables as

1. Global, amodal, *perceptual qualities* (intensity level, motion, number, rhythm)
2. *Categorial affects* (angry, sad, happy . . .)
3. *Vitality affects* (dynamic, kinetic—surging, fading away, fleeting, explosive, drawn out, etc.). (53–54)

Each of these variables contributes to our understanding of gesture, but vitality affects, with their dynamic and kinetic aspects, have already drawn the attention of music scholars. Michel Imberty (2000: 459–60) has applied Stern's ideas by noting what he calls "dynamic vectors" in music. The notion of a vectoral field is fruitful, and I will return in subsequent chapters to the ways in which music can create a virtual environment akin to the forces acting on our bodies in the world, in turn fostering an analogous sense of embodied gesture, as individually generated movements react to the constraints of virtual field forces akin to gravity. From another perspective, one might observe that the deformations attributable to field forces reveal the profile of an agent's actions and their relative strength.

Colwyn Trevarthen (1986a, 1986b, 1999) has perhaps most thoroughly explored the range of interactions between infants and their caregivers. His observations confirm those of Stern while going a bit further. Trevarthen realized early in his career that the emergence of sophisticated cultural communicative competencies in humans required a developmental investigation of the ongoing, affective interactions between the infant and a solicitous mother or father, and he has gathered these competencies under the umbrella concept of *intersubjectivity*. Intersubjectivity, as interactive communication between infant and primary caregiver, "requires coordination between evolving states of attention, changing emotions and cognitive adjustments" (1986a: 218). Trevarthen observes that humans not only perceive their own bodies' internal states (*proprioception*) and objects or events in their environment (*exteroception*), but also the expressiveness of others, which he terms *alteroception* (218). Besides perceiving that expressiveness, the infant attempts to maintain contact with the caregiver, as in Stern's affective attunement, and further models her own behavior in a manner consistent with the sharing of emotion and social bonding. Thus, many of the infant's movements, from hand gestures to vocalizations, share with the caregiver's a similar (gestural) shaping and timing. Trevarthen argues that this social turn-taking foreshadows the interactions of language. Even before language emerges, however, these kinds of gestural communications enable the participants to align their own motivations "with the expressed feeling or purpose" of the other (218). From the very beginning, then, communication is involved in the development of the architecture of the brain. Infants integrate perceptual and motor capacities into a single functioning system at the level of interactive communication and shared affect.[12]

Children who lack these capacities or are denied their development are termed *autistic,* a condition defined as an intersubjective disorder by Trevarthen (1989) and Hobson (1993). Temple Grandin, the autistic doctor of veterinary science made famous by Oliver Sacks (1996), was unable as a child to pick up the rich social and affective signaling of her playmates. In an evocative image, she compared her quandary to that facing an "anthropologist from Mars." Children with normal intersubjective development routinely acquire these competencies, and Trevarthen and others claim that they include the perception and enactment of rhythm and contour.[13]

Categories of Gesture Accompanying Speech

I turn now to the symbolic and paralinguistic uses of gesture in the context of language, specifically, gestures used to enhance spoken language.[14] This is an important area of research into gesture, and it focuses on intentional, signifying actions by the hands, arms, face, and body. My own, broader concept of gesture is not restricted to these sites, but includes the intonational contours of language itself. However, a brief overview of paralinguistic gestures will reinforce the concept of intermodality and suggest other useful ways to categorize expressive, energetic shapings through time.

Gestures as associated with speech are richly varied. Ekman (1999) outlines five principal categories: emblems, illustrators, manipulators, regulators, and emotional expressions. *Emblems* are socially learned, quasi-lexical items, such as circling thumb and forefinger to signify "OK." *Illustrators,* also socially learned, serve to illustrate speech. These include *batons* (a beatlike accentuation of speech by a sudden downward arm movement with pointing finger, slicing hand, or fist; or an upward or downward motion of the brow), *ideographs* (tracings with the hand and arm of the "path" of thought), *deictic movements* (pointing to an immediate object), *kinetographs* (depicting a bodily action), *spatial movements* (depicting a spatial relationship), *pictographs* (drawing a picture of a referent), and *rhythmic movements* (depicting the rhythm or pacing of an event). *Manipulators* are perhaps unwitting movements (scratching, licking one's lips) that vary from individual to individual. *Regulators* are coded actions that are used to maintain contact during conversation (regulating *phatic* communication, which involves those means used to keep the communicative channel open and active). These include *agreement* (head nod, smile), *calls for information* (raised brow), *floor holders* (holding the hand out), and *turn seekers* (leaning forward, beginning lip movement). Finally, *emotional expressions* are involuntary signals (though selected through the evolution of social communication) that include facial expressions for basic emotions (anger, fear, disgust, contempt, surprise, sadness/distress, enjoyment, embarrassment). Of course, one can attempt to fake an emotion, and *referential expressions* are facial movements that refer to an emotion not felt by the person communicating it. Interestingly, even when faking an expressive gesture, the body experiences changes in the autonomic nervous system similar to those occurring when the emotion is genuine (Levenson, Ekman, and Friesen 1990). Related discoveries underlie the acting theory of Delsarte (Stebbins 1894) and Manfred Clynes's (1977) interpretation of his *sentic forms* (see Chapter 6). What is important here is the system-wide (hence, at least interactively modal) character of emotion, which can be selected by gesture as well as reflected in gestures.

A theoretical weakness in Ekman's categorization is that it does not indicate varying degrees of conventionality. David McNeill (1992: 37) cites Adam Kendon (1988) as his starting point for a slightly different categorization of gestures along a continuum, with conventionality measured by closeness to language: Gesticulation, Language-like Gestures, Pantomimes, Emblems, and Sign Languages. *Gesticulation*—the gestures with which McNeill's own research is most concerned, and the basis for his "growth points" (see below)—are "idiosyncratic spontaneous movements of the hands and arms accompanying speech" (37). Clearly, from McNeill's examples, these are motivated actions tied to the meaning of the discourse: "the hand rising upward while the speaker says 'and he climbs up the pipe'" (37). Thus, gesticulations are akin to Ekman's illustrators. *Language-like gestures* can fill slots in a syntactic chain, replacing words. McNeill's example is "the parents were all right, but the kids were [gesture]" (37), in which one might imagine, for example, a "so-so" hand tilt (or worse) filling the linguistic slot. *Pantomines* are depictions of objects or actions in which speech is not obligatory, but pantomimes can create sequences, whereas gesticulations generally do not combine. *Emblems,* following Ekman, are language-like in that they have conventions of well-formedness; these include the familiar signs for insults. *Sign languages,* of course, are complete linguistic systems, characterized by segmentation, compositionality, a lexicon, a syntax, paradigmatic oppositions, distinctiveness, arbitrariness, utterance-like timing, standards of well-formedness, and a community of users (38–39).

Within the category of gesticulations McNeill outlines the following types, based on their meanings and functions (1992: 76–77):

1. Iconics—referring to concrete objects and events
2. Metaphorics—referring to abstract concepts and relations
3. Deictics—referring to orientations and reorientations
4. Beats—referring to discontinuities.

Interestingly, the first two types would fall under Peirce's category of Firstness (based on similarity at various levels), and the next two types under Secondness (based on indexicality and dynamic association). For McNeill, *Iconic* gestures represent aspects of the situation or scene as described in speech; hence, these gestures are complementary to speech (not merely duplicating it). This is one of the reasons McNeill claims that "gesture and speech jointly comprise a single integrated expression of meaning" (79). *Metaphoric* gestures go further than iconics, in that one must interpret the represented object metaphorically. *Deictics* may either point to a concrete object, or in the case of narrative pointing, to a relative location in the gestural space that corresponds to the relative positioning of events in narrative time. *Beats* (akin to Ekman's *batons*) "do not present a discernible meaning" (80) but are used for emphasis. Their prototypical movement is in two parts, up and down: "small, low energy, rapid flicks of the fingers or the hand" (80).

Two fruitful oppositions emerge from McNeill's categorization: "events that iconics illustrate inherently progress in temporal and causal sequences in the real or fictive world, while beats occur at points of significant discontinuity in discourse and function to highlight atemporal relationships" (93). Furthermore, "abstract pointing occurs chiefly with narrative clauses, whereas metaphorics appear chiefly with extranarrative clauses" (93).

Another illuminating gestural typology is that offered by Nespoulous and Lecours (1986). Based on "degrees of arbitrariness between gestural segment and referent" (55), their typology (58) can also be correlated with Peircean categories (see my bracketed additions).

a.	Arbitrary	+ distance	− transparency	[symbolic]
b.	Mimetic	+ distance	+ transparency	[iconic]
c.	Deictic	− distance	+ transparency	[indexical]

"Arbitrary" means that a gesture cannot be interpreted without being learned, and hence it lacks "transparency," or obviousness stemming from the context of the gesture. "Distance" means that the referred object of the gesture is not actually present during the time of the gesture. Only deictic gestures *require* the presence of the object, as in the prototypical pointing gesture. But even deictic "pointing" may have multiple functions—designating the particular object, designating the class of objects by reference to a token of the type, or even designating the function of the object (58). Nespoulous and Lecours recognize that arbitrary gestures may have been "somewhat transparent at some stage of their social history," although "their diachronic evolution turned them into more and more opaque segments" (51). They also wisely note that a given gesture may implement functions from more than one category—that categories are nonexclusive (59-60).

A preliminary application of these categories to music can readily be imagined, although a more careful consideration will be given in Chapter 6, where I discuss David Lidov's important and related categorization of musical gestures. For now, arbitrary gestures may be understood to include highly formalized or ritualized conventions (dance meters, for example) as well as gestures that take their meaning from our understanding of the conventions of tonal syntax. Mimetic, or iconic, gestures "sound" like or have analogous structure to the objects or events or states they represent or suggest. And deictic, or indexical, gestures are dynamically involved in the action upon their objects—including various forms of rhetorical "pointing" by which a composer or performer highlights a particular musical event—as well as dialogical responses to other gestures. Deictic gestures may vary in meaning depending on context, like pronouns in language; Roman Jakobson (1963) referred to these linguistic signs as "shifters."[15] We will see that the indexical category can be expanded to include more than deictic gestures.

The gestural categories outlined by Ekman, McNeill, and Nespoulous and Lecours are, indeed, only part of the story of gesture and speech. Intonation curves and various rhetorical emphases in spoken language have gestural properties that serve to enhance the informational chain of meaning attributed to syntax and semantics.[16] Furthermore, significant vocal gesture includes sounds that are not strictly verbal, though they may play a linguistic role.[17] In the following excerpt from *True at First Light*, the fictionalized Hemingway has just given advice to two Masai elders: "After receiving this message the two elders spoke together and then to me and I grunted knowingly throughout their speech with that peculiar rising inflection grunt that means you are giving the matter your deepest attention" (1999 [1953–54]: 30).

As is the case with intonational emphases in spoken language (whether verbalizing or "grunting"), each of the gesticulations defined by McNeill can be emphasized or inflected through (a) degrees of intensity (force), (b) exaggeration (spatial dimensionality), (c) unique shaping (of contour), (d) specific timing (duration, rhythmic character, etc.), and still other variables. Thus, besides their informational content, the gestures of the hand can convey something of the emotional state of the speaker, or the emotional attitude of the speaker toward the message or the listener (recall the "affect attunement" of Stern, where matching was governed more by affect than by imitation).

The integration between gesture and speech has been underlined by McNeill (1999: 80), who hypothesizes a "growth point" as a basic theoretical unit that "consists irreducibly of both imagistic [gestural] and linguistic [symbolic] forms of information at the same time." McNeill notes that "this combination of different modalities is the key to its potential for . . . change." Growth points, like the perception-action categories of Thelen and Smith (1994) and the actions defined by Kugler and Turvey (1987), reflect the interrelatedness of modalities at a fundamental level in the brain. McNeill takes that interaction to a higher cognitive level by integrating the conceptual system of language. As units that enable us to communicate, McNeill's "growth points" package meaning across modalities, with a "dynamic unfolding that is characteristic of consciousness" (86). Imagery, in the form of gesture, is important in that it provides grounding for the conceptual categories of language, which functions both as "a system of classification and a way of patterning action" (80). For music, this concept will be relevant to a discussion of how gesture and musical syntax (the more "symbolic" level) interact in the service of a singular, rhetorical musical event. A focal example is found in the first movement of Beethoven's Op. 109 (discussed at the end of Chapter 7).

The growth points of David McNeill reinforce the importance of intermodality at higher cognitive levels. One might conceive of intermodality in several ways; the following hypotheses address how different sense modalities might cooperate in their representation of gesture. The first three emphasize interaction at various levels, and the latter two, analogous representations at different levels:

1. There are finely tuned interactions among human perceptual and motor systems.
2. There are close interactions among perceptual systems (vision, hearing,

touch, taste, smell, and proprioceptive and kinesthetic senses), which also entail motor action as part of an active search for enriched perceptual information.

3. There are strong interactions among different communicative modalities (e.g., gestures of the hand and speech), integrated to achieve a communicative goal.

4. There are analogous intensities and shapings in the representation or interpretation of meaning through different channels (e.g., an intense gesture typically accompanies an intensely enunciated word); this is the level of McNeill's "growth points."

5. There are analogous topological mappings in the sensory neuronal fields of the brain, either (a) analogous to features of the objects represented,[18] or (b) analogous among the mappings of different sensory modalities.

Clearly, to speak of *interactions* among modalities is not as compelling as to claim *analogous modes of representation* in the brain, but the latter is not as crucial a claim for my theory as the general hypothesis that all sense modalities have ways—however analogous—of identifying, representing, and replicating the basic energetic structure of a gesture as a flow event. Recall my definition of gesture as perceptible and significant energetic shaping through time, regardless of modality or channel.

Gesture, as we have seen, involves a complex of elements, yet it may be considered a basic category, since its perception and cognition, like that of other significant objects and events, is characterized by rich intermodal syntheses. We are evolutionarily designed, and developmentally conditioned, to interpret and synthesize complexes of sensations into the following emergent meanings:

1. Object or event
2. Plausible agency or cause-effect relationship
3. Movement/direction/intensity/character
4. Emotional valency
5. Any necessary responses (e.g., survival, reflexes) as well as any desirable ones (e.g., socialization, aesthetic pleasure).

A prototypical gesture (one that takes shape in the perceptual present) entails a fusing of two gestalts: the *imagistic* (e.g., facial features; timbre and sonority in music) and the *temporal* (e.g., movement; melody, rhythm, and in general, progression of any element in music); together these provide configurational depth and breadth. The interpretation of a gesture often appears to be immediate since these emergent cognitive inferences are so richly implicated in perception, with its biologically attuned, senserimotor integration.

Finally, to return to our starting point, a gesture can draw upon a prelinguistic wealth of qualitative experience; language can, at best, provide a conceptual label for a gesture at the level of the *type,* and a partial articulation by adjectives and qualifiers at the level of the *token.* Thus, gesture can be more precise than language in that it can emulate those precise energetic shapes that hold expressive meaning for us. But language itself is built upon a stratum of gestural communication: the intonation curves, intensities of stress and climax, and other prosodic features of speech. Along with the gestural shapings of streams of phonemes, speakers have recourse to still other gestures—facial, bodily, and in particular those paralinguistic gestures accompanying speech, as cataloged variously by Kendon, Ekman, McNeill, and Nespoulous and Lecours. Thus, an account of human speech communication that omitted the gestural in deference to the symbolic or syntactic would be greatly impoverished from the start. As we investigate music in the next chapters, we will observe that even the syntactic dimensions of music theory—harmonic progression, voice-leading, and the like—maintain close connections to gesture, perhaps even more intimately than in the case of gestures accompanying speech.

The interdisciplinary insights presented in this chapter are summarized here as a set of foundational principles for a theory of gesture. Although I will not refer to every principle in my subsequent investigation of musical gesture in Chapter 6— nor in my more focused interpretations of style, performance practice, and expressive meaning in Chapters 7–10—the reader should bear these principles in mind as serving to ground my interpretive claims.

1. Gesture is most generally defined as *communicative* (whether intended or not), *expressive, energetic shaping through time* (including characteristic features of *musicality* such as *beat, rhythm, timing of exchanges, contour, intensity*), regardless of medium (channel) or sensory-motor source (*intermodal* or *cross-modal*).

2. Expressive gesture develops *prior to language* and develops interactively in infant-caregiver exchanges. The *intersubjective* grounding of meaning for members of a particular *culture* yields a stable set of *categories* with *expressive* meaning.

3. Expressive movement and interpretation creates *natural categories of dynamic motion* through the brain's sensorimotor mapping of functional units of the body. Perceptual *binding (synthesis, integration)* of the welter of sensations enables us to interpret *objects* (their *unity, coherence, constancy* across change) and *events* (their *continuity, functional coherence, and/or cause/effect relationships*); objects and events are thus *foregrounded* against the background of other sensations/objects/events, and thus initially *marked* as significant.

4. *Prototypical* gestures (those that occur in the *perceptual present* of working memory) have aspects of both object and event and thus integrate two syntheses of perception: the *qualitative depth* of an *imagistic gestalt* (crucial to facial perception, for example) and the *continuity* of a *temporal gestalt* (as featured in body movement, or the contours of expressive vocalization, for example).

5. The basic shape of an expressive gesture (qualitative and energetic temporal shaping; Clynes's sentic form) is *isomorphic* and *intermodal* across all systems of production and interpretation. At a higher, more symbolic cognitive level, the representation of gesture may be considered *amodal*, in that it is not restricted to any particular modality.

6. Based on their origin in expressive movement (whether of hands, face, vocal tract, or other body movement), gestural shapes are constrained by the *dynamics* of a *gravitational field* or *vectoral space* (whether actual or virtual). Gestures are negotiated

within that physical orientation, and their expressive effects exploit potential contrasts or energetic expenditure with respect to the forces in their field/space.

7. Emotionally motivated expressive movements develop a systematic *markedness* of oppositions (grief = down, heavy; elation = up, light), creating so-called basic emotion categories that may be universal across cultures. Cultures further mark the degree to which emotions may be displayed, the appropriate contexts, and any ritualized modifications of the biological expression of emotion.

8. Cultures (along with language) develop gestures within the Peircean typology:

   a. *Iconic* (including pantomimes and metaphorical gestures)
   b. *Indexical* (including pointing gestures)
   c. *Symbolic* (including emblems and other conventionalized gestural expressions).

6   Toward a Theory of Musical Gesture

The second movement of Schubert's Piano Sonata in A Minor, D. 845, opens with the theme for a set of variations in C major (Example 6.1). Its first eight bars display a straightforward harmonic and phrase structure (4 + 4), with the second phrase moving to the dominant to complete the first half of a rounded binary form. The melody is in the alto voice, and the soprano reiterates a dominant pedal point, creating a somewhat veiled effect. Topically the theme is a stylized *Ländler*, with accents on the downbeats of the first two bars of each phrase.

When I first studied this sonata in the mid-seventies, my critical faculties had been shaped by the thematic complexities of Brahms. I could not fully appreciate Schubert's theme because it seemed too formulaic harmonically, despite its subtle textural design. But simplicity in a theme that will be subject to variations is often a virtue. Furthermore, Schubert treats his theme to a progressive series of diminutions that ultimately flower in transcendent fashion, not unlike Beethoven's own C major variations in the finale of his Piano Sonata, Op. 111. While I admired the expressive outcome of the variations, I could not escape my initial impression of the theme as disappointingly trite. Recognizing that my playing was less than committed, my teacher sat down at the piano to demonstrate a more sympathetic approach.[1] It was a revelation I will never forget. Tears welled up at the poignancy and beauty of Schubert's gestures, which I had completely overlooked in my reductive dismissal of its melodic and harmonic design. With a delicacy of touch, and a characteristic *rubato* that marked the accents and shaped the meter of this stylized *Ländler*, my teacher not only brought Schubert's musical world to life, but captured an implied inner agency's poignant evocation of lost innocence as well.

Years later, drawing on my work with musical meaning in Beethoven (Hatten 1994), I could suggest several justifications for the heightened expressivity of this theme, which I now heard as "exquisitely naive." These included the cueing of the pastoral as topic or mode (the dominant pedal and simple harmonic structure); the elevation of a rustic pastoral dance to the sublime (the *pianissimo* setting and contextualization as theme for a set of diminutional variations that would emerge as transcendent); and the suggestion of poignant reminiscence (the stylized treatment of a *Ländler*, with its associations of an idyllic time that can only be regained through the imagination). But even after tagging each of these separate contributions to a more symbolic articulation of the theme's musical meaning, I had not fully captured the quality of emotion it evoked, an emotion that seemed to be generated by the character of the movement itself, and its gestural shaping. Unlike the opening theme of the Cavatina from Beethoven's String Quartet in B♭ Major, Op. 130 (interpreted in Hatten 1994: 203–23), this depth of emotion was not enhanced by an interpolated expansion of the phrase leading to a climactic reversal.

Example 6.1. Schubert, Piano Sonata in A Minor, D. 845, second movement, opening theme.

Rather, particular qualities of the performance itself appeared to be triggering my deeper response. Yet my teacher's gesturally realized performance was composed of the very elements I had analytically treated as separate components. The difference was in their *synthesis*, their *continuity* beyond the mere sequence of enchained pitches and rhythms, which fostered an *emergent* expressive interpretation far richer than I had been able to achieve in my own playing. It is this *synthetic gestalt*, and its *emergent expressivity*, that will be central to my study of musical gesture.

David Lidov (1993) insightfully defines artistic gesture as movement that is *marked* for significance, whether by or for the agent or the interpreter. Similarly, human gestures in general may be defined as those movements marked by their potential for meaningful interpretation. However, a movement need not be intentionally produced to be interpreted as significant.[2] For example, when I detect subtle movements indicating that another is bored by my conversation, that person's movements need not be conscious to take on gestural significance. By including unintended but significant movements as gestural, I go beyond Adam Kendon's more limited stricture on the term:

> A gesture is usually deemed to be an action by which a thought, feeling, or intention is given conventional and voluntary expression. Gestures are thus considered to be different from expressions of emotion, involuntary mannerisms, however revealing, and actions that are taken in the pursuit of some aim, however informative such actions may be. (1981: 28)

For the most part the inferred musical gestures to be discussed in the following chapters are ones for which intentionality may be argued. But in cases where the composer may not have specified a gesture through notation, aspects of style and compositional rhetoric may nevertheless imply a particular gestural realization.

Presumably, every technical movement a performer makes is already marked as relevant to the production of "significant" sound—hence, as artistic gesture. But, in fact, many movements observed in performance appear extraneous to the gestural interpretation of the music, and even among those movements that are expressively motivated, some may appear more significant than others. We are more likely to attend to those gestural movements that create either *thematic* or *rhetorical* gestures. A thematic gesture is marked by initial foregrounding and subsequent development. A rhetorical gesture is marked by its disruption of the otherwise unmarked flow in some dimension of the musical discourse (see Chapter 7 for the elaboration of these types of gesture). But other, less-focal movements may contribute gesturally to the expressive character of a passage: unmarked background textures, or conventional cadential materials in the Classical style, convey a significance that emerges from their qualitative musical motion, even when it is not foregrounded.

I should emphasize at this point that musical gestures, while inferred from notation, are also inferred from performance. In the latter case the motivation for a musical gesture may be *heard*—its source in a human performer's movements need not be seen to be inferred (recall the evidence for intermodality in Chapter 5). When hearing a performance with our eyes closed, or when listening to a recording, we can readily reconstruct the kinds and qualities of motion that give character to musical gestures. A digital recording breaks up the analog continuity of music by discontinuous, discrete sampling (much to the distress of those with extremely acute aural perception), but it cannot disable the capacity of most listeners to hear the seamless flow of a gesture's "energetic shaping through time." If the samplings are close enough, the ear is satisfied, just as the eye will interpret discontinuous frames at a sufficient speed in terms of the continuities of visual motion, as in a film. Indeed, creating the illusion of *legato* from discrete pitches that fade after being struck is a common dilemma for pianists, whose instrument demands the creation of a gestural illusion by the even dynamic control of attack points, as much as by the overlapping of releases.

Precedents for a Theory of Gesture

Given the importance of gesture to interpretation, one might reasonably ask why there is no comprehensive theory of gesture in music. Historically one reason may be that musical notation, which is also largely digital or discrete in its symbols, cannot adequately represent the continuities of gesture.[3] The history of the slur, the smoothly analog curved line connecting two or more notes, gives evidence of one attempt to represent not merely continuity of sound, but more importantly continuity of gesture (see Chapter 7). Conventions of style and the apprenticeship of instruction in earlier times also helped guarantee that performers created gestural continuities beyond those explicitly represented in the notation of a score.

But theorists have also attempted to clarify the intuition of an "energetic" dimension, as Lee Rothfarb (2002) amply documents.[4] Rothfarb notes that an application of the metaphor of gravity to music is found already in Rameau (1737), who modeled the tonic as center of gravity surrounded by dominant and subdominant on either side, and considered gravity as a motivating force for harmonic progression. Fétis (1858 [1844]) contributed the metaphor of a dynamic force field within which energetic tones operate, and Zuckerkandl (1956) theorized a "dynamic field" based on the scale, as guiding tonal motion. Riemann (1884) wrote of the "life force" found in the motive, and Schenker developed the "biological urges" of tones (1954 [1906]) into an organicist conception of voice-leading as the source of life for motive and melody alike (1921, 1979 [1935]).

However, it is in the work of Ernst Kurth (Rothfarb 1988, 1991) that the energetic conception most nearly anticipates one key feature of my own view of musical gesture (as energetic shaping through time): the insight that the gestural energy of a melody is phenomenologically more fundamental than the sequence of pitches of which a melody is comprised. Gesture presupposes the continuity of motion through a path for which tones provide the landmarks, analogous to the points outlining a smooth, curvilinear function on an X–Y coordinate graph.[5] As Rothfarb (2002: 940) explains, "for Kurth . . . melody occurs between the tones, in the sweep of kinetic energy that flows through them and becomes dammed up, as potential energy, in chords."[6]

Strikingly, in his conception of musical energy Kurth gives priority to the dimension of pitch, both melodic and harmonic; he views rhythmic energy as dependent on melodic energy. By contrast, I will address each of the elements of music—including the oft-neglected dimensions of dynamics, articulation, and pacing—as interdependent and often equally important means of creating a musical gesture. Furthermore, Kurth's prototypical "kernels" of melodic energy are found in what he calls "developmental motives," those patterns of ascending, descending, spiraling, and oscillating figuration that he identifies in Baroque sequential and developmental passagework. Although these may have been the easiest patterns to describe in energetic terms, they will not figure prominently in the gestural classes introduced in Chapter 7 (nor, for obvious reasons, in examples drawn primarily from the Classical style).

Historically, practical manuals for performance typically cover the full range of signs and their execution, from accents and slurs to dynamics and tempo markings, with attention to expressive issues scattered throughout. Although these sources respond to the changing technologies of musical instruments and their stylistic employment, their treatment of notated (and non-notated) elements is often partitioned according to discrete categories, whether viewed from the perspective of *processive strands* (suggesting the image of a cable with multiple strands) or that of *structural segments* (implying a hierarchy of discrete sections).

Processively, discussion of analog notational signs (slurs, *crescendi, ritardandi*) is relegated in performance manuals to separate chapters or sections dealing with topics such as articulation, dynamics, tempo, and the like, with very little overlap.[7] Stylistic assumptions about how to convey expressive subtleties, if broached at all, are often covered in separate sections on *rubato* (flexibility in pacing), accentuation (flexibility in the marking of tones or musical events), articulation (flexibility in beginnings and endings), and dynamics (flexibility in intensities). Chapter divisions of current books such as Sandra Rosenblum's (1988) superb study of Classical piano performance practice, or Clive Brown's (1999) exhaustive overview of performance practice from 1750 to 1900, exhibit similar divisions for practical reasons, but these authors differ in how they integrate categories of notation. For example, Rosenblum offers a chapter relating dynamics and articulation, and Brown features one that integrates accentuation and phrasing. Rosenblum's narrower historical scope justifies her summary application of historical insights to the performing interpretation of just one work (Beethoven's Bagatelle, Op. 126, no. 5), but even this culminating interpretation is in outline form, partitioned among categories of notational signs.[8]

Segmentally even the presumed gestalts of phrasing are often treated as mere slices of a temporal continuum comprised of discrete motivic or metric units, or as segments in a phrase hierarchy (incise, phrase, period, double period). Meyer's (1973: 89) image of "hierarchies of closure" suggests a more functional approach, but the mapping of articulated units of form is pervasive in line diagrams of movements. Although gestures may be subsumed as parts of larger gestures (at least metaphorically), a description of gestures as discrete units in a formal hierarchy cannot address the continuities of gesture across segmental boundaries. Furthermore, performers strive to create a shaping and shading of each gesture or phrase that is more than the sum of the motivic or harmonic units of which they are composed.

But is human gesture merely imposed by the performer to achieve a sense of vivid involvement, or to "communicate" one's feelings? How can one claim that gesture is implied by, or encoded within, the fabric of a score? To begin with, the dynamic environment in which we experience our bodies and their gestures has its virtual counterpart in music. At least for Western classical music, meter functions like a gravitational field that conditions our embodied sense of up versus down, the relative weighting of events, and the relative amount of energy needed to overcome "gravitational" constraints (as in an ascending melody). Rhythm, as well as melody and harmony, plays with and against the metric field in a way that suggests human energy and flexibility (recall point 6 from the summary at the end of Chapter 5).

Besides meter, other systematic dimensions of a musical style can contribute to the experience of embodied gesture in a work. With respect to diatonic tonal space, Steve Larson (1993, 1994, 1997, 1997–98) has defined three forces that constitute what I would characterize as *virtual environmental forces:* gravity (the tendency of tones to descend toward a pitch considered as a base, such as a tonic), magnetism (the attraction of tones toward more stable tones, which becomes stronger as the interval to the stable tone gets smaller), and inertia (the tendency of a pattern of motion to continue in the same way, even past a point of stability).[9] In considering these musical forces as environmental, I mean to suggest that Larson's model could be usefully complemented with the addition of a perceived or implied *source* of gestural energy—in many cases, the motivating force of an implied *musical agent.*

A spontaneous or "willed" individual gesture may be understood as being subject to various forces as it traverses tonal and metric fields, environmental forces which act upon it in various ways. The gesture may be deflected from its energetic direction, or it may be fulfilled by reaching a point of stability within the operative fields of tonality and meter.[10] My view acknowledges the embodied interpretation of listener expectation, or stylistic implication, in Meyer's usage, and extends it to a virtual, experiencing body.[11]

The first two of Larson's forces (gravity and magnetism) are like dynamic field forces that act upon a body, as revealed by its responses. Gravity suggests a pressure to descend; our sense of down versus up in pitch space is mapped onto down versus up in the lived world. Magnetism reflects tendencies to resolve or arrive at stable scale degrees as goals of motion.[12]

The third force, inertia, is different in that it does not exert a constraint on movement the way gravity and magnetism do. Inertia offers no impedance to the implied energy of the gesture itself, but merely reflects its tendency to continue. As defined in physics, inertia is the tendency of an object in motion or at rest to continue in its prior state. With respect to musical motion, Larson's inertia may remind the reader of the Gestalt "law of good continuation," applied to music by Leonard B. Meyer (1956).[13] But as Larson has recently noted (2003), Meyer's application of the Gestalt law is typically as a continuation to a goal, which is more akin to Larson's magnetism, as opposed to inertia, which exerts force even past a stable goal. It would be interesting to imagine a musical equivalent of environmental "friction" which could gradually deplete the inertia of motion. From the perspective of motivated gesture, however, inertia might be complemented by *momentum* (defined as "strength or continuity derived from an initial effort"),[14] in order to emphasize the effort of a virtual agency as the source of that energy.

Insightfully Larson describes cases where his three forces are in conflict, which leads him to an evaluation of their relative weighting in various contexts. The ultimate direction taken by an individual gesture (or a melodic contour) will thus reflect the influence of these sometimes competing forces. I would caution only that the internal energies and intentionality of musical gestures need not be pre- or overdetermined by Larson's forces, at least when considered as environmental. For example, Larson (1997–98) has elegantly demonstrated how the three-, five-, and seven-note basic melodic structures found in Schenkerian upper lines and structural motives (neighboring and passing figures oriented around stable tonic triad tones) may all be accounted for in terms of the regulative action of these forces—a striking indication that they are indeed the most stable, kernel "paths" through tonal space. From the perspective of motivated gesture, however, I would emphasize that the "deeper structures" these stable kernels provide (as in a Schenkerian analysis) may be viewed as resulting from the predictability of their motion in accordance with the constraints of a tonal environmental field; within that field, however, motivated gestures may more freely extend and elaborate their energies. Considered in this way, reductions do not explain the initial *motivations* for a foregrounded gesture, even when they reveal one important aspect of its *structure*—the default path from which it departs and in relation to which it achieves both expressivity and coherence.

When interpreting the expressive meaning of a gesture, taking environmental forces into account can be an important stage of the investigation. However, one must also address the unique energies, intentional actions, and extended continuities of those individually motivated shapes. It is this latter stage of investigation that will be the primary focus of my interpretations in Chapters 7–10. To summarize, then, gestural character and quality *emerge* for the listener from an interaction with tonality and meter as environmental fields with implied forces and orientations.[15]

How do pitch and tonal spaces interact with meter? Schachter (1976: 313) notes that metric expectations are drawn from basic tonal relationships, resulting in what he calls tonal rhythm. Tonic stability is typically correlated with a metric downbeat. Thus, upon beginning with a tonic chord, and in the absence of any contradictory information, a listener will assume that the initial chord is "grounded" both tonally and metrically (on a downbeat). If not, the character of the gesture will be appropriately affected by the contradiction—yielding an expressive effect that Meyer noted was the result of any violation of expectation, or implication.[16]

A clear example of the regulative effect of meter on expressive quality may be found in the opening theme of the third movement of Brahms's Third Symphony (see Example 4.12). The initial, three-note rhythmic motive could have been reiterated as an upbeat to m. 2, rhythmically sequencing its metric placement in m. 1.[17] But Brahms suspends the next upbeat of the one-bar rhythmic gesture to the following downbeat, thereby creating not only a pull from the lengthening of the motive, but also a physical sensation akin to being lifted by a wave: going over the top of the downbeat with a rhythm that *contradicts* without *contravening* the metric field. That embodied experience is easily correlated with an inner state of feeling; the swell of a restless, yearning emotion is an almost unavoidable interpretation.[18]

If meter and tonality each afford analogies to gravitation, or more broadly, *vectoral* space, together they enhance an experience of *embodied motion*, in that they provide the listener with dynamics and constraints comparable to those the body experiences in a natural environment, including its orientation as up or down.[19] Within the virtual dynamics of music's metric and tonal fields, analogous energetic shapings through time (as learned in earlier biological and cultural attunement) may be accessed, and their prior expressive meanings may issue almost transparently. The expressive potential of musical gestures may, however, be further realized by thematization and development within the constraints of a style and the strategies of a work.

The energy and flexibility we acknowledge as artistic implies the freely willed intentionality of an implied agent—the locus of our experiencing of gesture, regardless of stylistic forces that may be acting upon that agent in the virtual physical environment of music. These individualizing actions (leaps, articulations, reversals, syncopations) counteract what might otherwise devolve into the dull regularities of the frame (the triteness of tonal formulae, the tyranny of the bar line, or the justly criticized conception of meter as mere grid).[20] Individual configurations of gesture emerge in a composer's play with the regulative syntax of a musical style. But, as we saw with the Schubert variation theme (Example 6.1), sometimes these tonal and rhythmic energies and flexibilities are not immediately evident from the syntax alone. Significant characterization of gesture may also be heard in the subtle warpings of metric placement and accentuation in performance. This is especially true of much popular music, where microstructural variations in timing result in a very subtle and sophisticated rhythmic shaping that might be entirely overlooked by the scholar focusing on the notated rhythm and meter alone.[21]

For an interpreter to achieve a "top-down" gestural integration at the piano of separately notated elements, she must also integrate in a goal-directed fashion all the separate muscles in the arm and hand. There are thirteen degrees of freedom in the movement of the arm alone, and to date no machine can accomplish the sophisticated coordination of that many possibilities, whereas trained pianists exhibit such refined motion without a second thought. On the other hand, only a dogmatic pedagogue who has not observed a number of superb pianists would assume that a single "correct" combination of weight or muscular involvement throughout the body was required to achieve a given goal or expressive effect (recall the studies of functionally coherent human actions cited in Chapter 5). Analogously, expert (technically and stylistically competent) performers will exemplify individual or unique integrations or syntheses of the microstructural variables of performance (tempo, timing, articulation, dynamics, phrasing—and for the piano, pedal).

Thus, it would be counterproductive to try to describe and hence define musical gestures with respect to some precise recipe for performance, combining their musical components and their muscular embodiments. Clearly, different combinations can achieve similar effects. Furthermore, similar effects may not always be desired. To adapt an argument from Edward T. Cone (1968: 35–36), we may tire of what was once an illuminating interpretation and come to appreciate another interpretation that brings out other, equally valuable relationships.

Refinements in one's performance, as well as in one's theoretical understanding, can be achieved through a pedagogy such as Alexandra Pierce's (1994) that addresses physical movement as artistically conditioned by the constraints of a musical style and the unique configurations of a musical work. Her approach, to be outlined below, offers not only a way to refine, but also to discover gestural structuring at several levels. Pierce extends the concept of gesture beyond the muscles to include the expressive intonations of the voice, relating the feeling in a spoken word to the characteristic "feelings" (physical *and* emotional) implied by a musical passage.

Although gestures are high-level syntheses, they are also typically conceived as basic-level categories, characterized by the immediacy with which we identify primary expressive units.[22] Smaller gestures, however, can be subsumed by larger ones, and gestural performance can benefit from a Schenkerian analysis that coordinates larger phrase structure, as Alexander Pierce and William Rothstein (1995) have demonstrated.[23]

Much important work is being done on music's "microstructure," those variables in sound production that fall between the cracks of our discrete notational systems. Manfred Clynes's (1995) "composers' pulses" are individualized warpings of the framework of common-time meter, with a consistent timing and dynamic differentiation of each beat serving to distinguish the characteristic pulse frameworks of Haydn, Mozart, Beethoven, and Schubert. Clynes has tested the validity of his hypotheses by designing various warpings of actual themes generated electronically with these adjustments, and his expert listeners—concert artists—apparently prefer (or consider as more stylistic) his ideal pulses over other possible warpings. One might question whether these warpings fully capture the holistic character of gesture, but they may contribute to one strand of this twisted cable, to invoke my earlier image. But how might variances in rhythmic timing, as conditioned by unique gestural interpretations of motives, be negotiated within such a fixed warping of the frame? Should we attempt to prescribe a given composer's pulse and insist that others adopt that "groove" if they wish their performances to be valid? Such performances would likely sound stilted. Nevertheless, Clynes's experiment has profound implications, and experiments by Bruno Repp suggest that "musical structures have kinematic implications that not only compel performers to modulate their tempo in certain ways but also induce corresponding perceptual biases in (musically trained) listeners" (1998: 125). Importantly, these "adjustments" need not be conscious attempts by a performer to be expressive: "unlike expressive timing in performance, which is under cognitive control ('interpretation'), the perceptual biases elicited by a piece of music may reflect a precognitive, obligatory response to implied musical motion" (125). Repp's experiments address a level of expressive timing that reflects a performer's awareness of the background virtual fields of meter and tonality, as opposed to the more marked expressive gestures that I would consider as strategic for a particular work. In other words, Repp's experiments offer evidence that the vectoral fields provided by meter and tonality have entrained Western musicians with habitual expressive responses to their forces, prior to the novel energetic demands of individualized or motivated gestures.[24]

A theory of musical gesture may draw on what we can learn of culturally conditioned human gestural languages, especially those that are preserved due to their artistic or rhetorical development (dance, mime, styles of oratory, social posturing in aristocratic courts), as described in manuals or inferred from artworks and illustrations. Interesting work has been done on Baroque dances (Little and Jenne 1991), eighteenth-century acting gestures (Barnett 1987), and the rhythmic gestures of Classical dance types (Allanbrook 1983). But it is also important to recognize that some information may be missing from performance practice sources, perhaps because it was considered obvious enough to be assumed. Clues to a gestural realization (whether "natural" or "stylized") may also be inferred from a stylistically competent interpretation of the notated score.[25] One hears too many performances that fail to realize the potential expressive and motivic significance of articulation markings, or that fail to distinguish potential differences (for Schubert) between the markings of *decrescendo* and *diminuendo* (see Chapter 7).

If we grant that musical works can thematize gesture, should we consider the motivic structure of a phrase to be equivalent to a gestural "articulation" of the texture? To be sure, motivic boundaries may coincide with gestural boundaries, and slurs and other articulatory indications may help us recognize the proper segmentations, but how do we find the right "groove" (Keil and Feld 1994) that projects both motivic character and ongoing development in an expressive, embodied way? If a gestural idea can coordinate motivic development across a larger span, contributing to a dramatic scenario, then clues to its "just so" realization may come from interpretation of an overarching expressive genre, as pursued in my own work on musical meaning in Beethoven (1994). I will offer such interpretations in Chapters 8 and 9.

Interrogating One's Own Gestures

Consider how a pianist initially accesses a work's gestures by the simple heuristic of sitting down and trying them out—feeling what the hands must do to cover the notes at the right times, gauging the flexibility that leaps or sudden shifts demand, and then inspecting one's bodily engagement for clues as to expressive correlates. Improvisation depends on such experience, but an ongoing heuristic investigation is more difficult (and painful) when one is first learning to improvise (Sudnow 1978).

A heuristic approach is often the best one can hope for when learning an avantgarde composition, ironically, since one might expect the music of one's own age to come with a gestural realization transparently encoded in the style as well as the culture. But as many performers have experienced, playing an abstractly conceived work often "goes better" if the composer has provided gestural or expressive clues, and especially if the composer is present to coach the work. However, if the composer demands a "cool" performance (or one unladen with "baggage from the past"), the performer may opt to introduce gestural meaning from a personal imaginative store, if only in order to achieve an adequate sense of continuity among "segments" in the work.[26] Fragmentation of contemporary culture and musical styles makes historical reconstruction of a gestural language for Beethoven easier than for many modernist compositions. To counteract this gestural estrangement, many contemporary composers incorporate gestural and expressive "connections" with which the performer (or listener) has greater familiarity—·the topical use of popular styles, for example. This semiotic, at times *intertextual* grounding of expression, is an important motivation for twentieth-century composers' incorporating music of the past, whether the composer treats the familiar topic or material with Stravinsky's ironic objectivity or John Adams's postmodern sensibilities.[27]

Given the additional problems encountered with twentieth-century (and later) music, I have chosen to address the more familiar music of Mozart, Beethoven, and Schubert, with a focus on the instrument I know best (the piano), in order to demonstrate what an approach to gesture might be able to achieve, and how a more comprehensive theory of gesture might be conceived. The piano offers a particularly acute case of a musical instrument where a subtle gestural realization is absolutely necessary to produce the illusion of *legato*. We can learn a great deal about the role of continuity in gesture by studying its realization through the discrete mechanisms of keys and hammers. I have concentrated on Mozart, Beethoven, and Schubert since they offer a range of comparisons and contrasts within the larger Viennese Classical performance tradition. In particular, the late works of Beethoven and Schubert manifest an increasing concern for gestural configuration and its structural role in thematic development and emerging form.

That I know and play these works presents obvious advantages, especially since a theory of gesture—even more than the symbolic theory of musical meaning I introduced in my book on Beethoven—requires a kind of subjective involvement that may be variously conceived as experiential, embodied, or personally manifested. Finding the common ground in such personal experience is important for gestural interpretation. But when exploring conventionalized gestures, my approach will at times appear to be more phenomenological than strictly semiotic in gauging the immediacy of my own physical realizations and my subjective assessment of that experience. Communicating such states is part and parcel of any apprenticeship with a master teacher in the studio. If part of what might have been commonly shared by performers in the age of Mozart, Beethoven, and Schubert has been lost, then making subjective experience explicit within the framework of an intersubjective theory may help restore our sense of what a stylistic realization of a musical work can entail, in terms of physical embodiment and spiritual engagement.

Embodying Sound: The Role of Semiotics

If gesture is movement that is interpretable as a sign, how might a semiotic theory address the subtleties of a gestural sign, given that sign's uniqueness and the analog character of its continuities? Roland Barthes, in a series of essays from the 1970s and early 1980s (1985), broached this concern with respect to the more structuralist model of contemporaneous French semiology. An amateur pianist, Barthes emphasizes embodied gesture as beyond the grasp of a semiology focused on discrete structures in music. In his famous essay on Schumann's *Kreisleriana* (1985 [1975]) he identifies several significant "corporeal" categories ignored by a music semiology modeled after structuralist linguistics. A telling example is "*quasi parlando*," which "*speaks but says nothing*: for as soon as it is musical, speech—or its instrumental substitute—is no longer linguistic but corporeal; what it says is always and only this: *my body puts itself in a state of speech*" (1985 [1975]: 306). As Barthes elaborates:

> Such are the *figures of the body* (the "somathemes"), whose texture forms musical *signifying* (hence, no more grammar, no more musical semiology: issuing from professional analysis—identification and arrangement of "themes," "cells," "phrases"—it risks bypassing the body). (307)

For Barthes, music is best considered as "a field of signifying and not a system of signs" because "the referent is the body" and "the body passes into music without any relay but the signifier" (308). Music, then, is not semiotic in the sense of "an order of articulated signs each of which has a meaning" (311), because "musical *signifying,* in a much clearer fashion than linguistic *signification,* is steeped in desire" (312). Barthes does not deny that semiology is capable of treating the "system of notes, scales, tones, chords, and rhythms," but what he finds most meaningful in Schumann goes beyond such systematic theoretical explanation. Instead, Barthes seeks to interpret "the effervescence of the beats" (ibid.), to cite but one of his many evocative images.

While Barthes's interpretations are often insightful, his bald opposition of system and body denigrates semiotic theory as an encumbrance—a typical maneuver in the critical dialectic and poetic rhapsodizing with which he engages our sympathies. Lacking training in music theory, Barthes is unable to integrate the depths of meaning that issue from style, structure, and form with his attractive, if fanciful, figures of the body. And lacking a semiotic theory of gesture, he is unable to show how the corporeal might also be accommodated theoretically.

David Lidov, in his important article "Mind and Body in Music" (1987), offers just such a compelling theoretical account of how we can understand the gestural in music from a semiotic perspective, drawing on the Peircean categories of icon, index, and symbol.[28] Lidov describes an ongoing process through which the immediacy of kinesthetic and somatic association (described so poetically by Barthes) is *sublimated* into signs functioning in a formal system (71). According to Lidov, the indexical in music is that which is most particular but least articulate, specifically the gestural contributions of "tempo, rubato, nuance of intonation, and dynamic level" (73). The indexical is thus directly expressive in a physical sense (much as Barthes attempted to describe). The iconic, however, is already once removed, in that articulated shapes may be interpreted as "the isomorph or trace of some object or force not immediately in contact with it." It is the performer who then "reconnects them (indexes them) to the body" and thereby "reveals their force." Finally the "symbol is an articulated arrangement of articulated materials" that are furthest removed from the body, existing as "abstract types" (ibid.). Such abstract types can substitute "formal relations [in place of] physiological values ([such formal relations including] the developmental calculi of fragmentation, inversion, transposition, et cetera, which can be but need not be subordinated to images of feeling)" (74). The remainder of Lidov's article is a classic demonstration of the many kinds of meaning that can be brought to bear in interpreting Chopin's Ballade in A♭ Major, with a focus on the gestural.

Lidov's processive model addresses the gap between the elusive particularities of gesture and the typological demands of a semiotic theory, but he in turn overemphasizes an opposition between the immediacy of gesture and the abstractness of musical categories. To consider symbolic gesture as an abstract motive subject to developmental calculus is perhaps too formalist a view of the symbolic level. Instead of the sublimation of gesture into motive, I would substitute the concept of *emergence,* since thematized gestures more fully particularize expressive meaning. And instead of abstraction I would substitute the concept of *generalization,* since gestures may be interpreted as tokens of stylistic gestural types—or as unique exemplars of newly generated strategic types. Furthermore, actual performance, while critical for the aural manifestation of a gesture, is not the only source for the kinds of interpretive inferences that we can make about notated gestures. Even when the criteria for gestural performance are inadequately notated, a richly stylistic and strategic context is available to guide interpretation. We can intermodally explore a "natural" gestural performance even as we reconstruct those contexts that contribute further (emergent) meaning.

To summarize, if a gesture is *thematized* (foregrounded as a motive and used consistently in a work):

1. It need not be abstracted from its gestural motivations; rather, it may be generalized as a motive (strategic) type.
2. Its modes of its development will result not merely from the "developmental calculi of fragmentation, inversion, transposition"—techniques governed by compositional craft—but from the unfolding of its gestural and implied expressive meanings.
3. Its character may be inferred without re-creating it in performance, although the latter is certainly important as a heuristic means of probing a wealth of interpretative nuance.

Ultimately a theory of gesture entails, and demands for its relevance to analysis, a stylistic theory of expressive meaning. Unless we are committed to interpretation and explanation of more than the syntax of a work, we really do not need a rich theory of musical gesture, and we can default to the category of "motive" as a more abstract stand-in for gesture. But if gestural expressiveness is an essential motivator for compositional form and structure—and I will argue that this has consequences for our understanding of style and style change as well as for the interpretation of a work—then we must find a way to incorporate gesture in all of its particularity, in all of its continuity, in all of its analog character, and in all of its temporal shaping and shading, as part of the very foundation of structural analysis. We must also preserve those qualitative contributions to meaning at the highest levels of interpretation.

Beyond the limits of notation, one seeks the elusive precision of artistically conceived *emotion*—which is so often our instinctive and immediate interpretation of *motion*. In Chapter 5 I argued that we are biologically attuned to categorize nuances far beyond those for which we have labels in our language. Paul Churchland (1995: 84–91) and others have demonstrated how neural networks can "learn" quite subtle discriminations without "knowing" what it is they discriminate. Unfortunately Manfred Clynes (1995), with his hypotheses of temporal and dynamic "warpings" or "composers' pulses" (p. 119, above), attempts to establish too fixed a *rubato* for each composer's measure. Gesture is not reducible to such stereotyped images of (at best) composers' individual profiles with respect to the environmental field of meter. Clynes's earlier work (1977) on sentic shapes offers a powerful demonstration of the cross-cultural consistency with which we identify particular movements with particular emotional states, and with which we produce particular movements to illustrate those states. For Clynes, precision in gesture leads unwaveringly to precision in a listener's interpretation, and while one might agree with that observation in principle, one need not accept his proposed warpings of duration and accent within given meters as prescriptive for proper performances.

It is interesting to compare Barthes and Clynes as two sensitive listeners who early on both recognized and attempted to address the significance of gesture for music. Notice how capturing the distinctive and qualitative aspects of gesture led them to such extremes of treatment: from Barthes's poetic and nonsystematic "figures of the body" to Clynes's scientifically measured and systematic "composer's pulses." In an attempt to avoid the theoretical problems associated with either extreme, I wish to propose a more historically and theoretically grounded approach. I will argue that stylistically constrained musical expressive meaning can help orient and contextualize the kinds of meaning that a musical gesture might be called upon to convey, and suggest ways in which a performer might reconcile the competing demands of highly configured gestural landscapes, especially as found in Beethoven's and Schubert's late styles.

In the summary outline shown below, I present my foundation for a semiotic theory of musical gesture. Lidov's processive view of the sublimation of the physical into the musical may be qualified (as seen in point 4) along the lines of the Peircean categories (from which his icon, index, and symbol are derived) to avoid the notion of abstraction that I find problematic. The scientific evidence presented in Chapter 5 provides further grounding for my claims.

1. Interpreters can *translate from their cultural gestural competency to achieve a basic level of musical understanding* (it is also the *default* level of interpretation in the absence of stylistic competency). Meter and tonality each afford analogies to gravitation or dynamic vectoral space, making possible the experience of *embodied motion* subject to dynamics and constraints comparable to those affecting the body in a natural environment.

2. Musical gestures are characterized as

  a. *Analog,* as opposed to digital or discrete
  b. Hence, *continuous* in a productive sense of continuity (i.e., not necessarily continuous sound, but continuity of shape, curve, motion across silence, etc.)
  c. Possessing *articulate shape*
  d. Possessing *hierarchical* potential
  e. Possessing a significant *envelope* (pre- and postmovement can substantially affect the quality of the sounding gesture)
  f. *Contextually constrained and enriched,* both stylistically and strategically
  g. Typically *foregrounded*[29]
  h. *Beyond precise notation* or exact reproducibility but
  i. Amenable to *type-token* relationships via cognitive categorization or even conceptualization, and thus
  j. *Potentially systematic* to the extent of being organized *oppositionally* by type, as in gestural "languages" or ritual movements.

3. Musical gesture is *movement (implied, virtual, actualized) interpretable as a sign,* whether intentional or not, and as such it *communicates information about the gesturer* (or character, or persona the gesturer is impersonating or embodying). Another way of specifying gesture is as movement that is *marked* as meaningful (Lidov 1993). The particular dimension of relevant meaning may be marked biologically and/or culturally.

4. That information (whether or not the intended signification) may be classified following C. S. Peirce's categories (with the understanding that a single gesture may be multiply motivated), as

a. *Qualitative* (Firstness), in that it concerns the *attitude, modality, or emotional state* of the gesturer (or presumed agent)
b. *Dynamic/directional/intentional* (Secondness), in that it reveals *reactions, goals,* and *orientations* and
c. *Symbolic* (Thirdness), in that it may rely on *conventions* or *habits* of interpretation (in contexts such as artistic styles) to convey a wealth of extra meaning beyond the directness of its qualitative and dynamic characteristics. This "extra" may at times displace or be *emergent* from more immediate sources of meaning.[30]

5. Conventionalized *music-stylistic gestures* (which must be learned, often by direct apprenticeship with musicians competent in the given style) are also relevant at all levels of structure and form. In other words, as gesture enters into the *symbolic* level of musical style, it can have consequences for musical form. For example, gestures may be associated with beginning, middle, or ending functions at different levels of a formal hierarchy (J. Kramer 1988; Agawu 1991).

6. A musical style constrains to some degree the creation of *strategic* (work-specific) gestures, which may range among the overlapping categories of: *spontaneous, thematic, dialogical, rhetorical,* and *tropological* (these will be elaborated in Chapter 7 and following). Composers use *spontaneous gestures* to access cultural expressive meaning immediately (e.g., the nose-thumbing, *buffa* gesture that opens the finale of Beethoven's Second Symphony). A gesture may also be *thematized* and become the basis of a compelling musical discourse. Thematic gestures may be treated like motives, but they are not limited to pitch-structural or even rhythmic formation—articulation, dynamics, and timing may be as pertinent. As motivic, thematic gestures may be subjected to developing variation and thereby contribute to the strategic (formal and expressive) structure of a musical work. *Rhetorical* gestures, by disrupting the unmarked flow in one or more dimensions of the musical discourse, help direct the dramatic trajectory of an expressive genre. This may result in distinctive manifestations of standard formal types, hybrids, or even new forms. Some thematic strategies (dialectical opposition) or textures (imitative or thematic counterpoint) may involve *dialogical* gestures (e.g., the conversational character of a Haydn quartet). And under special conditions, gestures may be *tropologically* combined to create new meanings.

7. Musical gestures may also be generalized as parts of higher-level syntheses, such as *topics,* which may involve characteristic "rhythmic gestures" (Allanbrook 1983). I interpret the characteristic rhythmic gesture of dance and march types as creating *alternate metric fields,* with their distinctive gravitational or vectoral properties. Such characteristic treatments of dynamics and timing in the metric field may be an iden-

tifying feature of ensembles—the "grooves" discussed by Keil and Feld (1994) for rock and polka bands, or even composers—the "composers' pulses" claimed by Clynes (1995).

8. Gesture "under a fermata" is akin to *posture*. An apparently "frozen motion" or pose may reveal the energy and affect with which it is invested, including that required to move into the pose (imagine a bodybuilder's routine, or certain histrionic actors in outdated acting styles). The posture thus "reverberates" with the resonance of the implied gesture of an *agent*.

With the invocation of one of Alexandra Pierce's key terms (reverberation) I anticipate the next section, which treats her comprehensive approach to gesture as a means of analyzing and interpreting music on the part of the performer-as-theorist.

Embodying Sound: The Role of Movement in Interpretation

What can we learn about gesture from the standpoint of actual embodiment by a performer? Alexandra Pierce, Professor Emerita of Music and Movement at the University of Redlands in California, is a composer and pianist who has devoted her career to exploring gesture in very practical ways, not only in her own composing and performing, and in collaboration with her husband, Roger Pierce, with whom she teaches expressive and "generous" movement in everyday life,[31] but most importantly for a theory of musical gesture, in her pedagogy of movement for performers as well. I had the opportunity to study with her for five days in March 1995, and we have collaborated on demonstrations for the Society for Music Theory and the Semiotic Society of America.[32] Her definitive article on this pedagogical approach is entitled "Developing Schenkerian Hearing and Performing" (1994). The early-twentieth-century Viennese theorist Heinrich Schenker's approach to music analysis is best characterized as hierarchical, drawing on the basic contrapuntal and harmonic patterns of tonal motion to interpret layers and levels of pitch organization in Western tonal music (Bach to Brahms). Mapping the best gestural realization of these hierarchical structures is difficult because of the metrical and durational hierarchies in which pitch structures are also embedded.

In a general sense one may speak of two levels of expressivity in a tonal work of music. One arises from the regular periodicities of meter, phrase rhythm, and harmonic progression, occurring when stylistic expectations are fulfilled in timely fashion. The other arises from the inevitable freedom with which the composer plays with periodic stylistic expectations, by deferring their realization (Meyer 1973) and/or by creating various irregularities and asymmetries. These striking events challenge a simplistic interpretation and thereby expand the expressive potential of the work. What we call music theory is primarily concerned with regular features and expectations in a style; music analysis, at least its current manifestation as critical analysis, is more concerned with the irregular and unexpected as these relate to a horizon of expectations. In a Schenkerian analysis the background is comprised of stylistic "types" or patterned structures and processes which exemplify stylistic "principles" of organization. The foreground might best be understood as revealing a composer's innovative strategies of tonal motion. In my own interpretive work this is also the site of marked events that imply "new" meanings by their coherent departure from previous, familiar structures and processes, and by their evasion or deferral of immediate expectations.

What Pierce offers her students is a nuanced pedagogy that accounts for the expressivity of both regular and irregular processes in musical works—both those that issue straightforwardly from the style, and those that strategically deflect the interpreter from such a straightforward reading. Accounting for these stylistic and strategic meanings involves not only traditional analysis but also interpretation, and Pierce's interpretation is enhanced by insights that emerge from the heuristic of physical embodiment, both at the instrument and away from it. Pierce's exercises enable the performer to explore, gesturally, the background coherence and foreground configuration of a work, and to sense kinesthetically the pulls and releases implied by organic phrases in their unique encounters with tonal and rhythmic forces. Ultimately the performer learns to translate gestural character into sound, through the medium of the body's corresponding (intermodal) gestural realizations. Learning how to perform is thus inseparable from learning how the piece is structured, how it has expressive meaning, how one can physically manifest that meaning in one's body, and how one can then transfer that bodily gestural meaning to the instrument. The goal is to achieve in sound the expressivity and implied meaning one has previously explored and experienced through the embodied analytical exercises.

Pierce typically begins with the rhythms of pieces as they work elastically within and beyond the regular frameworks of meter and four-bar phrases (hypermetric units). One exercise enhances the experience of a regular beat, or pulse, through pendulum-like, swinging motions ("arm swings") away from the instrument (1994: 102–103). The point of this exercise is to embody the full motion required to produce what in overly abstract terms might be called an "attack point" for an event that occurs "on the beat." One begins to shape the upswing and the after swing (as the next beat's upswing) with as much attention as one calculates the precise arrival of the arms at the bottom of the arc, which signifies the beat as an ictus. Thus, what happens between beats is as crucial to the experience as the arrival, and the expressive vitality of even an undifferentiated steady pulse becomes a part of one's kinesthetic awareness. One can then transfer this awareness of energized timing to a "straight" metric performance of a passage (or a regular metric reduction of the passage), generating a wealth of gestural expressivity even before one has fully explored the passage's unique rhythms and contours.[33]

Another preliminary exercise, "contouring" (103–109), focuses on the melodic line, which is easier to follow than the subtleties of structural harmonies in aural analysis. Here one draws with the hand (using sustained arm weight) an analogue to the shape of the melody, transferring pitch and rhythm into tracings of space that correspond—in their highs and lows, their sudden and sustained movements—to what one hears as a continuous line connecting the successive pitches of a se-

quence. It is natural to hear melody as though it were a single force or line travers-
ing a space, rather than a sequence of distinct sound events (recall Kurth's theory
of musical energy, mentioned above). Indeed, one might argue that this perception
of musical motion is crucial to our experiencing of successive sounds as music,
rather than as mere acoustic phenomena. In any case our evolutionary training has
biased our perceptual systems to link sounds with objects and agencies in our environment, as was noted in Chapter 5.

Pierce's contouring has an interesting precedent in the work of Eduard Sievers
(1924), Gustav Becking (1928), and Alexander Truslit (1938) in Germany, as discussed by Patrick Shove and Bruno H. Repp (1995: 65–72). Truslit (1938: 144) presents a "kinematic interpretation" of the opening theme of Brahms's Op. 79, no. 2
(reproduced in Shove and Repp, 70) that comes closest to the kind of dynamic
mapping that Pierce proposes with her "contouring." As Shove and Repp describe it:

> [The] height in space [of Truslit's curves] tends to follow the pitch contour of the
> melody . . . with the speed of movement and the consequent relative tension being
> governed mainly by the curvature of the motion path. That is, a slowing-down and
> commensurate increase in tension in the music is portrayed by a tight loop, whereas
> faster, more relaxed stretches correspond to relatively straight movements. (71)

As opposed to the abstracted individual composer's pulses of Becking (and his
spiritual heir, Manfred Clynes), Truslit's curves are "work-specific" and give a primary role to the smooth flow of the pitch sequence in the melody (ibid.).

Just as one must negotiate the gestural projection of regularly occurring events
with the aperiodic events that constitute the unique dynamic shape of a work,
one must in performance find a way to physically negotiate the complementary
claims of, for example, a chord's vital presence and its subsumed role as part of a
temporal sequence. Whereas the arm swings introduce something of the duality
or co-presence of harmonic sound and progression, Pierce addresses this complementary requirement for more complex musical passages in her concepts of "coalescence" and "middleground rhythmic vitality":

> Coalescence in physical movement refers to the weight of the body as it *settles* into an
> integral stage of action or gesture. Middleground rhythmic vitality refers to the man-
> ner in which weight *passes* continuously throughout an action, its energy intensifying
> and diminishing, setting up a pattern in time. (1994: 73)

The physical means of embodying these complementary dynamics is called
"stepping"—not coincidentally, a play on Schenker's concept of *Stufen,* or scale
"steps," upon which the structural harmonies of a passage are built. Reducing a
musical passage to its essential harmonies may produce a rhythm that is out of
synch with the regular divisions of time suggested by meter and four-bar phrases
(hypermetric groupings). Thus, physically stepping the structural bass line will
challenge a performer far more than regular metric arm swings. As the performer
shifts weight from foot to foot, she must also gauge a number of irregular temporal
spans, as well as map the approximate pitch intervals between bass notes by the
size and direction of her steps. Once she is able to embody the unique "structural

rhythm" of the harmony, she can return to the instrument and move more confidently in her performance, with better preparation and follow-through. As a consequence, there will be a marked aural difference in the gestural persuasiveness of the passage.

At this point the student has advanced to a level of performance analogous to a proper declamation of the accents in a poem, as opposed to a sing-song rendition of an iambic pentameter. The final stages of preparation involve, to pursue the analogy, internalizing the intonational curves and climaxes that shape the sense of the poem, and embodying the peculiar character or tone that carries the poem's implied emotional affect(s).

These two essential expressive attributes may be practiced separately as "spanning" and "tone of voice" (Pierce 1994: 87–101). Spanning is embodied in two exercises, the first of which is stretching the hand from a loose fist outward to its full extent, timed to a felt climax in the music, and then gradually releasing the tension in the hand after the climax (87–91). Besides discovering that the felt point of climax is not precisely where one might have analyzed it mentally, one soon realizes that "performance phrases" often go against the grain of the regular hypermetric structures (four-bar, eight-bar, sixteen-bar units). The exercise is also useful in determining whether one is dealing with the proper-sized musical unit for a performance phrase. If one cannot find a "convincing climax," then "the phrase level chosen may be too small to have developed compelling harmonic motivation, or too long to sustain the elasticity of a single harmonic-structural purpose" (85). In this sense Pierce shares fellow Schenkerian William Rothstein's understanding of a phrase as "a directed motion in time from one tonal entity to another; these entities may be harmonies, melodic tones (in any voice or voices), or some combination of the two" (1989: 16). In other words, if the first four measures of the "Blue Danube" Waltz (in Rothstein's example) merely prolong a single harmony, they cannot constitute a phrase; indeed, Rothstein's analysis demonstrates that only the first thirty-two measures qualify as a "complete tonal motion," or performance phrase, in Pierce's terminology.

Pierce's second exercise for determining climax and performance phrase is "arcing," which involves a stretch of the whole body directed by an arm that moves in a large, sweeping motion, as though outlining a giant clock face. The climax in this case is the point of maximum extension of the arm diagonally from the body, peaking around 1:00 or 2:00 on the clock face if the right arm is arcing in a clockwise direction. As Pierce describes the exercise:

> Just enough momentum is spun forth to match the kinetic energy heard from the musical phrase as it continues, intensifies, subsides, and finally releases into completion. Effort washes out into stillness, without there necessarily being any lapse of time before the next phrase begins. (1994: 92)

Such practice away from the instrument (but nevertheless mapped onto a recording or another student's playing of the passage) can help one realize the "elastic play of foreground against deeper levels," and thus spanning is "perhaps the most purely 'Schenkerian' of the movement processes" (95).

Alexandra Pierce's final exercise may well be the most difficult (speaking from my own personal experience), since it is also the most intimate or personal. "Tone of voice" is her term for "the wash of affect in a piece of music" which "suffuses the sound with hue and the player with expressiveness visible through the entire body" (1994: 96). In Chapter 5 I noted that there are two useful (and intermodal) sources for our understanding of musical gesture—the physical movements of the body and the intonation curves of language. Tone of voice draws on the latter for its inspiration, but an intonation cannot be achieved without an intention. Intention requires a semantic and pragmatic context, represented in this exercise by a word, with all its symbolic richness of denotative and connotative meaning. One might begin by choosing an adverb (e.g., "boldly"), saying it with a characteristic tone of voice, making a comparable bodily gesture, freezing it into a momentary stance, then taking that gestural pose to the instrument and saying, "If I were speaking, it would sound like *this*—," and performing the passage (100). The student will thereby transfer not merely kinetic energy but a particular *quality* of energy to her performance.

But the pedagogical difficulty lies in helping the student overcome a natural reticence to express character in a word, and to express it with full feeling in an intimate setting. In listening to my cassette recording of the session in which Alexandra introduced me to tone of voice, I became aware of how my voice dropped considerably in dynamic power when I intoned my chosen word, perhaps reflecting my uncertainty or lack of confidence in the exercise. A commitment to the meaning of a single word may also have been in conflict with my prior (wordless) expressive sense of the passage, and thus I may have been fighting against the limitations of my own word choice. Ironically, despite having written a book on musical expressive meaning, I was unable at first to connect with this most semantically loaded of exercises, as much as I could appreciate its usefulness from a theoretical standpoint. Later, in our staged demonstrations for music theory and semiotic conferences, we were able to illustrate tone of voice as it affected my tone in the melodic line from a Chopin *prélude.* Here the word I had chosen was "sinking," which already encompasses a fluid intermodality between feeling and motion, as well as invoking its typical usage in teaching piano technique (as in the expression, "sink into the keys").

In concluding this brief exposition of Pierce's approach, I must emphasize the limits of theoretical and even descriptive language for conveying the subtle nuances of gesture she helps students achieve. I have witnessed the remarkable transformations in expressive performance that ensue from these exercises, from my observation of her teaching, as I have experienced them in my own playing, and as I have myself taught them to students.[34] Those who are familiar with the music and movement pedagogy of Émile Jaques-Dalcroze[35] (one of Alexandra's inspirations in her own movement research) will appreciate the insights that can emerge from such efforts to embody the dynamic meanings of music. What Pierce offers both students and sophisticated performers is a heuristic for exploring the dynamic projection of expressive meaning, as it is interpreted physically in conjunction with a detailed analysis of complex musical materials. In realizing the implied "choreography" of the score (rather than counterpointing it, as one finds in most artistic ballet choreography), the performer re-creates the dynamic movements and gestural meanings as moving performances.

The Embodiment of Gesture in Music

The following chapters will inevitably make reference to specific ways of performing gestures, but my principal focus will be on interpreting gestures as implied by the notation of scores, interpreted both stylistically and in terms of their strategic deployment in a work. My evidence ranges from the competencies of style, including stylistic conventions of notation, to the thematic role that certain gestures play (in negotiation with the environmental forces of tonality and meter) in creating a unique expressive trajectory within the coherent frame of a formal and expressive genre. Embodiment, then, is understood as broader than that which is literally manifested through a body. We do not have to perform to understand and experience the embodiment of a gesture—we embody gesture imaginatively as participating listeners, or even more imaginatively in silent audiation of a score. Indeed, the intermodality of gesture leads ultimately and naturally to its categorization as a form of thought.[36] Furthermore, just as in social discourse an overly obvious gesticulatory style may undergo refinement under social pressures (Efron 1941), so in music the attenuation of the overtly physical can lead to increasingly subtle, but highly developed, symbolic gestures that remain potent for those competent in the style.

Notation has its limits and must be allied with an awareness of stylistic meaning; I will explore some familiar signs and their subtle potential in the next chapter. One might view stylistically interpreted notation as a *script* whose representations imply the gestures needed to realize those musical ideas for which we have other supportive evidence. As in a dramatic script, various realizations are possible that will satisfy gestural and rhetorical implications. But fortunately, musical scores are much more revealing of the kinds of gestural performances that will satisfy their dramatic trajectories than are the written texts of most plays. Musical notation can draw upon a more subtle set of gestural specifications than are usually found in written language.[37] Poems may share metric structure with music, and caesuras and enjambment may serve the analogous functions of phrasing, but gesture entails more than these alone. In his freer (blank) verse, Robert Frost attempted to supply gestural information for his readers through the use of "sentence sounds," familiar phrases with well-known intonational realizations. Bertolt Brecht, especially in his collaborations with Kurt Weill, attempted to characterize the "gestus" through which one could best deliver his dramatically shaped phrases, and thus to provide Weill with clues for their effective musical setting. Janáček often based melodic contours directly on speech patterns, and Steve Reich derives motives from the actual intonational curves of recorded speech (e.g., in *Different Trains*). But musical gestures need not ride on the intonation curves of language to achieve meaning. As I will demonstrate in the next chapter, other kinds of cultural gestures may help ground those qualitative, intermodal shapings of energy through time that constitute music's most direct form of communication.

Indeed, musical gestures need not correspond to any particular culturally encoded gesture to be meaningful, based on the tendency we have as biological creatures to interpret any energetic shaping through time as gestural and hence as potentially significant. The indexical intensities and iconic shapes of musical gestures may be projected through melodic contour or harmonic progression, and negotiated within the gravitational fields of tonality and meter, to produce an equivalent of embodied gesture that we can recognize as expressive of an imagined agent (whether or not we co-body it experientially). That basic transaction is all that is required, initially, to ground meaning in music. What the following chapters will reveal is how such a basic form of communication is further enriched by the symbolic levels of a style and the structural dimensions of a work. Ultimately the enrichment—not sublimation—of gesture leads to a lively reengagement with "energetic shapings through time" at all levels of interpretation. The human capacity to encode and interpret gestural meaning in any modality allows music to exist even without sound. A sufficiently imaginative world of inner audiation, such as enabled Beethoven to transcend deafness, is available to us all.

7 Stylistic Types and Strategic Functions of Gestures

> When I left out something in a passage, a note or a skip, which in many cases he wished to have specially emphasized, or struck a wrong key, he seldom said anything; yet when I was at fault with regard to the expression, the crescendo or matters of that kind, or in the character of the piece, he would grow angry. Mistakes of the other kind, he said, were due to chance; but these last resulted from want of knowledge, feeling, or attention.
>
> —Ferdinand Ries, on his piano lessons with Beethoven
> (Sonneck 1926: 52, cited in Rosenblum 1988: 29)

Beethoven's insistence to Ries on the importance of expression and character when performing a work can be interpreted in terms of the appropriate shaping and shading of musical gestures. Mistakes in expression resulting from lack of knowledge or feeling (as opposed to mere lack of attention) typically occur when a performer is unable to recognize implied gestures in the notation of a score, or to interpret them stylistically. In this chapter I investigate the stylistic competency that ensures a performer's sensitivity to gesture and gestural meaning.[1] Specifically I will examine how the Classical style and performing tradition both constrain and condition our understanding and expression of individual musical gestures.[2]

I begin with some preliminary considerations. Stylistic types of gestures, regardless of their common attributes, are individually realized in musical works.[3] Each such manifestation, more or less original, may be understood as a strategic token of its corresponding stylistic type. Whereas common features determine the affiliation of a token with a type, the distinctive or original features of the token may also be interpreted as significant, especially from a gestural perspective. Interpretation at this level becomes highly contextual, linked to an evolving conception of the expressive intent of an entire movement or multimovement cycle.

Since I am exploring gesture in the realm of Western classical music, I will presuppose the hierarchies of meter and tonality and the complementary dynamic-vectoral fields that enable an embodied experience of musical gesture, as detailed in Chapter 6. Meter and tonality condition our temporal experience of rhythmic shape, melodic contour, and voice-leading within a virtual gravitational field, thereby enabling listeners to experience musical analogues of bodily orientation, movement, action, and gesture in everyday life. In turn, the expressive attributes of culturally learned gestures are associated with analogous musical gestures.

In considering the various gestural competencies implied by the Viennese Classical tradition, I have drawn upon evidence from performance practice studies and contemporary accounts of performance. Historical performance manuals are limited, for reasons already suggested in Chapter 6. First, their authors' recommendations cannot be stitched together into a completely consistent and stable set of instructions for reconstructing a single composer's style or interpreting a particular work in that style. Writers of the time may be radically opposed in their interpretation of articulatory or expressive markings.[4] Second, performance manuals are constrained by limits of space from addressing the intricate contexts of individual musical gestures. Thus, for practical reasons we typically find general recommendations for interpreting signs, rather than guides for reconstructing the work-specific *synthesis* of separately notated elements that make up a musical gesture. Third, performance manuals are not equipped to fully comprehend, much less address, the work-specific role such musical gestures might be called upon to fulfill as subjects of musical discourse, or as means of highlighting a larger voice-leading structure.[5]

Subsequent chapters will document the thematic evolution of marked musical gestures through the course of complete movements or even entire sonatas. Here I am more concerned with establishing the contexts and constraints on interpretation as they arise from conventions of musical practice—including such prefabricated syntheses (dances, marches) as topic theory assumes, as well as the less familiar syntheses (strategic gestures) that composers create.[6] Although my theory will address general functions and stylistic types of gesture, my interpretations of musical excerpts will go beyond the more general expressive correlations of conventional types. This is to be expected; excerpts of sufficient aesthetic value to capture our interest are not likely to be straightforward or transparent manifestations of stylistic types. The spontaneous creativity of great composers is reflected in the unique ways they find to manipulate the conventional elements of a musical style and achieve individuality in their gestures. Individualized gestures are often "original" in the sense of their adaptation of convention, but they may also expand the style.[7] When an individual impulse finds expression within the stylistic constraints governing a work, a more or less original musical gesture is the result. Since it must be expressed within the constraints of a style, it is likely that the "new" gesture will be understood as a token of an established stylistic type. If other, similarly distinctive tokens of that type are created, then it may be possible to generalize a new (sub)type from the set of distinctively configured tokens, resulting in style growth. It is impossible to determine the precise historical moment that the original features of a set of similar gestural tokens carve out a new gestural type. As a working hypothesis, however, the distinction speaks to a reality even if that reality can be only theoretically reconstructed.

On the Strategic Functions of Musical Gesture

Besides their stylistic type affiliations as gestural shapes with general correlations—both expressive (gracious, grieving) and structural (opening, closing, etc.)—gestural tokens may be broadly characterized by a range of strategic functions with respect to a given work. Of the possible strategic functions gesture may serve, I will explore the following: spontaneous individual expression, dialogical interplay, motivic or thematic foregrounding and development, rhetorical marking of the discourse, and gestural troping.

The category of spontaneous gesture accounts for the unique energetic shapes composers introduce that may appear as fresh and original inventions, although their negotiation with a style will generally provide some affiliation with broader gestural types, as mentioned earlier. Spontaneous gestures provide an avenue for the expression of individuality, and they broaden the expressive range of a style. The emergence of subjectivity in Mozart, and its further development in Beethoven and Schubert, is due in no small part to the spontaneity and individuality of their gestures.

The dialogical function of gesture is characteristic of both Haydn's "conversational" style in his string quartets[8] and Mozart's dialectical oppositions in opening themes of works such as the *Jupiter* Symphony or the Piano Sonata in C Minor, K. 457. Equal dialogue is a marked feature in Beethoven's development of the cello sonata,[9] and the dialogue characteristic of quartet as well as concerto genres is often imported into the solo piano sonata. Indeed, the dialogical convention originates in the Baroque *concertato* principle,[10] and it is further enhanced as a dramatic or witty opposition between the individual and society in the Classical concerto.

The range of rhetorical gestures, which includes both the expressive fermata in the slow movement of a sonata as well as the cadential $\frac{6}{4}$ that marks the break for a cadenza in a concerto, is expanded by strategic reversals, undercuttings, or shifts in level of discourse, such as the ones explored previously in Beethoven's Andante from the String Quartet in B♭ Major, Op. 130 (see Chapter 2).[11] I will define this function more broadly as *any event that disrupts the unmarked flow of a musical discourse.*

Perhaps the most important function of gesture, however, comes from its thematization as motivic idea. A gesture becomes thematic when it is (a) *foregrounded as significant,* thereby gaining *identity* as a potential thematic entity, and then when it is (b) *used consistently,* typically as the *subject of a musical discourse.* In a coherent musical discourse, the gesture may be varied without losing its affiliation to the original form (its identity, perhaps generalized as a schema), as long as the stages of its evolution are progressive (no huge gaps in degree of development or variation) and temporally associable (no huge gaps in time between instances of the gesture).[12]

A thematic gesture is typically designed so as to encapsulate the expressive tone and character of the work or movement; thus, its expressive properties help the listener understand and interpret musical meaning at higher levels as well. What might otherwise appear accessory—the articulations, dynamics, and temporal character of a motive—are potentially structural in that, by their embodiment in thematic gestures, they contribute to the shaping of an emerging expressive trajectory. As will be seen, unusual features of the resulting forms may be expressively motivated by the progressive evolution of thematic gestures.

To complete this brief overview of strategic functions, I address the constraints on gestural troping, along the lines of the troping of topics explored in Chapter 4. The possibilities that emerge from a creative fusion of different gestures would appear to be endless, but a note of caution is in order. Gestures are already such distinctive syntheses that in order to interpret a gesture as an amalgam of two separate (and presumably contrasting) gestures, the gestures in question must already possess established (stylistic) expressive correlations, or else be (strategically) familiarized as thematic, before they are combined. Another criterion might be that each can be heard as making its own contribution to the expressive meaning that emerges from their synthesis or fusion. These are stringent criteria to meet. I will note one example of gestural troping below and return to the subject in Chapter 10.

The following outline summarizes the foregoing discussion of classes and functions of musical gestures. It should be kept in mind throughout the subsequent discussion that a single gesture may be viewed from each of these perspectives. A spontaneously creative or individualized gesture may be featured thematically, involved in a dialogical play with another gesture, used to mark a rhetorical shift or stage in the dramatic trajectory of a work, or troped with another gesture. If similar gestures are used in other works, a new stylistic type may emerge, at least for a given composer.

1. *Stylistic gestures,* as conventional energetic shapings through time.

   a. Presuppose tonality and meter as "gravitational" background fields.
   b. Appear in ritualized genres such as dances and marches. Provide the gestural syntheses of *topics.*
   c. Entail conventions for interpreting articulation, accentuation, dynamics, tempo, timing (performance practice issues).
   d. Comprise a wide variety of *stylistic types* (e.g., the two-note slur).

2. *Strategic gestures,* as constrained by the stylistic, may be understood as *tokens* of preexisting stylistic types, and may even be generalized as new (sub)types.

   a. *Spontaneous* (individual, original, creative), as negotiated within a meter and tonality. These novel mappings of expressive gesture to sounding forms are often marked and subsequently thematized.
   b. *Thematic,* as subject of discourse for a movement. May be treated to developing variation.
   c. *Dialogical,* as gestures between agencies, or within a single agency. In the Classical style, suggestive of a conversation among equals (string quartets incorporating Haydn's new style of thematic counterpoint), or oppositional ideas (thematic dialectics), or oppositions between individuals and larger groups (*concertato* effects).
   d. *Rhetorical* gestures, marked with respect to an otherwise unmarked musical discourse or flow.
      1. Are used to foreground stages of an expressive genre, giving it a dramatic or narrative character.
      2. Include sudden or unpredicted pauses, changes, or shifts.
      3. May highlight tonal reversals or textural undercuttings.

    4. May mark a shift in level of discourse, perhaps fostering a Romantic ironic interpretation.
  e. *Troping* of gestures occurs when the character of two separate gestures is blended into an emergent gesture.

In the chapters to come I refer to these *overlapping* classes of gestural functions with an eye toward interpreting their expressive—and structural—role in works of Mozart, Beethoven, and Schubert. Understanding musical gestures will be seen as crucial in interpreting the irreducible significance of the surface, as well as comprehending the deeper structural levels that they help shape.

Stylistic Gestural Types

I begin my closer examination of musical gesture with a consideration of stylistic gestures in the Classical style, and it is here that recent scholarship on performance practice is relevant—most notably, for the repertoire I will be examining, Sandra Rosenblum (1988) and Clive Brown (1999). It would be impossible to do justice to their splendid and exhaustive summaries here. Rather, I have selected several musical examples in order to examine how the related styles of Mozart, Beethoven, and Schubert might have developed their own gestural repertories, in terms of local articulation tendencies and larger phrases.

Accentuation

Heinrich Koch (1969 [1782]) is one of the most important sources for accentuation in the Classical style, and as Rosenblum (1988: 90) has observed, accentuation "played a role in structural clarification . . . as well as in expressivity." Koch's basic categories of accentuation are the grammatical (metrical) and the oratorical (expressive), with the latter subdivided into the rhetorical and the pathetic. The pathetic, for Koch, is more emphatic than the rhetorical. Since expressive accents are often not notated, Koch notes that they may be added according to the performer's taste. Clearly, however, that taste should be grounded in a stylistic competency, and, indeed, Koch recommends emphasizing events that could be considered marked in the style (with the exception of the often unmarked slur, which takes an initiatory accent by virtue of convention, whether or not the event itself is marked). Rosenblum summarizes Koch's recommendations as follows:

> Notes that receive expressive accents in Classic music include those that are dissonant or that prepare dissonant intervals, those that are chromatic or syncopated, those distinguished by their length or by their high or low pitch, and those that are first under a slur. (92)

Clive Brown observes that within the Classical era, Koch's rhetorical and pathetic accents were rarely distinguished:

> The majority of writers made no firm distinction between accentuation that emphasized phrase structure or rhythmic features, thus clarifying the rhetorical meaning of

the music, and accentuation that was essential to its emotional content (since phrase structure and rhythm are inextricably linked with expression), yet it seems clear that this sort of notion lay behind the tripartite division of Koch and others. (Brown 1999: 8)

In Türk's *Klavierschule* we find a hierarchy of accents that Rosenblum calls phrase-rhythm accents. These would be considered hypermetrical by most theorists today. Türk indicates them with small crosses (anticipating David Lewin's vertically aligned dots, as adapted by Lerdahl and Jackendoff 1983), in which a four-bar phrase (hypermeasure) has, on successive downbeats, +++, +, ++, and +, reflecting a similar hierarchy of accents in a measure in common time.[13]

Whereas metric (and hypermetric accents in Türk's analysis) need only be subtly marked, rhetorical and pathetic accents should be realized, in Koch's view, "in part from an increased strength of tone" (i.e., dynamic accent) and "in part from a certain expressive lingering through which it appears that the accent note has been held an instant longer than its notation requires" (i.e., agogic accent) (*Lexicon*, cols. 49–50, cited in Rosenblum 1988: 90). This flexibility in realizing an accent suggests that the most important consideration is that certain notes are *marked expressively.* Bringing out those notes may involve more than one dimension of performance. Koch cannot specify the precise recipe of ingredients (dynamic and temporal in this case), nor would that be desirable. But we have evidence that a gestural realization for Koch involved a *synthesis* of at least two elements. We will explore further stylistic guidelines to the integration of these elements across a range of contexts.

Aesthetic Considerations

Aesthetic justification for the integration of musical elements into a coherent and expressive gesture is found in Sulzer's *Allgemeine Theorie der schönen Künste* of 1771 (Christensen and Baker 1995). As Christensen observes in his perceptive introduction, for Sulzer, "the origins of music lie in the movements and rhythms associated with quotidian human activities, to which are coupled vocal utterances engendered by our feeling associated with these activities" (21–22).[14] The virtue of music is in taking those original, quotidian feelings to a higher moral plane. Thus, an aesthetic sense of beauty is based on "a moral resonance in the soul rather than either a rational judgment of the mind or an epicurean stimulation of the senses" (12). The expression through music of these moral sentiments can "provide [man] with a moderate degree of sensibility as well as establish a good mixture of dominating temperaments in his soul" (29).

Although admirable, Sulzer's moralizing is not the central issue here; rather, it is his attempt to clarify how music can embody such meaning. If "expression is the soul of music," then "every passion must be seen not simply in respect to its idea, but in respect to its particular character: voice, register, tempo, and rhetorical accent" (Christensen and Baker 1995: 51). Here we find what amounts to a vision for a theory of expressive meaning in which musical gesture might play a leading role, integratively enacting the "voice, register, tempo, and rhetorical accent" of a given passion. Sulzer offers a suggestive list of means by which a composer might capture the particular character of a passion, but except for harmony he is short on specifics. Furthermore, as is the case with more pragmatically oriented performance manuals, there are no guidelines for integrating these various elements into a synthetic, expressive gesture. Nevertheless, the list is suggestive in including not only harmony, melody, meter, and rhythm, but also dynamics, texture, and timbre (I will add articulation in the following section):

> Every passion is actually a series of moving impressions. . . . Music is perfectly suited to portraying all kinds of these movements [and thus, their corresponding passions and moral sentiments] and making them sensible to the soul via the ear. . . . These means are: (1) The basic progression of harmony without regard to meter. This harmony should be light and unconstrained so as to express gentle and pleasant affections. . . . However, to express violent or other vehement affections, the harmonic progressions should be interrupted by modulations to distant keys; there should be greater intricacy, the use of many unusual dissonances, and quickly-resolving suspensions; (2) Meter, by which the general character of every kind of movement may be imitated; (3) Melody and rhythm, which are themselves capable of portraying the language of all emotions; (4) Changes in the dynamics of notes, which may contribute much to expression; (5) The accompaniment and particularly the choice and mixture of accompanying instruments; and finally (6) Modulation to, and digression in, foreign keys. (Sulzer, in Christensen and Baker 1995: 52–53)

Although Sulzer's suggestions are directed toward would-be composers, they have relevance for performers as well. If the musical motion implied by a score is meant to represent the energies of a given passion, then a performance would have to reproduce the same quality of motion, in order to achieve the same emergent meaning.

Sulzer's encyclopedic treatise also includes entries on specific musical genres by J. A. P. Schulz. Notably, the one on "Sonata" appears to dismiss the aesthetic qualm attributed to Fontenelle ("Sonata, what do you want of me?") with a single sentence: "There is no form of instrumental music that is more capable of depicting wordless sentiments than the sonata" (Christensen and Baker 1995: 103). Note that Schulz simply assumes the intentionality of such wordless sentiments (*whose* grief, and *why*) in his interpretation of a "monologue marked by sadness, misery, pain, or of tenderness, pleasure and joy"—or a "passionate conversation between similar or complementary characters." Agency is presupposed, as.well as the capacity of music to project two agencies in dialogue.

Sulzer provides strong contemporaneous evidence for the capacity of music to convey expressive meaning (passions, wordless sentiments) through an energetic shaping through time (movement) that captures the integrative character (voice, register, tempo, and rhetorical accent) of those passions. Schulz adds the notion of a musical discourse composed of a sequence of varying sentiments (monologue, conversations), which implies agency (similar or complementary characters). Together, this evidence suggests a concept of musical gesture along the lines I have been developing here.

The Slur and Its Gestural Meanings

I turn now to a common gestural type in the Classical style, one that is cued by a notated symbol of articulation, in order to explore how its stylistic and strategic employment expands the range of its possible expressive meanings. Quantz (1985 [1752]), C. P. E. Bach (1949 [1753]), and Leopold Mozart (1951 [1756]) are consistent in specifying that the slur should be interpreted with a small accent at the beginning and an unaccented release and shortening of the note at the end of the slur. This integratively gestural interpretation of a short slur, I would argue, is more revealing than its association with *legato* merely as a form of articulation. Rosen (2002a: 17–19) highlights the notational ambiguity of the Classical slur as indicating both *legato* and accent, and the end of a slur as "implying either a release of sound or simply an unaccented note." He also recalls Beethoven's famous comment about Mozart's performing style at the piano ("zu gehacktes," too choppy), which has been taken to refer to the earlier composer's typically *non legato* mode of performance in the absence of a phrase slur (28).[15] Although Beethoven apparently preferred a more connected style of performance for passages without phrase slurs or other indications, he shares with Mozart (and Schubert) a concern for subtle, gesture-enhancing articulations of longer thematic ideas. In this sense the shorter slur, along with the staccato or stroke, is typically used as a gestural marker. Stylistically, Mozart's keyboard melodies are marked by frequent internal articulations by shorter slurs, and their realization should emulate the bowing of a string instrument or the verbally articulated breath of a singing voice.

The prototypical slurred gesture of the *galant* style is the stepwise, descending, two-note (or two-event) slur. Interestingly, this slur need not be interpreted as a plaintive sigh, as in minor-mode laments.[16] While the slur as sigh remains a significant expressive type, more often the short, two-event slur appears as the musical analogue to such ritualized social gestures as bows, nods, inflections of the wrist and hand, and other aristocratic social graces. A characteristic location of the two-event stepwise slur is on the weak-beat galant cadence (Example 7.1a). Such cadences were inaccurately termed "feminine" by critics and scholars; more accurately, the weak-beat galant cadence captures the qualitative character of all gracious social gesturing in the eighteenth century, male and female alike.

Overuse of the galant gesture in such conventionalized cadences, often with suspension of the dominant-seventh chord in the upper voices over tonic resolution on the downbeat in the bass, made it less expressively focal in the style, and hence unmarked. But an example from Schubert illustrates how a figure which is stylistically unmarked may be strategically marked by thematic foregrounding.[17] In opening the second movement of his Sonata in A Major, D. 664 (1819), Schubert echoes the galant, weak-beat final cadence of the first movement (Example 7.1b). When late in the second movement the composer elects a similar weak-beat ca-

Example 7.1. Schubert, Piano Sonata in A Major, D. 664.
a. First movement, final cadence.
b. Second movement, opening theme.
c. Second movement, final cadence and codetta.

dence (m. 70), the elision with the head motive of this theme reinforces the motive's original derivation (Example 7.1c).

The two-note stepwise slur may be extended to include increasingly larger motivic units, and the same gestural shape is applied to its more extended instances: light initiatory accent, smooth follow-through, and unaccented release. The "sigh" motive is extended into a more elaborate galant gesture in the rondo theme from

RONDO.

Poco allegretto e grazioso.

Example 7.2. Beethoven, Piano Sonata in E♭ Major, Op. 7, finale, opening theme.

the finale of Beethoven's Piano Sonata in E♭ Major, Op. 7 (Example 7.2), which features an anacrustic, anticipatory sigh before the initiating sigh on the downbeat, thus doubling the expressive effect. Here the two-note gesture combines galant graciousness with the sigh, troping the two gestural meanings to yield an effect that is neither superficial in its conventional graciousness nor tragic in its emotional context. Expansive, gracious, and with a touch of poignant longing, the Romantic effect of this gesture emerges from the strategic treatment of a Classical stylistic type, exploiting its potential for further interpretation.

Physically the "down-up" motion of the wrist used to execute a two-note slur at the piano corresponds (intermodally) with the smooth arc of a bowing stroke, and as noted above, the keyboard sign is derived from the slur indicating a bowing stroke in string music. The physical analogue for an entire instrumental phrase, derived from the art of singing, is that of being carried on a single breath. Just as a sung phrase is articulated by the text—from the alternation of consonants and vowels to the effects of prosodic features—the instrumental phrase can be articulated in declamatory fashion by bowings, tonguings, or motions of the wrist. This exceedingly "natural" phrasing and articulation is at the core of Mozart's style. A performer may, however, overdo the gestural articulations of a Mozartean theme and lose the overall gestural flow of the phrase. An appropriate hierarchy of nuances must be established from the contours of the articulations within the phrase, as negotiated with elements of melodic contour, harmony, and the like. This can be a problem in interpreting Mozart's notation, since the long phrase slur (and correspondingly more uniform *legato* style of performance) was not often employed in themes.[18]

As an illustration of hierarchical gestural nuances, consider the slow movement of Mozart's Piano Sonata in D Major, K. 311.[19] In mm. 1–2 (Example 7.3a) the initial theme has many inner inflections; but the performer must also maintain its overall gestural continuity as a short phrase.[20] In mm. 8–11 (Example 7.3b) another theme—functionally closural but also expressive marked as thematic—is not articulated by slurs. Instead, the left-hand Alberti bass has an extra quarter note stemming on each first sixteenth, implying a continuous bass line and a broader-breathed thematic phrase. It would make sense to play the melodic line (except where notes are repeated) with an analogous degree of continuity, though a *legato* is not specifically notated. Even if stylistically available, a *legato* slur would have been rather fussy, given the obviously *cantabile* character of the line. Notably, at the end of the movement Mozart "orchestrates" the closing theme with octave couplings in the both hands, thereby underlining the closing theme's already more continuous and enriched texture in m. 8 (in contrast to the opening theme's articulations).

The eventual second theme of this movement (Example 7.3c) also features an expressive bass line, but its progressive descent is not marked with quarter-note stems, possibly because the implied bass line in m. 20 accelerates to a dotted-eighth/sixteenth followed by two eighths. In mm. 21–22 Mozart highlights a marked progression (also found in Beethoven; see Hatten 1994: 59–63) that involves the reversal from G♯ to G♮ (♯$\hat{4}$ to ♮$\hat{4}$) in the bass. The exquisite moment is created by an expressive turn figure around A in the melody at the point of the reversal. The euphoric sweetness of the (conventional) turn figure is imaginatively coupled with the more dysphoric chromatic reversal, yielding the expressive trope of abnegation, a blend of resignation and willed (positive) acceptance. The two gestures (conventional turn in melody and unconventional chromatic reversal in bass) spark a dissonance, the cross-relation between the hands of G♯ and G♮, before merging in acquiescence to the yielding V$_2^4$ to I^6. Thus, a kind of gestural troping contributes to the intense poignancy of this moment.

While Mozart's articulations enhance the gestural expressivity of a "singing" style in his themes, Beethoven extends notational conventions by specifying a hierarchy of nuances that can only be inferred in Mozart. A striking example is found in the first movement of the Piano Sonata in A Major, Op. 101 (Example 7.4), where the thematic gesture beginning in m. 16 is notated with two levels of slurs.[21] In this case the larger slur is needed to guarantee that the third eighth note, marked with a stroke, is not unduly accented. Instead, it is released as part of the same gesture that releases the second eighth, thereby preserving the lilt of the $_8^6$ meter. The stroke on the third note implies a still shorter duration, but the larger four-note motivic grouping guarantees gestural connection to the following downbeat. Although the marked melodic reversal created by the fourth note is a questioning drop of a minor seventh, its metric placement, duration, and function as reversed goal to the rising stepwise motion require a significantly fresh accent, and thus Beethoven cannot place it under the larger slur. The continuation of this passage treats the thematic gesture *dialogically* by imitation, and *dialectically* by inversion. In this example Beethoven does not use the longer slur found so often in Chopin to indicate an overall *legato* continuity. Even within a longer *legato,* however, internal articulation may be achieved by dynamic emphasis (as implied by the harmony) or agogic accent (as implied by the rhythm).[22]

In the Classical style, as long as the interior is uniformly *legato* and corresponds to the gestural shape of the slur, tapering from an initiating articulation to a graceful release, relatively longer slurs may be used, as in the opening theme of the finale of Beethoven's Piano Sonata in B♭ Major, Op. 22 (Example 7.5). Compare the theme of the finale of Op. 7 (Example 7.2): the Op. 7 theme might have been placed under a longer slur, were it not for the paired sigh figures, which require individual

Example 7.3. Mozart, Piano Sonata in D Major, K. 311, second movement.
a. Opening theme.
b. Thematic extension of the close of the first theme.
c. Second theme.

Example 7.4. Beethoven, Piano Sonata in A Major, Op. 101, first movement, beginning of the second theme.

Example 7.5. Beethoven, Piano Sonata in B♭ Major, Op. 22, finale, opening theme.

articulation. Observe that although the motivic incises occur *after* each tie, Beethoven expressly notates his slurs over these incises, to maintain *legato* continuity.

According to contemporary reports, Beethoven cultivated a more connected *legato* for his *cantabile* melodies than did Mozart.[23] But Beethoven did not always use a long slur to indicate an extended *legato* even when he intended *legato,* as is evident in the opening theme from the Adagio cantabile of his *Pathétique* sonata, Op. 13 (Example 7.6a). It would not make musical sense to shorten the releases at the ends of each melodic slur, as in Mozart's incises; rather, the slurring must be understood as indicating the placement of initiatory weight as a form of accentuation, and hence inner articulation, of an essentially *legato* melody. Thus, the downbeats of mm. 2, 5, and 7 do not receive weight (or some other form of perceptual emphasis), whereas the downbeats of mm. 1, 3, 4, 6, and 8 do.[24]

Beethoven's inner articulations provide a layer of rhythmic and expressive counter-

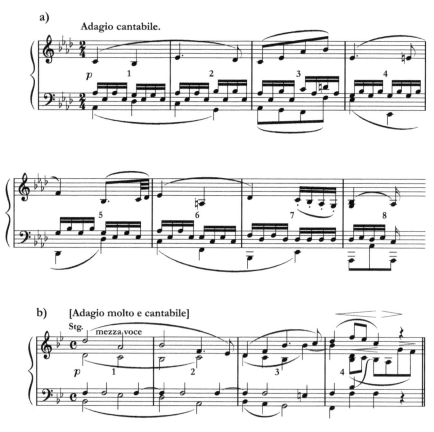

Example 7.6a. Related Adagio themes by Beethoven.
a. Piano Sonata in C Minor (*Pathétique*), Op. 13, second movement.
b. Symphony No. 9 in D Minor, Op. 125, third movement.

point against an unmarked gestural interpretation shaped by the metric field itself, with its regular, wavelike oscillations of up and down. These unexpected articulations individualize the melodic line, giving it a more self-willed agency that can shape its own way against the gravitational fields of meter and tonality.[25] Indeed, the strong sense of subjectivity that emerges in Beethoven's music may be related to his tendency to counter the unmarked metric flow with a layer of surprise accentuations and *subito* dynamic changes. If sufficiently marked as disruptions, such dynamic cross-currents may also be considered rhetorical in their function (see the finale of Op. 102, no. 1, discussed in Chapter 9).

The first slur in the Adagio cantabile theme also supports what I have called the "yielding" harmonic progression, V_2^4–I^6 (Hatten 1994: 57), enhanced by relaxing into the resolution to I^6 rather than accenting it. This same slurring occurs in the opening theme of the Adagio molto e cantabile of the Ninth Symphony (Example 7.6b), which was modeled on the Op. 13 theme in the sketches before being modified melodically to mirror that theme's opening bass line.[26] In performing this *mezza voce* theme, there is even more reason to de-emphasize the second downbeat, since the resolution occurs by step in the melody as well as the bass. One can observe a similar counterpointing of fourths and steps between melody and bass in this theme and in Op. 13, but in Op. 13 the upward melodic leap of a fourth counters the harmonic "yielding" of V_2^4-I^6. A tropological interpretation of this dual aspect might be "resigned nobility"—quiet heroism (upward fourth) in the face of loss (yielding bass). The willed energies implied by the rising fourths are enhanced in both themes by the similar ascending (or striving) arpeggiations in their third bars.

The stylistic gesture of a slur on the downbeat, linked to the dissonant-consonant resolution of an appoggiatura as an expressive prototype, is but one of many typical uses of slurs in the Classical style. Another type is the slur from an upbeat, commonly used to counteract the "squareness" of groups that would otherwise be in exact phase with the meter. The effect of smooth overlapping helps mask the "tyranny" of the bar line. In the opening theme of Beethoven's Piano Sonata in D Major, Op. 10, no. 3 (Example 7.7a), the slur reduces an otherwise strong downbeat emphasis on the first bar for a motive that is "on its way" to a climactic metric downbeat in m. 4.[27] Beethoven exploits the gesture's opening hint of grouping overlap in the coda (Example 7.7b), where the motivic fragmentation and liquidation of the main theme into four-quarter-note groups is placed accentually against the downbeat and under a four-note slur. By leveling out the underlying accentual hierarchy of the meter, Beethoven enhances the gradual dying away signaled by this motivic echo of the theme.[28]

The "leveling" accentual effect of overlapping grouping and meter can also contribute to a sense of graciousness, as is clear from its marked use in the first theme of Op. 14, no. 2 (Example 7.8), where three sixteenths overlap the meter. There is sufficient ambiguity of accentuation in stylistically executing the slur gesture such that it takes a while for the correct meter to register (see also the ambiguous grouping in the left hand). However, unless the performer gives a slight stress to the notated downbeat, the "default" meter (in which the second sixteenth would be interpreted as the downbeat) sounds hopelessly trite.[29] The use of an expansive grouping (and gestural) overlap at the beginning contributes to the pastoral haze of the opening pedal point and the equally expansive harmonic rhythm. Melodically the embellishing chromaticism enhances what sounds like a freely improvisatory, alternating contour. Together with the implied pastoral topic, these gestural elements suggest the qualities of ease and graciousness that are expressive prerequisites for an effective performance.[30]

Keyboard Articulations

The standard articulations (or "touches," in the telling metaphor for pianists)—*staccato, non legato, portato,* and *legato*—form a gestural continuum from disconnected to connected. But regardless of the degree of surface continuity

Example 7.7. Beethoven, Piano Sonata in D Major, Op. 10, no. 3, first movement.
a. First theme.
b. Intensification of the gesture in the coda.

Example 7.8. Beethoven, Piano Sonata in G Major, Op. 14, no. 2, first movement, opening theme.

Example 7.9. Beethoven, Piano Sonata in C Minor, Op. 111, first movement, progression from *non legato* through *portato* to *legato*.

of sound, any of these articulations can be dynamically shaped to imply gestural continuity of movement (just as, conversely, a *legato* melody may be articulated by use of varying accentuation or weight, as discussed above). Different articulations may also be used effectively in sequence as a means of transforming the gestural character of a motive. Rosen (2002a: 39) illustrates the gradual transition from detached to connected in an excerpt from the first movement of Op. 111 (Example 7.9) and notes that dots under a slur (*portato*) also typically imply a *ritenuto*.[31] Because of the gentle, reinitiatory movements it requires (involving separate wrist and/or arm strokes), *portato* not only requires more time but also provides a tactile sense of "palpability." *Portato* may be used to create a consoling effect, in that it mimes the series of calming, monorhythmic touches (pats on the shoulder) that one might make to reassure another. Typically *portato* involves the same or similar rhythms, and often the same pitches, which emphasizes the repetitive, gentle action of this touch. Of course, for repeated pitches under a slur the composer utilizes dots to avoid notational confusion with a tie.[32] Thus, purely pragmatically, *portato* is the best *"legato"* available for repeated notes on a keyboard instrument without a double-escapement mechanism. Example 7.10a, from the finale of Op. 13 (the second of two themes appearing in the B section of this sonata rondo), is instructive—if pedaled, continuity of sound results, but the separate strokes demanded by the *portato* nevertheless articulate that subsurface continuity.[33]

Beethoven's *portato* on repeated chords may also be part of a "reverberant" gestural strategy, as seen in Schubert's second theme from the first movement of D.

Example 7.10. Comparison of *portato* in themes by Beethoven and Schubert.
a. Beethoven, Op. 13, finale, second theme in the second theme group.
b. Schubert, Piano Sonata in A Major, D. 959, first movement, second theme.

959 (Example 7.10b). Here the effect is as though a single chord were resonating with reverberant vibrations—not fast, as in a tremolo that sustains a single sonority, but slowly echoing and dying away. Of course, all chords die away after being struck and held on keyboard instruments—that is the unmarked condition of keyboard sound. What Schubert achieves is a marked effect that foregrounds the decaying resonance of a chord. The Romantic image of sound as vibration, radiating in fading waves from an initial event like the wave radiating from a rock dropped into a body of water, may also carry connotations of inner spiritual reflection (see Chapter 8).

One may, of course, describe gestures according to features other than articulation, and, indeed, a more complete interpretation would weigh the contribution of other elements. I do not recommend, however, a return to the scale-degree motives for which Deryck Cooke (1959) provided emotional labels. Elsewhere (Hatten 1994: 49) I have noted the problem in this kind of taxonomy, which strives for a kind of lexical status of the *type* that neglects counterexamples of the *token*. Pitch contour alone does not provide uniform results, given the many variables affecting our interpretation of such contours: metric placement and rhythmic duration, harmonic setting, articulation, dynamics, timing (both tempo and pacing), orchestration, and the like. On the other hand, a gestural accounting for all of these variables, at least as a "fuzzy set" (i.e., without specifying exact boundaries of each variable) can help us evaluate their contribution to an emergent affect.

Dynamics

In performing *Winterreise* I was struck by the care with which Schubert distinguishes *decrescendo* versus *diminuendo*.[34] *Diminuendo* consistently occurs in locations where a very slight slowing down is appropriate (as, for example, a dying-away effect at the end of a song). *Decrescendo,* by contrast, would then imply the absence of any retarding of the tempo. Since *decrescendo* may also occur at the end of a song (for example, "Gefror'ne Tränen," "Auf dem Flusse," "Rast," and "Täuschung"), under this hypothesis one might interpret the repetitive or ostinato-like rhythmic figures of these songs as having an "inexorable" quality—an effect that would be undercut were one to slow down progressively at the end. Thus, Schubert elects the neutral "*decresc.*" instead of the more expressively loaded "*dim.*" Interestingly, the last five bars of "Rückblick" have a "*decresc.*" to *pp,* followed by "*dim.*"

Schubert had recourse to other terms that could specify a combination of dynamic decrease and tempo relaxing. Early in his career, in the Adagio and Rondo in E Major, D. 505/6 (Op. posth. 145) of 1817–18, Schubert used a variety of signs in a sequence that is revealing. *Calando* appears several times at the ends of sections. A final codetta marked *tranquillo* and *dolce* begins *p* and then sequentially offers five expressive markings: *dim., pp, sempre smorz., ppp,* and *morendo.* By the end of his life, however (as is evident from *Winterreise*), Schubert had gravitated toward just two verbal signs for decreases in intensity: *decrescendo* for strictly dynamic decay, and *diminuendo* (in place of *calando* or *morendo*) when a slight slowing down was also desired.

It is tempting to look for this subtle distinction in other nineteenth-century composers, but Chopin provides a useful counterexample. In the closing twelve bars of his Nocturne in F Minor, Op. 55, no. 1, Chopin notates *dim. ed accel.* (*decresc.* is not used at all in the work). We can only conclude that in this context *diminuendo* is strictly a dynamic indication—but note that the context is one in which a more "characteristic" term is appropriate, as opposed to the more objective labeling of *decrescendo.* The nocturne "diminishes" like thread spinning off a spindle, getting faster as it disappears into nothingness. On the other hand, Chopin's use of *dim.* simultaneously with the declining wedge in mm. 49 and 68 of his Nocturne in B Major, Op. 62, no. 1, suggests to the sensitive performer a hierarchy of nuances, not a mere redundancy.[35]

Strategic Gestures and Their Overlapping Functions

There are limits to generalized stylistic gestures, and composers delight in the spontaneous and idiosyncratic as ways of creating striking and memorable musical ideas. Beethoven is replete with such distinctive gestures. The finale of the Second Symphony (Example 7.11) opens with one that, despite its originality, nevertheless recalls the world of *opera buffa*—a scurrilous rascal thumbs his nose at us (or makes another appropriate Italian gesture). Broad topical categorization

Example 7.11. Beethoven, Symphony No. 2 in D Major, Op. 36, finale, opening theme.

("the world of *opera buffa*") grounds a narrower interpretation of this spontaneous gesture ("thumbs his nose"). The more marked such gestures are, the more likely they will be treated as thematic, since they provide the very individuality or "personality" that distinguishes a work. In this case the *buffa* gesture, a wonderfully evocative "opener," seems unpromising for thematic use; but the final two notes (*subito forte*) mark the "cadence" of the opening phrase with that same unbalanced, and hence comic, abruptness (Example 7.11, m. 6). This immediate reference to an otherwise isolated, initiatory (or even framing)[36] event is crucial if we are to understand it as thematic. Thematization at its most basic involves the elementary markedness of reiterated use.[37]

Mozart, Piano Sonata in C Minor, K. 457, III

Although an unexpectedly abrupt initiation suggests spontaneity, premature breaking off also has a source in the sigh figure itself. The sigh releases naturally in its prototypical form, but by breaking up a line it can add *empfindsamer* poignancy that is derived from such emotion-laden "gasps" or even "sobs." How might this gesture be spontaneously marked beyond its typical stylistic use? The rondo finale of Mozart's Piano Sonata in C Minor, K. 457 (1784), is instructive. It begins with a fourth-species-derived sequential treatment of the conventional sigh motive, usually creating suspensions on the downbeats (Example 7.12a). The gesture is expressively marked as obsessive, and already thematic in its consistent use. Note that the gesture contributes to a larger sense of continuity from the very regu-

Example 7.12. Mozart, Piano Sonata in C Minor, K. 457, finale.
a. First theme.
b. Closing theme of the first theme group featuring rhetorical disruption.

Example 7.12. Mozart, Piano Sonata in C Minor, K. 457, finale.
c. "C" theme with multiple formal functions.

Example 7.12. Mozart, Piano Sonata in C Minor, K. 457, finale.
d. Rhetorical breaking up of the second phrase of the first theme on its final return.

larity of its broken releases. Note also that there is nothing unusually abrupt about the releases, in which the notated quarters on each second beat could be realized anywhere from eighths to dotted eighths, according to conventions of performance practice (prior to Türk).

How might this idea be expressively developed? Rhetorically, obsessiveness is intensified in a furious passage hammering on the dominant (Example 7.12b), and unexpected abruptness is achieved by the disjunct, *Sturm und Drang* outbursts of vii°⁷ to i to V⁶₅ and sudden silence prolonged by a fermata.[38] The suspenseful break, a rhetorical gesture that disrupts the impending cadence, is bridged with a thematically marked melodic leap of a diminished seventh, leading to the proper cadence.

Stylistic Types and Strategic Functions of Gestures 155

This rhetorical rupture is so intense that Mozart forgoes a transition section to the B section of his modified sonata-rondo, modulating to E♭ by the simple device of a sudden (and rhetorical, though less marked in intensity) departure from a cadence in C minor to dominant seventh of E♭.[39] The theme of the B section follows immediately. Although in singing style above an Alberti-type broken-chord accompaniment, this theme has latent associations with the rondo refrain: its two-note slurs of tritone and M2. These will become more expressively relevant when the theme is resolved into C minor upon its return.

When the A section returns, Mozart fashions a new idea (Example 7.12c) that sounds at first like it might serve as a closing theme, then like it might mark a truncated middle or C section in the unfolding sonata-rondo design. But the idea soon reveals its transitional function, as it modulates back to C minor for the resolution of the "second theme" from the B section. As a closural theme that becomes transitional, the C theme tropes on all three formal functions of Classical material—thematic, transitional, and cadential (Hatten 1994: 115–21)—and it has an equally spectacular expressive effect. The theme begins with a mysterious Alberti-bass oscillation between i and vii° in F minor, preparing a desolate background for the dissociated single-note gestures that emerge as its "melody." This is an extreme instance of *Empfindsamkeit,* marked expressively by single-note sighs[40] and extensive rests that represent not merely gasps but utter emotional exhaustion. The "stuck" harmonic oscillation also develops the theme of obsessiveness. Only when the melody musters enough energy for a full sigh figure, echoed up an octave, does the bass finally begin to descend in a conventional lament pattern (like an extended sigh descending by step from $\hat{1}$ to $\hat{5}$). But a false move to D♮ sparks a renewed chordal outburst, and the theme starts over, sequentially up a step in G minor. It appears to be stuck in a melancholic spiral of despair, not really going anywhere, until G minor is suddenly transformed to G major as dominant preparation for the resolved return of the B section. Expressively the second theme's sigh figures realize their latent, tragic potential by transposition to C minor. Arriving after the single-note gestures of the previous "theme," we hear new poignancy in the repeated G's of the opening two bars of the B theme, and a possible derivation of the C theme is revealed. The *portato,* repeated-note anacrusis to a decorated sigh in the B theme now recalls the tragic weight of its more desolate variant. Clearly, developing variation of the opening gestures is providing expressive continuity for this tragic movement.

The rhetorical gesture of disruption is also developed by being inserted into the final return of A (Example 7.12d). Here the counterstatement fragments into two-bar gestures, landing on a series of fermatas. The *a piacere* designation indicates the flexibility of pacing demanded by this series of rhetorical disjunctions, in which the experiencing agent is allowed to step out of the relentless and obsessive metric/temporal pacing of the theme, as if feeling the full weight of each tragic gesture.

The effect of a choked-off release, as strategically developed by Mozart with the isolated notes and sighs in both the middle section and the *a piacere* return section of his C minor finale, is used often enough to become stylistic, as we can see in an example from Beethoven (for Schubert's use of the abrupt release as a crucial the-matic marker, see the discussion of D. 784 in Chapter 8). Beethoven makes consis-tent use of the abrupt release into silence in the opening theme to second move-ment of his Piano Sonata in C Major, Op. 2, no. 3 (Example 7.13a). Each one-bar gesture is isolated by a rest, and by notating endings in eighth notes, Beethoven enhances the effect of abrupt release, since these will be performed stylistically as even shorter values. Each internally articulated unit sounds like a larger sigh, choked off as though in repression of grief, and lending a sense of stoic response to tragedy—even in the context of major mode.[41] The repressed grief will be al-lowed to speak with the move to the parallel minor at m. 11 (Example 7.13b), as the opening hymnlike topic gives way to a more rhapsodic gestural dialogue between stoic bass in octaves and pleading treble. But the intensity of passion behind that stoic repression is revealed only with the sudden, rhetorical outbursts in mm. 53–54 and 71–72 (Examples 7.13c and 7.13d). One last, impassioned *forte* isolates the yearning ascent at the extreme high register, answered (in a kind of dialogic reso-lution) by the *forte* B in the bass, before "dissolving" into the reassurances of a galant cadence (Example 7.13e).

As my highlighting of other gestural functions has emphasized, it is impossible to speak of a purely spontaneous gesture in Classical works—any such gesture will have stylistic precedents, even at a very general categorial level, and its markedness will likely make it a candidate for thematic, if not also dialogic or even rhetorical, treatment. At the very least, such gestures will be integrated into the expressive language of the movement. Even Beethoven's *Beklemmt* episode in the Cavatina from Op. 130, perhaps the most extreme case of broken-off sighs and metrical dis-sociation of melody from accompaniment, echoes gestural contours from previous themes (Hatten 1994: 202–23).

It can be revealing to examine the juncture where creativity goes beyond the prototype to explore the expressive individuality of the token. An exquisitely poi-gnant gesture is created by Gluck in the trio added to the 1774 Paris version of "Dance of the Blessed Spirits," one of the ballets from his opera *Orfeo*. Here the solo flute may represent Eurydice, who despite an afterlife in Elysium still longs for Orfeo. The emotional crux of this highly expressive soliloquy arrives in mm. 40–42 (Example 7.14a), marking the modulation from D minor to F major with what at first appears to function as a closing gesture. The gesture will be reiterated in the second half of the binary trio (although there are no repeats, the form reaches its midpoint at the end of m. 44), and the gesture builds in expressive intensity with its transposition back to D minor (Example 7.14b). I will refer to this gesture as the "lift" gesture.[42]

The underlying schema for this gesture involves an energetic rise to a point where energy and gravity seem poised in the balance, a hovering on a released and perhaps lightly repeated pitch, and then a subsiding fall, either by resignational drop or by a mediated descent. Unlike typical climax structures, there is a sense of weightlessness at the "apex" of this gesture, and the corresponding drop gives it a sense of vulnerability and pathos that is quite extraordinary in Gluck's realization. As the expressive crux of the movement, it is appropriately reiterated for maximum

Example 7.13. Beethoven, Piano Sonata in C Major, Op. 2, no. 3, second movement.
a. Opening theme.
b. Contrasting theme in E minor.

Example 7.13. Beethoven, Piano Sonata in C Major, Op. 2, no. 3, second movement.
c. Rhetorical disruption at the cadence.
d. Internal rhetorical disruption.
e. Rhetorical treatment of the closing measures.

Example 7.14. Gluck, *Orfeo ed Euridice,* act 2, ballet, "Dance of the Blessed Spirits."
a. Lift gesture in the close to the first part of the trio (flute, mm. 40–42).

b)

Example 7.14. Gluck, *Orfeo ed Euridice,* act 2, ballet, "Dance of the Blessed Spirits."
b. Modal intensification of the lift gesture in the second part (flute, mm. 48–50).

Example 7.15. Bach, Sinfonia in G Minor, BWV 797.
a. Lift gesture and its suspension in the opening bars.
b. Imitative treatment of the lift gesture in mm. 11–14.

effect: "Must one let go? Yes, one must"—a species of poignant and sorrow-filled resignation that one might attribute to Eurydice as one of the "blessed spirits" who is still mourned by Orfeo. Gesturally it might be performed as though rising on a wave, lifting for a moment, and then subsiding, but the lift may also be experienced as a weightless release and hovering. The poignancy comes from the moment's suspension before the drop—as though one could have sustained a fleeting hope. Although there is no slur marked on the descending seventh, repetition of the motive clearly defines its gestural boundaries, and whether or not the soloist chooses to interpret the falling portion of the gesture as a *legato* descent (in effect, an expansive sigh), the final note must be played softly enough to satisfy the gestural envelope of a declining dynamic.

A similar "lift" gesture may be inferred from Bach's Sinfonia in G Minor, BWV 797 (Example 7.15a, b).[43] This exquisite character piece draws on the topic of the *siciliano,* and it benefits from an articulation that, although not specifically marked by Bach, may be defended as an appropriate gestural interpretation. It involves releasing the principal motive (in the right hand, mm. 1–2) just before the downbeat of the second measure, giving the swooping gesture just enough energy to suggest a weightless gap before lightly landing on the downbeat (see also mm. 11–15). Bach provides for gestural variation through the use of ties that prevent this articulation, creating instead contrapuntal chains of suspensions (see mm. 3–5). The suspension is expressively enhanced by gestural "suspension" of the expected "lift," and the "landing" articulation on the downbeat is shifted to the contrapuntally paired voice.

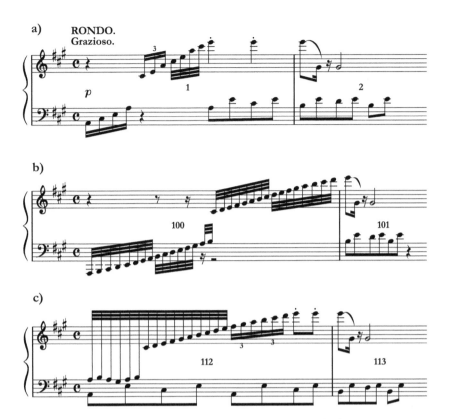

Example 7.16. Beethoven, Piano Sonata in A Major, Op. 2, no. 2, finale.
a. Opening version of the lift gesture.
b. First diminutional variant.
c. Second diminutional variant.

Beethoven offers the most extreme development of the lift gesture, now interpretable as a sweeping and gracious galant gesture, in the finale to his Piano Sonata
in A Major, Op. 2, no. 2 (Example 7.16a). The further development of the idea
features an extravagance that is in keeping with its projection of *le beau geste* (Example 7.16b, c).

The compositional working out of thematic gestures is the focus of Chapters 8
and 9. Before turning to dialogical gestures, however, I would note that although a
movement must be marked to be gestural, gestures must be further marked to be
thematic. Although the movements of the performer will always contribute a qualitative character to any movement in tones, and although stylistic markedness will
account for the relevance of many sonic movements as musically gestural, not all
musical gestures are strategically marked as subjects of musical discourse. When
gestures become thematic, their embodied meaning becomes thematic, as well, affecting the expressive character of the ongoing musical discourse.

Dialogical Gestures

Dialogical gestures are those that appear to respond to each other, along the lines of a conversation among equals (Haydn quartets), a dialectical opposition of themes, or a textural opposition (*concertato* effects). Mozart often employs dialectical opposition in first-movement opening themes (*Jupiter* Symphony, Piano Sonata in C Minor, K. 457), and Beethoven followed his lead (Piano Sonata in C Minor, Op. 10, no. 1). Although each gesture can call forth its own meanings—whether stylistic, spontaneous, thematic, or some combination—there is a new level of meaning that emerges from a dialogue with another "voice" or opposing agency.[44] In dialogical gestures part of the thematic signification emerges from the dramatic role played by the gesture. If a dialectical opposition is involved, each gesture is also defined, and characterized, by what it specifically is not—the opposing gesture. Thus, dialogical strategies enhance meaning both dramatically and qualitatively. Schubert expands the dimensions of two oppositional thematic ideas in the first movement of his Piano Sonata in A Major, D. 959 (see Chapter 8, Example 8.2a), but he secures a dialogical interpretation by immediately combining the opposing ideas to create thematic integration (Example 8.2b). Mozart also links his opposing ideas in the counterstatement of the first movement of the *Jupiter* Symphony, by means of a descending scale that bridges the gap between the two.

Whereas opening dialogical opposition often leads to integration, the opposite process is also effective. In the coda to the finale of K. 457 (Example 7.17), Mozart breaks up the line by extreme registral opposition. Gesturally, although the same hand performs the "line," the extravagant cross-hand move marks another voice—fateful in response to the more pleading high register, and implacable as it takes over for an inexorable cadence in the lowest register.[45] Note how the stylistically unmarked cadence formula in the bass is here strategically marked by this dialogical context and raised to a higher expressive value: unmarked "formulaic close" is marked as "inexorable fate."

The relationships among subjects and countersubjects in fugal textures, while obviously dialogical in the give and take of their counterpoint, are often tropological as well, especially when contrapuntal integration supports an interpretational fusing of what may be contradictory topics. Recall Raymond Monelle's (2000: 199–206) interpretation of Bach's Fugue in A♭ Major, BWV 901 (WTC II), in which a *galant* subject is paired with a countersubject that projects a chromatically descending lament figure (see Example 4.1). Monelle's reading moves beyond the trope of contradictory topics to an allegorical and even deconstructive account of the entire fugue.

Rhetorical Gestures

Rhetorical gestures (as already analyzed in the finale of Mozart's Piano Sonata in C Minor) may also be defined as those highly marked musical events that direct our attention to some aspect of the ongoing musical discourse, perhaps dramatically redirecting our path through the form or genre.[46] In the latter case the

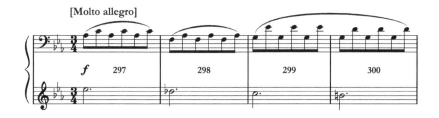

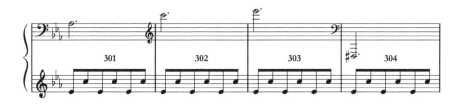

Example 7.17. Mozart, K. 457, finale. Dialogical and rhetorical intensification in the coda.

composer may either (1) rhetorically mark the initiations, arrivals, and closures of an unmarked formal scheme, or (2) mark strategic departures from the expected tracking of events according to such formal schemes, by such strategies as reversals, undercuttings, and shifts in level of discourse.[47] In either case rhetorical gestures are characterized by sudden changes in energy, force, direction, and character, and hence imply the marked presence of a higher, narrative agency. As Barth (1992) argues, in such cases the pianist takes on the role of an orator. These rhetorical gestures may or may not be specifically marked by signs in the music, but they must be understood from our knowledge of form and syntax—that is, as means of playing with stylistic expectation.

The finale of Beethoven's Piano Sonata in A Major, Op. 101, features a rhetorical juncture between the end of the recapitulation and the beginning of the coda (Example 7.18). At first the questioning dominant seventh is answered by a vehement octave drop of a third, recalling the defiant gesture that launched the development section. But instead of proceeding with another *fugato*, Beethoven echoes the gesture, suggesting a moment of doubt that is marked by a shift to the lowered submediant. At that point he appears to "reflect" in F major with the opening fragment of the fugue subject (I–V), which is then answered by itself (V–I). The passage is

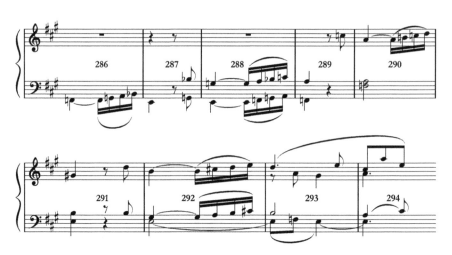

Example 7.18. Beethoven, Op. 101, finale. Rhetorical shifts.

completely circular and sets up what might be termed a "thematic fermata": the subject fragment is reiterated, but this time the harmonization turns F into VI and ultimately iv^6, resolving to V of A minor. The decision to return to A, marked by a progression that is also marked in the style (the Phrygian half cadence, iv^6–V, with its portents of fatefulness), needs time in performance—not just because it is a marked progression, but because it has a great deal of rhetorical work to do. It is not quite a "decision made with difficulty" (as in the introduction to the finale of Beethoven's String Quartet, Op. 135), but rather one that poses a rhetorical question: Where do we go from here? The home key then just slips in, as though it were ready to happen at any minute—but the effect of this return is like yielding to the safe haven of the pastoral. Taking a bit of time in performance for the Phrygian half cadence allows the subsequent yielding to bear weight at a narrative level (emphasizing the ultimate return home) as well as at a locally expressive level. This kind of thematized rhetorical gesture is narrative in that it helps tell the story, not merely enact the drama, by giving extra emphasis to significant hinges in the dramatic trajectory of the movement. The danger with narrative gesturing of this sort,

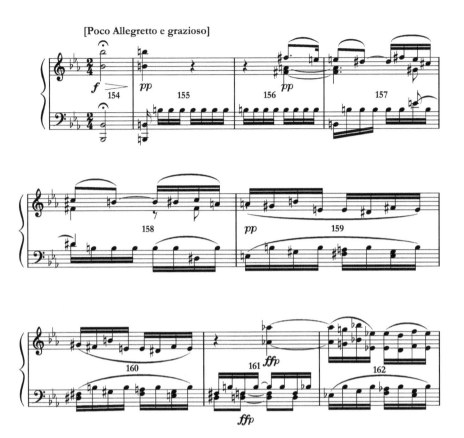

Example 7.19. Beethoven, Op. 7, finale. Rhetorical shift (expansion of the Neapolitan).

of course, is that it may lead to an overly didactic performance in which too much is pointed out.[48]

Consider another rhetorical gesture, also harmonic, that Beethoven liked to use in his codas. The shift to the Neapolitan key area in the coda of a finale appears in his first publicly acknowledged composition, the Piano Trio in E♭ Major, Op. 1, no. 1, as well as in Op. 2, no. 2 (IV), Op. 7 (IV), and Op. 10, no. 1 (III). The device returns in late works such as the coda of the finale of Op. 102, no. 1, the coda of the first movement of Op. 102, no. 2, and (as prepared earlier and expressively marked) the coda of the slow movement of Op. 106 (discussed in Hatten 1994: 16, 25). This rhetorical harmonic shift is thus used often enough to become a style type for Beethoven, and its typical location suggests that one of its rhetorical roles is to mark impending closure by means of the most radical escape from that closure (the Neapolitan is a distant key relationship and has a "mystical" character, often emphasized by enharmonic modulation, as when a German augmented sixth in the home key is reinterpreted as a V[7] in the Neapolitan key area). Thus, an effec-

Example 7.20. Beethoven, Piano Sonata in E♭ Major, Op. 31, no. 3, opening theme as four stages in a drama.

tive gestural realization must give a sense of stepping out of the piece into another realm, and that move is usually supported by differences in other elements as well (dynamics, register, etc.). The boundaries of a tonicized Neapolitan insertion may thus be marked by slight delays in timing that serve to acknowledge the tonal (and psychic) distance traversed.

In the coda to the finale of Beethoven's Piano Sonata in E♭ Major, Op. 7 (Example 7.19), B♭ yields mystically to B♮ to launch a parenthetical Neapolitan expansion; the sudden *sforzando* marks the tonal moment where B♭ pulls the listener back into reality, and an effective realization will create the sensation of pulling against the grain of an alternate world.[49] This effect can be achieved if timing is expanded to compensate for the dynamic "pull" of the *sforzando*.

The first movement of Beethoven's Piano Sonata in E♭ Major, Op. 31, no. 3 (Example 7.20), provides a miniature dramatic trajectory in its opening theme, which is instructive in the way topics can be used rhetorically. There are four stages in this mini-drama of a theme. First, mm. 1–2 feature an accepting drop of a fifth on a minor seventh chord in first inversion that is most plausibly interpretable as ii$^6_5$ (due to the strong associations of the mm7 sonority with supertonic-seventh function in major). The soft dissonance of the minor seventh chord, however, can be enjoyed for its own sonority's sake; it has a pastoral quality, and Beethoven repeats the gesture to foreground it thematically.[50] The second stage of the drama, mm. 3–5, features a chromatic intensification of opening sonority, now interpretable as vii°⁷/V. The *ritardando* and *crescendo* suggest impending drama, as appropriate to the semiotic status of diminished-seventh sonorities. Topically the move is from pastoral to *ombra*.

The third stage (m. 6) releases the diminished-seventh tension into what I have called an arrival $^6_4$ (see Chapter 1 and Hatten 1994) that reaffirms consonance and major mode, reversing lowered $\hat{3}$ to raised $\hat{3}$ (technically this is also a cadential $^6_4$, but its rhetorical effect as an arrival is conspicuously marked here). At this point a heroic or at least noble affirmation has been achieved, and the shadows of *ombra* have been dispelled. But a fourth topic undercuts the grandeur of the arrival $^6_4$ with a comic cadential gesture in mm. 7–8. The cadence deflates the pretensions of the preceding topics (pastoral, *ombra,* noble/heroic) with a thoroughly *buffa* gesture. This opening theme, made up of a series of increasingly rhetorical gestures, pro-vides in effect a microcosm of dramatic and narrative form, even ending with a Romantic ironic annihilation of the heroic. Given that this is "just" the opening, we can expect sudden shifts and reversals (characteristic of *opera buffa*) through-out the movement, and each will demand a gestural realization that supports its narrative and rhetorical labor, as well as its local expressive role.

Rhetorical Gesture as Thematic: Beethoven's Piano Sonata in E Major, Op. 109

I turn now to an extended example that realizes the thematic potential of a rhetorical gesture. The first movement of Beethoven's Piano Sonata in E Major, Op. 109, features one of the most celebrated of extreme gestures. It achieves *rever-sal* by means of an *undercutting* that implies a *shift in level of discourse*—in effect, combining all three means of dislocating the expected trajectory of a form. This gesture, negotiated with tonal and topical elements, creates a massive rhetorical dis-ruption, but one that is also marked as thematic for the movement.

After beginning with an unmarked theme in continuous sixteenths,[51] a quick modulation in the second phrase implies an arrival in the dominant in m. 9 (Ex-ample 7.21). Instead, tempo, meter, rhythm, texture, voice-leading, and harmony all shift in a gesture of radical annihilation. The syntactic (voice-leading and har-monic) shock is created by the reversal of expected voice-leading, as the new lead-ing tone A♯, which should have resolved to B, is instead pulled down to A♮ and harmonized by a dissonant diminished-seventh chord. But the gestural surprise goes still further than mere harmonic underlining of voice-leading reversal. There is also textural change (the sudden arpeggiation of a thicker sonority), tempo change (to Adagio), topical change (to fantasia), and, as the listener will eventually realize, metric change (to $^3_4$).

Tonally, the initial shock is "rationalized" when the diminished-seventh chord resolves to C♯ minor, which is retrospectively understood as ii in the sequential transition to B major (vii^{o7}/ii to ii, vii^{o7} to I). Thus, B major, the key that was de-ferred by the rhetorical reversal in m. 9, has the last word.[52] The surprising shift at m. 9 is also ultimately rationalized by the consistency of the Adagio tempo and $^3_4$ meter that follow, and absorbed motivically by the patterning of the sequence. But these retrospective rationalizations do not render the experiential effect of m. 9 any less shocking.

In tracing the compositional order of the decisions to undercut the interactive

Example 7.21. Beethoven, Piano Sonata in E Major, Op. 109, first movement, exposition. First edition (Berlin: Schlesinger, 1821), reproduced from the copy in the Austrian National Library, Hoboken Collection, S. H. Beethoven 440. (Reproduced here by permission of Tecla Editions, www.tecla.com.)

syntactic and gestural continuities preceding m. 9, one might consider two contra-dictory hypotheses: (1) given the highly marked syntactic reversal from A♯ to A♮, a gestural underlining was needed to signal thematic intention, and (2) the decision to create an extreme gestural shift demanded a sufficiently marked violation of syntax that could be thematized and developed with consequences for form.[53] But how can we determine the direction in which Beethoven's inspiration might have flowed—was the syntactic or the purely gestural shock first to be conceived? It may be more helpful to reframe the question, by considering the *expressive intent* as pri-mary, and considering how both gestural and syntactic dimensions interact to achieve the rhetorical effect of reversal.

A similar reframing of the relationship of bodily gesture to spoken language and its syntax led David McNeill (1999; McNeill and Duncan 2000) to propose an analysis according to "growth points," functional units based on specific commu-nicative intentions which may draw upon hand and arm gestures as well as verbal discourse in ever-varying combinations and alternations to achieve those ends (see Chapter 5). Kugler and Turvey (1987) proposed a similar functional unit in their characterization of human action, in which the goal of an action is its intent, and any number of muscular means may help the agent achieve that goal. One advan-tage of an analogous model for gesture and syntax in music is that it gives priority to the expressive motivations underlying musical structures. Another, more prag-matic advantage is that the particular mix of gestural and syntactic elements re-quired to achieve a rhetorical effect is not determined in advance, nor need it be prescribed as a stylistic given. While one may readily categorize syntactic reversals according to their scale-degree or harmonic ingredients (e.g., the class of $\sharp\hat{4}$ to $\natural\hat{4}$ reversals), this initial categorization is only a starting point for contextual interpre-tation in environments such as m. 9, where the effect depends on so many different elements undergoing radical shifts.

How, then, might one interpret the local expressive effect, and the rhetorical contribution to a global dramatic trajectory, that are typical of Beethoven's so-nata movements? Formally most sonatas maintain a single meter and tempo, de-spite the much-observed multiplicity of rhythmic affect that is possible in a single movement. If one finds such a contrast, it is typically in the opposite direction, from slow introduction to Allegro. Thus, it is plausible to interpret the expressive shift as analogous to a shift between the unmarked, ongoing character of everyday life and a sudden crisis that throws everything into another temporal space, one that is highly charged and inwardly directed. If this is a shift in level of discourse, it is unlike the Romantic ironic shifts I analyzed in Chapter 7 of *Musical Meaning in Beethoven* (1994: 172–88). Romantic ironic shifts are reflexive, commenting upon previous musical discourse by shifting to a higher plane, along the lines of the shift between unmarked story and marked narrative commentary in the novel. This shift is to another level, but not primarily to comment upon the first eight measures; rather, it is more like a lateral shift, taking us to a more intimately expe-rienced thought or feeling that sounds interpolated, like a dramatic aside, within the otherwise prevailing discourse.

The related problem of *agency* (to be addressed in Chapter 10) is intriguing: is this shift self-willed, as the result of a sudden insight, or is its impact on the experiencing agent of the work initiated by an outside agency, such as a sudden external crisis? In any case the experiencing of that shock is immediate and filled with internalized passion.

However we may interpret the expressive effect of m. 9, it is clearly important as a formal premise and a thematic expressive idea. Many analysts (Schenker and Rosen included) consider the Adagio section as a whole to comprise the "second theme" of the movement. The principal argument for this interpretation is that in the recapitulation the entire section returns (although slightly varied), transposed down a fifth (registrally up a fourth). But transitions may also be transposed down a fifth such that they arrive at the tonic key instead of the dominant. The music from mm. 9–10 certainly has a transitional character, both tonally and texturally (note the dialogical play of dissonance versus consonance and loud versus soft). Furthermore, it is only when we reach B major in m. 11 that a melodic idea is introduced—one that might have been expanded into a more prototypical second theme. But just as it is about to cadence prematurely,[54] this sliver of a theme slips chromatically into another rhetorical reversal. Again, A♯ is pulled against its will to A♮, supported by a diminished-seventh chord, and gesturally a rhythmic acceleration leads to an expansive arpeggiation of that diminished-seventh throughout the registers in m. 12. Clearly the idea of reversal is itself becoming thematic. A sudden piano undercutting at the end of m. 12 leads to a third marked shift, now enharmonic, to D♯ major (m. 13). D♯ is V of G♯ minor, the relative of B major, and G♯ minor will be featured in the development section. But the D♯ major triad is also a chromatic third away from B major. When a fourth reversal at the end of m. 13 magically restores B major as a direct chordal shift—*not* by means of a syntactic progression—the chromatic third relationship draws upon its stylistic correlation as a mystical transformation, one that is not "earned" but "received" by the agent. The thematic fragment from m. 11 now returns, up an octave and with variational diminution (a brief moment of plenitude), reflecting its transcendence as an unearned moment of insight or grace, depending on one's secular or sacred choice of interpretive label. This time it is not reversal but gentle, blissful liquidation that dissolves the atomized theme into a series of cascading, euphoric triplets, overflowing without the trauma of the vertiginous drops in mm. 12 and 13. By the end of m. 15 the highly truncated exposition has ended, and the development begins with the opening theme in the dominant.

Given the brevity of the exposition (and thus of the entire movement), one might ask to what extent that brevity was already implied by the initial eight bars. Do those texturally unmarked measures nevertheless reveal, upon closer inspection, anything that could be said to anticipate a reversal, perhaps even predicting one of its features? Note how the second phrase (beginning in the last half of m. 4) would require an extra bar in order to complete its harmonic progression. The interior grouping of the consequent phrase is thus two plus three bars. The shift to a three-bar grouping might be heard as anticipating (or preparing for) the local shift of meter to $\frac{3}{4}$, with the Adagio tempo rendering one bar of $\frac{3}{4}$ roughly equivalent to three bars of $\frac{2}{4}$ in perceived duration.[55] The expansion of the second phrase could also be viewed as setting up a larger hypermetric downbeat for the arrival of B major in m. 9, which marks that moment (retrospectively, at least) as ideal for just such a disruptive event. It is hard to imagine how the music would have continued if Beethoven had instead arrived on B major. Thus, given the *crescendo* and registral expansion, the syntactic and gestural reversal can appear almost inevitable.

Now compare the series of successive reversals that give the rhetorical device its thematic weight. Mapping mm. 12–14 onto mm. 9–11 is revealing, in that the same structural upper line descent in mm. 9–10 appears in mm. 12–13, simply expanded to include the enharmonic shift that supports the chromatic passing F×. (On this basis, one could indeed argue that the second theme begins at m. 9; such varied repetition gives formal weight to the passage.)

Consider next the expressive effect achieved by the contrasting topics in these two sections. The first theme, a bagatelle in its earliest sketch appearance (Kinderman 1995: 218), opens with what I call the deceptive sequence in alternating first inversions (I–V⁶–vi–iii⁶–IV–I6). This sequence is venerable enough to carry a hint of the high style. But the third movement of Op. 79 (Example 7.22a) begins with the same sequential progression, where it hardly sounds high in style, and thus the hypothesis is in need of further support. Interestingly, Beethoven uses a corresponding ascending sequence, which I have elsewhere termed an elevation or transfiguration sequence,[56] for the transformational passage in the development leading to the climax of the first movement of Op. 109 (Example 7.22b). In any case the familiarity of the opening deceptive sequence suggests its unmarked status in the first theme, and perhaps its association with the familiar suggests the security of an unbroken state of consciousness. Certainly the perpetual-sixteenth realization conveys a strong sense of continuity.[57]

The material beginning at m. 9 (return to Example 7.21) is clearly within the realm of the exotic—*ombra* and *fantasia,* to draw on Ratner's (1980) topical labels. In fact, Kinderman (1995: 218) notes that the section was originally labeled *"Fantasie"* by Beethoven in the Grasnick 20b incarnation. But the dramatic contrast between the transitional instability (mm. 9–10) and the brief nucleus of lyrical stability in what I have labeled the second theme fragment (m. 11) suggests a drama that is not limited to one topic.[58] Indeed, the parenthetical nature of the entire passage from mm. 9–15 is also noted by Kinderman (1995: 219). Registrally (if not metrically) the development picks up precisely where the first theme is cut off. Such parentheses have their own interior logic, but how might Beethoven attempt to integrate these two radically opposing levels of his discourse, given that each has thematic weight in the movement?

The coda (Example 7.23) provides one answer. It begins parallel to the development, by closing the parenthesis around the second theme area. But the main theme is now literally expanded (by an extra bar and a half) and again interrupted. This time the interruption is a reversal without sound—a rhetorically charged rest on the downbeat that reverberates into a chord on the offbeat. Clearly the unstable transitional/second theme is being invoked, with similar diminished sevenths and expansion of the supertonic. Beethoven places the material in the tempo and meter

Example 7.22. Comparison of sequences in Beethoven piano sonatas.
a. Piano Sonata in G Major, Op. 79, finale, opening theme.
b. Piano Sonata in E Major, Op. 109, first movement, development section.

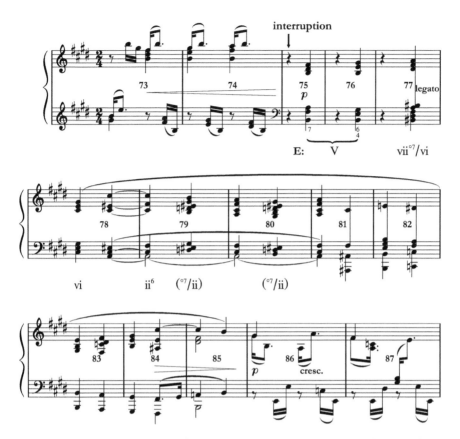

Example 7.23. Beethoven, Op. 109, first movement, interruptive launching of coda with integrative treatment of Adagio section.

of the first theme, and even liquidates the rhythmic setting to relatively constant quarter-note motion, but the slower values and transformed topic reveal a treatment that is almost religious in character. This hymnlike reconciliation of the tensions of the charged passage retains just enough poignancy to convey a retrospective summing up of the disruptive episode. The last statement of first theme's texture echoes the parting sigh of this chorale-like thematic transformation, and the final one-bar sighs ascend like cherubs in a Renaissance ceiling.

The many examples I have chosen to illustrate strategic functions of gesture also demonstrate how difficult it would be to classify gestures on the basis of a single such function. Although it is possible to distinguish functions such as the thematic, dialogic, and rhetorical, any given gesture may, and typically will, implement more than one function. Even the boundary between the strategic and the stylistic is constantly in flux, both historically and analytically. In most cases of apparently spontaneous or original gestures it is possible to trace at least the influence of a conventional stylistic gestural type. Despite these inevitable barriers to a stable functional inventory of gestures, one can make a strong case for gesture's role as both expressive and structural element. In the next two chapters works drawn from the late styles of Beethoven and Schubert will provide still further evidence of the structural and expressive potential of thematic gestures.

8 Thematic Gesture in Schubert: The Piano Sonatas in A Major, D. 959, and A Minor, D. 784

In the previous chapter I concentrated on individual gestures with only occasional reference to their development in a movement (e.g., the finale of Mozart's Piano Sonata in C Minor, K. 457, and the first movement of Beethoven's Piano Sonata in E Major, Op. 109). Here I will consider the evolution of thematic or strategically marked gestures across whole movements and cycles of movements. Thematic gestures are those that play a significant role in the drama of a work, as subjects for musical discourse. To review the theoretical argument:

1. Gesture is the synthesis or integration of many musical elements, and (as bodily *index* and/or *icon* of movement shape/force) offers an immediate connection to expressive meaning.
2. Gesture may be thematized (as a strategic type, hence not merely iconic or indexical but also *symbolic*). Its articulations, dynamic shading, and temporal shaping may be as important, or even more important, than its pitch-motivic relationships in the unfolding thematic discourse.
3. Gestural ideas may be subject to developing variation in the course of that unfolding discourse, often providing an expressive or dramatic link between or among otherwise contrasting themes or theme groups.
4. By contributing their particular expressive meanings to the ongoing thematic discourse, gestural motives can help shape the *expressive genre,* or the dramatic trajectory of a movement or work. Gesturally derived expressive meanings can motivate striking departures from, or manipulations of, typical formal schemes or conventional formal expectations. (These will often be achieved by means of rhetorical gestures.)
5. Interpreting the evolution of thematic gestures suggests that form is not an end in itself, but a vehicle for projecting expressive meaning.

In Western music themes are often considered as subjects of musical discourse. Depending on genre and compositional choice, a theme may be either *varied* (which implies that its length or form is preserved), or its motive(s) may be broken out and *developed,* perhaps in a counterstatement that becomes transitional, perhaps in a separate section devoted to development (as in sonata form). Arnold Schoenberg is credited with observing a third kind of thematic process, a more continuous evolutionary process that he termed *developing variation.*[1] In a famous essay Schoenberg (1947) highlights Brahms's masterful use of such an evolutionary thematic process, dubbing him "progressive" for having achieved an ongoing *thematic* coherence. Schoenberg argues that a similar concern for unfolding motivic relationships helps provide coherence in the absence of functional tonal progression—that is, in his own atonal works. In Schoenberg's examples, and in much of the literature on thematic analysis, the focus is on a group of pitches shown to be the essential thematic seed for the composition. This *Grundgestalt* (basic shape, or fundamental idea) may be transformed through such standard developmental techniques as inversion, interval expansion, fragmentation, or reorientation with respect to the meter. However, by focusing on continuous motivic evolution, one may also discover that a contrasting theme is the result of a logical series of transformations of an original idea.

Developing Gestural Variation in Beethoven, Op. 90, and Schubert, D. 959

Schoenberg finds developing variation not only in Brahms, but also in the earlier Viennese Classical music of Mozart. I will demonstrate a similar kind of developing variation in the sonatas of Beethoven and Schubert, but my focus will be on gesture, not merely a configuration of pitches. As an initial point of comparison, consider the evolution of a similar articulated gesture in the first movements of Beethoven's Piano Sonata in E Minor, Op. 90, and Schubert's Piano Sonata in A Major, D. 959.[2] Although Beethoven's first movement is more tightly developed than Schubert's, it shares a similar strategy of developing variation. However, Beethoven and Schubert may be seen to shift the focus from pitch structure alone (as is often the focus of Schoenberg's *Grundgestalt*) to the syntheses of articulation, dynamics, and timing that comprise thematic gestures. The resulting "gestural motivation" of form guarantees immediacy of affective meaning, as projected by the synthetic gestures of a performer. Furthermore, the listener can be guided securely through the discourse of a movement by the gradually unfolding, affective trajectory of thematic gestures. The unique realization of a conventional expressive genre (as in the path from tragic struggle to triumphant victory, transcendent acceptance, or ultimate devastation) is often dependent on the affective course mapped by the developing variation of thematic gestures.

Beethoven's Op. 90 (Example 8.1a, m. 1) and Schubert's D. 959 (Example 8.2a, m. 8) both feature what on the surface appears to be the same *stylistic* gestural type: two sound events in an upbeat-downbeat, short-long, and released-held articulatory configuration.[3] Dynamics and tempo suffice to create an enormous difference in affect, and the two movements develop their *strategic* gestures in strikingly individual ways (compare Examples 8.1 and 8.2 in their entirety). The expositions of both sonatas exhibit an ongoing evolution of their gestures, but one would be hard pressed to claim in either case that a particular pitch cell (or contour) was the "kernel" from which variants emerged. The thematic discourse might better be understood as having been generated from the gesture's properties and their potential.

If a thematic gesture is progressively varied, the derivation process relates the

Example 8.1. Beethoven, Piano Sonata in E Minor, Op. 90, first movement. Stages in the developing evolution of a thematic gesture.
(*Continued on the next page.*)

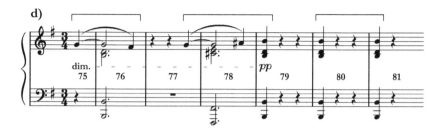

Example 8.1. Beethoven, Piano Sonata in E Minor, Op. 90, first movement. Stages in the developing evolution of a thematic gesture.

variants by means of a single "genealogy," even if a later variant is so transformed that it projects a radically different affective character. This continuous identity of a constantly evolving thematic idea is important if we are to infer a dramatic agency, or even persona, from the dramatic evolution of a gesture. Beethoven progressively alters the articulatory relationship, the durational length, and even (most impressively) the metric orientation of his initial gesture, yet the coherent linkage of developing variation allows the listener to follow, and identify bodily, with each stage of the drama.

The compression of events in the opening exposition of Op. 90 reflects a strategy Beethoven pioneered as early as his first acknowledged solo piano sonata (Op. 2, no. 1, in F Minor). Beethoven's choice of passionate depth over monumental breadth creates a propulsive and highly dramatic discourse, culminating in a continuous wave of Romantic intensity. The dialectical contrast in Op. 90 of dramatic and lyric modes (already hinted in the opening shifts between *forte* and *piano,* minor and major) is coordinated as part of a larger span directed by the gestural evolution.

Schubert's exposition (Example 8.2) is also dialectical in its initial thematic contrasts. Schubert ends his first theme (mm. 1–6) on the dominant, shifts to a radically different idea (mm. 7–15), then mediates the opposition in a counterstatement (mm. 16–21). Thematic integration, my term for such mediation, can be a useful developmental strategy in relating contrasting themes. Here the integration supports a dialogical interpretation of the two themes, in which mm. 7–15 are heard as a hesitant response to the more dynamic opening bars.

Since we possess Schubert's first continuity draft of the movement (Example 8.3), we know that the gesture in m. 1 appeared compositionally only at a later stage. The gesture in m. 8 was clearly conceived first, and this evidence also suggests that the gesture in m. 1 was conceived in dialectical opposition to the later one. Both are two-event, articulated gestures; however, in the first gesture the two events are downbeat-upbeat, equal in length, separated by a large leap, and *forte* in dynamic, whereas in the second gesture the two events are upbeat-downbeat, short-long, separated by a step, and *piano* in dynamic. The first gesture is intertextually related to the opening gesture of Beethoven's *Hammerklavier* sonata, Op. 106, but Schubert's intervallic inversion and registral reversal express a more stoic kind of heroism, under the "stiff upper lip" of a pedal on A that yields only to the lead-

Example 8.2. Schubert, Piano Sonata in A Major, D. 959, first movement. Developing variation of the bracketed thematic gesture.
a. Contrasting first themes.
b. Integrative counterstatement.
c. Closing theme for the first theme group.
d. Transition.

Example 8.3. Excerpt from the continuity draft for the first movement of Schubert, D. 959. (Note absence of left-hand gesture in mm. 1–2; articulatory gesture in m. 8 is already complete.)

ing tone at the half cadence. The dialogical response of mm. 7–8, on the other hand, implies freedom from dutiful constraint (the arpeggiated descent from a higher register, suggestive of inspiration from outside the encapsulated sphere of the opening) and a more tentative, questioning, and palpably humane response (the articulated gesture's hesitancy) to a serious conflict (V^7 to iv^6 suggesting a reversed Phrygian half cadence, with its fateful connotations). I would go further in suggesting that in his late sonatas Schubert is plumbing the depths of existentially profound questions, experienced by a subject whose agency the listener may readily grasp. Although we should not label this subject or agent as Schubert himself, we can nonetheless hear a fictive protagonist undergoing an epic inner or outer struggle with respect to an indeterminate situation at the heart of the discourse. Nor can we label the precise referents of the drama; music is not determinate in that sense. But situational precision is irrelevant to our sense of the significance of the music; we can readily imagine a suitable scenario or do without such specificity. What matters is the precision of the work's affective meaning—and that meaning can be "too definite" for words, as Mendelssohn would soon claim.[4]

Schubert works out the consequences of his articulated gesture in the exposition, skillfully combining the two opposing gestures (mm. 1 and 8) into a larger, three-note gesture created by their overlap. This three-note gesture is the basis for a lengthy "predevelopment" section (mm. 82–115) inserted between statements of the second theme in the exposition. Having exhausted the traditional developmental *fugato* here, Schubert must find an alternative compositional strategy for his actual development section, and his solution is stunning: a musette-like theme in the high register that features oscillation between C major and B major, a descent to a rustic dance in C minor and A minor, and a long dominant prolongation. This topically motivated and tonally static development section captures, especially in its opening oscillations, the character of Romantic reflection, in opposition to the willful energies of the earlier *fugato*.

The first movement's primary gestures contribute to subsequent movements as well. Schubert draws on the articulatory character of the second motive, in the metric setting of the first, for both the accompanimental figure at the beginning of the Andantino second movement (Example 8.4a) and the declamatory melody at the beginning of the fourth movement finale, marked Rondo: Allegretto (Example 8.4b).[5]

One of the few performances I have heard in which the articulatory character of these gestures was consistently projected was by Malcolm Bilson, in a live fortepiano recital.[6] Most recorded performances either blur these distinctions or observe them so inconsistently as to negate any sense of developing variation in the gestural motive. This unfortunate tendency may be the result of several factors. One is the bias of Romantic School piano playing, which emphasizes thick, *legato* melodic lines and continuous pedaling. Such homogenized playing reflects a lack of awareness of the subtleties of articulation in the Viennese Classical tradition. Although the modern piano may not offer the same absolute dynamic or timbral values as the fortepiano, it nevertheless can emulate the articulatory aspect of Schubert's gesture with relative success. Another reason some performers miss the gestural discourse of a movement, even after adjusting for the modern piano, is their bias for pitch-oriented motivic development. This bias factors out articulations as mere surface detail—expressive, to be sure, but lacking in structural significance and thus left to the performer's spontaneous discretion. It is no wonder that the resulting performance fails to project the progressive evolution of thematic gestures.

Another thematic element in Schubert's sonata, again traceable to Beethoven's influence, involves the overtone resonance of the instrument, which is, relatively speaking, quite prominent in the fortepiano.[7] The peculiar technique implied by Schubert's notation involves a more forceful accent and release of one or more bass notes beneath a sustained chord in the right hand. Overtones from the bass pitch(es) are thereby reinforced by sympathetic vibration with the undamped strings in the treble, creating an eerie enhancement of sound all the more remarkable in an instrument characterized by sonic decay. Examples may be found in all four movements of the Schubert sonata, though in varying degrees of approximation (Example 8.5). In what sense might one consider this instrumental effect a ges-

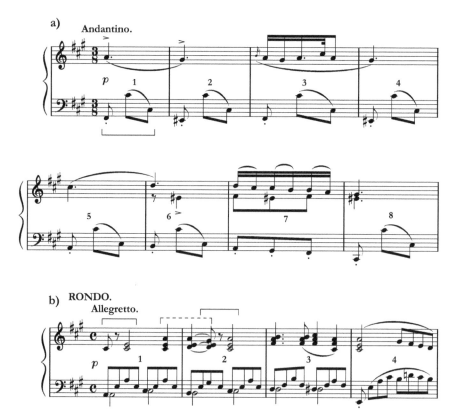

Example 8.4. Variants of the articulatory gesture in later movements of Schubert, D. 959.
a. Second movement.
b. Finale.

ture? Certainly, human gestures are required to create the effect, and these will convey their proper "sentic" significance, as further enhanced by the visual component in live performances. But is virtual human gesture cued in this case? Consider the expressive role of the idea, which is foreshadowed already in the opening theme of the first movement (see Example 8.2a). Here the left hand's "stoic-heroic" gestural motive (shifted to the downbeat) is punctuated such that it enhances the resonance to the right hand's sustained chords. The parallel thirds of the latter strive upward by step until the phrase relaxes into a half cadence in m. 6. In this opening the determined will of a persona is clearly implied and gesturally projected. But when the theme returns in the coda (Example 8.5a), up an octave, *pianissimo*, with the overtone effect more clearly pronounced, then the theme (though still requiring accurate gestural performance) no longer appears to have the same immediacy of human agency. Instead, it takes on an ethereal character, transcendent in that it sounds from beyond the body, as if suggesting a spectral reminiscence—although it may still reflect the noble, spiritual character of a persona. The reverberation of

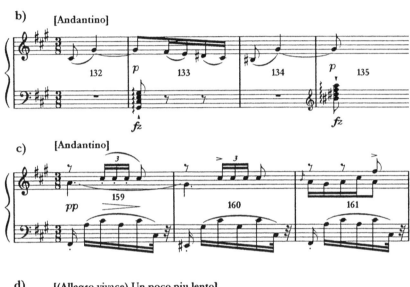

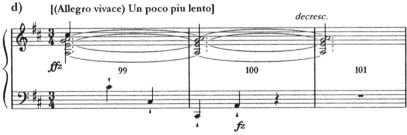

Example 8.5. Examples of thematic use of the overtone effect in Schubert, D. 959.
a. First movement, coda.
b. Second movement, transition to the return of the principal theme.
c. Second movement, return of the principal theme.
d. Third movement, Trio, dominant prolongation before return of the theme.

each chord may capture the "resonance" of a spiritual association, but the heroic, physical component is severely attenuated by the *pianissimo* dynamic, especially when compared to the forceful embodiment of the opening theme.

Composers often represent aspects of the inanimate world, and as Peter Kivy observes (1984: 124–42), musical representation or illustration can project expressive features. But the illustrative features of a passage of musical representation need not always be expressive of a developed persona. In similar fashion I would suggest that musical ideas, while embodied in performance and hence expressive due to the character of any embodied performance, need not always draw their significance from the association between performing body and assumed persona in the work. Compare, on the one hand, Barthes's enjoyment of Schumann's "physicality" (discussed in Chapter 6), and on the other, the gestural character of the Kontarsky brothers' performance of Pierre Boulez's *Structures* for two pianos. The latter is an emergent property of a work conceived in more abstract terms—a work in which every variable (including those associated with expressive performance, such as dynamics or articulation) is strictly controlled by a precompositionally designed series.

For Beethoven and Schubert, gestural developing variation can help generate the structure and motivate the expressive meaning of major works in sonata form. In the next example I will demonstrate how gestural shapes interact with pitch-structural strategies in the creation and working out of the thematic premise for a work. The thematizing of gesture entails expressive identifications with the character of the gesture as physically performed, and these in turn may be mapped with considerable individuality onto an expressive genre, as negotiated within the schema of sonata form.[8]

Performers knowledgeable about historical performance practice (e.g., Bilson) are more likely to project articulations and subtle details that realize characteristic gestures in a way that is stylistically consistent with their implied expressive meaning and ongoing development. Romantically schooled pianists are less likely to adjust to these stylistic constraints, perhaps due to differences in the modern piano, a bias toward unbroken continuity of (melodic) line, and/or a bias toward pitch-generated structural motives. Whereas the movements of the performer will always contribute a qualitative character, and stylistic markedness will account for the relevance of many of the movements contributing to musical meaning (as examined in Chapter 6 with reference to Alexandra Pierce's pedagogy), not all musical gestures need be strategically marked as subjects of musical discourse. But as we have seen, physical movement must be marked to be gestural (Chapters 5 and 6), and musical gestures must be marked thematically to contribute their embodied meanings to an ongoing musical discourse (Chapters 7, 8, and 9).

A strategically marked or thematic gesture is not merely an abstract or sublimated motive subject to developmental logic.[9] Its individual affective character is focal to our primary level of attending, and its expressive structure (as premise) may directly influence the kinds of treatment it receives, as part of an expressively conceived musical discourse, culminating in one of several expressive genres. Thematic gestures also reveal the embodied physical energies, dynamic motivations, and affective stances of the (implied) agents that listeners typically infer in Classical or Romantic works, an issue to which I will return in Chapter 10.

Developing Thematic Gesture in Schubert's Piano Sonata in A Minor, D. 784

Schubert composed the A minor sonata, D. 784, in 1823, perhaps in response to a foreboding of death from having contracted syphilis. The last five years (1823–28) of Schubert's short life were in any case marked by a turn toward serious composition of major works in the genres of piano sonata, string quartet, symphony, and song cycle; and many of these works plumb the depths of the tragic. The Piano Sonata in A Minor, D. 784, is a remarkable example of Schubert's use of gesture to pursue an at times obsessively tragic scenario throughout a three-movement work. Its allusion to perpetual motion in the rondo theme of the finale (as in the rondo-finale of his four-movement Piano Sonata in A Minor, D. 845, of 1825) may have been inspired by Mozart's thoroughgoing perpetual-motion finale in his own tragic Piano Sonata in A Minor, K. 310.

Schubert achieves another kind of obsessiveness in the first movement of D. 784 through the ostinato-like reiterations of a particular gestural configuration (see Example 8.6). The character of this gesture, which first appears in mm. 2 and 4, is given topical specificity beginning in m. 9 as part of the minor-mode, iv–i progression characteristic of a funeral march. The gesture involves a held downbeat and accented half note slurred to an abrupt release on an upbeat eighth note[10] and typically involves a downward melodic drop. In m. 9 the first event is a low-register, closely spaced triad, and the second is a single note. As a heuristic guide to interpretation, a pianist can kinesthetically explore the sense of heaviness in the accented chord and the almost "shrugged off" quality of the transferred release onto the single pitch. Through the immediacy of intermodality, a listener can also access the affective quality of the gesture: heaviness of grief that is not expelled by force (as in the emotion of disgust), but "sighed off," only to return with an insistence that suggests its implacability. "A weight that is too heavy to bear and must be constantly shrugged off with a sigh" is but one attempt to capture in words what is a much more palpably immediate sense that can guide the pianist to an effective dynamic shading and articulatory timing of that gesture. Of course, the precise performance cannot be prescribed, since various mixtures of dynamics, voicing, timing, and articulation may achieve comparable gestural effects. With a clear expressive sense in mind, acquired both heuristically from the notated gesture and topically from the associations of the funeral march, the performer will be led to reject and refine various less adequate physical realizations. Certainly, maintaining the continuity of a single physical gesture would appear to be crucial to a proper realization of the motive's expressive sense. For example, the performer might try sinking deeply into the chord and transferring part of that weight into the smoothly sequenced release of the chord to a single pitch, rather than employing two motorically disjunct attacks.

Example 8.6. Schubert, Piano Sonata in A Minor, D. 784, first movement, exposition. (*Continued on the next page.*)

This physically conceived (indexical, even iconic), gestural motive is part of a higher-level (symbolic) design involving developing variation. Certain pitch configurations also play a significant role in conjunction with the articulated gesture. The first appearances of the abruptly released gesture occur with the striking D♯–E, ♯$\hat{4}$–$\hat{5}$, in m. 2 (the D♯ is treated as a Classical thematic dissonance), and with the drop of a third, C–A, in m. 4 (the descending third plays a thematic role in transitions and prefigures important tonal key relationships as well).

The two seeds of the thematic gesture—accented (or "weighted") beginning and

Example 8.6. *Continued*

a)

Un poco più moto
Stg.
tutti

pp   1   cresc.   2   *fz* ⎯⎯ *p*   3

Example 8.7. Schubert, *Fierrabras*, two excerpts from the finale of act 1.
a. Opening of Fierrabras's recitative and aria (scene 9).

abrupt release—are themselves detachable motives that support a consistent approach to the texture, lending the movement (and the work) a coherent expressive
character throughout. For example, after the *tutti*-like (*forte*) counterstatement of
the opening two-bar motive we hear a series of parallel $^6_3$ chords in dotted rhythm
(Example 8.6, mm. 27–29). This passage alludes to a martial style (suggesting determined energy), and the parallel $^6_3$ chords thicken a single line. When the passage
ends on a metrically weak eighth note, the entire outburst not only sounds parenthetical, but as though it were a "filled-in" response to the opening motive, prolonging the gesture to a similarly abrupt release.

Intertextually, evidence for the expressive purport of both ideas may be drawn
from Schubert's opera *Fierrabras*, which dates from 1823, the same year as the sonata (see Example 8.7). In the finale of act 1 the Moorish noble Fierrabras is in a
state of torment; he loves Emma but tries to suppress that love, since he recognizes
that she loves the Christian knight Eginhard. He will later accept an unjust accu-
sation of having attempted to seduce Emma, to provide an alibi for Eginhard.
Schubert may well have identified with the "outsider" Fierrabras's self-sacrificing
love and his sad fate as the one unpaired lover at the end of the opera. In any
case Fierrabras's suffering in his solo scene is expressed by a similar dropping gesture to that found in the opening of the sonata (see the two-note motive in Example 8.7a). At the point in the subsequent text where Fierrabras sings of bearing
his sufferings stoically, like a man, we find the descending dotted-rhythmic motive
that here suggests an energetic, controlled-heroic, "pumping up" of one's resistance
(Example 8.7b). In the sonata a similarly heroic outburst is equally frustrated in
the face of an implacably tragic situation.

The second theme in the sonata's first movement (Example 8.6, m. 61) is a study
in contrasts. It features two topics—pastoral (pedal, subdominant emphasis) and
hymn (four-voice chordal texture)—in a serene major mode (to be discussed below). The second theme is motivically related to the opening theme; the intervallic shape of the melody in m. 62 is a diminution and contraction of the opening
two-bar motive. But just as importantly, the second theme draws on the downbeat accent that is associated with the opening gesture, even while oppositionally
attempting to ameliorate its abrupt release and tragic connotations. The compromise articulation achieved here is not a fully sustained one; instead of *legato*,

Example 8.7. Schubert, *Fierrabras,* two excerpts from the finale of act 1.
b. Climactic section of Fierrabras's aria.

the important *portato* (slur over dots) notation hints at the potential for a more abrupt release, which indeed occurs when the second theme begins to break up into registrally disjunct echoes of the sudden-release gesture (mm. 76, 78). These changes anticipate the horrifying, *fortissimo* intrusions in minor by the tragic gesture (mm. 79, 83); it has now fully infected the initial, repeated-chord serenity of the second theme with the fateful heaviness and abruptness of its manifestation in

m. 9. The initial juxtaposition in the second theme of a pastoral, hymnlike *topic* with a grief-laden *gesture* suggests a *tropological* effect of meaning that I would interpret as one of undermined hope. The emotional effect is extremely poignant when this serene, E major hymn is understood as being too fragile to endure, as if it were unsuccessfully trying to cover up or repress the grieving gesture it presumes to displace.

Having suggested how interpretations of gesture, topic, and trope can be integrated, I turn to their interaction with tonal structure, first by examining expressive motivations for unusual tonal design in the exposition of this sonata. The counterstatement of the main theme (Example 8.6, m. 26 ff.) begins to lead transitionally away from the tonic, but in the wrong direction (m. 30 ff.). The funereal march emphasizes plagal harmonic motion; its grief-laden expressive character appears to motivate analogous tonal motion into the darker and less-energetic subdominant region—from A minor to the key of D minor, with its own minor subdominant chord, G minor.

Although mm. 42–46 imply a turn back to A minor, the *subito pianissimo* in m. 47 marks an unexpected (and nonsyntactic) shift of the descending-third gesture down a whole step to B♭–G, recalling the earlier subdominant of the subdominant. From this dark impasse of an emotionally failed transition, we are suddenly thrust up a half step with a *forte* tremolo and *fortissimo* fanfare in E major. The expressive purport of this tonal reversal is signaled by the use of a fanfare topic, suggesting the heroic, and strong dynamic gestures, implying a self-willed projection of force. But note the persistence of the grieving gesture in mm. 53–54, which is repressed by an even more forceful diminution in mm. 57–58. When the energy of the fanfare subsides into cadential whole notes, the second theme appears as a serene, hymnlike expression of tender joy.

Stylistically we might have expected the minor dominant at this point, as substitute for the relative major. Beethoven in his tragic piano sonata movements often uses the minor dominant for his second theme—for example, the first and third movements of the *Tempest,* Op. 31, no. 2, and the last movement of the *Appassionata,* Op. 57. The major dominant is not coherent in a Classically conceived sonata form; thus, we are led to interpret its use here as associational and dramatically oppositional. As a mutation of the minor dominant, E major is an explicit reversal of the tragic obsessiveness that would have persisted had the minor dominant been selected.[11] Schubert's reversal of mode, and the dramatic reversals by which the surprising key is motivated, provide a lesson in the importance of expressive motivations for unusual tonal forms—and the style growth or change that they foster.

Compare the transition in the recapitulation (Example 8.8).[12] The shift from E♭ to E♮ in m. 216 happens without the sudden infusion of heroic energy. Instead, Schubert enharmonically reinterprets E♭ as D♯ (perhaps recalling the D♯ of m. 2), as part of a German augmented-sixth chord (m. 215), and resolves it to an arrival/cadential $^6_4$ in A major (m. 216). This mystical transformation from depressed, falling thirds in minor to a glowing, positive major mode is more miraculous than willed, more transcendent than heroic. Dynamically the transformation never breaks the soft surface, since the noisy fanfare is deleted. Note that the changes to the tran-

Example 8.8. Schubert, D. 784, first movement, recapitulation, transition, and return of the second theme.

sition are not motivated by a need to stay in the tonic key. Schubert had already rewritten the earlier part of the transition to keep it down a fifth, and the E♭–C depressed third could easily have been reversed by a heroic E–C♯ outburst, exactly parallel to the exposition. Instead, the compressed transition creates a dramatic foil to the exposition's sudden reversal. The transformation is not achieved through heroic effort of the will (as suggested by a blustery fanfare), but by something that transcends effort: spiritually, an unexpected moment of grace; or mentally, a sudden illumination; or emotionally, a melting change of heart—but in any case a seemingly unearned and sudden transformation into a more positive state.[13]

When the second theme appears, resolved to the tonic major, a new rhythm is also introduced (see Example 8.8, m. 218). The triplets are gesturally motivated, as appears clear from both their late appearance and a complementary textural detail: the opening chord features a doubled third in the right hand. This unbalancing of the norm is used by Beethoven in major-key contexts to enhance the contrastive serenity and sweetness of major (Hatten 1994: 50–54). The triplet quarter notes in turn subdivide the initial half note of each measure, deflecting the power of the underlying tragic gesture by fractioning the direct force of its initial accents. By this "reverberant" gestural strategy, Schubert suggests that the implacable, fateful character of the gesture is somewhat absorbed or mollified by a more resilient version of the second theme. Even the *fortissimo* interjections cannot sustain quite the same degree of disruptiveness, suggesting that gestural amelioration contributes to "expressive resolution" in this passage, a strategic innovation that goes beyond conventional (stylistic) tonal resolution.

The coda to the movement (Example 8.9, m. 259 ff.) combines both heroic and transcendent outcomes to fulfill the expressive or dramatic genre of the movement. First, the transitional thirds, again on E♭–C, are subject to augmentation within a dark, diminished-seventh chord (mm. 259–62), and the subsequent acceleration gives the effect of double diminution (mm. 263–66)—a considerable heightening of negative energy that enhances the sense of heroic reversal to triumphant fanfares in A major (mm. 267–70). What was missing in the recapitulation is thus restored in the coda—a familiar compensatory strategy in sonata forms since Haydn.

At this point a third appearance of the second theme is only hinted, in the closural cadence pairs in mm. 277–84. These chords echo the gesture in contrasting extreme registers, absorbing it within a tonic pedal that recalls the transcendent serenity of the second theme as it appeared in the recapitulation. Only the sudden *fortissimo* interruption—a double-augmentation of the descending third—in mm. 285–88 serves notice that these triumphant and transcendent achievements may be short-lived.

The second movement (see Example 8.10a) begins auspiciously in F major. This key was utilized several times in the development of the first movement, most tellingly for the integrative version of the second theme. The half-note accompanimental harmonies in the opening of the second movement (mm. 1–2) are released halfway through each bar, leaving the melody vulnerably exposed. And the half-note chords in m. 3 release to an eighth-note tonic in m. 4, hardly a typical durational resolution. Clearly the first movement's tragic gesture is motivating these textural details. But the most compelling evidence for a continuation of the gestural premise of the first movement occurs after the release in m. 4. An uncanny, parenthetical figure is notated *ppp* and *sordini* (muted). These indications would have been realized on the fortepiano through the use of the moderator pedal, and the resultant sound—muted and hair-raising—would provide a haunting depiction of this intrusion of negative agency. The melodic figure, presented in octaves between the hands, is a chromatic turn around the dominant degree, emphasizing with its dotted-rhythmic configuration the $\hat{5}$–$\sharp\hat{4}$–$\hat{5}$ motive from the opening theme of the first movement. Furthermore, the figure releases on an eighth note, preserving the same gestural character as the enigmatic opening to the first movement. This motive takes on a fateful character in the Andante, undercutting the expansive gestures of F major with an otherworldly reminder of something less desirable. The additional chromatic twist provided by the upper chromatic neighbor ($\flat\hat{6}$)

Example 8.9. Schubert, D. 784, first movement, coda.

Example 8.10. Schubert, D. 784, second movement.
a. Opening theme with parenthetical insertions.

lends this motive a serpentine shape that in the *Affektenlehre* of the Baroque was associated with Satan in his iconographic representations as a snake, worm, or serpent. Although one cannot know Schubert's intent in this regard, the thematic association suffices to establish, if not a specifically evil connotation, at least a reminder of the lurking force of the tragic behind the beauty of the surface. I find the motive's appearance analogous to William Blake's image of the worm in the rose, in his memorable poetic line "O rose, thou art sick."

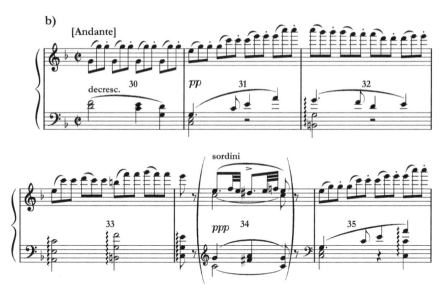

b. Diminutional variation of the opening theme in the dominant.

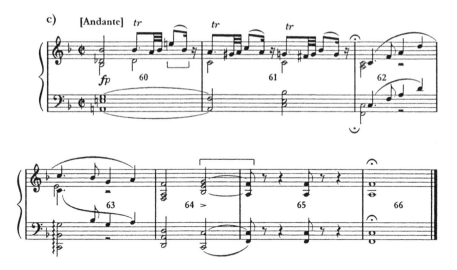

Example 8.10. Schubert, D. 784, second movement.
c. Transition and final return of the opening theme.

A grandiose transition passage is inaugurated by this "serpent" motive's emergence in m. 19, effecting a sequential modulation to the key of D♭ major in m. 21,
down a third from the tonic F major. In the first movement Schubert had moved
to F major in the development, also down a third from the tonic A minor. The
ensuing transitional passage utilizes the deceptive sequence (I–V–vi–iii–IV–I; also
employed in the opening of Op. 109—see Chapter 7) to build to a climax. The

deceptive sequence—with its venerable associations—enhances the heroic grandeur of thicker texture and stronger dynamics, as a powerful antidote to the serpent's venomous interpolations. Schubert also introduces an element of struggle
that climaxes in sequential motion up from G♭ major, through a "crisis" vii^{o7}/V over
a dominant pedal, and ultimate resolution to V of C major. The climactic outburst
of this transition section appears outside the horizon of expectations arising from
the placid opening theme. Its sheer weight suggests that the tragic premise from
the first movement is still being addressed.[14]

Having established the dominant key, Schubert re-presents his opening theme
(Example 8.10b, m. 31 ff.) in an integrated texture similar to the one used for the
integrative treatment of the second theme in the first movement's development section. This texture is characterized by a tenor melody in the left hand, echoed in
diminution by the right hand in a high register. Strikingly the parenthetical "serpent" motive is maintained (mm. 35 and 38) but "ameliorated" tonally, by scale-
degree variation and full harmonization. Instead of $\hat{5}$-#$\hat{4}$-$\hat{5}$, the motive undergoes
scale-degree transposition to $\hat{3}$-#$\hat{2}$-$\hat{3}$, emphasizing the "sweetness" of the major $\hat{3}$
by means of a far less enigmatic, embellishing chromaticism. When E ($\hat{3}$ of C ma-
jor) threatens to become $\hat{5}$ of A minor in mm. 36–37, a dissonant B diminished-
seventh chord over E pulls us back to the realm of C major just in time for the
cadence. Modulatory sequencing on this strategic idea returns us to F major, and
the remainder of the movement is an extended closing section in which the serpent motive plays an increasingly prominent role. Despite having regained F major,
there are further expressive harmonic digressions within the coda. A return to the
opening four bars (Example 8.10c), with its abrupt cadence onto an eighth note
(mm. 64–65), serves to cap a movement that has apparently lost its way. We are left
with a sense of unsatisfied resolution, despite the last-minute absorption of dissonant harmonies.

The finale features a perpetual-motion rondo theme in A minor (Example
8.11a). Imitative treatment alludes to the learned style, with its connotations of
seriousness and authoritativeness, but the close *stretto* and overlapping of hands
also draws us back into the intensity of the first movement's tragic premise. I will
focus on the contrasting theme of the episode, which appears nearly identically
three times, in F major, C major, and A major. Example 8.11b presents the opening
measures of its first appearance. This contrasting theme is extraordinary for the
multiple thematic integrations that enrich its role in the drama in a way analogous
to the role of the first movement's second theme. The melodic opening provides an
allusion to the serpent motive of the middle movement, but as it appeared in its
"ameliorative" setting on scale degree $\hat{3}$. The key and the arpeggiation in the melodic continuation (m. 52) suggest a link with the F major opening theme of the
slow movement as well. The drop of a third and the long-short *legato* linkage in
the next measure (53) recall the first movement's principal motive. The inner pedal
point C may even allude to the pastoral pedal point of the second theme from the
first movement. Finally, the left-hand accompanimental pattern features the now-
familiar abrupt release on an eighth note.[15]

a) Allegro vivace.

a. Perpetual-motion rondo theme in A minor.

b) [Allegro vivace]

b. Episode theme in F major.
Example 8.11. Schubert, D. 784, finale.

The integration of gestural ideas into the *Ländler*-like theme of the episodes carries expressive significance for the overall dramatic trajectory of the work. Beginning with the tragic first movement's serene second theme, each attempt at consolation or relief has been undermined in some way.[16] The entire work, not surprisingly, ends neither triumphantly nor transcendently, but with an implacably fateful climax in A minor. The perpetual-motion rondo theme is sounded *fortis-*

simo in octaves in each hand, overwhelming the listener with what amounts to a tragic peroration. What the lyric theme of the episode attempts to achieve, I believe, is yet another amelioration of the tragic, but the effort is even more vulnerably exposed from the start.

The "serpent" fragment with which the episode begins (Example 8.11b, m. 51) is not only ameliorated in its scale-degree setting on $\hat{3}$ of F, but it softens the chromaticism by use of diatonic neighbors (B♭ and G). A hint of the chromatic upper neighbor occurs in the next measure, where lowered $\hat{6}$ (D♭ in m. 52) is the last note of a rising arpeggiation that falls to C. The gestural drops of a third and a second (mm. 53–54) are marked with articulatory sighs, but they are not abruptly released. Their downward sighs expressively complement the upward arpeggiation to the poignant ♭$\hat{6}$. Despite these thematic echoes, the key to the vulnerability of the passage is the repeated gesture of the accompaniment, with its detached measure units broken off on the fifth eighth. When the ear detects a motivic echo of the melodic line in the third and fifth eighths of the accompaniment in mm. 52–53, then the abrupt releases in the left hand begin to inflect the melody's *empfindsamer* sighs with an even greater gestural association to the tragic opening motive of the first movement. To experience the fragile episode theme's attempt to reconcile the tragic while lacking full support from the accompaniment is to experience an even greater expressive effect than would be gained by the direct representation of a stylistic gestural type correlated with grief. Our reaction to the pathos of a theme that cannot achieve what it attempts is a more complex and deeper kind of tragedy than that created merely by playing a theme in minor. It is this heartrending vision of the desired within the context of the impossible that makes the episodes so dramatically effective.

I have demonstrated that it is only by combining gestural evidence with traditional motivic, tonal, harmonic, melodic, and rhythmic analysis—all within the context of a dramatic trajectory that expressively motivates the developing variation of ideas, topics, and textures across the entire work—that we can begin to interpret the richness of Schubert's compelling late style. The ongoing developing variation of a gesturally inspired motive involves negotiation with the more symbolic, stylistically coded elements of a style, even as it helps support their strategic manipulation in a unique work.

9 Thematic Gesture in Beethoven: The Sonata for Piano and Cello in C Major, Op. 102, no. 1

Beethoven's Sonata for Piano and Cello in C Major, composed in 1815, opens a window onto the ways that gesture will inform his later style. As in the first movement of Op. 90, thematic gestures are subject to developing variation. And as in Schubert's Piano Sonata in A Minor, D. 784, the evolution of thematic gesture coordinates the expressive trajectory of a work in contrasting movements.

The opening Andante in C major unfolds in pastoral serenity, its freely varied treatment of the theme leading to a plenitude of textural fulfillment. After a brief cadenza, the close to tonic is not allowed to fade into silence before an Allegro vivace in A minor intrudes. This serious sonata-form movement is in dialectical opposition to the improvisatory opening Andante with which it is paired. It is followed by yet another improvisatory movement, this time an Adagio in C major that reveals its transitional function when the opening of the first movement suddenly appears, as a visionary quotation, and a transcendent dominant preparation is topically disrupted by the unexpected comic finale, still in C major. Throughout, gesture motivates the musical discourse, and the implied four-movement cycle fully resolves its gestural issues only in the final measures.

Op. 102, no. 1, was composed a year before the Piano Sonata in A Major, Op. 101, with which it shares numerous formal and expressive innovations. Both sonatas feature an opening movement in a moderate $\frac{6}{8}$ meter and a weightier second movement in an unexpected key. The piano sonata moves from a highly concentrated and lyrical sonata-allegro in A major to a dramatic march in F major, whereas the cello sonata suspends its first movement with an expanded fermata on V^7 of C major, but resolves to tonic (unlike a typical slow introduction) before a disruptive *attacca* in A minor launches the Allegro vivace second movement. Both sonatas feature the cyclic return of the opening theme before the last movement, as part of a strategy in which a potential slow movement transforms into a poetic transition to the finale.

There are important differences as well. The cello sonata features a sonata-allegro form as its second movement, as opposed to the first movement of the piano sonata, and whereas the overall cycle of the piano sonata projects toward a weighty finale with an extensive *fugato* in the development, the comic finale of the cello sonata is a deflatingly ironic *expressive doubling* (L. Kramer 1990: 21–71; see also Chapter 2 of the present book) of the tragic second movement in A minor. But this comic finale has sufficient energy and weight to achieve an expressive resolution for the cycle as a whole.

Perhaps it is not surprising that Beethoven first worked out this unusual cyclical scheme in a cello sonata, since he virtually invented the genre. Both the early Op. 5 cello sonatas have large slow introductions and forgo a slow movement proper. The Op. 69 cello sonata has a scherzo-trio-scherzo-trio-scherzo middle movement, and a potential slow movement, Adagio cantabile, that loses interest in its theme before the cello has finished its turn, evolving, as in Op. 102, no. 1, into a transition to the finale. Only with the fifth and final cello sonata, Op. 102, no. 2 in D major, do we find a full-fledged slow movement, in D minor. Its second theme has a turn figure that is remarkably close to the one in the truncated slow movement of Op. 101 (see Example 10.1d, mm. 11–12). Both sonatas treat the motive imitatively. The D major cello sonata also ends with a full-fledged fugue, anticipating the extensive fugal development section in the finale of Op. 101.

In the C major cello sonata, gestural motives are generative, and they evolve across the whole sonata cycle. The source for these ideas is the opening of the Andante. The cello begins with a two-bar phrase (Example 9.1a, mm. 1–2). Topically there is a hint of the pastoral in the simplicity of major, diatonic, stepwise motion in $^6_8$. Intertextually the theme shares the pastoral character of the opening theme of Beethoven's Sixth Symphony (Example 9.1b). Each theme features a poetic articulation that gently undercuts the intensity of the melodic apex. Such undercuttings are quintessentially pastoral (see Chapter 3 and Hatten 1994: 92). The two themes differ in that the symphony's motto suggests a more dancelike provenance,[1] whereas the cello sonata's motto is more reflective.

Inspection of the opening motive (Example 9.1a) reveals a wistful descent from tonic to dominant, followed by renewed energy leading to a marked gestural configuration. Notice how the cello's articulation provides a release on the repeated G's in m. 2; this is another instance of the "lift" gesture described earlier in Bach, Gluck, and Beethoven (Examples 7.14–16). It is as though the energy of the scalar ascent had momentarily lifted into weightlessness before subsiding. In performance this articulation should be foregrounded, but not at the expense of the background flow of the meter. The metric flow, or "wave" (Zuckerkandl 1956: 168), is also significant expressively, as Alexandra Pierce also reminds us (Pierce 1994). One senses the embodied energy it takes to move within the virtual gravitational field of meter (Chapter 6). We experience the sense of weightlessness at the top of an energy curve, as well as the relapse into gravity at the close of this gesture. In an ideal performance of this opening theme, then, the relaxed descent in m. 1 from $\hat{1}$ down to $\hat{5}$ is reversed by the energy required to ascend in scalar fashion from $\hat{5}$ back to $\hat{1}$ and beyond to $\hat{3}$. "Stepping back" from $\hat{3}$ to $\hat{1}$ coils the energy to spring forward from $\hat{1}$ to $\hat{5}$. The melody then releases lightly on the higher G and floats across the gap until "caught" by the declining three-note gesture. As embodied movement, the melody has immediate expressive character and an elementary dramatic shape. We can interpret it even if we have never experienced this particular, spontaneous token of the gestural type. Most of us have experienced the physical sensation of a wave near the shoreline swelling underneath our body, lifting it for a moment of

Example 9.1. Comparison of Beethoven opening themes with lift gesture.
a. Sonata for Piano and Cello in C Major, Op. 102, first movement.
b. Symphony No. 6, Op. 68, first movement (first violin only).

exhilarating weightlessness, and then bringing us down more quickly to rest. There is pleasure in such an experience, but Beethoven is offering us more than a *bodily arabesque*, to extend Hanslick's (1974 [1854]) visual image to choreography. Much of the meaning we experience in our first encounter with a melodic shape relates to its modality of action, which traces the shape of a lived experience as we *move through* the tones.

As the opening theme's most characteristic motive, the lift gesture is soon echoed by the piano's left hand (m. 3^2), but not before the right hand enters with an echo of the subsiding notes of the theme (m. 3^1). The *ars combinatoria* or mosaic character of this unfolding motivic discourse is striking. The detachable motives, characteristic of Classical developmental procedures (Rosen 1972), are also engaged in dialogue. Before exploring the other fragments, consider how the gestural "lift" motive is extracted and subject to development. First, it is marked thematically by reiteration and isolation, and the leap is reinterpreted from a perfect fifth to a questioning diminished fifth (mm. 4^2–5^1), and then to a yearning seventh that is frozen at the very point of release—suggesting a sense of longing that is sustained before subsiding (m. 5^2). The "suspension" of this exquisite moment recalls Bach's use of ties to sustain the lilting release of his *siciliano* gesture in the Sinfonia in G Minor (Example 7.15). A final, spectacular variant of the gesture occurs in the piano (Example 9.2, m. 24). Note that elements of the contour are preserved, although chromatically compressed: the sixteenths are now atomized into trills, and the repeated G has migrated to the bass. Note also that the fermata features the dominant seventh's expanded interval of a seventh, extravagantly filled in when compared with m. 5^2.

The movement resolves the dominant seventh to tonic, but in a way that does not satisfactorily resolves the enigma of the "lift" motive or the tonal tensions it implies when suspended over the dominant. Also, the theme has been somewhat submerged by the progressive saturation of doublings, pedals, and counterlines. The ensuing state of *plenitude* may be understood as an expressive motivation for the variation-like treatment of this theme (recall the Andante movement from Op. 130, interpreted in Chapter 2). The C major shimmer of tonic (end of m. 24 through m. 27) provides syntactic tonal resolution of the V^7; however, the lingering, and questioning, melodic third will be taken up with a certain repressed vehemence in the Allegro vivace (Example 9.2, m. 31). The *attacca* into the Allegro vivace (and, significantly, the absence of double barring between the two sections) suggests that the relationship between Andante and Allegro is indeed a close one. The Allegro vivace not only shifts abruptly to A minor, but its energetic initial motive (mm. 28–32) reverses the opening Andante's contour; it ascends in scalar fashion from tonic to dominant before marching down to the subdominant and ending in open suspense on the dominant.

The gesturally oppositional second half of the theme (Example 9.2, mm. 32–35), though soft at first, features quick releases—flickers of energy that expend themselves without resolution, maintaining intensity across the vast gestural range of the theme. Gesturally these releases are not on $\hat{5}$ until m. 35, and their "lift" is rather a frustrated "shrugging off" of a tragic heroic energy that cannot seem to progress beyond $\hat{5}$. The collapse down to m. 31 engenders a negative climax on the rising third foreshadowed at the end of the Andante.[2] As the double neighbor to the dominant pedal which follows, this motive suggests something implacably fateful, with its stylistic lowered $\hat{6}$ to $\hat{5}$ highlighting of the tragic. The motive that emerges above the pedal $\hat{5}$ is also a variant of the double neighbor, but it marks its relationship to the Andante's lift gesture by doubling its energy, with dual releases and imitative treatment. These flickers of energy, however, cannot escape the pressure of the fateful E pedal, and even the counterstatement of the theme ends questioningly with a descending tritone, shifting to G for a contrasting transitional theme.

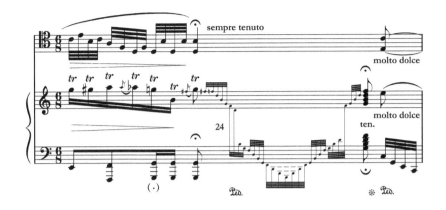

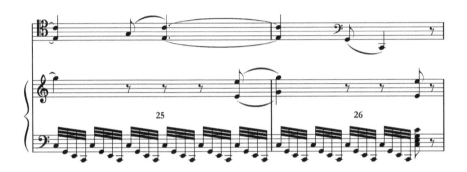

Example 9.2. Beethoven, Op. 102. End of Andante and beginning of Allegro vivace (*attacca*) in A minor. (*Continued on the next page.*)

Example 9.2. *Continued*

The transition begins with a more lyrical fragment in the cello (Example 9.3a, m. 40), derived from the last half measure of the Andante's two-bar theme.[3] There its subsiding gestural quality could be interpreted as gently resignational; here the resignational character is enhanced by harmonization through the "yielding" V_2^4 to I^6 (Hatten 1994: 57–58). This fragment cannot properly close; instead, it overlaps with a variant of the filled-in fourth with which the work began, but in the rhythm of its inversion (m. 41, right hand of the piano; compare m. 1). Together with the gestural derivation from the first movement's theme, there is clear evidence for expressive doubling in the quick repression of this pastoral oasis. It gives way to tragic sequencing in E minor, where frustrated releases become vehement outbursts in the development of the subsiding gesture. The repressed, low minor third is further exacerbated here as a diminished third (mm. 50–52), and the exposition becomes increasingly dissonant with a contained but obsessive fury. Only two brief moments suggest attempts at positive transcendence. In m. 61 (Example 9.3b) A♯ is enharmonically reinterpreted as B♭, and the arpeggiation in the bass outlines V^7 of F major (the Neapolitan of E minor), which might have offered at least an illusory

Example 9.3. Beethoven, Op. 102, Allegro vivace.
a. Transitional theme in G major.
b. Tonal reversals in the transition to E minor.

surcease of tension (recall Beethoven's use of Neapolitan expansion in his codas, discussed in Chapter 7). At the last minute, however, the chord is reinterpreted as a German augmented sixth (in diminished third position), resolving in m. 64 to an arrival $^6_4$ in E major, with the raised third in the cello. This hint of transcendence is palpable, even though the chord is quickly interpreted as V/iv, pulling us back to the more tragic field (compare the similar passage in m. 53, where the G♯ is delayed until the second beat, avoiding any hint of major arrival $^6_4$ and functioning solely as vii°$^6_5$ of iv). Beethoven tries again, with an even more transcendent arrival $^6_4$ in positive G major on the downbeat of m. 65. Note that this downbeat $^6_4$ is preceded by the dominant seventh, and thus its sense of arrival above a reiterated dominant in the bass is palpable. But the continuation is a chromatically heightened deceptive move, vii°^{7}/vi to vi (again, compare the similar passage in m. 54, where a tied D across the bar line undermines the effect of an arrival $^6_4$ on G). This deceptive undercutting of potential transcendence in G major wrenches us back into E minor for the closing theme.

What is spectacular about the tonal progression in mm. 63–65 is the number of rhetorical reversals that Beethoven achieves in such a small space. The highly concentrated harmonic language creates a sense of slippage as two brief visions of transcendence are immediately undercut. Unlike the consoling episodes in the Schubert Piano Sonata in A minor, D. 784, discussed in the previous chapter, these brief windows barely have time to register. What emerges from the obsessive *ostinati* (as in mm. 60–61) is a wrenching back and forth between potential relief and relentless tragedy—again, a more effective dramatic heightening than would be achieved by a straightforward use of the minor mode. The interruptive closing theme, derived from the octaves and the abrupt character of the opening theme, is an appropriate capping of this rhetorical struggle.

Despite moments of mystical transformation in the development (m. 90 ff.) and the coda (m. 146 ff.) the movement ends tragically. The pastoral opening Andante and the tragic Allegro vivace thus form a dialectical pair of movements marked by oppositional use of related thematic gestures, as well as by contrasts in topic, tempo, meter, and mode.

The Adagio, returning to C major, picks up the mystical thread suggested in the previous coda and weds it to the pastoral. This movement features the resignational three-note drop that closed the Andante's opening theme (bracketed in Example 9.4a, m. 1). Sixty-fourth-note gestures serve to fill the gap between G's in a reference to the Andante's cadenza-like close. The tragic aftermath of the Allegro vivace also infects the continuation here (mm. 3–6) with rhetorical diminished sevenths and *sforzandos* that recall the half-repressed frustrations of the A minor movement. When the music clears to C major in m. 7 (Example 9.4b), it is clear that the pastoral will prevail in this fantasia-like movement. The resignational three-note subsiding gesture appears several times in echoing statements of a closing theme (m. 7^4 in the cello; m. 8^4 in the right hand of the piano). Beethoven seals the pastoral contract, however, with a return of the Andante theme (Example 9.4c), transcendently appearing in the piano's higher register (mm. 10–11). The quota-

a)

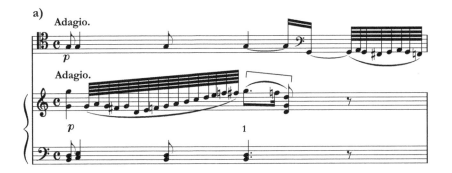

b)

c)

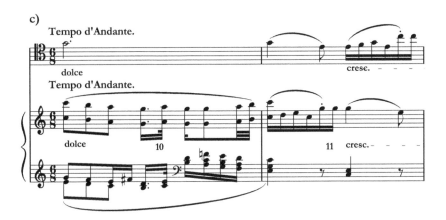

Example 9.4. Beethoven, Op. 102, Adagio.
a. Opening theme with falling gesture.
b. Closing theme with falling gesture.
c. Quotation of the opening theme from the Andante (varied).

tion is enriched by textural plenitude: the parallel $^6_3$ doubling recalls m. 17 of the Andante, and the rhythmic embellishment suggests impending action. Subsequent diminution and imitation in three parts add further textural saturation.

As in the finale of the Piano Sonata in A Major, Op. 101, the cyclical quotation of the opening pastoral theme provides a dramatic transition from an incomplete slow movement to a culminating finale, here in C major. The second Allegro vivace might also be understood as an expressive doubling of the earlier Allegro vivace in A minor, and it achieves a definitive closure in terms of gestural resolution, despite its surprising shift to the high comedy of wit and irony.

When the Andante theme returns as a quotation, it is still in search of gestural and tonal resolution. The beginning of the finale (Example 9.5a) provides immediate tonal resolution from $\hat{5}$ to $\hat{1}$, utilizing a *spontaneous* motivic gesture derived from the Andante theme's second beat.[4] But the tonal resolution is ironically deflated—the tonic is flippantly released on a weak beat. As witty as the finale's opening theme may be in addressing the issue of tonal resolution, Beethoven has left the gesture sufficiently open in other dimensions to provoke a series of playful variations on the problem of definitive closure. The first clue that the composer is taking the witty gesture seriously (*thematically*) is when the cello *dialogically* picks up the C and sustains it after the piano has released it—as if to say, "No, wait, there is a train of thought, even here." If the Andante's "lift" gesture motivated this more dynamic release, then the subsiding motive is replaced here by a more dynamic "catch" by the cello. This marked gestural fragment is expanded to a full theme by varied reiteration as the cello and piano reverse roles and then proceed in sequence, creating a full-length phrase. A series of contrasts and sudden dynamic changes serve to inject drama while preserving the disjunctive character of the motive. Even when the cello begins continuous sixteenths in earnest, the piano accompanies with a comically augmented version of the motive, filling from C down to G and back, and mirroring the disguised motive in the cello (Example 9.5b, mm. 39–41). For the first time we hear potential metric closure, since augmentation delivers the tonic on the downbeat in m. 41, but the phrase does not stop there. Cello and piano join forces in mirroring the motive, shifted dangerously to A minor at the end of m. 42 in a tonal echo of the first Allegro vivace. The obsessiveness of the perpetual sixteenths may recall the earlier movement, but here the madcap frenzy leads quickly to G major for a remarkably dislocating cadence (m. 73).

The abrupt *rhetorical* gesture of this (texturally disruptive) tonic close is enhanced by a dramatic pause, which allows the cello to embark on what seems like a completely different train of thought: the world of the pastoral emerges with the cello's drone fifth (on E♭), and the piano acts as an irritant by *rhetorical* disruption with the motive (Example 9.6). Instead of a releasing gesture, however, Beethoven dramatically accents the point of arrival (although not on a metric downbeat). The cello can only echo the gesture at first, as if failing to enter on time (m. 79)—a comic use of *dialogical* gesture that also achieves a *troping* of pastoral and *buffa* topics. Rhetorical silences isolate sequential reiteration down by thirds, as a search for an appropriate tonal level emerges from this playfully grotesque troping of pastoral and comic elements.[5]

Example 9.5. Beethoven, Op. 102, finale.
a. Opening theme and rhetorical undercuttings.

On the third try, the piano launches a more lyrical and imitative (more fully *dialogical*) version of the gesture, this time sustaining the goal tone in a legato sequence; Beethoven expressly writes *tenuto* over the fourth note of the motive (m. 91). A new trope also emerges from the fusion of singing and learned styles. Inevitably tension begins to mount, and the motive is truncated to three notes in juxtaposed sequences, leading to a climax. Having first accented and then length-b)

Example 9.5. Beethoven, Op. 102, finale.
b. Augmentation (and inversion) of the thematic gesture.

ened the goal tone, Beethoven now eliminates it altogether, and the remaining three notes (m. 104 ff.) sound abruptly "cut off" (recall the discussion of choked-off gestures in Chapter 7, and the abrupt releases in Schubert's D. 784, in Chapter 8). The development has pulled us from timeless pastoral, through comic interruption, to lyric and learned intensification, and finally back to the comic for the reprise. Although one might analyze the foregoing gestural variants in strictly formal motivic terms, I would counter that the primary motivation for this section is the expressive development of a *thematic* gesture.

The recapitulation undercuts the effect of the restored motivic gesture by overlapping echo imitations in its full thematic setting. This *stretto* continues the textural plenitude that guided the development, and the return reverberates with similar gestural play. The coda brings back the drone fifths and descending-third sequence of the opening of the development, but this time the piano shifts *rhetorically* into the Neapolitan for a dreamy, transcendent treatment of the imitative portion. After returning to C major, the original motive reappears, but with variation of texture: cello and piano are in unison. This unison serves to resolve their *dialogical* competition, and the piano enhances the effect by enlarging the registral compass to four simultaneous octaves (Example 9.7, mm. 237–38 and 241–42). Note that two last echoes of the gesture in augmentation enable it to resolve on a metric downbeat (mm. 243–46), this time cadentially. As the gesture counterpoints the closing melodic descent in mirror inversion, we hear stepwise closure from $\hat{5}$ to $\hat{1}$ in both directions. The final rush to the finish also brings back the "subsiding" motive (introduced by the Andante in m. 2^2), employed here as an integrative riposte. It resolves to C major for the first time in the entire cycle, and on a downbeat as well (mm. 247–48).[6]

Thus, Beethoven convincingly realizes gestural implications that have spanned an entire multimovement work—one whose strategies of unfolding have been motivated by the potential of a gesturally conceived theme. The articulation of this

Example 9.6. Beethoven, Op. 102, finale. Abrupt cadence ending the exposition and rhetorical shift to the development section. (*Continued on the next page.*)

Example 9.6. *Continued*

thematic gesture is no longer a mere accessory to performance, but is instead a crucial premise that shapes the musical discourse. With thematized gesture, then, we discover a potential *Grundgestalt* that cannot be reduced to pitches alone—an *Idee* that synthesizes pitch structure, pitch contour, rhythmic structure, metric placement, articulation, dynamics, timing, and all the subtle variables of performance that so often elude notation. And we find that the developing variation of that gesture is in turn motivated by its salient features—the premise of an articu-

Example 9.7. Beethoven, Op. 102, finale, closing peroration.

lated "lift" in the Andante becomes the premise of unsatisfactory closure in the finale.

An effective performance must balance the foregrounded thematic gestures with the background gestural flow and continuity of patterned regularities: meter, hyper-meter, grouping patterns, and the like. Thematic gestures create a counterflow against this background, and rhetorical gestures can disrupt the emerging conti-nuity of thematic evolution or development. Unexpected dynamic markings alone can play a rhetorical role. Beethoven is hardly the first to use unexpected dynamics for rhetorical effect (recall the finale of Mozart's K. 457, for example), but his extensive deployment of *subito piano* (mm. 28, 36, 51) and *fp* (mm. 39, 40, 43, 44, 47, 48) in the finale of the cello sonata is striking. These dynamic reversals and accents mark otherwise unmarked syntactic events, and they thus qualify as rhetorical even though there are no textural breaks at these locations. Besides injecting cross-currents against an otherwise unmarked flow, these dynamic jolts occasionally suggest another level of discourse, marked in this case by a constant intrusion that appears to offer commentary on the prevailing motivic discourse. In the Mozart finale the discourse-disrupting rhetorical gestures came early, and they motivated the rhetorical pauses in the final return of the main theme. In the Beethoven finale, on the other hand, the thematic gesture motivates the rhetorical gestures. The dynamically marked, *subito piano* undercuttings of perfectly syntactical half cadences are suggested by the premise of the $\hat{5}$–$\hat{6}$–$\hat{7}$–$\hat{8}$ thematic gesture, whose "cadence" (scale-degree closure) is unsupported by metric or durational weight. In this sense, even when the exposition closes with a strong, dynamically supported authentic cadence, another kind of rhetorical gesture must be found to undercut it. Beethoven opts for the abrupt release (and rhetorical gap) that is also inherent in the thematic gesture itself. Such rhetorical gaps at significant formal boundaries open up the possibility of a shift to something radically different, and Beethoven's enigmatic drone fifths mark not only a shift to the pastoral, but also the beginning of a topical and even tropological development of the thematic gesture.

To summarize, the character of the gestures and their ongoing development in this sonata support an agency of willfulness and indecision, comic wit and tragic defiance, which one can dramatize by embodiment in actual physical gestures. Indeed, Romantic ironic subversion and commentary on the discourse imply a kind of narrative agency that may also enhance the dramatic life of thematized gestures and their development, in that the narrative agency can be physically manifested through contrametric accents and rhetorical gestures. I will explore agency and its varieties in the following chapter.

By focusing on the thematic, dialogical, and rhetorical role of marked gestures, I have demonstrated how one can ground a gestural/emotional interpretation in the structures of the work. Instead of accepting disembodied philosophical metaphors of profundity based on abstract or abstruse syntactic relationships, one can directly engage with the drama of human agency as revealed in gestures and their ongoing discourse. For the analyst (formalist or Schenkerian) and the interpreter (theorist, performer, or listener), the lesson is that structure at all levels may be expressively motivated by elements that are often overlooked as less essential parts of a musical "surface."

10 Gestural Troping and Agency

Gestural Troping

Consider the upbeat-downbeat articulated gesture which launches the finale of Beethoven's Piano Sonata in A Major, Op. 101 (Example 10.1a, m. 1). This gesture is a token of the type that Beethoven also employs in the opening theme of his Piano Sonata in E Minor, Op. 90 (Example 8.1); and Schubert, as we have seen, thematizes the type in his Piano Sonata in A Major, D. 959 (Example 8.2). In Op. 101 Beethoven prepares this gesture by introducing it within the extended anacrusis of the second theme motive from the first movement (Example 7.4). The articulated separation of upbeat and downbeat also pervades both the march and pastoral trio themes in the second movement (Examples 10.1b and c), it is echoed in the brief turn motive from the third movement (Example 10.1d, mm. 11–13), and it is clearly foregrounded in the fragmented, *stringendo* fragments of the quotation from the first movement (Example 10.1a, mm. 25–27) leading to the finale proper. The finale trumpets the *forte*, upbeat-downbeat fanfare motive in a *stretto* imitation between the hands (Example 10.1a, mm. 1–4), and the musette-like continuation also begins with a softer version of that anacrusis (mm. 5–8).

Besides the integrative effect of this cyclic use of gesture, three topics appear in the eight-bar theme of the finale: (1) fanfare, correlated with the heroic/victorious, (2) learned style, correlated with the authoritative, and (3) pastoral musette, correlated with graceful simplicity (Hatten 1994: 107, 170). Each topic contributes to the overall tropological interpretation of the theme, and the movement further develops the trope. In order to warrant tropological interpretation, the concatenation or juxtaposition of established correlations must meet the following criteria (170):

1. The trope must emerge from a clear juxtaposition of contradictory, or previously unrelated, types. (Here one would not expect to find a concatenation of heroic, learned, and pastoral topics.)
2. The trope must arise from a single functional location or process. (Both the locational and material functions of the finale's eight-bar theme provide a formal and processive frame within which the creative fusion of topical correlations may take place.)
3. There must be evidence from a higher level to support a tropological interpretation—beyond mere contrast, or the more interesting case of dialogic (or dialectical) opposition, which I will treat in the next section. In the finale the opposition has been prepared by the earlier contrast between a pastoral first movement and a heroic/learned second movement march with pastoral trio. Furthermore, the Baroque-inspired Adagio (with

Example 10.1. Beethoven, Piano Sonata in A Major, Op. 101. Thematic gesture.
a. Quotation of the opening theme from the first movement, transition, and opening theme of the finale.

Example 10.1. Beethoven, Piano Sonata in A Major, Op. 101. Thematic gesture.
b. Second movement, opening theme of the march.
c. Second movement, beginning of the trio.
d. Third movement thematic imitation.

learned imitation) leads, via quotation of the pastoral first movement's main theme, to the finale. Hence, the drawing together of these contrasting topics in the opening theme of the finale is an integrative culmination for the cycle as a whole, and it enhances the positive outcome of the cycle's pastoral expressive genre.

Indeed, the fusion of topics in the opening theme of the finale creatively engenders a tropological meaning that is *emergent,* or beyond the mere sum of the correlations of each topic. As the theme moves from the outward determination (*mit Entschlossenheit*) of the authoritatively (learned) victorious (heroic fanfare), it elevates the graceful (pastoral musette) to a higher spiritual realm. One possible tropological interpretation would thus be "an inward victory of the spirit"—a richer and more subtle outcome, to be sure, than the "outward triumph of the will" characteristic of Beethoven's heroic middle style.

In the continuation the finale tropes the low-style pastoral musette with the high style implied by *stretto* imitation (mm. 29–32, not shown). Still further, the play of low versus high is humorously troped when a characteristic pastoral horn-fifth figure is quoted (*pianissimo,* as if from a distance) and then mockingly dismissed (*forte,* mm. 57–58) before being displaced by a rollicking folk dance variant of the opening motive (in imitation, mm. 59–66).

A contributing factor to the tropological fusion of these contrasting topics is the articulatory gesture itself, which continues to return in various guises and takes on an expressive role as more than mere anacrusis. Its isolation as a fragment (mm. 74–75) in the closing theme of the exposition leads to its brutal punctuation as a descending third that launches the fugal development in A minor. The harmless transformation of that fateful third into the cadential, cuckoo-like echoes of perfect fifths in the coda (mm. 308, 310, and 312–14) provides a final example of gestural developing variation, lending coherence to the tropological merging of topical oppositions (tragic/learned high style and comic/pastoral low style). And just as gestural development in this movement is directed by an underlying trope of contrasting topics, gestural development in turn supports the creative integration of the trope by providing a thematic link among the various topics.

But does the finale of Op. 101 provide as clear an example of *gestural* troping as it does *topical* troping? We can apply the same constraints on gestural troping as were outlined for topical tropes. In the case of the finale, since a single gesture is being transformed as needed to fulfill several topical roles, rather than two contrasting gestures merging to create a new gesture, there is no troping of gestures. Are there, indeed, any situations that would warrant the tropological interpretation of two or more *gestures?* The next two examples (from Hatten 1998) may help clarify what might be involved in making such a claim.

Several years ago I performed Schubert's *Winterreise* with Prof. Norman Spivey of the voice faculty at Penn State University. One of our students noticed that at a certain point Norman's body appeared to spiral upward as he sang a yearning melodic contour, while his eyes remained downcast, as though miming a gesture or posture of grief. Although these physical "extras" are not directly specified by the score, they are effective means by which a performer may complement and enhance a gestural trope as implied by the music. The contrast between overall mood (the heaviness of grief) and local emotional response (the pull of yearning or hope) might suggest a tropological interpretation. In this example of actual physical gesturing, the three constraints of troping are met: there are (1) two incompatible or contrasting gestures that (2) "come together" in a single functional location, and (3) there is a compelling reason to consider the trope as motivated by a higher-level expressive intent: these emotional states had been individually introduced prior to the moment of their creative fusion, grounding the highly poignant intensity that emerged from the fusion of their individual correlations.

Machado de Assis, the nineteenth-century Brazilian writer, introduces what might appear to be an oxymoronic trope in his novel *Epitaph of a Small Winner*, when he speaks of the "voluptuousness of misery" (de Assis 1952: 72). The combination of grief, and a luxuriant wallowing in one's feelings of grief, may indeed constitute a striking literary trope, but in real life such a literary trope may prove illusory. Psychologically the two separate kinds of feelings may remain distinct. The "voluptuous" feeling suggests the psychic reward one might obtain by shutting off all normal (and fatiguing) daily activity and immersing oneself in one's feelings of grief—a savoring which is all too rare in the normal course of events. Thus, psychologically one may have "mixed feelings," but these will not necessarily fuse (or "trope") into an emergent emotional state. Instead, one might more typically experience an oscillation between feelings: the unalloyed suffering of grief, and the psyche's provision for relief by means of the satisfying catharsis of freer emotional expression. Note that in my critique of what is nonetheless an effective literary trope, I have moved the discourse to the level of psychological realism, thereby— perhaps unfairly—suggesting that the literary trope might be suspect in its applicability to human experience (but see below). My psychological analysis belongs more to the realm of critical valuation than interpretation, and yet it is just this challenge that artistic tropes must face, if their creative fusions are to succeed in producing the sense of rightness characteristic of an artistically achieved moment of insight.

Consider once more the remarkable second theme from Schubert's Piano Sonata in A Minor, D. 784 (Example 8.6, m. 61), this time from a tropological perspective. Recall that the second theme presents a relatively sustained, pastoral + hymn topical trope, supported gesturally by the gentleness associated with the palpability of a *portato* touch. The theme suggests a vision of serenity, even of spiritual grace, emerging after the tortured expressions of raw grief have been willed away by means of the heroic fanfare reversal in the transition. But there is also a trace of the earlier grief gesture, referenced by marked accentuation on the first of each pair of *portato* half-note chords—a contradictory gestural type, given its potential distortion of the placid and even hymn prosody, to say nothing of its prior affective association with grief. What happens when these two contradictory gestural types are fused in a single functional location? The hymnlike vision, while foregrounded, appears to be subtly undermined by obsessive echoes of grief. This interpretation is strongly supported by later events in the second theme: the isola-

tion of the two-chord grief gesture with a release of the second chord, its registral echo with poignant mixture, and its *fortissimo* disruption, again with modal
mixture. The expressive trope hinted already in the opening of the second theme
is thus confirmed by its dramatic development. In my interpretation the trope
achieves a greater sense of expressive poignancy due to the vulnerability of its vision of serenity and peace. A performer who accepts this tropological interpretation must somehow convey a fusion of gestures—seemingly impossible, but surprisingly achievable in performance. My own solution is to allow the accents to
slightly distort the otherwise placid surface of the theme, and to respect the slight
separations indicated by the *portato* as a subtle trace of the grieving gesture's more
abrupt release.

Schubert's expressive meaning in this second theme should not be confused with
de Assis's "voluptuousness of suffering," a trope that Oscar Wilde and Richard
Strauss realize more convincingly (in psychological terms) with the character of
Salome—and with our own reactions as voyeurs. The trope of voluptuous suffering
(here as grief plus desire) is realized in Salome's final monologue, especially in
Strauss's musical setting. The effect of lurid decadence is expressively enhanced for
the audience through the contrast between the repulsiveness of Salome's actions
and the seductiveness of her genuine desire. Since Salome does not realize the re-
vulsion her actions trigger, this trope is also an example of dramatic irony.

My far less extreme interpretation of Schubert's second theme is also psychologically plausible: a visionary release from suffering that is rendered fragile and
unsustainable by an underlying, and unsettling, sense of inescapable grief. Consolation is fused with tragic import by the creative force of this musical trope. Compare my earlier interpretation of the finale's episode theme (Example 8.11b), another vulnerable moment of relief:

> To experience the fragile episode theme's attempt to reconcile the tragic while lacking
> full support from the accompaniment is to experience an even greater expressive effect
> than would be gained by the direct representation of a stylistic gestural type correlated
> with grief. Our reaction to the pathos of a theme that cannot achieve what it attempts
> is a more complex and deeper kind of tragedy than that created merely by playing a
> theme in minor. It is this heartrending vision of the desired within the context of the
> impossible that makes the episodes so dramatically effective.

Such an interpretation is clearly tropological. But how might a performer convey
that tropological significance? In my own performance of the theme, I convey the
lyricism of the melodic line in the first two measures (the "ameliorated" serpent
theme) by an unbroken *legato*. I then express the "sighs" in the third and fourth
measures with greater declamation (a slight break after each two-note sigh). During these four measures I play the accompaniment by releasing the fifth eighth note,
as written (without carrying over the sound with the pedal, as in a more "Romantic" style of performance). But the third and fifth accompanying eighth notes
create their own sigh motive, which I bring out as an inner line that first anticipates (in inversion) and then echoes the sighs in the melodic line. Thus, the troping here is more complex: several motivic elements carrying expressive associa-

tions from earlier movements are ameliorated and undermined at the same time, and the gestures which might underline that opposition—smooth singing style and breathy accompaniment—are each modified in the direction of the other. The *legato* melody admits the slight discontinuity between sigh gestures, and the released accompaniment figure features the internal continuity of each *legato* two-note sigh motif. Again, I would like to think that I can convey this complexity in performance—at least for informed listeners. But, as Leonardo da Vinci warns, "the supreme misfortune is when theory outstrips performance"! In any case my tropological performance merely ratifies what Schubert has already achieved in his compositional "performance," and any attempt to realize this admittedly complex theoretical interpretation will at least enhance the subtlety with which this fragile theme "speaks" to the listener, regardless of how the listener understands the expressive significance of the passage.

One might counter that the texture of the accompaniment is merely configured so as to suggest an instrumental realization by strings, possibly to support a dance topic, such as might be found in a trio of a minuet. But Schubert's trios that feature flowing eighth-note accompaniments (including those few in the waltzes for piano) typically promote continuity, often with one or more pedal points, rather than releases—and even his implied releases are not notated with rests in these works. A rare instance of this kind of rhythmically notated release is found in the accompaniment in the return section of the second movement of Schubert's Piano Sonata in A Major, D. 959. In Beethoven's Alla danza tedesca fourth movement from his String Quartet in B♭, Op. 130 (Example 2.4a), the rhythmically notated releases of the opening thematic gesture evoke the touching gestures of a simple German folk dance. In the finale of D. 784 the dance topic already supports an appropriate, episode-like contrast between Schubert's second theme and the obsessive, perpetual-motion character of his rondo theme. But the written-out release in the accompaniment is also motivated by the thematic gesture of abrupt release that has been strategically exploited throughout all three movements of the sonata.

The play of topical tropes may also involve the characteristic gestures of those topics, especially in the case of topics like dances and marches, as seen in Chapter 4. There I cited a charming minuet from Mozart's *Linz* symphony (Example 4.8) in which a topical march competes with the minuet both gesturally and metrically, and an asymmetrical hemiola accommodates the march's characteristic quadruple-meter motive and cadence. Schubert plays a similar game by importing a fanfare figure and a polonaise-derived rhythmic gesture into the context of two waltzes (one of which is reproduced as Example 4.4a). The contradictory gestures are part of a larger strategy of alternation between loud, martial, or ceremonial waltzes and soft, dreamily intimate ones. Although stylized or topical gestures may be involved in tropes, these tropes may lack the expressive originality and depth of thematically created gestures such as those found in the two Schubert sonatas (D. 784 and D. 959) discussed in Chapter 8. The play of incongruity in Mozart's minuet/march may be witty on the surface, and Schubert's fanfare/waltz may also function to signal the ceremonial closure of a waltz sequence with the pomp appropriate to a formal dance. But do these juxtaposed topical gestures really fuse into something that is creatively more than the sum of their individual contributions? As in language and literature, the most valued tropes are those that engender a unique interpretive insight or experience that goes beyond the mere sum of their expressive correlations.

Gestural Agency

How might we interpret contrasting gestures when their tropological fusion does not appear to be warranted? Such gestural contrasts may imply more than one agency, and may be interpreted as dialogical. Of the many presuppositions about musical gesture offered in Chapter 6, the third point is fundamental to the issue of agency: "Musical gesture is *movement (implied, virtual, actualized) interpretable as a sign,* whether intentional or not, and as such it *communicates information about the gesturer* (or character, or persona the gesturer is impersonating or embodying)." When musical events are heard as gestural, then the implication of agency is inescapable. In the finale of Beethoven's Op. 101 we sense an agent who not only experiences an inner, spiritual victory, but also, in a *performative* sense (Austin 1962; Searle 1970), *achieves* it by affirmative utterance.[1]

The enactment of meaning by gesture, however, also carries with it the symbolic significance of more systematic stylistic correlations. It is not enough that we hear the opening of the finale played "with determination"; we also need to hear the imitation that triggers the learned style; then, after the shift to a "softer" contrasting gesture in m. 5, we must recognize the pedal point and continuous swirl of sixteenths that cue the pastoral through the musette topic. In other words, we still need to be able to identify topics, as well as the details of harmony and voice-leading, rhythm, and meter that support their cueing in the context of a musical phrase. And we must recognize the stylistic expressive correlations which these topics bring to the creative synthesis of a musical trope. Not all of these elements of musical meaning are necessarily communicated through the Firstness or Secondness of gesture as performative realization, but they may depend on our knowledge of style conventions at the level of Thirdness.

Analogously one may process musical events without taking full account of their gestural agency, and indeed, the history of music theory demonstrates this possibility, with its traditions of formalist analysis. Recall Hanslick's (1974 [1854]) image of the arabesque. One is hard pressed to account for an "arabesquer" in that poetic conceit, to say nothing of whether or not an arabesque is expressive of a particular emotional state. And his image of "tonally sounding forms," while superficially similar to a part of my definition of gesture (as "energetic shaping through time"), also lacks the fundamental connection with agency, and hence with the modalities of affective experience.

I do not assume that the gesturer or agent of a composition is simply the composer, or the performer—despite the example of Liszt, who appears to have embodied both roles in conceiving his music within an aesthetic of Romantic self-expression. Nevertheless, one need not dismiss relevant biographical evidence for compositional intentions as revealed in the work.[2] Instead of assuming the composer as agent, however, I will propose four kinds of agency that may be variously weighted in the interpretation of score and its manifestations in performance. As a way to highlight the need for multiple kinds of agency, I will consider the difference between tropological fusion (implying a single agent) and separation into two agents. In the following example the juxtaposition of contradictory gestures does not lead to their fusion as a trope, but rather to a dialogical play of agencies.

Alkan's *Le Festin d'Ésope* or "Aesop's Banquet," Op. 39 (1857), is the last of twelve "etudes" in all the minor keys, and it comprises a lengthy set of variations on an eight-bar theme in E minor. Variations 21 and 22 form a double variation in E major. The hunting fanfare of Variation 21 continues in the right hand in Variation 22 (Example 10.2) with the gestural addition of a chromatic "riff" in the left hand (compare the opening of Mozart's *Jupiter* Symphony). But the riff is marked *Abbajante* ("barking"), and thus the gesture is already tropologically developed by a linguistic metaphor (a riff is to be "heard as" a bark). By shifting the representative connotation of the riff gesture from a snare drum or military drum figure to the unflattering baying of a hunting dog, the performance instruction tropes on the correlation of a style type. As the variation proceeds, the barking accelerates, hilariously disrupting the hunting horn fanfare, and ultimately displacing it for a measure before the fanfare's final, punctuated cadence.[3] Whereas I readily interpret a tropological effect of comic irony in this little drama (a "deflation" more blatant than that of the theme launching the finale of Beethoven's Cello Sonata in C Major, Op. 102, no. 1, Example 9.5), I am reluctant to consider it as an example of *gestural* troping, since the two relevant gestures (fanfare and riff) cannot fuse. Unlike the complex bodily gesture made by my *Winterreise* collaborator, these gestures do not merge into a single agency but instead maintain their separate roles. At best, the gestures contribute to a trope at the level of the *discourse:* their opposite meanings interact dialogically, and rather than fusing metaphorically into a third meaning, they may create a trope at a higher level, as ironic wit emerges from their unassimilated friction.[4]

In terms of agency, the two contrasting gestural types in the Alkan example suggest the roles of protagonist and antagonist in conflict dramas, or more neutrally, actant and negactant, to use the terms popularized by A. J. Greimas and introduced by Eero Tarasti (1994) in his narratological music analyses. Besides these two types of agency that gestures can imply, there are two others either implied by a score or generated by a performer while stylistically realizing, or interpreting, that score. The following outline distinguishes these four types of agency.

I. Interpreted score conceived as drama.
   A. Level of *story* (musical events in plausible, logical, stylistic sequence).
      Type 1. *Principal agent* (actant, protagonist, persona, subject, voice): the individual subjectivity with which we identify, whether as performer or listener.
      Type 2. *External agent* (negactant, antagonist; *or* depersonalized external force, e.g., Fate, or Providence): that agency which acts upon, or against, the principal agent.
   B. Level of (built-in) *narration*, derived from a *compositional* play with musical events or their temporal sequence or relationship, inflecting their significance,

Abbajante.

Example 10.2. Alkan, *Le Festin d'Ésope* (Aesop's Banquet), Op. 39, end of variation 21 and beginning of double variation 22.

or proposing a certain attitude toward them. This agency (Type 3) provides a "point of view" or filtered perspective.

Type 3. *Narrative agent* (the creator's persona, or the "teller's" persona): the sometimes invisible or transparent agency involved in ordering, arranging, and/or commenting upon the (sequence of) events of the story level. The narrative agency is cued by shifts in level of discourse (see Hatten 1994: 174–88 and Chapter 2 in the present volume).

II. Interpretation as realized in performance.
   A. Realizations in sound of Types 1–3 without overt intrusion of the performer's personality (beyond the performer's stylistic analysis and sonic reconstruction of the work and its implied agencies) but inevitably further inflected by:
   B. Narrativity of presentation.

Type 4. *Performer-as-narrator:*[5] directing the listener's attention (possibly overdidactically) to the structure and significance of events, although not changing or reordering the events themselves (exceptions: productions of operas, some twentieth-century scores offering the performer options). Commenting upon the events from the perspective of the individual point of view and prejudices of the performer as engaged participant in the "telling" of the story. May (over-)emphasize the characterization of actants (Types 1 and 2), or (rhetorically) mark especially unusual (narrative) reorderings or disruptions of expected events or event sequence (Type 3).

As explored in Chapter 7, gestures implied by the score but not notated must be interpreted, both stylistically and strategically, and especially with regard to the variable elements of tempo, timing, dynamics, pedaling, and qualities of articulation. Notational practices often tacitly presuppose certain gestural realizations, such as the characteristic temporal warping of triple meter in a Viennese waltz, or the "swing" of jazz. But beyond the characteristic gestures we might consider appropriately implied by the work in the context of an historical style, a performance may introduce additional gestures to clarify, or direct attention to, or emphasize certain features of the work. In this way the performer may inject considerable personality into the work, at all levels of agency. Performers' personal styles, or temperaments, are reflected in such "additions."

On the other hand, when encountering embodied performances which so match our ideal of a work that we consider them to be pure realizations of the composer's intentions, our biases may ironically lead us to praise those performers for selfless dedication to the work. Yet the performer may, even in such seemingly "pure" realizations, be narratizing by gestural highlighting, either through simple deixis (emphasizing a melodic apex or harmonic deflection) or the musical equivalent of abstract pointing, a type of gesture that accompanies speech (McNeill 1992: 173). According to psychologist David McNeill, abstract pointing is a gesture that highlights the frame, or disjunctive locations and times within the frame, of a story or discourse. An analogous example from performance might involve a pianist who highlights the retrospective character of a tonally relaxed coda by leaning back, as if suddenly removed from the temporal present and absorbed in the reverie of a memory. This visual gesture might be accompanied by subtle changes of tempo and dynamics that would place the section under a veil of reminiscence. Such postures may be seen in photographs and drawings of Liszt and Brahms performing at the piano, and although they may appear as caricatures to modern audiences, a performer's absorption in the act of expression is germane to Romantic aesthetics.

The temporal and dynamic nuances that may result from a performer's narratizing gestures may well be implied by the score (hence, Type 3 agency); recall the example of rhetorical gesture in the turn to the coda of the finale of Beethoven's Piano Sonata in A Major, Op. 101 (Example 7.18, mm. 281–91). Although no such *rubato* or taking of time is sanctioned by the notated score in this transition, any attempt to play through these measures in strict tempo would be, in my judgment, a failure to re-create the implied narrativity of the work as dramatically conceived, cued by such factors as harmony, texture, theme, topical contrast, and formal juncture (even the rests need rhetorical emphasis). In Bach we often encounter stylistically encoded rhetorical gestures. In the Prelude in E♭ Minor from Book I of the *Well-Tempered Clavier* (Example 10.3, Czerny edition), Neapolitan and V_2^4 harmonies are arpeggiated and set off by rests, rhetorically marking the presumed final cadence in mm. 28–29. The deceptive evasion of an authentic close is rendered that much more powerful in light of these rhetorical harmonic cues. Even when played on the harpsichord, subtle emphases of timing and articulation can gesturally enhance the rhetorical, or oratorical, effect. Czerny, whose edition is notorious for its added dynamic and other markings, is clearly responding to the rhetorical significance of these chords when he applies *crescendo* and *forzato* markings. His indications, though crude, exemplify a narrativity of selective emphasis. The performer should respond to these built-in rhetorical gestures, as implied by the style, but avoid the crudeness of Czerny's dynamic highlighting.

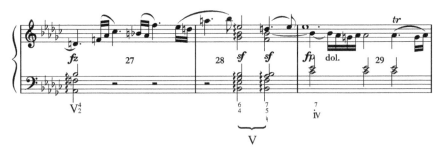

Example 10.3. Bach, Prelude in E♭ Minor, WTC I, from Czerny's edition (rhetorically motivated dynamics and accents).

Piano music also allows for multiple voices, hence multiple agencies, of which the simplest is the distinction between foregrounded actant (Type 1 or 2) and backgrounded environment (potentially agential), as found most obviously in melody and accompaniment textures. But it is also possible to interpret a single agency that is split between two *gestural fields,* as it were. An elegant and simple example is found in the opening of Debussy's *Des pas sur la neige* (Footsteps in the Snow), the sixth of his *Préludes,* Book I (Example 10.4). The opening ostinato in the left hand represents each footfall crunching into a crusted field of snow, and may be further interpreted (based on use of the minor mode, limited ambitus, and obsessive repetition) as expressive of grief or sadness. Debussy's three verbal directions leave no doubt as to his expressive intentions: *triste* appears twice and *douloureux* once. What makes this prelude peculiarly modern, however, is the fragmentary melody that emerges above the ostinato. By choosing not to begin segments of the melody on structural pitches in the mode of D minor (D and A), or the prevailing harmony (G in m. 5), Debussy creates the effect of a melodic line dissociated tonally from its accompaniment. It is but a short interpretive step from dissociated melody to dissociated consciousness, and the frozen surroundings add to the sense of dissociation as "frozen feeling," in the telling metaphor. This twentieth-century insight into grief is one compounded of repressed feeling and negated hope, and Debussy's combination of gestures achieves an appropriate tropological realization. The contour of the lines in mm. 2–4 and 5–7 suggests vague yearning in its echo of a Romantic ascent, rendered especially fragile by the one-note sighs in mm. 5–6. The two collapses of the melodic line in mm. 3–4 and 7 suggest that the apex of E is unsatisfactory as a goal or climax, and that the potential yearning toward a warmer

Example 10.4. Debussy, *Préludes,* Book I, no. 6, "Des pas sur la neige."

emotional expressivity cannot sustain its hopeful energies against the icy weight of frozen grief.

The two strands of this example, while implying different gestural realizations, are best interpreted as two parts of a single agency (perhaps implying a tropological fusion of meaning at that level, but not a specifically gestural fusion). The purposeful "split" between monotone, repetitive (bodily) motions represented by the ostinato and dissociated (emotional/thought) processes represented by the broken melodic line contribute two parts of an integrative state as experienced by a single agent (here the protagonist).

I have lightly sketched in the Debussy example a typical chain of interpretants that Western music has previously forged between representation and expression, and I will note parenthetically that the performer's gestures in representing any physical part of the natural environment (e.g., snow crunching underfoot) must also, again according to well-established linkages in Western music, reveal the expressive tone of the agent from whose implied perspective we are given the perception.[6] At times, the associative link may be forged in the other direction, as when a composer represents the turbulence of a stormy sea and we are led to infer a corresponding inner turbulence of an imagined agent. However, as Eero Tarasti astutely warns, in seeking for agency in music, "we run the risk that the subject we have found in the music is none other than ourselves" (Tarasti 1994: 109).

How does a composer distinguish between or among the first three types of agency—those implied by the score? Elsewhere (Hatten 1994: 9–28) I distinguished internal versus external agency as revealed by the slow movement of the *Hammerklavier*. For example, in the continuation of the second theme group the "willful" (stepwise ascending) search for cadential resolution is frustrated more than once before the desired cadence arrives unexpectedly, as if through an unwilled but providential event. The cues for interpreting this event as external to the efforts of the implied principal agent are the surprise modulation ("unearned") and the monolithic texture that follows ("authoritative" source). However one interprets that event—as a psychological moment of insight, a mystical epiphany, or an act of divine grace—it appears to have come unexpectedly from outside the principal agency.

There will inevitably be cases where it is not as easy to decide among types of agency. Consider an example that Raymond Monelle (1992: 269–70) uses to illustrate my own theory of markedness. In the recapitulation of the first movement of Beethoven's *Waldstein* sonata, Op. 53, the octave arpeggiation that in the exposition led dramatically to the dominant is shifted at the last moment up a half-step to A♭ (Example 10.5). This provokes a sequential echo on D♭, also ending on a "wrong" note, B♭. What follows in mm. 171–73 is a parenthetical three-bar modulation that returns to C major for the counterstatement of the main theme, powerfully punctuated with a *subito forte* in m. 174.

Beethoven's three-bar response to, and recovery from, these dramatically marked (rhetorical) moments almost seems to trivialize them, by treating them playfully and resolving their dissonant threats. The issue for interpretation, however, is whether the previous wrong notes are a fateful injection by an external agency—surprising, disrupting, and briefly deterring the principal agent's forward progress—or whether the principal agent has in some way "willed" the initial disruption, choosing to speculate upon it (the sequential reiteration of the gesture), and then demonstrating power over the discourse by jocularly dismissing the potential threat (the parenthetical, modulatory return to C major). Here a performer's gestures can be quite significant in projecting one or the other possibility. In the first, a Type 1 agent appears as surprised as the listener is meant to be, whereas in the second, a Type 3 agent acts like a powerful magician, delivering the unexpected A♭ and B♭ in the role of one who is "in on the surprise," and then provoking the listener's sense of wonder at the mastery that can transform a threat into a trifle. The second interpretation would be my choice here, and I think the composition supports it. There is a *pianissimo* dynamic and a perfunctory texture in the three-bar return to C, suggesting an ironic dismissal on the part of the principal agent, and leading to a recapitulation of the more heroic main theme. Note that the second interpretation shifts from Type 1 to Type 3 agency, that of the narrative persona which, in telling its own tale, can also direct its own adventures.[7] Note also my reference to the performer's "power" in projecting the second interpretation. The subjectivity that we might attribute to a principal agent, and perhaps assume for ourselves as

Example 10.5. Beethoven, Piano Sonata in C Major (*Waldstein*), Op. 53, first movement. Rhetorical parenthesis in the recapitulation of the first theme.

listeners or performers, may become that of a super-subjectivity—one that experiences not only dramatic power, as with heroic gestures enacted in the musical discourse, but also *narrative* power, as in the implied ability to control one's own virtual existence by provoking and then dismissing an imagined threat as harmless. Of course, as easily as we can appropriate such seductive, super-subjectivity for our own psychological ends (or needs), we can attribute it to a persona of the composer—here, Beethoven as hero, to echo Scott Burnham's (1995) profound study of the consequences of that attribution. What I call "shifts in level of discourse," which also imply Type 3 agency (internally narrative), are often cued in Beethoven by sudden stylistic changes, use of the "recitative chord" (major $^6_3$) and/ or topic, or other highly marked contrasts (Hatten 1994: 174–88; see also Chapter 2 in the present book).

I return now to the consequences of Beethoven's deliberate mixing of gestural agencies in the finale of his Sonata in C Major for Piano and Cello, Op. 102, no. 1 (Example 9.5), where the very presence of another performer introduces further dialogic complications. As discussed earlier, the opening gesture sets the comic tone. This is the first time in the work that a gesture has ended on the tonic note, yet its flippant release is hardly sufficient to accomplish closure. Unlike the similar motive ($\hat{5}$–$\hat{8}$) in the Alkan (Example 10.2), this is not a satisfactory drum riff since it does not resolve to a metric accent. The cello immediately grabs the released tonic, however, and sustains it, with a gesture that undercuts the witty release as though proposing a more serious, if still speculative, consideration of the tonic degree. That the piano and cello are virtual representatives of two interchangeable agencies, rather than defined and consistent characters in their own right, is obvious from the immediate reversal of roles in mm. 19–29: this time the cello releases and the piano catches the tonic to sustain it. Just as thought can be dialogical (even within a single mind), this play between cello and piano may also be interpreted as an inner dialogue within a singular agent or protagonist.

The finale contains many surprise undercuttings, as we saw in Chapter 9. Indeed, the (rhetorical) process of undercutting may justifiably be considered thematic in itself, and hence part of the ongoing drama, not merely a means of narrative manipulation of the dramatic sequence. But most of the undercuttings are mutual; both performers undercut a phrase goal with a sudden drop in dynamics, as in m. 28. Thus, both performers participate in a single narrative agency (Type 3), beyond their dialogically opposed individual agencies. Since this narratizing has been absorbed, as it were, into the very fabric of the thematic discourse, we may also experience the kind of super-subjectivity (Type 4 agency) that was only briefly engaged by the *Waldstein* example.

Gestural interpretation at this level is difficult to unpack, involving as it does a compression of multiple types of agency—and I have yet to treat the two performers' own instinctive additions as performers at the level of Type 4. But in terms of the implied agencies in the score, Beethoven's gestural and agential complexity is a significant innovation of his later period, stemming from the greater motivic or thematic concentration of events that many commentators have emphasized. Beethoven's practice, however, goes beyond mere temporal compression of ideas and their gestural contrasts. The specific density of Beethoven's late style is also a result, I would claim, of the multiply intertwined strands, and levels, of gestural agency, in that so much happens at the level of the story and at the level of the willful manipulation of that story. When such manipulations become integral parts of the thematic process itself, as in the finale of Op. 102, no. 1, or the openings of Beethoven's string quartets Opp. 130 and 132, then we are describing a technique that is ahead of its time.[8]

Conclusion to Part Two

Musical gestures include stylistic types and their correlations, as well as strategic tokens and their contextual interpretations. They may originate as spontaneous expressive movements translated into sound; and they may be treated thematically, dialogically, rhetorically, and/or tropologically. Musical gesture is a point of entry for listeners (a default level of understanding for those listeners lacking stylistic competency) and a point of entry for composers (a means of inspiration, or an interface between the creation of a musical idea and its representation of a particular emotional state, as mediated by gesture's energetic shaping through time). Thematic gestures, like motives, can affect the musical discourse, often through a process of developing variation, and help guide both formal design and expressive genre (the dramatic trajectory of a work). Gesture can also be generalized into higher-level syntheses, such as topics, or the most creative of syntheses: the speculative integration or fusion of tropes, which combine stylistic correlations in novel ways and enable new meanings to emerge along stylistically and culturally conditioned lines.

A gestural competency encompasses four fundamental aspects of musical gesture:

1. *Gestalt identity.* A musical gesture is the product of a single or coordinated set of represented and/or inferred (human) movements.
2. *Continuity.* A musical gesture bridges the discreteness of isolated acoustical events by providing coherent and nuanced shaping, shading, and/or consistency across possible highly variable parameters.
3. *Qualitative character.* Arising from (1) and (2), the perceptually dense and replete experience of a musical gesture can exemplify the qualities that it possesses.[1]
4. *Implied agency.* The qualitative character of a musical gesture, and its continuities, typically enables us to infer a precise (if unnamable) expressive motivation or modality, and thus, in many cases, an implied agency (or in special cases, a persona, or actant, or character) in an enacted (or in special cases narrated) drama or "story." Even the musical representation of natural objects (e.g., wind, or a storm) may be freighted with a human quality or amalgam of affective motivation (as when an agent experiences emotional turbulence analogous to the turbulence of a storm). Alternatively, the implied gestures of an agent may suggest reaction (responding with fear or anxiety), or the representation of a storm may contribute a background heightening of intensity as appropriate to the charged emotions of a portrayal.

There are two powerful sources for the gestural competencies outlined above. The first is physical: biological and cognitive. Our brains encompass a highly refined perceptual-motor awareness that over a long period of evolutionary development has successfully coped with visual, kinesthetic, and aural gestures, in terms of their intermodally linked shapings and shadings. Thus, our physical bodies are designed such that we quickly achieve (through experience and bodily learning) what soon appears to be an ingrained perceptual/cognitive capacity for identifying aural gestures, their continuities (and hence duration), their qualitative character (a skill essential for social interaction via utterances), and their implied agency (a skill essential for survival—escaping predators in situations where they are not visible).

The second source is social: cultural and music-stylistic. Culturally, we absorb typical bodily movements in response to typical social interactions, ranging from emotive expression in everyday life, to the intonations of a language, to the more ritualized gestures of cultural institutions ranging from social dance to civic ceremony and religious ritual. What a musical style clarifies and constrains is the identity of a gesture as thematic, its placement in a virtual environment of meter and tonality, its coherence in terms of these and other musical elements, and its contextualization in terms of other musical events and their cultural significance. What a musical work clarifies and constrains is the significance of a musical gesture in terms of its strategic role in the work. And what a musical gesture creates is a fresh embodiment of expressive energy, with the capacity to shape the work, to change the style, and to transform the listener.

Part Three: *Continuity and*
                 Discontinuity

Introduction to Part Three

The final two chapters explore one of the most fruitful consequences of a gestural perspective—the continuity of intentional action—as projected to other dimensions of musical structure and meaning. Continuity of texture and discontinuity of discourse are marked options with respect to the Classical style, where articulated textures and continuous musical discourse are the norm. Continuity (or discontinuity) may thus function as a thematic premise for an entire movement, not just as a salient feature of a thematic (or rhetorical) gesture. Nevertheless, our interpretation of textural continuity draws upon a basic competency in interpreting musical gestures, even as it introduces a new level of organization. I explore perpetual motion and plenitude as two possible premises with varying expressive consequences.

Discontinuity of discourse may be understood as intensifying the conflict that is at the heart of all drama, or as representing a postmodern fragmentation of the subject. In the final chapter I consider the advantages of the former over the latter interpretation of a late Beethoven quartet movement. If discontinuity is a premise for the first movement, then the continuity of the finale may suggest a strategically marked reversal of that premise. I address this opposition and another one, the absence of easily recognized topics, and I propose expressive motivations for each. My interpretation ultimately relates the different expressive genres of the two movements.

11 From Gestural Continuity to Continuity as Premise

Since continuity is so fundamental for music, it may be useful to sketch out some of the levels at which a comprehension of continuity most profoundly affects our interpretation of sound. The most obvious involves the cognitive musical ear taking discrete pitches and connecting them into the continuity of a melody or line. This is apparently a perceptual inevitability, discussed in Chapter 5 as a temporal gestalt, and it is from the basis of this perceptual phenomenon that another musical competency emerges—that of hearing a melody as *movement* through pitch *space*, not merely a coherent temporal gestalt of sequential pitches.

Hearing a sequence of pitches as *legato* further aids the ear, in that the *legato* is an articulation that binds discrete pitches in a continuity of sound. But as we have seen, the gestural mode of interpretation that is such a strong part of our musical competency enables us to hear gestural continuity across breaks in actual sound (recall the examples from sonatas by Schubert and Beethoven in Chapters 8 and 9). Indeed, according to Gestalt laws of perception, it is proximity and good continuation (in some parameter) that secures even the perceptual coherence of broken melodies in *empfindsamer* style, such as the "C" theme from the finale of Mozart's Piano Sonata in C Minor, K. 457 (Example 7.12c, mm. 148–53). As a more general principle, sufficient regularity of patterning enables us to take isolated events as units in a continuous chain at the next higher level. The chain of suspensions and appoggiaturas in the opening theme of the Mozart finale is instructive (Example 7.12a). Despite their gestural articulation into two-note units, the reiteration of a gestural pattern creates continuity at the next level of structure. This alternation between discrete and continuous operates throughout the perceptual hierarchy; discrete "units"—if reiterated in a given pattern—may thus be understood as the "grain" of the next level's continuity. A similar alternation may be observed between "closed" formal units and "open" processive levels in the hierarchies outlined by Meyer (1973) and Narmour (1977); indeed, it is this alternation that enables us to understand both closed patterns and open processes as interactively creating the hierarchy that ensures music's essentially temporal status. Meyer's "hierarchy of closures" might alternatively be viewed, from the perspective of gesture, as a "hierarchy of continuities."

On the other hand, the continuities of a voice-leading hierarchy in Schenker's inspired model are not always adequate to the analysis of discontinuities that may reflect dramatic structuring. Such disjunctions may undercut the unmarked flow of temporality in such a way as to demand a higher-level coherence. Coherence in this sense is understood not merely from reference to an evaded but ultimately subsuming *Ur*-structure, but from an entirely different conception of deep structure in which the coherent logic of *dramatic* continuity highlights those disruptions and conflicts in musical structure that are so easily "explained away" as mere delays of deeper voice-leading patterns. In a dramatically conceived form, closure must be achieved not solely by completion of syntactic harmonic patterns, but also by working out the possibilities of the material, or even, as in the first movement of Beethoven's Op. 130, exploring and exhausting the possibilities for reconciling two incompatible thematic ideas whose conflict is a basic premise for the movement (Hatten 1994: 134–45). Thematic integration, as a means of reconciliation akin to dramatic resolution, can play a role analogous to syntactic closure in a movement conceived according to a dramatic model (Hatten 1987).

Textural Continuity

Still another kind of continuity may be created texturally. One of the most striking differences between Baroque and Classical styles is found in their respective treatment of texture. Classical composers typically articulate texture by implementation of clear phrase breaks and introduction of rhythmic contrast, thereby breaking up the *Fortspinnung* and "single-affect" continuities characteristic of Baroque movements. Classical articulation provides several advantages, of which two are paramount. The hierarchical organization of discrete phrases and sections enables composers to construct larger movements with audibly coherent formal organization. But equally important, the introduction of rhythmic contrast supports the creation of highly dramatic oppositions in structure, and hence affect. These two aspects of Classical articulation are interrelated, in that a hierarchical organization of tonality and phrase construction provides a coherent framework in which extremely contrasting sections (or events) may be understood as interactive parts of a dramatic trajectory. Sonata form, with its deeply hierarchical tonal and thematic rhetoric, was a successful schema in which the competing demands of coherence and dramatic opposition could be reconciled, and in sufficiently flexible ways, such that characteristic features of themes might help determine aspects of the resulting form. Hence, the impression of deeper organic unity might compensate for the extremes of discontinuity in dramatically conceived surfaces, yielding a balanced integration of dynamic drama and coherent form.[1]

The discreteness of section, texture, and theme that gives Classical form such dramatic potential and expressive force is at times relinquished in favor of apparent textural or thematic continuities, which may in turn generate greater dramatic or expressive power. A movement featuring perpetual motion is the most obvious example of textural continuity as a thematic premise. Perpetual motion is marked in opposition to the unmarked, stylistically established articulations of texture. In other words, the salience of perpetual motion texture in the Classical style (psychologically marked as different or unexpected) contributes to its theoretical interpretation as a stylistically marked opposition, and eventually as a new style type.[2] But it is continuity in the broader sense described above, not simply the textural continuity we find in perpetual motion, that will be relevant to the inter-pretation of the following excerpts from Mozart, Beethoven, and Schubert. Fur-thermore, the treatment of textural continuity is one index of the gradual shift from Classical to Romantic aesthetic orientation.

An early example of marked textural continuity as a compositional premise oc-curs in Mozart's Piano Sonata in A Minor, K. 310. The third movement is an on-going, perpetual-motion finale. Already in the first movement the second theme and closing group (Example 11.1) unroll in nearly continuous sixteenth notes, despite clear divisions of function between presentational, transitional, and clo-sural types of material.[3] Subtle articulations of the continuous sixteenths are also achieved by the discrete rhythms of accompanimental chords and the shift of six-teenths between registers. The continuous sixteenths, at first decorous and galant (mm. 23–27), become increasingly obsessive in the continuation (mm. 28–35), and resume a galant cadential character to head toward closure (mm. 35–42). In the final drive to cadence, (mm. 42–49, not shown), the sixteenths take on a more fate-ful aspect in their relentless descent in the left hand to the lowest register; and the return of the dotted-rhythmic motive associated with the A minor first theme underscores their obsessive and fateful character.

At the beginning of the second theme group (Example 11.1, mm. 23–27) each measure appears motivically self-contained, creating the effect of additive phrase construction from the start. Yet the first four bars also establish an expectation of symmetry, based on their closed harmonic progression. Only in the continuation is this symmetry broken, by an interruption in m. 28 that embeds a new eight-bar phrase. Note that the accompanimental texture changes radically in m. 28, helping to underline the unusual phrase embedding, while the sixteenths maintain their continuous flow. The galant style shifts to the learned and bound styles (Ratner 1980: 1–30), *non legato* shifts to *legato,* and a circle-of-fifths melodic sequence is answered by a linear descending sequence with 7–6 suspensions. Ironically, this in-terruption may also be understood as enhancing continuity, since the interpolation (as an embedded phrase that continues by displacement) evades the hierarchi-cal formal articulation that would have emerged if the potential four-bar unit beginning in m. 27 had been completed. By forgoing regular symmetry, Mozart achieves an effect more akin to musical prose.

A related effect of interruption may be found in the last movement (Example 11.2a), a thoroughgoing perpetual-motion rondo in which four- and eight-bar phrases are the norm until the drive to cadence closing the second section in the relative major, C. As seen in Example 11.2b, chromatic disruption is employed to delay closure, promoting continuity by extending the phrase twice—first, in m. 52, by recycling the cadential progression, and second, in m. 56, by launching a sequen-tial, modulatory transition to E minor for an eventual restatement of the rondo theme.

That the continuity of motion draws something of its expressive force from al-lusions to the Baroque is clear from passages in the development section of the first movement and the middle section of the second movement, where minor mode,

Example 11.1. Mozart, Piano Sonata in A Minor, K. 310, first movement, second theme.

Example 11.2. Mozart, K. 310, finale.
a. Opening theme.
b. Cadential evasions of C major in the transition to E minor.

c)

Example 11.2. Mozart, K. 310, finale.
c. Musette episode in A major.

chain suspensions, and insistent, motoric repetition may be found. Allusion to a venerable style carries with it the connotation of authoritativeness, interpretable here as relentless and implacable fatefulness, which complements the tragic obsessiveness attributable to minor-mode perpetual motion. Mozart wrote the sonata just after his mother had died, which may well have influenced his cyclic use of textural continuity to express the obsessiveness of grief.

Minor mode and obsessive sixteenths characterize two well-known examples of perpetual motion in Beethoven: the finales of the *Tempest* and *Appassionata* sonatas (Op. 31, no. 2 and Op. 57). But the continuity of sixteenths in Beethoven's finales, or eighths in Mozart's, does not constitute the sole level of articulation. Mozart's rondo finale theme (Example 11.2a) offers a variety of rhythmic articulations from the start (the melodic idea features repetitions of a dotted-quarter-plus-eighth rhythm), and the minor-mode obsessiveness is relieved by a contrasting middle section in which a major-mode musette "vision" is laid on top of the continuous eighth-note generation in a variation of the original melodic idea (Example 11.2c).[4] In both locations the continuous-eighth-note texture might be understood as absorbing the dotted-quarter-plus-eighth-note repetitions into a thematic complex characterized by obsessive continuity. The fine-grained repetition of eighth notes thus complements the coarser-grained repetition of the bar-length rhythmic pattern.

In Beethoven's *Appassionata* finale the distinction between texture and theme is more striking (Example 11.3a). After offering a sinuous contour of continuous sixteenths as an unadorned theme, Beethoven creates a rhythmically varied theme by a process of layering, or lamination, on top of the continuous sixteenth-

Example 11.3. Comparison of perpetual-motion finale themes.
a. Beethoven, Piano Sonata in F Minor (*Appassionata*), Op. 57, finale.

note texture. The originally foregrounded thematic sixteenths are backgrounded against the emergence of the laminated idea, without ceasing to be "thematic" (and gestural).

Compare, with respect to the Mozart and Beethoven finale themes, the rondo finale of Schubert's Piano Sonata in A Minor, D. 845 (Example 11.3b), with its perpetual-motion theme. Although the perpetual motion is not sustained through-out the entire movement, Schubert attempts a more thoroughgoing continuity of thematic texture in his eighth-note theme.[5] Despite a slippery segregation into

Example 11.3. Comparison of perpetual-motion finale themes.
b. Schubert, Piano Sonata in A Minor, D. 845, finale.

compound lines, hinting at two-voice counterpoint, there is no clear sense of a foreground motive projecting against a background texture as in the Beethoven. More importantly, and in contrast to both Beethoven's and Mozart's finales, Schubert avoids symmetrical phrase construction from the very beginning. His fourteen-bar theme is constructed by an additive or paratactic process that features recycling (indicated by the parentheses in mm. 5–6 of Example 11.3b), shifting precipitously back to A minor from a premature move to the relative major (mm. 7–10), and spilling over the articulative half-cadence into the next phrase (mm. 14–15). The expressive effect of a *thematic labyrinth* is part of Schubert's effect. One may "get lost," and the thread of continuity is precariously woven in an expressive world where nothing is quite what it seems.

What emerges from these examples of continuity as a thematic ideal in sonata-form and (sonata-) rondo movements from Mozart, Beethoven, and Schubert are the first hints of a type that becomes so popular as to effect a change in style, fully achieved by the time of Schumann's rhythmically obsessive movements or those of Chopin's subtly structured *préludes* that feature textural continuity. What is marked in Mozart or Beethoven, as strikingly oppositional to the typically articulated textures in the Classical style, increasingly becomes the norm for the new Romantic style and is thus unmarked texturally (but still expressive). For Schubert, however, the stylistic situation is both transitional and flexible. I would suggest that continuity is still marked in Schubert, but that more exotic means (such as the additive and recycling phrase construction of this "labyrinthine" theme) must be employed to maintain the novelty.[6]

The move from discrete to continuous texture may itself be thematized, as suggested by many sonata movements of the Classical era in which dramatic contrasts in the first theme group and transition are evened out by the more consistent rhythmic/textural drive to the cadence in the second theme group.[7] In Schubert's Piano Sonata in G Major, D. 894 (1826), examined in Chapter 3, the thematization of the move from discontinuity to continuity is so remarkable that it apparently confused the generic perceptions of its first publisher, who appended the title "Fantasie" despite the movement's rather clear underlying sonata-form structure. But the surface may easily distract the listener from its underlying form. The motto-like first theme (Example 3.1) is introduced in isolation, then linked to varied statements by a five-eighth-note anacrusis, which becomes an important motivic part of the second theme (Example 3.3a). The inadequacy of continuity in the isolated statements of the first theme, also characteristic of the brief transition, is finally overcome by the second theme's extensive presentation over a dominant pedal in D major (see Example 3.3a, mm. 27–36). A diminutional variation with continuous sixteenths (mm. 37–46) leads to the highest register for a dynamically soft, ecstatic, and visionary effusion (as opposed to a traditional climax). A scalar descent (mm. 46–47) returns the visionary to reality, represented by lower register, thick harmonic stasis, and a forte dynamic level (m. 48). This disjunction also affects the haunting closing theme (mm. 49–52), in which a trancelike continuity attempts to restore closural periodicity.

"Perpetual motion" adequately describes only the diminutional variation of the second theme (from m. 37); we could as well speak of *plenitude* in the textural perfusion created by diminution (recall Chapter 2, and see below). The broader concept of textural continuity, however, can admit less uniform instances than the bald reiteration of a single rhythmic value—for example, the topical use of the waltz rhythm in the first statement of the second theme (Example 3.3a, mm. 27–36), where it appears on just the first and second beats of each broad four-beat measure. In turn, despite the uniformity of a pedal point (implied if not actually sustained over the twenty measures of the second theme, and resolving only at the end of each ten-bar unit), various harmonic and tonal motions offer a more discrete and varied rhythmic articulation of the upper strata.

Continuity (in this context, as opposed to the context of a more immediate musical gesture) must be defined in terms of *consistency of action at some level* (or "grain," to use the visual analogy introduced earlier) regardless of its possibly varied internal articulation. Thus, a sequence can create continuity from the most discontinuous of themes. And as we have seen, some kinds of interruption can promote continuity if they can be absorbed as phrase embedding, or phrase extending, since the previous phrase is not allowed to end with its predictably discrete articulation. Being "led on" is a basic ingredient of dramatic continuity. Unpredictability, as well as more predictable kinds of pattern change, can of course be used to break continuity. But strikingly, extended passages of continuity often incorporate their own unpredictability and yield expressive effects accordingly.

Such sections generally de-emphasize hierarchical organization in deference to more additive construction, as we have seen, and Schubert's ten-bar second theme is no exception. It begins with a motivically clear, symmetrical organization (1 + 1), repeated up an octave (1 + 1), followed by (1) + (1) + (1 + 1 + 1 + 1), yielding what can be heard as a two-bar extended variant of the *Satz* form.[8] But the aural impression is far from Classical because of the continuous one-bar motivic-unit construction, which conspires with the pedal point to produce an additive, hence somewhat unpredictable, effect of leisurely phrase growth—like an improvisation on a motive. The hierarchical structure of the $\frac{12}{8}$ meter encompasses the equivalent of four waltz measures: each $\frac{3}{8}$ unit at this slow tempo corresponds to a typical $\frac{3}{4}$ waltz (recall the discussion in Chapter 3 of this theme as a trope of pastoral and waltz topics). But the very length of the sonata measure makes the ultimate ten-bar phrase a considerable expansion of the *Satz* schema, since it constitutes the equivalent of forty "normal" measures. Thus, the temporal expanse of this single phrase foreshadows the stylistic shift from articulated Classical phrase hierarchies to continuous Romantic unfolding.[9]

The sequential elevation to a high register may be interpreted as analogous to an intuitively unfolding spiritual discovery. A searching or exploration is implied by the additive elevation of the motive, and it is thus expressively appropriate that the climax is not achieved in a singular crux, as often in Beethoven, but suffused over a broader stretch (note the placement of the decrescendo in m. 35, before the apex of the ascent). The gestural effect is that of an emotion welling up on progressive waves of feeling, and the welling itself—not any particular peak—is the goal. Thus, even the Classical notion of climax as having a discrete point—an apex, or an "expressive crux" (Hatten 1994: 59–60)—is diffused by means of continuity, and the expressive yield is appropriately transcendent.

A musical style that draws on topical and gestural associations, such as those triggered by the waltz topic, can ground emotion in motion that is both physical (the feel of an embodied waltz rhythm) and cultural (the stylistic correlations and intertextural associations of a musical topic). The progressive intoxication of a waltz, even one as slowed down and reflective as this, supports a comparable expressive interpretation of Schubert's more strategic compositional choices (the vast $^{12}_{8}$ metric frame, the pedal point, the additive phrase construction, the sequential ascent to high register). Together, these elements support an interpretation beyond simple physiological response to a reiterated motive, or the personal or cultural associations of a topic. Instead, something akin to spiritual exaltation is achieved in this passage.[10]

Continuity leading to trance, if not transcendence, is a strategy that achieves the status of a stylistic type in the emerging Romantic era. We can see how the technique, and its expressive motivation, has its roots in works of Mozart and Beethoven (and Haydn), where the continuous appears as highly marked texturally, and where its distinctiveness is used for spectacular expressive effect. Schubert takes the concept further, exploiting temporal expansiveness and the unpredictability of additive phrase construction to achieve a kind of timelessness. If, in certain exceptional works, the Classical composer sought to transcend the constraints of periodicity and articulation, perhaps the Romantic composer sought surcease from temporality itself.

Plenitude as Fulfillment: Textural and Gestural Motivations for Beethoven's Late Fugues

Plenitude as blissful expressive fulfillment was introduced in Chapter 2 as a textural topic and expressive goal of the Andante con moto movement in Op. 130. This desired expressive state is frequently achieved by progressive textural and rhythmic saturation of the main theme. It is a typical strategy in Beethoven's later variation movements, in which progressive rhythmic diminution often leads to a state of transcendent bliss. Superb examples are found in the slow movement of the *Archduke* Trio, Op. 97, and the finale of Op. 111. But as early as the Sonata for Piano and Cello in G Minor, Op. 5, no. 2, Beethoven was exploring the possibilities of plenitude and continuity. In the G major finale, the refrain theme (Example 11.4a) is introduced in a miniature rounded binary form without the repeats. Hints of diminution appear early on, and the contrasting strain (mm. 8–12) is treated in its subsequent appearances to *stretti* (double, then triple). The final peroration of the refrain theme (Example 11.4b) features continuous thirty-second notes in the piano, and the contrasting section of the theme in m. 264, featuring a triple *stretto* with one voice in inversion, now merges in seamless rhythmic continuity with the return of the initial section in m. 268. In this spectacular early example, plenitude is achieved through both diminution and *stretto,* and the saturated textural and thematic continuity between contrasting ideas creates a strong sense of fulfillment —a thematic or dramatic closure that goes beyond the syntactic demands of tonal closure alone.

The Adagio of the Ninth Symphony alternates between two themes, and each receives a progressively saturated textural enhancement in which diminutions play an important role. The contrasting theme is rather static, moving in sequential

Example 11.4. Beethoven, Sonata for Piano and Cello in G Minor, Op. 5, no. 2, finale.
a. Opening theme in G major.

waves over a tonic pedal, and plenitude as bliss emerges from its increasingly trance-like presentation. The use of parallel consonances (thirds, sixths, and tenths) to further sweeten, as well as saturate, the texture is also in keeping with the pastoral character of this theme.

Beethoven's increasing interest in fugue may have been stimulated in part by its potential for thematic saturation. Derivation of countersubjects from the subject, and *stretti* between two forms of the subject, are two highly integrative techniques found in the late style. *Stretto* is also one of the typical culminating (and rhetorical) thematic techniques in Baroque fugues, as are mirror inversion and augmentation. Mirror inversion is the most compressed of *stretti*, but its rhythmic coupling lessens the potential for rhythmic saturation. Augmentation, though expressively weighty and thus suitable for a closing peroration, would appear to be the opposite of the saturation achieved by rhythmic diminutions. But augmentation typically enters as a new rhythmic layer, and the resulting saturation of rhythmic values also supports a culminating rhetorical effect. Furthermore, when augmentation arrives in the low bass register, its authoritative weight is enhanced by registral expansion. In the fugue from Op. 131, Beethoven features *stretto* between subject and augmented subject as part of a culminating return to C♯ minor. The vertical saturation of pitch space complements the horizontal saturation of rhythmic space, enhanced through the accumulation of thematic and rhythmic layers.

In the *Missa solemnis*, Beethoven creates an appropriate musical trope for the text "Pleni sunt coeli," by surrounding the soprano subject with diminution in the violin and a reduction of the underlying 7–6 suspension sequence in the flutes (Example 11.5). Here the plenitude of heaven is suggesting from the beginning by three *reductive* as well as rhythmic layers. More impressive culminating effects may be found in the Credo fugue, with its intensifying diminution, but the "Pleni" opening is striking evidence of Beethoven's critical awareness of a technique that need not be limited to a Baroque-based rhetorical peroration.

Mutually supportive textural, thematic, and registral saturation may readily be

b)

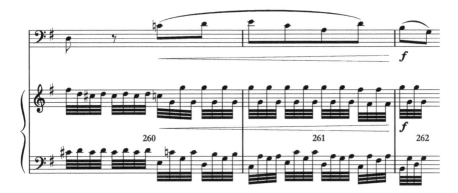

Example 11.4. Beethoven, Sonata for Piano and Cello in G Minor, Op. 5, no. 2, finale.
b. Saturated return of opening theme.

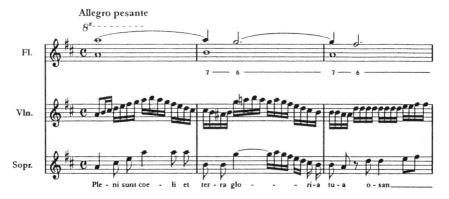

Example 11.5. Beethoven, *Missa solemnis* in D Major, Op. 123, Sanctus, opening of "Pleni sunt coeli" (theme, diminution, and reductive skeleton).

found as closural strategies of peroration in Bach's keyboard Sinfonias in G major, BWV 796, and B♭ major, BWV 800. Each features thematic intensification through *stretto*, along with a progressive filling of registral space. In addition, the textural space is suffused with the consonant sweetness of parallel thirds, sixths, and tenths, supporting the more blissful connotation of plenitude as expressive fulfillment.

This consonant closural strategy is employed to good effect in a Classically conceived fugue by Mozart (K. 394, Example 11.6). Having exhausted the typical culminating devices of augmentation and *stretto* earlier in the fugue, Mozart must find other means to achieve a comparable sense of fulfillment. A useful substitute for the textural saturation of *stretto* is achieved by doubling thematic ideas in parallel thirds or sixths. Note the suffusion of texture created by layering the countersubject in parallel thirds (mm. 56–57) and sequentially extending the subject in parallel sixths (mm. 58–60). Sequencing of subject and countersubject over a syncopated dominant pedal (mm. 60–62) implies imminent closure, but a swerve to the subdominant (m. 62) leads to a climactic peroration: the subject sequences in octaves in the bass, mirrored in the alto, with the countersubject on top in m. 63. The subject in parallel sixths is then presented against the countersubject in octaves in the bass in mm. 64–65, moving in a sequential descent to the crux of a precadential and Baroque-rhetorical diminished-seventh chord in m. 66.

Another rhetorically effective means of achieving plenitude (thematic as well as textural) is the definitive contrapuntal combination of several ideas; this is the culminating strategy in double or triple fugues, and it also conveys a sense of plenitude as fulfillment, both thematically and texturally. Beethoven adopts the double-fugue strategy in the *Hammerklavier* finale and the culminating, E♭ major fugue in the *Diabelli* Variations. Beethoven also integrates significant countersubjects or developments of subjects, often doubling in thirds, sixths, or tenths, to underline the affirmative value of his thematic integration in appropriately heroic and or transcendent fashion.

Example 11.6. Mozart, Fantasy and Fugue in C Major, K. 394: thematic and textural saturation in the closing measures of the fugue.

The Fugal Finale of Op. 110

The finale of Op. 110 is celebrated for its concatenation of a tragic *arioso* lament in A♭ minor and a more positive fugue in A♭ major. The drama is doubled, however, when the first fugue is wrenched back into the *arioso* as locus of inconsolable grief, in the distant key of G minor. The transformative second fugue, whose subject is the inversion of the first fugue's, also reverses minor to major, but must earn its way back from the distant key of G major to the tonic A♭. Beethoven dramatizes the expressive transition from dark to light with a progressive diminution, an innovative tempo modulation and *accelerando,* and a gradual registral ascent, justifying his appended instruction "Nach und nach wieder auflebend" (Little by little coming back to life). Before the spectacular metric "change of gears" takes place, however, Beethoven has already restored the normal contour of the subject, in augmentation in soprano and bass (Example 11.7a, mm. 152 and 160, respectively). These augmentations are contrapuntally combined with diminutions occurring in *stretto,* and the diminished form of the subject is soon thickened in parallel sixths and thirds over the bass augmentation (m. 160). Thus, the ingredients sufficient for a culminating statement are already present, with the exception of an appropriate dynamic level. But Beethoven then undercuts this too-early textural and thematic culmination with a Meno allegro section (Example 11.7b) that features *double* diminution in imitation and even *stretto* (m. 170), surrounding an inverted entry (mm. 170–74). This saturation of rhythmic levels makes the normal rhythm of the subject sound like an augmentation (see also the entry in the bass in m. 174, with its emphatic metric resolution to the downbeat indicated by the *sf*).

With the accelerando, the ultimate in textural diminution occurs, as double diminution begins to liquidate into a thematically contoured but now homophonic accompaniment to the subject—ultimately, a species of Alberti bass (Example 11.7c). In the *topical transformation* from imitative to homophonic textures, the subject entry in the right hand is thickened into chords and sequentially extended. The climactic registral ascent finally spills over into a full-registral arpeggiation—a saturation that is thematically motivated by its resemblance to the registral arpeggiation on the first page of the sonata. The close of the fugue thus achieves plenitude as apotheosis, with the thematic transformation from imitative to chordal texture in the right hand and buzzing diminutional sixteenths in the left. Fugue is formally and stylistically transcended by Classical lyricism and heroism, here blended into a trope of spiritual affirmation. In the "pilgrim's progress" from searching *ricercar* to triumphant melody and accompaniment, Beethvoen models *Kunstvereinigung* as spiritual allegory.[11]

The *Hammerklavier* Fugue, Op. 106, Fourth Movement

In the *Hammerklavier* fugue even the sequence of fugal techniques used for the principal statements of the subject (first augmentation, then retrograde, and finally inversion) may be understood as motivated by an overarching dra-

Example 11.7. Beethoven, Piano Sonata in A♭ Major, Op. 110, finale, second fugue.
a. Diminution and augmentation.

matic strategy that involves plenitude as its ultimate goal. The problem situation (Example 11.8a) involves a countersubject (m. 27 ff.) that is derived from the subject. The countersubject imitates the head of the subject in mm. 27–29, augmenting its sixteenths with a similarly contoured descent in eighths in mm. 29 and 31, and offering a more marked echo of the head's opening-leap gesture in m. 30. Where we might have expected a second countersubject to counterpoint the entry of the third voice (Example 11.8b), we find even less independent material—a refractive echo of the head of the first countersubject, followed by pairing of countersubjects in parallel sixths (m. 40).

Parallel sixths become thematic in this fugue that opens by surrounding the subject with its own offspring. Parallel sixths are strongly marked in mm. 72–75. A pastoral episode in G♭ (mm. 85–93) also "ameliorates" the intensity of the opening tenth in the subject head by filling its leap of a tenth in two stages; an arpeggiated bridging of the octave and a stepwise filling of the third. Stepwise sixteenths in contrary motion foreshadow the *stretti* to come. The first major treatment of

Example 11.7. Beethoven, Piano Sonata in A♭ Major, Op. 110, finale, second fugue.
b. Double diminution.
c. Harmonic thickening (diminution as Alberti bass).

Example 11.8. Beethoven, Piano Sonata in B♭ Major (*Hammerklavier*), Op. 106, finale.
a. Exposition, answer and first countersubject.
b. Exposition, subject and both countersubjects.

the subject, however, is augmentation (Example 11.8c). The same two counter-subjects are also augmented, but what gives this section its special character is the parallel-sixth thickening of the subject's descending sequence in mm. 97–100. In augmentation, these parallel sixths echo the similar treatment of the counter-subjects (compare m. 40 in Example 11.8b), thereby highlighting the derivation of the countersubjects from the subject. Thus, the first major treatment of the sub-

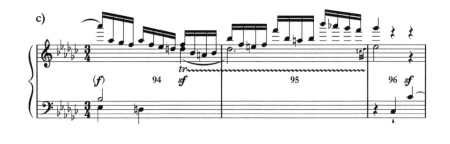

Example 11.8. Beethoven, Piano Sonata in B♭ Major (*Hammerklavier*), Op. 106, finale.
c. Augmentation.

ject was clearly forecast by Beethoven's design and treatment of the two counter-subjects.

The next important fugal technique emerges unexpectedly after a punctuated and overlapped half cadence in B minor (Example 11.9a). The expressive attention in m. 153 is directed not toward the retrograde we only later recognize as having begun (when we hear the rhythmic hiccup of the retrograde in mm. 155–57), but toward a new countersubject to that retrograde, a lyrical, *cantabile* line that also serves to foreshadow the definitive countersubject Beethoven is still seeking. That definitive countersubject will first appear as a subject, in the second exposition of this double fugue (Example 11.9b). Note that the *cantabile* line (Example 11.9a) descends through a fifth from F♯ to B under its first large slur. The second subject, in D major (Example 11.9b), will also descend lyrically through a fifth, this time from A to D, and mark its thirds even more prominently.

The dysphoric key of B minor—recall its dark oppositional role in the first move-ment, sardonically echoed at the end of the second movement—seems appropriate for the rare and bizarre use of melodic retrograde. Notice how B minor, the central dramatic dissonance of the sonata, is progressively ameliorated in this section—al-ready by the mysterious balm of the *legato* countersubject, and then by a shift to the relative major in m. 180 (Example 11.10a). Beethoven reinforces this euphoric turn by means suggestive of plenitude—the sequential motive from the subject is treated to both parallel tenths and *stretto*. Gesturally the *stretto* voice also "normal-izes" the rhythmic dissonance. Since both retrograde and inversion of the subject body's descending sequential lines are contour-identical, the rhythmic displace-ment of the *stretto* in effect transforms a retrograde fragment into an inversion

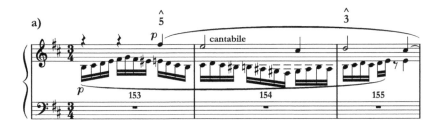

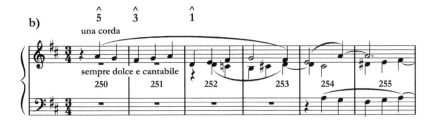

Example 11.9. Beethoven, Op. 106, finale.
a. Retrograde with new countersubject.
b. Second exposition, subject based on variant of new countersubject.

fragment. This rhythmic/metric resolution not only helps resolve the bizarre tensions of the retrograde, but also foretells the next major treatment of the subject—full entries in inversion beginning in m. 208. Thus, in a maneuver that both resolves the dissonant key of B minor to D major and begins the transition from retrograde to inversion, Beethoven expressively motivates the tonal plan and technical "invention" of his dramatically conceived fugue.[12]

The inversion entry section appears in G major, and it is followed by a move to Eb major as part of the large-scale descent-in-thirds strategy that is also thematic for the entire sonata, as Charles Rosen has demonstrated (1972). But what is interesting in Example 11.10b is a similar texture to that found in the earlier D major section.[13] Beginning in m. 230, the sequential sixteenths are once again featured in *stretto,* but this time the emphasis is on imitation in contrary motion. Textural saturation is achieved by a third voice creating mirror (simultaneous) inversion on the third beats of mm. 230–31, as well as by more continuous doubling or mirroring between the inverted entry and the two upper voices in mm. 233–34. A culmi-

Example 11.10. Beethoven, Op. 106, finale.
a. Retrograde fragments preparing for inversion.
b. Inversion.

nating *stretto* of the diminished head (mm. 243–46) leads to the first break in the continuous texture: a rhetorical half cadence on V of D followed by a rhetorical pause (mm. 248–49).

The key of D major, anticipated for its role in "resolving" the tensions of B minor, is now featured in the exposition (m. 250 ff.) of a new subject (see Example 11.9b). Not only can this new subject be read as the definitive version of the counterpoint Beethoven explored in the retrograde section, but, as I have observed else-where (Hatten 1994: 18–20, 27–28), it is also a direct allusion to the slow move-ment's second theme, also in D and featuring "resignational" drops through the triad. The second exposition proceeds after a short development to a recapitulatory double fugue, and this magical transformation happens precisely when a chromatic modulation slides into the home key of Bb major. The result is a definitive thematic integration that may be interpreted tropologically: the "heroic will" of the first subject fuses with the "resignational acceptance" of the second subject as true countersubject, creating a trope that is abnegational in its willed acceptance.

The double-fugal thematic integration is but the first of many strategies of plenitude employed in the final, culminating pages, which feature four major *stretti,* frequent doubling in consonant intervals, mirror inversional wedges, and three examples of harmonic enrichment of the subject head.[14] One spectacular subject entry features the principal subject varied in order to outline a diminished-seventh chord, along with both of the originally derived countersubjects, all over a double pedal (tonic trill plus dominant bass). After this much suffusion of tex-ture, however, Beethoven's ultimate close comes as a surprise: a stark return to uni-son and octave textures for sequential extensions of both the sixteenth tail and the head with trill. Rhythmic dislocation is thematized in the final cadential chords, which also achieve a written-out *ritard.* Texturally and rhythmically, then, this closure sounds strangely undercut, and it offers a more ironic perspective on "plenitude-as-resolution-and-fulfillment" than is found in the finale of Op. 110. A comparison of the *Hammerklavier* fugue's closing bars with those of the fugal finale of the Cello Sonata in D Major, Op. 102, no. 2, is telling; a suffusion of par-allel sixths and pedal trills in the latter is ultimately broken off for a similar se-quence involving bare octaves and tenths in the piano and cello.

The *Diabelli* Fugue (Variation XXXII)

The extended thirty-second variation of the *Diabelli* Variations, Op. 120, features a subject (Example 11.11a) that is structurally analogous to the opening subject of the *Hammerklavier* fugue. There is a marked head (a leap of a fourth from 1̂ down to 5̂ and repeated notes on 5̂), a clear body (a sequential stepwise descent to 3̂), and a tail (a *legato* extended turn figure leading back to 5̂). Unlike the *Hammerklavier* subject, however, this subject is paired with a distinctive counter-subject that complements the stasis of the subject's head, the sequential treatment of its body, and the melodic twist in its tail. The fugue begins with subject and countersubject as indissoluble contrapuntal associates. A potential second counter-subject is not as marked; it appears to be derived sequentially from the tail of the subject. It reaches a more definitive form with the third entry of the subject (be-ginning on the last beat of m. 14), with marked leaps of a sixth that complement the sequential body of the subject and first countersubject (labeled in mm. 17–18).

Stretto is featured early on (m. 29, head only), and parallel consonant thickening of the texture also happens rather soon (m. 46, doubling the subject in parallel sixths). These devices are combined to thicken the texture by m. 57; the principal

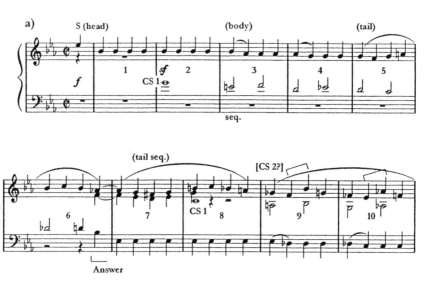

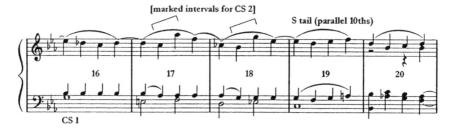

Example 11.11. Beethoven, *Diabelli* Variations, Op. 120, Variation 32 (Fugue).
a. Exposition.

countersubject is doubled in thirds and supports a complete *stretto* of the subject. An early, augmented bass entry at the pickup to m. 64 hints at closure, but the entry is in inversion, and it is too soon for closure. Next, the head is treated to *stretto* in inversion, with parallel thirds in the countersubject advancing the sequence and varying the harmonization of the head. All of these intensifying techniques lead to the first climax, a powerful half cadence in C minor that recalls the mode of the previous set of three variations (also heavily Baroque-influenced, especially by Bach's *Goldberg* Variations). But the fateful authority of this half cadence is quickly

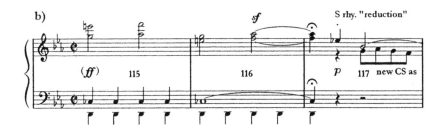

Example 11.11. Beethoven, *Diabelli* Variations, Op. 120, Variation 32 (Fugue).
b. Rhetorical climax and second exposition.

undercut by a dismissive, comic variant of the subject, shifted back to E♭ major. The parallel, chromatically descending thirds seem playfully to mock the monumental half cadence in C minor. The subject is then thickened in thirds (m. 87) while the principal countersubject is doubled in harmonic counterpoint to realize a circle-of-fifths progression as implied by the contrapuntal sequence in the body of the subject. A stentorian bass entry in octaves is inverted but not augmented, and it is sequentially extended to lead to the second major climax. This climax is thickened by parallel sixths and thirds (m. 109) and culminates in extreme registral insistence on the repeated-note gesture, outlining a rhetorical diminished-seventh chord (Example 11.11b) that also serves as vii°⁷ to return to the home key of E♭ major.

At this point something similar to the *Hammerklavier's* second exposition occurs—a new idea in continuous rhythmic values is introduced and treated to a full exposition—but unlike the *Hammerklavier* fugue, it is already being combined with a variant of the original subject (Example 11.11b, m. 117). The marked, repeated-note gesture of the original subject has been "liquidated" (or "congealed") by reduction into more sustained rhythmic values, thereby shifting our focus to

Example 11.11. Beethoven, *Diabelli* Variations, Op. 120, Variation 32 (Fugue).
c. Return of the subject in triple counterpoint, with doubling in thirds and tenths, leading to rhetorical undercutting (m. 160).

the new, more active countersubject. And this new countersubject is a diminished variant of the twisting tail of the subject. Intriguingly, this is also the source of the potential second countersubject from the opening exposition, material that had been neglected even after gaining a more marked form (mm. 17–18) with the third entry of the subject.

Another strategy of plenitude begins to emerge with the second exposition. The original subject was basically in quarter notes, the principal countersubject in half notes; with the new countersubject's eighth notes a third rhythmic level is activated, and the reduced subject's dotted half notes create a gap for the quarter notes of the original subject to fill. In Example 11.11c (m. 142) the definitive new countersubject (CS3) is coupled with a return of the original subject (head and body)—inevitably in the bass in octaves—and when the original countersubject joins in (m. 147), the effect is akin to a triple fugue. Not only are all three marked ideas thematically integrated (m. 146 ff.), but all three rhythmic levels are finally activated at the same time. Not surprisingly, couplings in parallel thirds (m. 154), tenths (mm. 155–57), and sixths (mm. 158–59) are added to further saturate the texture. The crowning touch, however, comes when Beethoven explicitly marks the derivation of his "new" countersubject 3 from the discarded *second* countersubject of the opening by means of the implied leap of a sixth—the marked leap that had brought the second countersubject to our attention in the original exposition (compare mm. 156–57 in Example 11.11c with mm. 17–18 in Example 11.11a). The "definitive" version of countersubject 3 (as derived from countersubject 2) is just being realized when the climactic plenitude of textural and thematic saturation is abruptly halted by another rhetorical diminished-seventh chord over tonic pedal (m. 160). The fugue, despite realizing every possible strategy of plenitude, simply cannot be allowed to have the last word in closing the variation set. Although the fugue had provided a heroic antidote to the tragic set of C minor variations that preceded it, E♭ is the wrong key for ultimate closure.

Beethoven's rhetorical undercutting at the end of the fugue is not ultimately a tragic reversal, however, since the fugue has accomplished its mission, achieving a reassuring plenitude that is deflected only in the interest of another, more appropriately mystical and poetic closure—one that William Kinderman (1995) and Charles Rosen (1972) have so touchingly described. The conventional minuet, with its sublimated qualities of Classical reminiscence, allows for a poignantly resignational leave-taking, transforming Diabelli's trite opening gambit into the quintessential gesture of galant sensibility. We are left with a transcendent sigh of acceptance as Beethoven completes his farewell in appropriately suffused diminutions.[15]

Plenitude as topic is achieved by techniques ranging from parallel imperfect consonances to *stretto*, from thematic integration to double and triple fugue, and from saturation of registral space to the diminutions and thematic layers that help saturate rhythmic and textural space. Furthermore, plenitude as premise can guide the sequence of techniques in a fugue (Op. 106), or the transformation from imitative to homophonic textures (Op. 110), or the developmental realization of a definitive countersubject as a strategy of thematic completion (Opp. 106 and 120). All of these seemingly formal procedures, far from being abstractly conceived, have arguable expressive or dramatic motivations. It is this aspect of "poetic content" that Beethoven sought to infuse into his appropriation of Baroque imitative textures and formal processes. Certainly one would not assume any less of Bach, but the dramatic energy and overwhelming intensification of Beethoven's epic trajectories draws from Classical developmental logic, hierarchical forms, and poetic visions. This aspect of creativity in Beethoven's late style may be understood as a further dramatization and elaboration of what was already present in Bach's own dramatic and rhetorical invention—the move toward plenitude as textural, rhythmic, registral, thematic, and ultimately expressive fulfillment.

Whether as blissful plenitude or (as in the minor-mode, perpetual-motion sonata movements examined earlier) tragic obsessiveness, textural continuity plays an expressive role as a marked feature in the otherwise highly articulated Classical style. But continuity is a larger concept than can be encompassed by texture alone, even in the broader applications given here. In the next chapter, surface discontinuities that threaten fragmentation of the musical discourse will be interpreted as potentially coherent stages of a higher-level dramatic continuity. The analogy with gesture's perceptual synthesis of discrete elements is a tempting one to draw. The question in the former case is whether dramatic continuity is imposed by the interpreter or earned by a composer testing the limits of coherent integration.

12 Discontinuity and Beyond

Fragmentary Subjectivity? Beethoven, String Quartet in A Minor, Op. 132, First Movement

Of the many elements of Beethoven's late style that have been interpreted as anticipations of twentieth-century musical approaches, perhaps the most often noted is Beethoven's extensive use of abrupt juxtapositions or disruptions. The resulting discontinuity in the musical fabric has been interpreted in radically different ways, which suggests that such meanings may be underdetermined, or else highly dependent on context. I will compare and evaluate different interpretations of expressive meaning stemming from Beethoven's disjunctive strategies in the first movement of Op. 132, and consider the kinds of evidence that both support and limit the analogies with modernist or postmodernist procedures.

The first movement of Beethoven's String Quartet in A Minor, Op. 132, offers one of the most splintered or fragmentary openings in Beethoven (see Example 12.2). Susan McClary (2000: 119–33) summarizes Joseph Kerman's (1966) and Kofi Agawu's (1991) approaches to this movement in developing her own interpretation, "an image of shattered subjectivity" (119) that is one step toward "the schizophrenic postmodern subject" (125). While Agawu (1991: 125) stresses the "absence of synchronicity between topic and harmony," McClary describes a "collage of . . . apparently unrelated topoi" in the opening bars, a collage that "destabilizes their meanings" (2000: 122). According to McClary's narrow reading (125), Agawu overvalues the coherence provided by the underlying harmonic structure (as interpreted in Schenkerian fashion), but in fact, Agawu emphasizes that the "dissonance between the domains" of topic and underlying tonal progression "gives the work its unique character" (1991: 125). McClary then appropriates Kerman's "more hermeneutic account" of the movement as a psychological journey of suffering and frustration, as supported by (but not highlighted in) Agawu's more "structuralist" interpretation, in order to demonstrate that the subsequent movements of the quartet each expand upon one of the isolated topics of the opening, hence preserving their traditional associations as conventional topics only outside the first movement proper. She concludes that the quartet thematizes the struggle of a conflicted persona with a "tangle of contradictory impulses" (129). If the wholeness or identity of the persona becomes the central theme in late Beethoven for McClary, it is "because such constructions had lost cultural credibility." McClary then considers Beethoven's various options for this fractured subjectivity: it "hovers without choosing among the illusion of unity, the lure of blind faith, the potential of disciplined force, the expression of alienated self-pity, and a hope against hope that makes continuation possible" (133).

What are the kinds of evidence involved in the interpretive claims of these authors? First, some notion of thematic material that draws on the associations of conventional topics, gestures, and stylistic allusions. Second, a series of strikingly different musical ideas and textures which not only juxtapose but often also interrupt or displace each other. Third, and this is the area most carefully mapped by Agawu, a lack of congruence between the implications of these topics or ideas and the underlying tonal structure, specifically with respect to conventional points of tonal/formal articulation.

Interpretation then proceeds more or less conservatively or radically, depending on the degree of cultural or ideological emphasis each author brings to the task. McClary is heading toward a larger vision of music history in which Beethoven plays with what she calls "counterconventions."[1] Kerman proceeds as an intuitive and intelligent critic who captures Beethoven's experiments with form and expression by comparisons between pairs of late quartets, emphasizing common or opposing treatments of compositional strategies, such as the initial dissociation and subsequent integration of thematic materials. Agawu hesitates at the gates of expressive interpretation, unwilling to go very far beyond an accounting of noncongruence between labeled topics on the surface and underlying harmonic coherence, but more willing than Kerman to accept an ultimately unresolved or nonunified ending to the quartet. Both McClary and Kerman create a rudimentary plot to account for the successions: McClary's based on a fractured subjectivity, and Kerman's on an objective account of suffering within the context of a psychological sequence.

I would now like to propose six other ways one might conceivably interpret disruption, disjunction, or discontinuity in Beethoven's late style.

First, disjunctions may signal *combinatorial play,* in the somewhat abstract or witty sense of Mozart's *ars combinatorial* minuets. An example is found at the end of the fourth movement of Op. 130, where the *Ländler* theme's measures are presented in scrambled order (see Example 2.5a). But permutations need not occur disjunctively; compare the opening eight bars of Op. 132 (Example 12.1), which treats $\sharp\hat{7}$–$\hat{1}$–$\hat{6}$–$\hat{5}$ in minor in a continuous motet-style texture, despite its various permutations: transposition, inversion, and interversion (switching of note pairs).

Second, interruption may be interpreted as *humorous undercutting* or diversion, one of the staples of the *buffa* style, and central to an understanding of many of Haydn's disruptions.[2] In the finale of Beethoven's Op. 101 (Example 12.1), a pastoral emblem of horn fifths (mm. 55–56) is played almost as a reminiscence before being solidly rejected by a disruptive gesture that sets up an "alternative" pastoral allusion in the form of a rustic dance topic. Other examples abound in the comic finale of Beethoven's Cello Sonata in C Major, Op. 102, no. 1, interpreted in Chapter 9.

Third, disjunctions may imply a *shift in temporality.* The chief exponent of this view is Jonathan Kramer (1988), whose hypothesis of nonlinear or gestural time informs his interpretation of the first movement of Beethoven's Op. 135. In his analysis disjunctions of temporality are related to the temporal implications of themes and gestures, which may radically depart from the temporal functions of formal locations. I would not go so far as to claim that the strong authentic cadence

Example 12.1. Beethoven, Piano Sonata in A Major, Op. 101, finale, pastoral vision and comic dismissal.

in m. 10 is actually the ending of the first movement, as opposed to its anticipation (1988: 151), but clearly there are ways in which sudden contrasts between radically different kinds of music (from eventful to static, for example, or conventionally in the expansions of fermatas and cadenzas) trigger a shift in our processing of piece time.[3] The most straightforward examples of such radical juxtapositions are the parenthetical ones that William Kinderman analyzes in his book on Beethoven (1995). As Kinderman notes:

> Beethoven's complex use of thematic foreshadowing and reminiscence contributes a dimension to his music that transcends a linear temporal unfolding. And his special interest in techniques of parenthetical enclosure, whereby contrasting passages are heard as an interruption within the larger context, further enriches the temporality of his musical forms, helping to open up narrative possibilities rare in instrumental music. (1995: 12)

The first movement of Op. 109 (Example 7.21) is one of Kinderman's examples; he notes that the Vivace material returns at the same registral location where it had been disrupted by the parenthetical Adagio espressivo. But as I noted in Chapter 7, two further parentheses (in m. 12 and again in m. 13) disrupt the attempted emergence of a second theme before it is prematurely liquidated (mm. 14–15) within the Adagio itself.

Fourth, disruptions or disjunctions may imply a *shift in level of discourse* (Hatten 1994: 174–84). If the disruption or shift involves sufficient contrast in style, or sufficient differentiation along other dimensions, it may suggest not only a shift in temporal experiencing, but also a shift in the discourse itself, generally to a higher level that comments or reacts to the ongoing, unmarked discourse of piece time.

Such shifts as, for example, from minor to parallel major at the end of the finale of Op. 132 may even imply Romantic ironic commentary (but see below, p. 285).

Fifth, extreme juxtapositions may trigger a *trope* (Hatten 1994: 161–72), in which the disruption is interpreted as the juncture between two incompatible ideas, for which an overarching relationship may nevertheless be found. A tropological interpretation may be suggested by the larger context or premise of the piece, such as the "all-embracing" trope in the finale of the Ninth Symphony, in which the low-style Turkish March undercuts the sublime moment of "steht vor Gott" not as a grotesque travesty of the sacred, but as an enlargement of the realm of brotherhood—embracing everyone, regardless of social station or nationality.

Sixth, and most common, disruptions may function as parts of a dramatic trajectory based on a premise of thematic contrast or conflict. By this interpretation, disjunctions are redeemed by the overarching coherence of a dramatic trajectory.

Any of these disruptions may be marked by rhetorical gestures; indeed, the act of shifting lends rhetorical significance to whatever material immediately follows, even if that material did not help provoke the shift, as did the A♮ in m. 9 of Op. 109 (Example 7.21). For example, if one theme is simply cut off and a new one enters, the new theme may not have been rhetorically marked internally, but in this context it acquires the markedness of the rhetorical shift.

Many disjunctive or interruptive events involve extreme stylistic or topical contrast, as we have seen. Sometimes the contrast is achieved by means of intertextual quotation or stylistic allusion, which also suggests a shift in level of discourse, if not in temporality as well. In the transitional slow introduction to the finale of the *Hammerklavier*, Op. 106, the three successive pastiches of Baroque imitative textures are heard as sudden intrusions from another realm. Of the numerous ways one might interpret this transition, an attractive hypothesis is the modeling of emerging creativity or invention. The pastiches suggest windows into another style, as though they had arisen spontaneously in the mind of the creator and had dispersed just as spontaneously. This representation of a creative consciousness need not imply a splintered subjectivity, however. Instead, the unpredictable shifts of musical thought may be understood as part of an ultimately integrative process, reflecting the composer's *Phantasie*, a term Beethoven poetically applied to his inspired creativity.

Using this example as a model, let us return to the first movement of Op. 132 (Example 12.2) and see if a closer examination will reveal a more coherent subjectivity —as opposed to a simple-minded representation of psychological unity—in the *Phantasie* of this disruptive thematic exposition. I will argue that surface disjunction is motivated by a coherent dramatic strategy (supported by significant motivic interrelationships), and that both slow and fast music participate in an emergent scheme that combines the objective and the subjective (as in Kerman's interpretation) as fateful and passionate forces in a tragic "expressive genre" (Hatten 1994: 77–90). I will reference topics—as in Agawu, McClary, and implicitly in Kerman— in terms of their expressive suitability to the emergent drama, but in place of McClary's splintered subjectivity I will argue for a dialogical interpretation that enacts a coherent subjectivity (with the capacity to make sudden shifts in con-

Example 12.2. Beethoven, String Quartet in A Minor, Op. 132, first movement, mm. 1–29.

sciousness, but to integrate otherwise contrasting perspectives) as it engages with itself, and against an external agency. That external agency may be interpreted as immutable, tragic Fate—in the ancient Greek sense as well as in its more Romantic manifestations.

The opening eight bars set the enigmatic tone with a four-note cell (P1) that features the paired half steps, $\sharp\hat{7}$–$\hat{1}$–$\hat{6}$–$\hat{5}$, in A minor. Its transposition to $\sharp\hat{4}$–$\hat{5}$–$\hat{3}$–$\hat{2}$ in mm. 3–4 will support a strong connection to P2, the principal theme or motive in the cello, mm. 11–12, which features half steps from both the original cell and its transposition ($\hat{1}$–$\sharp\hat{7}$ and $\hat{3}$–$\hat{2}$), in counterpoint with the other half step of the original cell ($\hat{6}$–$\hat{5}$). Thus, the motet-like topic of the "slow introduction" is related to the "main theme" of the movement as its generative source. The P2 motive (mm. 11–12, cello) is a march in Kerman and Agawu, but an aria topic in McClary.[4] The motive's dotted rhythms support a subsequent affiliation with a more typical march topic, drawing on its sense of "determination," as indeed emerges more clearly in m. 20. But Agawu (1991: 114) also observes that while this motive "is clearly a reference to a march," its "narrow range and sighing effect hint simultaneously at singing style." McClary is not alone, then, when she observes that P2 has the solo character and stepwise line of a more subjective lyricism, at first rather circumspect and then, spilling down from the first violin's sustained E, more passionate in its yearning. I would suggest that P2 is interpretable as a *trope* that creatively fuses in its initial gesture elements of P1 (the tragic half steps), march (the dotted rhythms), and aria (the stepwise line, solo character, and appoggiatura treatment of the half-step sigh that leaves the motive open).

The texture of mm. 9–10 is cadenza-like, and suggestive of the recitative in its individuality of expression. Contextually it functions both as a prolongation of the diminished seventh of V (hence, a suspension of time, an embellished fermata) and as a disruption of the character of what has come before (by sudden rupture of texture and extreme acceleration of tempo). This passage is also a trope of different topics, and it may be further interpreted as a personal response (solo instrument, implied recitative intimacy) in a state of agitation (fast figuration, cadenza brilliance) to the looming intensification in m. 8 of the "fateful" emblem of the tragic. Thus, the movement begins with a strong shift in level of discourse that sets up what I consider to be a dialogical relationship between the objective, fateful opening and a more personal, passionate response.

Agawu takes special note of the resolution to i^6 at the end of m. 10, treating it as one of several instances of noncongruence, since tonic arrives before the theme in m. 11. But I would counter by noting that the F–E appoggiatura on that last beat of m. 10 clearly echoes the P1 cell and thus anticipates the P1-based counterpoint that will ensnare P2 like a fateful web (see mm. 13–14 and mm. 23–24 for clear examples). Furthermore, i^6 rounds off the agitated reaction as a kind of undercutting: Kerman (244) dramatizes this premature resolution as sounding like "a hand clapped over the mouth [of a] scream." The pattern of outburst and repression is thus established for subsequent disruptions.

We can see the outburst-repression pattern prepared in a less disjunctive way in the treatment of the main theme (mm. 11–18). Although the theme starts periodically in two-bar units, its passionate yearning leads to sequential intensification as a one-bar unit (in mm. 17 and 18), and the broken periodicity leads to a liquidation of the theme in frustrated dotted unisons descending relentlessly through a Neapolitan, marking the frustrated outburst. The dotted rhythms herald the march topic of m. 20, another trope interpretable as tragic, fateful determination; it combines implacable quarter-note staccato chords (march, hence "with resolve") with a chromatic bass (tragic lament, hence "fateful") to the arrival on a cadential $^6_4$. Thus, the outburst is unfolded progressively, and the expressive effect is one of increasing frustration leading to grim resolve. The interpretation of this emergent march idea as tragic and inexorable is reinforced by the melting away in the first part of the "fermata" created by the poignant Adagio and its "repression." In turn, the more objective reflection on the tragic of the Adagio spurs a second reaction in the form of a compressed version of the agitated response from m. 9, now on a more stable V^7 to prepare for a proper arrival of the P2 theme.

This version of the theme begins with the definitive package of P1 and P2, and a reinforcement of P2 in octaves. Marking the structural downbeat of the Allegro proper, the doubling of second violin and cello recalls an orchestral *tutti,* despite the continued *piano* dynamic. But just when we think the movement is finally underway and the main theme will be completely presented, the same intensification leads to frustration and a *forte* Neapolitan descent. When we land on an intense grinding of the motive over a repeated Phrygian half cadence, iv⁶–V (Example 12.3, mm. 30–33), we realize that a modulation to F minor has taken place. Phrygian half-cadences correlate with the fateful in Beethoven's style.[5] This warning, however, yields to a more positive F major, supported by increasingly lighter and more playful figuration (Example 12.3, mm. 34–39). Before these playful cadential progressions can resolve to tonic, however, intensification leads to another Phrygian half cadence on V of D minor (m. 40).[6] This second one brings the playfulness to a halt by diverting to the relative minor. The use of a gavotte topic—which in Agawu's account appears unaligned and at a structurally subsidiary point with respect to the preparations of V of F—functions quite effectively as a somewhat pompous (imitative) response to the implied seriousness of the push to D minor, and the energies in the second bar of the gavotte motive betray a more playful or ironic spirit. After two statements of the gavotte motive, with imitation, D minor is in turn displaced by V/F, and an excited, near-chromatic ascent leads in m. 47 to a climactic A and the cadential $^6_4$ of a definitive close in F major.

Clearly the second theme that follows in F major is a radical departure from the tragic atmosphere of the opening, but just as clearly, and neglected in the three interpretations I have cited, Beethoven has carefully worked out a convincing transition to this oasis of serenity, by progressive infusions of positive energy along the way. McClary's interpretation of this theme as "[radiating] hope, escape, or nostalgia for a lost arcadia" (123) is appropriate; but her more radical elaboration, in the spirit of Adorno, is perhaps less warranted. McClary claims that the theme "comes to invoke a sense of longing for the arcadia of the Enlightenment, even though the irrationality of such devices [the use of a nonconventional second key area] marks them as irrevocably alienated from the Edenic world of the previous generation" (123). Although I would agree that the theme suggests an expanded pastoral mode (see Chapter 3), this theme is not so atypical, nor does its key suggest alienation. Beethoven's use of the subdominant (F major) of the typical relative major (C major) for topical contrasts in a work in minor mode (either for the second theme or the slow movement)[7] has become a Classical convention that is well supported by two kinds of stylistic growth: (1) the use of form-building progressions of descending thirds (Op. 7, II; Op. 34; Op. 106), and (2) the choice of a subdominant-oriented area for its associated reduction of tension. Since the subdominant in a minor key is also minor, the convention substitutes the (major) subdominant of the relative major (or VI in minor) for the slow movements of works

Example 12.3. Beethoven, Op. 132, first movement, mm. 30–58.

Example 12.4. Beethoven, Op. 132, first movement, coda, mm. 228–64. (*Continued on the next page.*)

in minor—as in Op. 13 (*Pathétique*), Op. 31, no. 2 (*Tempest*), and Op. 57 (*Appassionata*). This choice of key for slow movements was easily adopted for the second key area in a minor-mode work whenever that area implemented a more positive topical opposition to the tragic first theme group.

I will set aside the problematic aspects of larger form in this movement and turn instead to the coda (Example 12.4), where a characteristic thematic integration counters Agawu's claim that the work ends without resolution. The kind of thematic resolution I find is one in which the essential conflict between P1 as objective Fate and P2 as passionate subjective response reaches its dialogical climax. Since the tension between the two is exacerbated to an almost unbearable degree, it would appear that Agawu's interpretation has clear grounds. But such heightening of tension is characteristic of thematic or strategic resolution of a dramatic premise in a coda (Hatten 1987). What matters for thematic resolution is whether the dramatic argument is clinched, and with this coda Beethoven achieves perhaps the most convincing tragic closure since the *fortissimo* cataclysm that brings the *Appassionata* to its fiery end. First, in the final peroration of P2 (beginning in m. 232) the motive is extended, presumably for a cadential summation (mm. 241–46), but expanding into a passionate outburst, with the half-bar fragment being treated to increasingly expressionistic leaps. At the *fortissimo* climax (mm. 247–48)

Example 12.4. *Continued*

the P1 + P2 thematic package is emblematically summarized, and a subsequent liquidation of its appoggiatura subsides dynamically, harmonically, and rhythmically (mm. 249–53) for one last fateful crescendo above a thematized dominant expansion (mm. 254–57). That crescendo leads to the *forte* peroration of the tragic march, now combined with the metric resolution of P2 in a cadential pattern that hammers A minor with inexorably tragic vehemence.

The dynamic structure of this coda might best be understood with the help of an operatic image: the tragic-heroic protagonist singing in passionate extremity before impending doom, then marching implacably to utter annihilation. Or one might view the fateful web of the enigmatic P1 cell and the emergent march topic as finally immobilizing the protagonist, with P2 captured by the march and led to an inexorably tragic end. Whether or not one chooses to interpret this ending programmatically (I offer these images only as a form of "poetic criticism," in Schumann's sense), it is clearly coherent with respect to the dramatic trajectory implied in the opening. As Kerman and McClary note, the consoling second theme is not allowed to stand; indeed, its final resolution to A major (mm. 223–30) is denied—it slips back into A minor even *before* being disrupted by the coda in m. 232.

McClary claims that Op. 132 "enacts the tension between, on the one hand, a loss of belief in the very conventions upon which Beethoven himself had earlier relied and, on the other, the desire to speak despite obvious skepticism that speech is possible." Her ultimate interpretation is intended as "a kind of reconciliation between Kerman's humanist interpretation and Agawu's formal analysis" (2000: 119). But in attempting to turn Beethoven into a skeptic with respect to the vitality of conventions, and in viewing Op. 132 as a step on the way to the postmodern splintering of subjectivity, she has moved beyond historical reconstruction to a present-day appropriation of Beethoven. I would counter that Beethoven works quite consistently within the conventions of his extension of Classical style principles. Beethoven's conventions have also accrued expressive meanings over the course of his compositional career, and they enabled him to maintain coherence even when exploiting extremes of discontinuous discourse. If it appears that he is struggling with outworn Classical conventions, it may be because we have assumed too limited a model for those conventions, which Beethoven was in the process of transforming—and often strengthening—already in his first mature works from the 1790s.

McClary wants to justify the expressive meanings that may be inferred from a disruptive surface against the claims of deeper meaning that are typically referred to a Schenkerian analysis, and this perspective also warps her critique of Agawu. As I have shown, there is dramatic coherence to be found even in Beethoven's surface discontinuities, but that coherence is not merely topical. And it is negotiated with not only underlying tonal progressions but also (neglected in McClary's account) cogent motivic and gestural relationships that can support our assessment of agency or subjectivity.

I would maintain that Beethoven is not postmodern in his self-conscious play with all the conventions at his disposal; there is too much that is ultimately integrative in his treatment of even the most disparate materials. But there is certainly a link to modernism, in that Beethoven was concerned with expanding the resources of musical expression to the extent of a self-conscious awareness of the very conventionality of his language (as Adorno and Rosen, among others, have observed). Later composers might find new materials with which to expand the expressive resources of their styles, perhaps promoting aesthetic goals that would have appeared foreign to Beethoven, but they would encounter much the same struggle to cue multileveled meanings—temporal, discursive, and expressive—by means of stylistic and other disjunctions, especially when the resources of functional harmony were no longer available. Disjunctive strategies analogous to Beethoven's may be found in twentieth-century composers from Stravinsky, who rejected Beethoven,[8] to Schnittke, who embraced him. Indeed, twentieth-century composers have employed disjunctive strategies in support of radically differing expressive ends and degrees of subjectivity—from objective and ironic wit to extremes of apocalyptic tragedy, both as personally experienced and dispassionately represented. Beethoven's forging of a musical language capable of levels of tragedy and irony thus presents a challenge for twentieth-century styles that would approach a comparable depth of meaning—as well as for those postmodern styles that are content to play with surfaces.

Beyond Topics and Discontinuity: Beethoven, String Quartet in A Minor, Op. 132, Finale

Topics, as we have seen, are stylistic categories or types that can accommodate a wide range of creative and varied tokens. Although we tend to think of prototypes when imagining a topic, and the analysis of topics has naturally concentrated on works where clear-cut topics or topical blends are central to the discourse,[9] there are, of course, many works where the contrastive play of clear-cut topics may not be foregrounded. One such example is the sonata-rondo finale of Beethoven's String Quartet in A Minor, Op. 132. The finale begins with seamless continuity, and although thematic contrasts will follow, they do not create the radical disjunctions found in the first movement. Furthermore, the finale's "topics" are not prototypes, whereas in the first movement—even discounting contradictory labeling of the main theme of the Allegro as march or aria (see above)—few interpreters would deny clear traces of these and other defined topics. The following analysis will extend interpretation beyond familiar topics and introduce *strategic types* that may elude clear topical identification, instead emerging from Beethoven's creativity at the level of the token.

The finale (Example 12.5, mm. 1–39) begins with a clear melody and accompaniment texture, but "singing style" as a topical label fails to capture the character of this theme. Perhaps we could widen the topical interpretation by noting that the theme features a dance-derived $\frac{3}{4}$ meter, and that the Romantic melody sings above a mesmerizing, hurdy-gurdy accompaniment. But the character of this theme is haunting for other reasons that have less to do with such topical flavorings and

Example 12.5. Beethoven, Op. 132, fifth movement (finale), mm. 1–39.

more to do with other kinds of types, both stylistic and strategic—including some unique to Beethoven.

The recitative which ends the previous movement's eccentric march clearly serves as topical transition to set up the theme, now interpretable (in response to recitative) as an aria endowed with personal expressiveness. But the recitative also prepares the thematic $\hat{6}$–$\hat{5}$, F–E, from the first movement. Upon the *attacca* into the finale, that sigh will become a haunting ostinato and one ingredient in the obsessive accompaniment figuration. The melody's first structural move is A–G#, and with the accompanimental F–E the first movement's enigmatic cell is complete. Thus, we are led to hear the finale of Op. 132 as reengaging the expressive world of the first movement.[10]

In Op. 132 the opening movement ends with inexorable tragedy. The initially quiet finale, on the other hand, sounds like an aftermath; it is unable to escape the fateful net of the four-note chromatic cell. But then something extraordinary happens. In m. 7 the bass yields G# to G♮, which supports a V^4_3 of the subdominant in C, and the melody swells to G♮ as an appoggiatura to that subdominant. The modulation to the relative major is not at all remarkable for a rondo theme in binary form. But the modulation is strategically transformed here into a highly marked expressive moment, one that gesturally "opens up" the obsessive and cramped confines of the A minor theme and allows, in an embodied sense, more breathing room, along with a sense of relief or release into a more euphoric mode. With this liberating gesture the dramatic goal of the movement is foreshadowed. Note that my interpretation here owes less to topical influences than to expressively motivated progressions in the melody and harmony of the theme, and their registral expansion. Nevertheless, the topical ingredients of this theme provide an appropriate setting for this expressive action.

The opening-up gesture of the finale's theme cues an expressive genre leading from tragic to transcendent; but this dramatic trajectory is rarely unproblematic. In the finale the second strain of the theme moves through more troubled chromatic reversals in the bass, as applied dominants yield their leading tones in an unsettled sequence (mm. 20 and 22). As soon as the theme cadences, what I have elsewhere analyzed as a primal scream erupts (Hatten 1994: 54–55). This raw outburst (m. 35, again in m. 39) is marked by unusual doubling, exacerbating the dissonant ninth-plus-octave in the first violin. The F–E motive is here verticalized, and its dissonance is thematic—a clear reminder of the tragic vehemence of the first movement. This is not a topic, however, and the effect is uniquely Beethoven's.

The punctuated eighths that round off the scream into a proper eight-bar period (mm. 40–42) recall the marchlike staccato quarters in the first movement. Beethoven invokes topical character by thematic reference, since a march is not prototypically in $\frac{3}{4}$ meter.[11] But the second time (Example 12.6, mm. 49–50) these purposeful eighths lead us to G major. Notice the smooth transition as these same eighths, *subito piano*, lead in learned imitation to a galant/pastoral idea treated to a sequential descent in thirds. Is this the B theme? And is this an instance of developing variation, since each idea evolves out of the previous one? In any case the "theme" sounds like a calming response to the preceding screams, but it becomes transitional in function when its eight-bar sequence accelerates and lands on a fateful, Phrygian half cadence to V of E minor (mm. 58–59). The cadence is progressively deformed in two varied repetitions, as Beethoven first suspends the previous G, producing an augmented sonority in m. 61, and then introduces an F♮ in m. 63, which creates a grindingly dissonant augmented sixth with the D#. By also suspending both C and G in the viola, Beethoven creates the most complexly dissonant sonority thus far. Because of the varied repetition, we can hear the chord as a dis-

Example 12.6. Beethoven, Op. 132, finale, mm. 49-68.

torted V in E minor, even though it resolves as a V^{+4}_{2} of VI with a C pedal. This dissonance sets up an inexorable cadential progression with obsessive, ostinato figuration, very much in the character of the closing page of the first movement.

Again, these are not topics, but their significance can be interpreted if we have a theory of musical meaning that goes beyond obvious textural and stylistic types to those unique formations that create what Leonard B. Meyer (1989) calls an *idiolect*. I do not mean to deny conventions here—indeed, I have drawn on conventions of form and harmony, as well as typical attributions of tension to dissonance and the tragic to the minor mode, in grounding my expressive interpretations. Not surprisingly, one of Beethoven's focal motives is $\hat{6}$–$\hat{5}$ in minor, a stylistic type with a long history signifying the tragic, as Deryck Cooke (1959) claimed years ago. Even "unique" events may have conventional pasts—if at times the conventions are ones that Beethoven has established for his own style.

In the next episode (Example 12.7), the central development section of the sonata-rondo form, fragments of the main theme swirl over a slow harmonic rhythm (V^6_5 of IV and V^4_3 in C) that, from this verbal description, might suggest a pastoral moment (mm. 125–36). But the aural effect is hardly pastoral. Indeed, considered stylistically, the status of the pastoral as a topic is somewhat ambiguous in this example.

I argued for broader consideration of the pastoral field as a topical *mode* in Chapter 3. It is not surprising to find, in this expansion of the topic, that pastoral cueing is now no longer necessarily prototypical or even entirely "characteristic." Here the development of fragments of the first theme begins with incidental, galant-based chromaticism, and the textural intensity (typically associated with development sections) is not so much propulsive as it is frenetic. The fragments gain in intensity not by progressing but by sounding trapped within a static mechanism; Ratner's (1980: 391) "clockwork" topic comes to mind. Upon the reiteration of textural and melodic inversions (m. 145), an intensification of harmony leads to diminished-seventh expansions (m. 153). Due to the tension of this harmonization, the slow harmonic rhythm attributed to the pastoral mode fails to achieve the potential pastoral oasis that we might expect as one stage in this expressive genre. Instead, the effect is that of being trapped inside the fateful web with which the movement began. The expressive development of this sonata-rondo appears to be motivated, then, not by conventional topical meaning, but by Beethoven's ongoing creative responses to the initial premise of the movement.

The recapitulatory return of the rondo theme (m. 169 ff.) is suitably elided, given the emphasis on continuity in this movement, and it features three false entrances of the first two bars of the theme in the subdominant before the tonic takes over. The second entrance reverses the ending C♯ to a C♮, in anticipation of A minor, and the third restores that C♯ to add another two bars of the theme before the definitive entrance in A minor (with C♮) effectively displaces it. These multiply false returns are perhaps motivated by a similar inability to escape the tragic web. The expressive continuity in this movement recalls something of the obsessiveness of perpetual motion, but Beethoven's means are more subtle here.

The exposition's A and B sections are recapitulated as expected in sonata-rondo

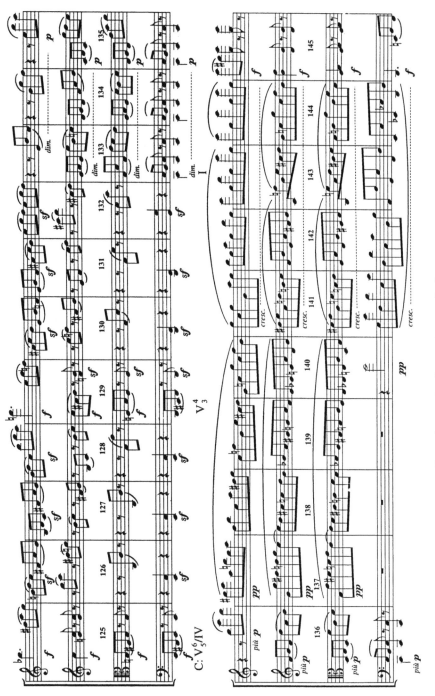

Example 12.7. Beethoven, Op. 132, finale, mm. 125–45.

Example 12.8. Beethoven, Op. 132, finale, mm. 242–48.

form, with the second group appropriately transposed down a fifth. Whereas in the exposition the B section collapsed back into the rondo theme, in the recapitulation it reaches a surprisingly final cadence in the upper three voices on F, above a pedal dominant in the cello (Example 12.8, m. 244). The cadential motive played by the first violin in mm. 242–44 is then given speculative treatment, cueing the learned style by means of imitation in the cello and viola (mm. 244–48). Such treatment is typical of a development, or at least a transition, and this section ultimately functions as a transition to the final statement of the rondo theme. Although the section begins closurally, reiterating the cadential gesture within a *pianissimo* web, this trancelike, euphoric reflection cannot be the coda, since both the sonata-rondo form and the tragic-to-transcendent expressive genre demand one more dramatic encounter with the main theme. Beethoven sets up the return marvelously, gradually infusing the closural episode with bits of the rondo theme, and shading the closural reflection into a modulatory transition (Example 12.9). In m. 260 a rhythmic delay hints at the F–E ostinato rhythm and contour, and in m. 265 the head motive slips in. This triggers an accelerando and crescendo, emotionally heightened by "heartbeat" *pizzicati* in the cello (mm. 267–76) and minor-ninth intensifications of the F–E motive in the first violin (mm. 272–83).

The main theme emerges, *Presto* and *forte*, in m. 281, with the cello forcing the melody to sound out from beneath the first violin's expressionistic F–E insistence. The tragic apotheosis of the theme in A minor is elusive, however, in that the violin shifts to support the cello for the phrase that modulates to C major (pickup to m. 285), dramatically displacing the fateful F–E motive with the more positive portion of the theme, and highlighting its registral expansion. After a single statement of the theme a definitively transcendent moment arrives (pickup to m. 296). A lengthy coda in A major begins before the refrain theme can fully cadence. The spiritual liberation of this coda is experienced as a sudden breakthrough, and its hushed *piano* dynamic is indicative of the unearned character of this moment of grace.

Example 12.9. Beethoven, Op. 132, finale, mm. 260–97.

Unlike what I have called the addendum to the finale of the "Serious" Quartet (Op. 95), an extreme, Romantic ironic dismissal in its shift from a previously tragic discourse (Hatten 1994: 186–88), the extensive coda to the finale of Op. 132 is thematically and expressively integrated as a logical outcome to both the movement and the quartet. Beginning with the modulation in the first theme at m. 7, we have glimpsed the potential of this ending. The coda's release achieves the euphoria hinted in both the pastorally inflected development section (Example 12.7) and the imitative codetta/transition (Example 12.8) that prepared the climactic return of the rondo theme.

To summarize, although topics provide benchmarks for interpretation, much more is required to properly interpret those movements whose topics are far from prototypical. What we have observed in the finale of Op. 132 is a greater concern with continuity, and a perhaps compensatory move from the foregrounding of topics as subjects of discourse to the foregrounding of marked moments in themes that are less characterized by underlying topics.

Conclusion

In the conclusion to my first book, *Musical Meaning in Beethoven*, I summarized musical meaning as difference, correlated by means of structured (marked) oppositions, and further interpretable according to a range of contexts (thematization, expressive genre, tropes, intertextuality) that move interpretation beyond the more stable hierarchies of correlation in a musical style. Although I defended the iconic as a motivation for musical signs, I maintained that "the ultimate status of the musical sign is symbolic" (1994: 275). In the present study I have explored the ways in which indexical as well as iconic aspects of musical gesture provide more direct motivation for expressive meaning in music. I have also expanded my investigation into the symbolic, but more in the realm of the synthetic, in particular those familiar stylistic types known as topics. And I have explored ways in which new musical meanings emerge at either end of the spectrum: from spontaneous gestures that find individual musical settings, to creative tropes that emerge from the combination of well-established stylistic or strategic types. I have suggested how musical oppositions (for example, those that differentiate grief and joy) provide musical gestures with a degree of systematic coherence within a style. But I have probed more deeply into the other side of gesture—its internal character as an indivisible, or molar, unit of "energetic shaping through time." From this perspective musical gestures may be understood as synthetic entities with emergent affective meaning, even prior to their incorporation within a musical style and their subsequent positioning within a hierarchy of stylistic correlations.

The phenomenological character of my investigation into the qualitative aspects of musical gesture (iconic, indexical), even before its systematic codification in a style (symbolic), has surely not gone unnoticed.[1] My heuristic exploration of the biological or psychological aspects of musical gesture included considering the way a musical gesture might enact a universal physical expression of grief, as in the tragic thematic gesture of Schubert's Piano Sonata in A Minor, D. 784. But my interpretation of that gesture was, from the start, inextricably intertwined with stylistic categories (such as the funeral march topic, or the drum roll of a cortège). Even those musical gestures that appear to be original and spontaneous immediately encounter the virtual environments of meter and tonality (and, if presented at the beginning of a movement, they may help to create the meter and tonality that is understood as providing that environment).

Although the purely phenomenological experience of musical gesture may be an illusion, it is a fiction supported by composers when they help us hear the familiar as fresh or novel. When Beethoven opens a piano sonata with a mm$^6_5$ chord (Op. 31, no. 3, Example 7.20), we can easily predict that it will be treated as a ii$^6_5$ within the syntax of tonal progression (and the E♭ seventh will eventually resolve to the leading tone of the dominant). But for a brief, shining moment the isolation of the gesture and its immediate reiteration impels us to reflect upon the chord as pure sonority, a sonic event that is qualitative and expressive in itself. Indeed, we may hear the sonority as suspended in a tonal environment where nothing demands immediate resolution.[2] We may then integrate this sonority into the synthetic gesture of the entire measure: hearing the softly dissonant but warm minor-minor seventh sonority as supporting the "acceptance" of the descending fifth in the melody, the "calling forth" of its dotted rhythm, and the gentle "insistence" stemming from its downbeat metric placement. These connotations are supported by—or in turn motivated by—the gentle dynamic level, the smooth slur and falling sigh figure, and the rhetorical rests that follow, which imply a more *rubato* pacing. All of these elements come together to create a musically emergent experience.

Note that this quintessentially Romantic attention to sound is achieved within a Classical performing tradition. The reiteration of the entire gesture, like an echo or reverberation, contributes to our singling it out for reflection. As we attend to it, movement becomes pose—an animated stillness, as if under a fermata. A sense of the pastoral (potentially as mode, although as we have seen, the movement veers abruptly toward the comic mode) also emerges from this constellation of gentle, gestural qualities (sonority, contour, rhythm, dynamics, articulation, duration, and pacing) and their treatment as thematic (isolation by rhetorical rest, emphasis by reiteration).

But what, the reader will inevitably ask, does this gesture "mean"? Throughout this book I have ventured verbal interpretations of gestures and their contribution to the musical discourse and its resulting expressive genre. Just now, in attempting to characterize the contribution of a number of elements in this gesture, I resorted to an analytical parsing. Nevertheless, I would insist that the emergent meaning of this opening gesture eludes a mere summing up of its connotations. To venture an intermodal conceit, what I hear is an exquisite recipe of ingredients that are baked into a unique expression—recognizable enough to be comprehensible, and distinctive enough to be satisfying—yet I have no word that could translate that aural "taste" into language. I could choose a word, and utilizing Alexandra Pierce's "tone of voice" heuristic, perhaps come closer to the affective modality that I sense. Indeed, by pursuing her other exercises, I could perhaps discover how to convey the "just so" character of this musical gesture in all its dimensions—its inner "wit." And then I could perform the opening in a perfectly convincing way, but be no closer to explaining just what the meaning of the gesture might be, in any literal sense. Perhaps a purely synthetic approach to the explanation of synthetic categories such as gesture is as impossible as the purely phenomenological experiencing of gesture. Or perhaps the problem is that we tend to think of all theoretical explanation in terms of the analytic. Perhaps a more poetic texture of words is needed to suggest those movement images and affective meanings that most closely correspond to one's musical experience.[3] But at some stage we must move beyond the subjective to provide stylistic and interpretive evidence to support our claims that such meanings are both historically plausible and intersubjectively accessible. Or to go still further (as in Chapter 1), one might draw on several methods of analysis, several kinds of evidence, even several modes of explanation to converge on an interpretation that is intersubjectively apt, from the perspective of contemporaneous competencies, for historian, performer, and theorist alike. Given that this degree of explanation is impractical to provide for every musical gesture, some of my own interpretations may appear impressionistic; nevertheless, by concentrating on a limited repertoire, I have been able to provide an interconnected web of examples, interpretations, and theoretical evidence that I trust has strengthened the plausibility of my claims.

I began my comments on the opening gesture of Beethoven's Op. 31, no. 3 with the conventional bias toward pitch—both as sonority and melodic contour. As illustrated by my discussion of rhetorical gesture in the first movement of his Op. 109, we can rarely know which comes first in the compositional process: the gesture, with all its complex synthesis of energies, or the unusual tonal procedure (or violation of tonal syntax) that forms just one part of that gesture. What matters in interpreting Op. 109 is that we understand the tonal reversal as part of a larger rhetorical gesture that is multiply motivated and that becomes thematic. I have argued that a striking gesture may motivate unusual pitch events, or evocative uses of sonority. The traditional approach, on the other hand, gives priority to the manipulations of tonal syntax, perhaps with attention to their rhythmic and metric features, while the gestural treatment of dynamics, articulation, and pacing are relegated to the role of highlighting those "motives."

To be sure, each premise—the pitch-specific violation and the comprehensive gesture—is an expressive one. Each may be understood as thematic, and each may have structural consequences, at least in the hands of a sensitive composer. However, when the pitch dimension is *unmarked* in its syntactic treatment, then other dimensions of the gesture—perhaps neglected aspects of articulation, dynamics, and pacing—will be even more crucial for interpreting a theme's expressive character and structural consequences. For example, the syntactically conventional iv–i progression was interpreted as a grieving gesture in the Schubert piano sonata (Chapter 8), and the straightforwardly diatonic ascent from $\hat{5}$ to $\hat{1}$ was interpreted as a comic gesture in the finale of the Beethoven cello sonata (Chapter 9). But in the latter example the weak metric location of the "resolution" to tonic suggested ultimate syntactic closure as an expressive goal to be achieved. And in both the Beethoven and Schubert examples, unusual tonal events had a role to play as well in the unfolding of their respective expressive genres.

In urging a more synthetic approach to musical meaning, then, I have not neglected the role of pitch (and rhythm) in the more inclusive category of gesture, even when I have selectively focused on thematic gestures in which other elements have played a more significant role, as evidenced by their subsequent treatment. The working out (and evolution) of an articulatory gesture in the first movement of Schubert's Piano Sonata in A Major, D. 959, is a compelling example. The synthesis of musical elements in a thematic gesture, as I argue in Chapter 8, counterbalances the structural priority given to a pitch cell, whether in a Schoenbergian *Grundgestalt* or an even more abstract set class. And a gestural approach offers as well the necessary complement to more traditional analyses of motivic structure, with their emphasis on pitch and rhythm. Thus, I would propose expanding the concept of motive or *Grundgestalt* by defining it in more comprehensive terms as a thematic gesture.

A musical gesture is far more than a "tonally sounding form," in Hanslick's (1974 [1854]) memorable image. One cannot fully understand compositional design without addressing expressive content and its motivation of structure. Hanslick reveals his formalist bias in his other memorable metaphor for music, the arabesque (those decorative designs that frame the picture).[4] A gestural approach avoids such marginalization and puts us in the center of the action. In our gestural encounters with music, both evolutionary history and individual human development have ensured that we will connect with the expressive—we can hardly force ourselves *not* to attend to significant energetic shaping as affective—but this sense of embodied expressiveness in music is enhanced by our ongoing engagement with the implied agency behind thematic, rhetorical, and dialogical gestures. In addition to recognizing gestures' expressive properties, and co-experiencing their synthesis through an embodied sense of action within the virtual environments of meter and tonality, we can identify at least one fundamental agency as created and sustained through the developing variation of a thematic gesture. We will experience its independent "life force" within gravitational fields, but also as an emerging individual subjectivity defined by interactions with other agencies (at least in those musical styles that treat thematic gesture as the "subject" of musical "discourse"). And the journey of that agency will create a trajectory—a dramatic arc and an outcome—as a unique realization of an expressive genre (at least, in the music I have explored).

An interpretation of musical gesture thus offers insight into a composition's remarkable integration of expression, subjectivity, musical discourse, and resulting expressive form. Gesture is not merely the default level of interpretation with which I began my investigation; it is manifested, embodied, and engaged at all levels of style and interpretation. A gestural perspective leads us to discover expressive motivations for the intricate structures and formal hierarchies that are often the stopping place for analytical inquiry. As coordinated with topics, enriched with tropes, and integrated with both the syntax of a style and its traditions of performance, the interpretation of musical gesture has much to contribute toward a more comprehensive practice of music theorizing. That practice will embrace the expressively grounded reconstruction of style competency, the expressively motivated explanation of style growth and change, and the expressively engaged interpretation of musical experience.

These interrelated tasks demand not only our intelligence, but our empathy and our poetic imagination as well. Thus, my closing gesture is also an opening one—an invitation to engage with that which is most human in our artistic inheritance, and to share in its vitality.

Notes

Introduction

1. This is a point Janet Levy (1981) first argued in 1975, with respect to the syntactic function of Haydn's gestures as opening or closing.

2. I will delineate these paths with reference to the work of a few individuals who have contributed representative, foundational arguments for each approach. The complete story, involving many forward-thinking music scholars, would require a separate book in order to fairly credit each participant. Instead, this introduction is meant to situate my own work as a music theorist relative to current trends in musicology.

3. McClary (2002: xviii) now claims that "the long-term legacy of *Feminine Endings* involves not so much the particular arguments it advances, but rather the fact that it granted North American scholars license to discuss meaning and to exchange interpretations." This overstates the case considerably, but then, much music-theoretical work on musical meaning is curiously absent from her references. Ironically, in claiming that "*Feminine Endings* has attained the status of a classic text" (xviii) and crediting it with a "paradigm shift" (xiii) in musicology, McClary apparently accepts the concept of a canon of individual and influential works (in musicology), and assumes the authoritative voice of an individual subject who can both create and evaluate her own place in history—hardly a sufficiently "contingent" set of positions for either a work or a subject, by the standards of the New Musicology. I agree that her book has become a frequently discussed text and that her work has helped promote a shift toward ideological interpretation. But hers was not the only new paradigm available for addressing musical meaning.

4. This presumed expansion of a work's meanings actually reduces the composer's role in creating and determining meaning. Note the parallel in McClary's reduction of the interpreting subject: "the Self can usefully be understood as a construction formed at the intersection of a wide range of discourses" (2002: xvi). For the problematic notion of a work defined as the intersection of codes, see Hatten (1985). Briefly, both positions tend to reduce the freedom of the creative agent (composer, author) to that of an unwitting pawn caught in the currents of cultural discourses or practices over which she has no real control. The result is a transposition of meaning to the level of cultural constructions; the scholar in turn is enjoined to "resist" an aesthetic that is too autonomously conceived (Krims 1998). In my own work I have demonstrated how one might pursue a less autonomous notion of aesthetic meaning without displacing the plausible intentions of a freely willing composer, as negotiated within a flexible and generative set of stylistic principles and constraints (Hatten 1994).

5. For productive hypotheses concerning such style growth and change, see Meyer (1989). Meyer also addresses the problem of autonomy in a way that preserves

both the cultural importance of *style* and prerogative of *choice:* "There is no such thing as understanding a work of art on its own terms. Indeed, the very notion of work of art is cultural. The choices made by some compositional community can be understood and explained only if relationships can be discerned among the goals set by culture, the nature of human cognitive processes, and the alternatives available given some set of stylistic constraints" (1989: 351). For Meyer, Romantic ideology includes the values of originality and individuality, and although he is keen to demonstrate how convention is often merely "disguised" in Romantic compositional extravagance, Meyer never doubts the capacity of the creative individual to play with, and extend, those conventions. Ironically, McClary's (2000) study of convention does not significantly acknowledge Meyer's work. I address one of McClary's interpretations in Chapter 12.

6. Just as I would not test the cognition of rich musical experience with subjects who are untrained (or unentrained) in the chosen musical styles, so I would not confuse historically and stylistically constrained kinds of meaning with the uses to which any signifying text can be put.

7. For an application of topics, expressive genre, and tropes to an interpretation of Bruckner's Fourth and Fifth Symphonies, see Hatten (2001). My inquiry responds to the problem of sectional discontinuity—Bruckner's "isolated cells," in Schenker's critique—by considering the expressive motivations for discontinuity within a larger dramatic scheme.

8. See Agawu (1996: 149), for example, who criticizes the dichotomy of structure and expression in Hatten (1994). Cook and Dibben (2001: 62–63) also find "the immediate impression of Hatten's working procedure is that . . . he starts with structural analysis, and then adds in the interpretation" (62), although they concede that the treatment of the Cavatina from Op. 130 (in a chapter entitled "Analysis as Synthesis") is "more even-handed," "mingles structural and expressive vocabulary," and "offers parallel structural and expressive interpretations." I would give three responses to these critiques of my use of structure and expression. Given what was still a rather formalist audience during the time I worked on the book, I felt compelled (as I still do) to ground my expressive claims with solid structural/analytical evidence—in effect, reinforcing the conceptual divide between structure and expression at the same time I was attempting to overcome it. Second, my strategy of presentation was pedagogical in its sequence—gradually introducing a series of expressive approaches—and thus the interpretation of the Cavatina in the last analytical chapter was intentionally the most fully realized in its integration of approaches. Finally, regardless of the novelty of one's approach, one's language must reflect a compromise with old terminologies if one hopes to be understood. I addressed the issue in the conclusion to that book, which I will cite in this section.

9. Nicholas Cook (2003a), in his proposals for "music as performance," goes so far as to suggest that the musical work can exist only as an "interpretive construct" (207) whose field of meaning includes its performances. Although conceding the "historically privileged" (207) role of autographs, scores, and editions, he insists on their notated status as *scripts* that choreograph "a series of real-time, social interactions between players," as opposed to ideal texts that are simply "reproduced in performance" (206). While I am in complete sympathy with the impor-

tance Cook places on interpretation, I differ by maintaining the regulative concept of a work (at least for the examples from Mozart, Beethoven, and Schubert that I address) as reconstructed not just through performances but other kinds of historical and stylistic evidence. The performative nature of music does not displace the work concept, or its status as hierarchically more authoritative, despite the ongoing task we face in reconstructing those stylistic competencies a work presupposes, and interpreting the kinds of contemporaneous meanings it could have supported. Without some regulative concept of a work (not just its structure but its potential meanings—or, to use Cook's felicitous image, those meaningful acts that it "scripts"), how could we evaluate which, among the vast pool of performances, deserve our attention as contributing relevant new interpretations or enhancing established ones? This is not to say that we cannot study mediocre performances for what they can teach us of human interaction as guided by a "script" in performance. It is rather to maintain that performances are inevitably evaluated according to a standard that goes beyond the immediate social fulfillment of performers or listeners. And it is to recognize that performers, like actors, strive to realize an admittedly idealized conception of the work, including those kinds of expressive meanings which scripted actions were intended to recreate. Granted, performers can fail to achieve that level and still have an extremely rewarding experience (at least, outside the demeaning environment of performance competitions), but we should not neglect, as theorists, the source of our discernment of value in performances. It is not just that they can teach us something, but that they have the potential to re-create what has been enfolded into a style and a musical work by the endless, relevant, intentional choices of a gifted individual, one for whom subtle differences in notation were meant to have certain consequences. And those consequences can be reconstructed without presuming a prescribed recipe for their realization in performance. In Part Two I demonstrate how one can maintain both theoretical rigor and flexibility in respecting those gestures implied by a notated score and a relevant stylistic competency.

10. Throughout the book I will make reference to the more familiar ideas of American philosopher and foundational semiotician Charles Sanders Peirce (1839–1914). The *Collected Papers* (1931, 1960) in eight volumes is being superseded by a chronological edition; six volumes out of a projected thirty have appeared (1982–2000). The original editor, Max Fisch, was succeeded by Nathan Houser under the auspices of the Peirce Edition Project at Indiana University–Purdue University at Indianapolis. The interested reader may wish to consult *The Essential Peirce*, edited by Houser and Kloesel (1992), as well as the glossary and index of Hatten (1994) for relevant definitions. Briefly, the *interpretant* is Peirce's term for the idea that arises for some interpreter from the sign-object relationship. It in turn may become a sign, which may give rise to another interpretant; this process may produce a chain of interpretants, which is characteristic of semiosis in general. The interpretant enables Peirce's theory of semiosis to avoid simplistic code-mapping and address the complexities of interpretation—an important advantage for the study of artistic works (as opposed to traffic lights).

11. "Diagrammatic" is Peirce's term for association based on isomorphism of structure, as opposed to similarity of properties. Both kinds of association fall into the category of the "iconic," which differs from the "indexical" in that the latter re-

quires association based upon a dynamic relationship between the sign and the (present) object. Indexical relationships include contiguity, synecdoche, cause-and-effect, stimulus-reaction, deixis (pointing), and ostention ("showing" a token as representative of its type).

12.   See Hatten (1994: 50–56, 257–68) for detailed examples and discussion of the various processes leading to the generation of a new type.

13.   Of course, one cannot assume that the text determines the meaning of the music, or that the music merely illustrates the text. As I have argued elsewhere (1994: 216), music's meanings may at times contradict the text, perhaps tropologically (e.g., ironically), and only a theory of musical meaning not tied to words and programs will enable one to establish such productive collisions and interpret their potentially tropological significance.

14.   The increasing agitation as the Queen recounts her daughter's abduction is reflected more directly in the music beginning in m. 13, which suggests the importance of the gestural as a more immediate source of meaning.

15.   For a more exhaustive treatment of musical troping, including irony, see Hatten (1994: 161–96).

16.   The work was originally composed in 1817 in the key of D♭ major, but was extensively revised and transposed to E♭ major in 1826.

17.   I analyze the dramatic sequence of topics in the opening theme of Beethoven's Op. 31, no. 3, in Chapter 7. In the Conclusion I examine more closely the qualitative significance of this theme's opening gesture.

1. Semiotic Grounding in Markedness and Style

1.   Schenker actually discusses this opening theme in his unfinished manuscript on performance, recently published in translation as *The Art of Performance* (2000 [ca. 1911]). His comments (to which I will return below, note 4) concern *rubato* and not voice-leading; he barely mentions the chord in m. 6, which he labels simply as VI (♭VI in D major, of course) (54).

2.   This effect, in which dysphoric $\hat{3}$ is transformed into euphoric $\hat{3}$, is lost to the eye in the so-called "doubly augmented German sixth," in which lowered $\hat{3}$ is misspelled as raised $\hat{2}$ as an aid to the performer. The reversal of a scale degree has a completely different significance from the chromatic move between scale degrees, especially when the latter moves "in the direction of the inflection."

3.   I will not attempt to fully explain these points in terms of stylistic correlations and markedness of oppositions, although in principle I could do so. For more on the trope of abnegation as it relates to this progression, see Hatten (1994: 58–63). See also in the same volume pp. 281–86, where I argue that the abnegational move underwrites a new expressive genre in both literature and music.

4.   It is here that I would object to Schenker's (2000: 54) suggestion for an *accelerando* to compensate for "an entirely unintended ritardando" in mm. 4–5. As Schenker argues, "Following the fury of the staccato eighths in the preceding bars, the sparse tones would simulate a slowing down, particularly since the rests between them suggest that they should be radically separated one from another. To counter this effect it is necessary to speed up until the VI appears in m. 6."

I would counter that the rhetorical effect of the sudden braking in mm. 4–5 (its uncertainty and dysphoric turn to minor) would be undermined by Schenker's proposed *rubato*. I also disagree with his interpretation of Beethoven's declining wedge in m. 6 as implying "a corresponding holding back," although that may be one way of marking the transformation that is to come, as F♯ gesturally melts into F♮.

5.   Still other interpretations of the "y" theme that might arise from chains of connotation or intermodal gestural considerations would include the "potential" character of the y theme, since it emerges over a dominant pedal, and the theme's "aliveness"—both interpretations are supported by the evolving treatment of the two-bar motive, which, though closed in itself, is treated rather "openly" as far as phrase extension through imitation, sequence, and fragmentation.

2. Expressive Doubling, Topics, Tropes, and Shifts in Level of Discourse

1.   Although I had illustrated shifts in level of discourse in short excerpts from the Andante of Op. 130 (Hatten 1994: 177–81), the impetus to offer a more complete interpretive accounting of this movement came from Yonatan Malin, during a follow-up seminar to my lecture at the University of Chicago in February 1999.

2.   Richard Kramer (1992) notes that the doubled G's at the end of the Cavatina enhance the rhetorical and narrative function of the quadrupled G's which announce the Ouverture of the *Grosse Fuge* finale. This linkage supports expressive doubling in that a reversal in intensity marks a shift to another realm of discourse, one that for Kramer turns the Cavatina into "an act of fantasy" (181). For an in-depth analysis of expressive meaning in the Cavatina itself, see Hatten (1994: 203–23).

3.   See also the insightful analysis of the first movement of Op. 130 by William Kinderman (1995: 299–303), and my own interpretation (Hatten 1994: 134–45).

3. From Topic to Premise and Mode

1.   Richard Will (1994: 166) notes that "the most common subject in Classical-period programmatic symphonies is pastoral" and that "it appears in nearly seventy symphonies and movements that range chronologically across the entire period, from Leopold Mozart's and Johann Stamitz's pastoral symphonies of the 1750s to Beethoven's of 1808." He addresses works with "pastoral titles" as well as those with further programmatic texts or indications; his catalog of the latter extends to 1815. Allanbrook (1983) convincingly demonstrates how pastoral topics create a dominant interpretive context in Mozart's opera *The Marriage of Figaro*.

2.   In a richly textured essay on the pastoral in Beethoven's music, Maynard Solomon (2003: 71–91) interprets Beethoven's final Violin Sonata in G, Op. 96 (1812–13) as a four-movement pastoral work in this sense. As in the case of Op. 101, there are no pastoral titles or programmatic indications on Beethoven's part, but the pastoral style in Op. 96 was recognized, as Solomon notes (258, n8), by contemporary critics such as Wilhelm von Lenz. Solomon also notes Beethoven's preference for pastoral in his lieder, especially *An die ferne Geliebte* (1816), where pastoral imagery serves "as a symbol, not only of the reunion of parted lovers,

but of their unity with nature and all of nature's creatures" (75). Elaine Sisman (2000) interprets some of the more striking pastoral moments in Op. 102, no. 1, and Op. 101 as "visions," from the Greek *phantasia* (considered here as a figure of thought, not a genre). These visions are ethereal, distant in time and place, and evocative of either past memory or future longing (63–76). A compelling approach to the pastoral for the latter half of the nineteenth century is found in Reinhold Brinkmann's *Late Idyll: The Second Symphony of Johannes Brahms* (1995 [1990]); the symphony unfolds as a "monumental" (54) and "melancholy" (46) idyll of "elegiac character" (28; 200–203).

3.   I am grateful to Yonatan Malin for this reference.

4.   Although musical contexts may not always be determinate as to the temporal perspective of pastoral visionary moments, in general the pastoral mode is past-oriented in its recall of lost innocence or of previous joy. A recent study by John Daverio interprets a "gestus of remembering" in Schubert's style, which Schumann recognized critically in essays on the Piano Trio in E♭ Major (with its poetic "memory" of the slow movement in the finale) and the late set of Impromptus, D. 935 (Daverio 2002: 48). Daverio cites Emil Staiger's differentiation of temporal perspective among literary lyric, epic, and dramatic modes in his pithy phrase "lyric existence remembers, epic existence presents, dramatic existence projects" (Staiger 1991 [1946]: 187).

5.   Compare Michael Beckerman (1992) for a set of pastoral features relevant to Mozart, including drones and parallel thirds (94), and their contribution of stasis or timelessness (97).

6.   Eero Tarasti (2002: 97) explores this aspect of what I consider the pastoral under the rubric of the "organic" in Sibelius's Fifth Symphony, noting the importance of the "field" created by repetition, in which a melody or theme "loses its character as a musical subject that distinguishes itself from its surroundings." This "deactorializing" process in turn captures nature's voice, as it were, in the relative stasis of such passages. In my interpretation, Schubert anticipates Sibelius in his creation of such "field" effects, but I will argue that for Schubert these pastoral spaces invoke very human reflection, or reminiscence, or wish-fantasy, and they achieve a certain poignance due to their contextual placement.

7.   According to David Neumeyer (private communication) the use of the dotted-eighth/sixteenth/eighth figure in a waltz (as opposed to a *siciliano*) is not common in early-nineteenth-century waltzes by composers such as Hummel, Lanner, and Strauss Senior. But Schubert appears to have used it eighteen times in 150 individual dances, "most often in a rhythmic context that is very like the composite rhythm of the second theme in the G major sonata: the dotted rhythm 'announcement' followed by smooth, regular rhythms." Neumeyer conjectures that the waltz association may have been more private, perhaps for the circle of Schubert's friends for whom he improvised waltzes, or perhaps "as a kind of Schubertian self-portrait." I am grateful to Prof. Neumeyer for sharing his research with me. For more on Schubert's dances "in 3" (and the problem of distinguishing between *Ländler, Deutscher,* and *Walzer*) see Litschauer and Deutsch (1997).

8.   This point is developed in Rosen (1995) and Hatten (1993) with respect to the development section of Schubert's Piano Sonata in A Major, D. 959.

9. The other option, transposition up a fourth, would have exceeded the range of Schubert's piano.

10. Consider, in this regard, the Aeolian harp effect of a tonic with added $\flat\hat{7}$, used to end Berlioz's "Les derniers soupirs de la harpe" (the fifth "movement" of *Lélio*) and Chopin's Prelude in F Major, Op. 28, no. 23. An Aeolian harp is imaginatively sounded by the action of the wind (from Aeolus, mythical god the winds; a completely different etymology from that of the Aeolian mode). The approximation of the natural overtone series by use of $\flat\hat{7}$ suggests a primordial sounding of Nature.

11. Anthony Newcomb (1997) explores the contrast between rustic (and clumsy) *Ländler* versus urban (and corrupting) waltz as two opposing action forces in the second movement of Mahler's Ninth Symphony. These indeterminate action forces may be interpretable as external forces, other virtual characters, or elements "within the protagonist's own personality" (141). I opt for the latter in my interpretation of the Schubert sonata, and I think that much Romantic music, concerned with hyper-individuality, is best understood in this way.

12. For example, the injection of a military fanfare into Schubert's Waltz in E Major, D. 145, no. 12, or a march in the finales of Schumann's *Papillons* and *Carnaval* cycles (see Chapter 4, Examples 4.4a and 4.4b).

4. The Troping of Topics, Genres, and Forms

1. Troping should not be confused with the generalized concept of metaphor that Lakoff and Johnson (1979, 1999) associate with any cross-domain mapping, and which has been appropriated for music to explain what I call correlations between musical structures and cultural meanings. My tropes involve music's capacity to bring together novel combinations of structures (and their attendant meanings) within the same domain (of music). The theory of conceptual blending (Fauconnier and Turner 2002; Zbikowski 2002: 63–95) is a richer model to explain the creativity of metaphor, as well as dead metaphors (e.g., the blend of computers and viruses) that have become literal meanings. Although it would be possible to model my musical tropes as blended spaces, it is important to note that the musical tropes I am investigating are more like creative metaphors in poetry, in that they are novel interactions between otherwise contrasting musical entities that spark new (emergent) meanings. Thus, high versus low pitch, or motion in music, while perhaps entailing a cross-domain mapping that was originally revelatory, are now quite literal with respect to our understanding of music, having lost any creative spark. For another perspective on our association of gestural motion with music, see Chapter 5.

2. J. N. Forkel, in his biography of Bach (1802, Chapter VI, cited in Little and Jenne 1991: 30–31, trans. David and Mendel 1966 [1945]: 323–24), praises Bach's capacity not only to capture the "precise character and rhythm" of every dance, but also to incorporate their rhythms into his fugues, "in a manner as easy and uninterrupted from the beginning to the end as if they were minuets"—an observation that might suggest an awareness of topical, if not fully tropological, use of dance gestures in other genres.

3. Peter Brown (1983: 439–40) emphasizes the importance of this theme in his

analysis of the symphony, and Walter Frisch (1984:130) labels it the "missing theme" (X) because of its absence from the return section of the Andante (perhaps to create an expectation for its later recall in the finale).

5. Foundational Principles of Human Gesture

1. For a more complete account of the range of signs that may be processed by an organism, see Thomas A. Sebeok (1972, 1976, 1977), who coined the term "zoosemiotics" for the field (Sebeok 1963: 465–66). Sebeok draws on the concept of an organism's "Umwelt" (von Uexküll 1928), which may be defined as the phenomenal world of an organism, comprised of all and only those impacts from the environment to which its sense organs can attend. Helpful summaries of von Uexküll's and Sebeok's ideas may be found in Thure von Uexküll (1987) and Baer (1987). For an interesting application to music, see Eero Tarasti (2002).

2. Edelman (1992: 87) emphasizes that maps of neurons are topographically connected and posits "a dynamic structure containing multiple reentrant local maps (both motor and sensory) that are able to interact with nonmapped parts of the brain." This global mapping "ensures the creation of a dynamic loop that continually matches an animal's gestures and posture to the independent sampling of several kinds of sensory signals" (89).

3. An example of such nonconscious perceptual functioning is found in what is called "blindsight" (Weiskrantz 1986), in which a subject who cannot report vision in a certain area nevertheless can "guess" a majority of correct answers when questioned directly about information shown to that blind area. This is due to a "second major subcortical pathway from the eyes to the brain, which is intact in blindsight subjects" (Tye 1995: 217). Thus, information reaches the brain, and the subject can access it in making such judgments, even though it is not directly available to the visual consciousness of the blindsighted person.

4. Bregman (1990) has pioneered "auditory scene analysis" to investigate, among other issues, how our hearing can distinguish coherent sound events and their generating sources from amid the welter of competing sounds. Applications to music include the well-known phenomenon of auditory stream segregation—how listeners parse successive pitches into coherent yet competing melodic lines.

5. Thus, event cognition goes beyond categorization based on attributes. As McCabe (1986: 13) argues, "categorization theorists do not indicate how ['bundles of perceptual and functional attributes . . . that form natural category discontinuities' (Rosch 1978: 31)] come to be bundled or correlated; their explanation implies that our knowledge depends on our perception of particular attributes (those with high cue validity) that by their particularity require some form of further organization." Furthermore, "models of memory and pattern recognition based on mental comparisons of various versions of then and now (templates, schemas, scripts) also attribute the order perceived in the world primarily to mental processes," and "it is unclear how these mental mechanisms might deliver on their promises to (a) aggregate separate features into integral wholes (association theories and networks beg the question), (b) compare present aggregations to past ones (what features of these aggregations are compared?), (c) augment present perceptions with past knowledge (on what basis is past knowledge selected?),

(d) specify when one aggregation ends and another begins (impute meaning), or (e) even select when the past ends and the present begins." McCabe concludes, "how can a world under constant transformation and change be represented by cognitive structures whose a priori nature can only be adjusted in saltatory leaps from static state to static state?"

6. Another perspective on intermodality involves comparisons of neural processes between sensory modalities. Gjerdingen (1999: 172) claims a strong analogy between low-level neural processes regulating our sense of apparent motion for both vision and music (how we hear a string of pitches as a "moving" melodic line, for example). He also notes that "visual parameters such as stimulus contrast, size, luminance, duration, color, and figural organization . . . have natural analogs in music (respectively, signal-to-noise ration, bandwidth . . . , amplitude, duration, timbre, and figural organization)" (ibid.).

7. Lakoff and Johnson (1999: 54–58) offer a neural modeling hypothesis for "primary metaphors," but the mapping, here conceived as neural connections between domains, is still considered metaphorical. As Auyang (2000: 90) counters, this is a rather "rigid notion of embodiment," and there is "no evidence that the projections [from sensorimotor areas] preserve entire activation patterns that are recognizable as sensorimotor inference or metaphors." Auyang suggests that to capture the appropriate isomorphism of Lakoff and Johnson's metaphors requires higher cognitive work—along the lines of a theoretical, not a metaphorical (in their sense), modeling (92).

8. For more on basic emotions, and the universal aspects of their facial expression, see Ekman (1972) and the helpful summary of his work in the first chapter of Ekman (2003).

9. McCabe (1986: 18), referencing Frykhold (1983), attests to the wealth of information that can be extracted from the physical dynamics of walking: "From a simple oscillating pattern produced by the motion of human walking and etched out in a space-time manifold, we can perceive nested information that specifies (a) the human species . . . (b) individual identity . . . (c) gender . . . (d) age . . . (e) intention, mood, and activity."

10. I address the issue of agency in Chapter 10.

11. Integration is also a fundamental property of consciousness itself, according to Edelman and Tononi (2000: 144, 146). If gesture is a physically perceptible projection of the kinds of things that go on in the brain, we might also find further analogies with Edelman and Tononi's characteristics of consciousness: subjectivity (or, more generally, agency in music), coherence, informativeness and high complexity, context dependency, flexibility, and continuity within change (146–52).

12. For more on the importance of culture in the evolution of the human brain, see Merlin Donald (2001).

13. See Trevarthen (1999) and Papousek (1996); Ian Cross (2001: 34) provides an excellent summary of their work. Trehub, Schellenberg, and Hill (1997) also cover a range of developmental issues, comparing infants' and young children's with adults' cognitive strategies for tonal and well as contour listening.

14. Although I will not pursue issues of gesture related to sign language, I highly rec-

ommend Armstrong, Stokoe, and Wilcox (1995) and Emmorey (1999, 2001) for discussion of the important issues surrounding the syntactification of gestures. American Sign Language (ASL), for example, is a true language with grammatical rules; although open to the addition of iconic gestures, these may not override the conventions of ASL grammar. For an instructive example, see Emmorey (2001: 169–70).

15. As cited by Nespoulous and Lecours (1986: 59).

16. Patel and Peretz (1997) have studied the relationship between intonation curves in speech and contour in music as part of a larger investigation of relationships between our cognition of music and language, and they conclude that "the processing of pitch contour employs some of the same neural resources in music and language, while the processing of tonality appears to draw on resources used uniquely by music" (208).

17. The multiple meanings of a single (gestural) vocal utterance are humorously analyzed by Patrick O'Brian in *The Thirteen Gun Salute* (1989: 279). A character named Loder (part of the diplomatic mission on board the ship) meets Stephen (the ship's doctor) after having been forced to miss the Captain's luxuriant dinner in the gunroom, due to his superior's (chief diplomat Fox's) feud with the Captain:
    " 'You seem to have had a very cheerful time in the gunroom,' said Loder.
    'It was most agreeable,' said Stephen. 'Good company, a great deal of mirth, and the best dinner I remember ever to have eaten at sea—such a turtle, such Java geese!'
    'Ah,' said Loder, meaning by this that he regretted the turtle and the geese, that he thought Fox's refusal for his colleagues an abuse of authority, and that he for one dissociated himself from the barbarous incivility: a considerable burden for a single 'ah', but one that it bore easily."

18. Damasio (1994: 103) cites a study by Tootell et al. (1988) in which "activity of neurons in early visual cortices will be topographically organized in a pattern that conforms to the shapes the monkey is viewing"—that is, one can tell whether the monkey is looking at a cross or a square, with Tootell's neuroanatomical imaging techniques.

6. Toward a Theory of Musical Gesture

1. My teacher at the time was Prof. Menachem Pressler on the faculty at Indiana University. The reader can well imagine the extraordinary effect of his playing of this Schubert theme by listening to his recordings of the Schubert piano trios with the Beaux Arts Trio.

2. My inclusion of unconscious gestures is in accord with David Epstein's: "By its very nature gesture (and gestures) involve motion—those movements . . . that often accompany and help to convey expression of feelings, and other motions that in their unconscious way are telling signs of character and personality" (1995: 485, n1). On the other hand, I do not follow Epstein when he subsumes gesture under the larger category of "motion, which as a generic term covers movement on all levels and spans of musical duration" (ibid.; see also 561, n7). First, gesture as I define it involves more than temporal shaping alone. Dynamics

and articulation, along with timbre, are also significant aspects of gesture, and they cannot be subsumed under motion or movement (terms which Epstein claims are interchangeable), hence, my definition of gesture as significant *energetic* shaping through time. Second, I conceive of gesture flexibly enough to embrace larger spans hierarchically, although I concede that the notion becomes increasingly metaphorical for entire sections of works. I would note, however, that although Epstein's study focuses on duration, his sensitive recommendations for expressive performance inevitably include discussions of dynamics and articulation.

3. An exception to this blunt critique is found in the nonmechanical and often gesturally vivid autographs or sketches of many composers. Newman (1988: 34–35) observes that this is particularly the case with Beethoven's manuscripts, where dynamic inflections and change of pace are reflected in the forward slant of stems and beams, the spacing between notes, and other distortions that could be considered, in my terms, direct indices of energetic shaping through time.

4. I draw from Rothfarb's superb chapter the following brief summary of theorists' treatment of tonal attractions, life forces, and kinetic energies in music.

5. Of course, my geometric point/line analogy is incomplete, in that tonal forces also play a role in Kurth's assessment of energies, not merely the phenomenon of "apparent motion" that gives temporal coherence to successions of tones.

6. Rothfarb (1991: 21) links Kurth to the Gestalt theorists that would follow, in his intuition of "dynamically organized, super-summative wholes" such as the coordination of tones that constitute a melody. As Kurth states, "the tones do not exist first and their connection afterwards; rather, the dynamic current is the primary element" and "the content is not to be interpreted as a (secondary) connection traced out subsequently from tone to tone but rather as the totality of the dynamic phase" (Kurth 1956 [1917b]: 17, 1917a: 85, cited by Rothfarb 1991: 21). Rothfarb then tellingly compares Gestalt psychologist Kurt Koffka's with Kurth's energetic concept of melody: "Melody is not a collection of tones but rather a primal continuity from which the tones are released" (Koffka 1935: 343–45); "The melodic element resides in the motion through the tones, not in the individual tones through which the motion flows" (Kurth 1917b: 18, cited by Rothfarb 1991: 21). I would simply add that the energetic continuity of motion theorized by Kurth and Koffka shares the character of, and may be interpreted as, human gesture, with the qualification that the implied originary force of such gestures is inflected by the virtual environmental forces created by tonal and metric fields.

7. Of course, there are exceptions. Quantz (1985 [1752]: 119–26), in his chapter on "Good Execution," stresses the importance of grasping the "dominant sentiment" of a piece, and indicates the role of mode, interval size and articulation, dissonant content, and tempo as clues to that sentiment, in order to "make his execution conform to it." Czerny (1991 [1846]: 54–57) in his explanation of types of Adagio movements (also based on their overarching expressive purport) provides a detailed set of suggestions for realizing notated and non-notated elements in several music examples. Clearly the notion of a synthesis of various expressive means leading to the emergence of a coherent sentiment underlies these inadequate but intriguing suggestions. See Chapter 7 for further discussion.

8. A more engaging summary interpretation, touching on the neglected category of rhetorical interpretation, is found in George Barth's *The Pianist as Orator* (1992).

9.   Candace Brower (2000) and Fred Lerdahl (2002) have incorporated these attractions into their own models of tonal pitch space. Brower relates these forces to the conceptual image schemas of Mark Johnson (1987). The sense of tonal gravity thus draws on a CENTER-VERTICALITY-BALANCE schema, and the sense of tonal motion on a SOURCE-PATH-GOAL schema. Interestingly, one of the entailments of the latter schema is that "motion is carried out by an agent who wills the motion to take place" (Brower 2000: 331). Brower also provides increasingly comprehensive models of pitch space that incorporate the three levels of tones, triads, and regions. Her interpretive approach includes a pattern-matching component that compares paradigmatic phrase structures and their variants, and a larger narrative component that integrates the implied dramatic trajectory of a work's hierarchical pitch structures.

     Lerdahl (2002) explores still further the multitiered modeling of tonal spaces, including chromatic as well as diatonic. He quantifies musical attractions based on the (cognitive) distance each tonal progression traces in its respective tonal space, factored with its hierarchical status and stability, as determined through the rule system of his "Generative Theory of Tonal Music" (see Lerdahl and Jackendoff 1983). Lerdahl (2002: 285–92) also explores the analogy of metric spaces, based on a grid concept of meter; this part of the theory is only lightly sketched, and Lerdahl points out the need to incorporate the influence of grouping structure on metric structure. Otherwise, the primary metric attraction is conceived as the tendency of a weak beat to progress toward a strong one (as Riemann claimed).

     Note that Lerdahl's formulation of metric space in terms of beat attractions within a grid differs from a gravitational conception; I find the latter offers a better analogy for both field forces and the orientation of up versus down affecting our experience of virtual human gestures. I am not convinced that quantification of forces will "add up" to what I consider the emergent qualitative aspects of musical gesture. Furthermore, Lerdahl offers no clear distinction between the primary force of a musical agent's intentional action and what might be understood as the secondary or environmental "resistances" imposed by a virtual tonal/metric field. However, Lerdahl has clearly focused his theory on pitch-event hierarchies, excluding "associational structure" (motives, and hence thematic gestures) because (a) hierarchy is a primary factor aiding learning and memory, (b) association depends in part on hierarchical status, and (c) "on a practical level, it is difficult to make a substantive theory of associations" (6). Furthermore, Lerdahl notes that although his "idealization of auditory experience is necessary for a clear account of cognitive musical structures, . . . much is lost in the process, including dynamic variation, expressive timing, textural density, and timbral modulation" (381). Lerdahl considers this loss as "critical when music does not employ stratified basic spaces" (381), as in some twentieth-century musical styles. I would argue that it is equally critical in tonal styles.

     Lerdahl acknowledges that phrase grouping entails an "emergent level of analysis" (2002: 248) that will ultimately require its own treatment, independently of (as well as interactively with) the analysis of the pitch-event hierarchy. Lerdahl (292–97) briefly explores the interaction of tonal and metric attractions in his quantification of Roger Graybill's (1994) qualitative analysis of a phrase of Mozart's in which implied tonal rhythm is out of phase with the meter. In his elegant article Graybill parses (two- and three-note) gestural groupings as they interact with brief Schenkerian prolongational groupings, and gesture helps account for the motion to and from focal points (especially when out of phase with prolongational groupings).

10. After making this conceptual distinction, I found its echo in a critique of cognitivist psychology by Fred Keijzer (2001: 13), who distinguishes *embodiment* from *situatedness*, the former including "both sensory capabilities as well as the capacity for movement," and the latter addressing "the environmental characteristics that bear on intelligence." Cognitivist psychology, in Keijzer's view, "tends to focus almost exclusively on the internal thinking apparatus, abstracting away from the concrete circumstances in which real cognitive systems operate." Larson's identification of what I would call virtual environmental forces stemming from tonality need not be considered part of a cognitivist understanding of music as completely internalized, but the analogy I have drawn between the interaction of environmental constraints and agential energies in music and a similar interaction in other realms of human experience is a compelling one.

11. See Meyer (1956, 1973). The distinguishing of a musical agent's motivational gestural energies from the environmental forces of tonal and metric fields that inflect them should be underlined as essential to my own approach. The agent can be realized both from the identification with primary energies and the awareness of their possible deflection by secondary forces or attractions which are not realized. Together, these energies and attractions can create distinctive gestural profiles, for which the gesturer is not totally responsible, but which reveal characteristics of the gesturer (i.e., whether enough "willful" energies were available to overcome the implicational attractions of tonal syntax or metrical gravitation).

12. One might subsume magnetism under gravity by considering it as a force arising from the "mass" of stable scale degrees such as the tonic in a scale-degree space. But Larson's reasoning is compelling—we live on earth, not in space, and our experience of gravity is earth-based as a downward force on our bodies; thus, we need another concept for other attractive forces, and magnetism offers a handy analogy.

13. More precisely, in physics inertia is defined as "the property of a body, proportional to its mass, by virtue of which it continues in a state of rest or uniform straight motion in the absence of an external force" (*The New Shorter Oxford English Dictionary* [1993]). Thus, the tendency of an object to persevere or resist change is the criterion, whether the prior state involves movement or stasis. The "object" here would be equated with the implied agent. Inertia is extended by Larson to the continuation of any strategic patterning. In my view this exceeds a purely environmental force, and for that reason Larson's inertia suggests a closer analogue to the Gestalt law of good continuation.

14. *The New Shorter Oxford English Dictionary* (1993).

15. The philosopher Jerrold Levinson (2002a) argues for the importance of spatial imagination in the interpretation of musical gesture, and his theses are supportive of the theory I have been developing. In brief, "musical expression of emotion presupposes the notion of personal expression of emotion and rests on the emergence of musical gestures"; both require "generic spatial imagination" (147). Levinson conceives of musical gesture as "a function of both performing gestures understood as the sources of musical sequences [as] heard" (i.e., "a sense of the

possible sources of sounds, not necessarily *knowledge* of their actual sources" [141]) and "perceived resemblances between musical sequences and behavioral expressions" (147). It is the latter with which I am most concerned in this book, and for which I have provided a range of motivations.

16. Meyer (1956, 1973). It is important to stress that these expectations are based on regularities, not requirements. The so-called rules are not proscriptions but generalizations about typical behavior based on stylistic principles (see Hatten 1994: 293). Rules, understood as regularities, help determine the expressive effect of irregularities, although there are of course conventions that are generally followed to avoid incoherent or improper syntax—but even here, exceptions can be expressively fruitful, if a composer can compensate for a "violation" at one level by a balancing resolution, for example, at another level.

17. In fact, the pianist providing music on the video of the early silent film *Pandora's Box* makes this amusing error!

18. I would argue that even if Brahms had (highly uncharacteristically) labeled this movement "Waves," his real intent would have been to use representation to achieve expression (compare Kivy's argument in *Sound and Semblance* [1984]).

19. The metric orientation up versus down does not always map in the most obvious ways onto culturally conventionalized dance steps. Little and Jenne (1991: 21) note that in the noble French style of Baroque dance, the *plié* (or "sink," in English)—a downward motion involving bending of the knees—is performed on the upbeat of the music, whereas the *élevé*—an upward motion to the balls of the feet—is performed on the downbeat.

20. For critiques of meter as grid, see Hasty (1997) and Krebs (1999). For arguments against an overly rhythmic concept of meter that slights its regulative role in creating and sustaining a virtual gravitational or dynamic field, see Hatten (2002a).

21. For illuminating examples and discussion of different "grooves" in popular music performance, see Keil and Feld (1994).

22. Lawrence Zbikowski (2002: 34) considers motives to be basic-level categories, and I extend that insight to gesture (especially for what I call thematic gestures). Basic-level categories are those we use most frequently, and they are generally in the middle of a hierarchical taxonomy—thus, a gesture may be composed of several tones, but (as argued in Chapter 5), we synthesize the significant event of the gesture instead of each tone. The two principles of this midlevel classification (Rosch et al. 1976; Rosch 1978) are *efficiency* (minimum demand on memory) and *informativeness* (maximum detail). The optimal compromise between these competing demands is found in basic-level categories. Gestures, like motives, are gestalt wholes that efficiently organize the details of tones into synthetic event structures that are memorable and easily manipulated. However, I would note that the analogy with basic-level categories in language suffers when it is translated to music. First, motives and gestures are often unique syntheses created by individual works. The basic-level category designation is even better suited to stylistic *types* of gestures, such as the sigh figure, that have greater familiarity. Second, motives and gestures are actually comprised of tones (and other lower-level elements); basic-level category words (e.g., bird) are not actually made up of the components of lower-level category words (parakeet, blue jay), but rather include them as subcategories. Nevertheless, as a basic level of psychological processing

(we capture this level of organization most quickly, and it has a preferred cognitive status), the concept is valuable for such basic shapes as Zbikowski's motives and my gestures.

23.   See Schenker's (2000 [ca. 1911]) own treatise on performance at the piano for many other insightful treatments of foreground expressive features (notably, articulatory touches, fingering, and modes of pedaling). Schenker's concern for continuity of gesture may be inferred from his discussion (65) of ways to continue a sense of motion across a phrase-internal rest (by analogy with the continuous movement of the violinist's bow through a rest). On the other hand, when a rest implies an abrupt release, that continuity of motion must be broken by a "thrusting-away motion" (65). We will encounter both kinds of gestures in Chapter 8, the former in Schubert's D. 959, and the latter in his D. 784.

24.   There has been a great deal of experimental work on expressive timing in performance, including Alf Gabrielson (1974, 1982, 1987, 1988), Manfred Clynes and Janice Walker (1982), and Eric F. Clarke (1985, 1988).

25.   For more on historical stylistic evidence, see Chapter 7.

26.   Compare a similar strategy applied to Balanchine's abstract ballet choreography by the renowned dancer Gelsey Kirkland (1987: 185).

27.   Peter Burkholder emphasizes the intertextual as a key to musical meaning in his study of Ives (1995a) as well as his recent proposal for a simple model of musical meaning (2002).

28.   An earlier application of Peircean categories may be found in Wilson Coker (1972). Coker's theory of gesture has been revived by Nicholas Cook (2003b), who draws on Coker's "performative" characterization of gesture: gesture creates meaning rather than merely representing it.

29.   However, obsessive repetition can level out the distinctive or marked character of a gesture and relegate it to the background, upon which another (emergent) gesture may arise. Examples would include Mozart's *Prague* Symphony, first movement, principal theme; Beethoven's *Waldstein* sonata, opening of the first movement; and the opening of the finale of the *Appassionata*. Conversely, that which appears backgrounded may, by choice of the agent or the performer, become marked as foregrounded. Or the interpreter may mark an otherwise unmarked gesture, reading in a certain significance, as in the case of an interpreter bringing a psychological need or desire to bear on the interpretation.

30.   Emergence entails those aspects of higher-level organization and expressive meaning which could not be captured by, or predicted from, the organization of lower levels. Gesture is already emergent in perception: the qualities (Firstness) and dynamic characteristics (Secondness) of gestures are not simply the sum of various stimuli, but, as we saw in Chapter 5, emerge as functionally coherent events. At the level of Thirdness cognitively emergent aspects of expressive meaning may in turn exceed what one might be able to predict from lower-level expressive qualities or dynamic attributes.
        Naomi Cumming (2000: 243–50) discusses three kinds of emergence which have concerned philosophers of aesthetics: (1) the musical sign as emergent from mere material description of acoustic properties (Scruton 1997), (2) expression as emergent from musical structure (Beardsley 1982), and (3) the embodied, affec-

tively complex subject as (culturally) emergent from the immediate expressive character of musical structures (Margolis 1974). Cumming also notes an important consequence of emergence for interpretation: "it is inherent in the exercise of describing emergent qualities that the description can never be final in its authoritativeness" (2000: 253).

Emergence as a feature of new levels of organization should not be confused with another use of the term *emergence,* as in the gradual emergence of a musical process, or a theme. This is the sense Meyer (1989: 198) intends in his characterization of (nonhierarchical) emergent structures in Romantic musical styles, which feature "continuous, seamless development," "mobility and openness," and unity based on the working out of a basic principle or idea (198–99).

31. Their two co-authored books are *Expressive Movement: Posture and Action in Daily Life, Sports, and the Performing Arts* (1989) and *Generous Movement: A Practical Guide to Balance in Action* (1991).

32. "From Gesture to Interpretation: A Demonstration and Dialogue," with Alexandra Pierce, for a session I organized under the title "Gesture and Music: Theoretical and Practical Considerations," Semiotic Society of America, San Antonio, October 20–22, 1995; and "Movement as a Model of Performance," with Alexandra Pierce, for a special session organized by David Lidov, "Musical Microstructure in Expressive Performance," Society for Music Theory, New York, November 2–5, 1995.

33. Recall the discussion, above, of Clynes's (1995) composer's pulses and Repp's (1998) conclusions concerning the "precognitive, obligatory response to implied musical motion."

34. For example, in an integrative seminar on gesture and performance I taught at Penn State University in 1997.

35. The interested reader may wish to consult the work of one of Alexandra Pierce's former colleagues at the University of Redlands, Stephen Moore: "The Writings of Émile Jaques-Dalcroze: Toward a Theory for the Performance of Musical Rhythm" (1992). Another movement theorist whose influence is acknowledged by Pierce (1994: 92, n27) is Rudolf Laban. See *The Mastery of Movement* as edited, revised, and enlarged by Lisa Ullmann (1971).

36. For more on music as a form of thought, see Levinson (2002b).

37. This is a problem that Alexandra and Roger Pierce address in their notated scores for gestural and dramatic performances of poetic texts.

7. Stylistic Types and Strategic Functions of Gestures

1. By "competency" I mean more than a familiarity with common processes and patterns in a style. A competent performer or listener has the capacity to interpret novel applications of stylistic principles, as well as unique disruptions of typical processes, and to gauge their expressive significance within the context of contemporaneous practice. See also Hatten (1994).

2. Although I will sample the literature on performance practice as well as studies on the performance of works by Mozart, Beethoven, and Schubert, I will not attempt to address the manifold issues pertaining to the emerging field that

306 *Notes to pages 126–133*

Jonathan Dunsby (1995: 17) identifies under the chapter title "Musical Performance Studies as a 'Discipline.'" Besides Dunsby, interested readers may wish to consult Cone (1968), Barnett (1972), Schmalfeldt (1985), Berry (1989), the essays in Rink (1995 [reviewed in Hatten 1996] and 2002), and for a philosopher's perspective, Godlovitch (1998). Rosen (2002a, 2002b) offers an informed performer's perspective. On the pertinent issue of whether a performer simply realizes what an analyst discovers, I have already indicated in Chapter 6 how important the performer's heuristic process of discovery is to the joint project of performer and analyst, namely, *interpretation,* and I have illustrated how this perspective is crucial to Alexandra Pierce's work.

3. For the concept of a style type, see Narmour (1977), Meyer (1989), and Hatten (1994).

4. Konrad Wolff (1990: 149) notes that for the performance of Beethoven's piano works, "Czerny and Schindler are our two principal witnesses, and they are diametrically opposed to each other on nearly every point of importance."

5. For a superb example of the impact of large-scale motivic connection on interpretation of musical gesture in performance (specifically, the *calando* in the fourteenth bar of the first movement of Mozart's Piano Sonata in A Minor, K. 310) see Schachter (2000: 49–52). Schachter notes that none of the eighteenth-century performance manuals advise us "to hold a dissonant or chromatic sound longer when we can't play it louder," but one can extrapolate this solution from their comments on *rubato* (C. P. E. Bach 1949 [1753]: 150) and accent through length (Türk 1982 [1789]: 327–29). The general principle, in my view, is that the performer is enjoined to find some way to bring out the significance of stylistically (or strategically) marked musical events, whether or not they are foregrounded by notational means (e.g., with a special accent or dynamic marking). In this regard, it is useful to keep in mind that "in the middle of the eighteenth century expressive accentuation and dynamic nuance [were] left largely to the discretion of the performer" and "composers relied on performers' taste and experience in applying generally understood principles of phrasing and accent" (Clive Brown 1999: 59).

6. Allanbrook (1992: 170) offers a valuable hint that topics might also be considered as gestures, although her main point in the following is that topics may have structural significance for an unfolding musical discourse: "We have not yet been able to contrive a topical syntax, in which principles for the combination of topics are laid out, and I have some doubt that such a thing is possible. But that the choice of gesture can have a strong influence on the working-out of a movement seems to me both indubitable and widely ignored; it has rarely been a working premise of musicological analysis." In practice, topics tend to imply one or more characteristic gestural types in their realization. HaCohen and Wagner (forthcoming) explore the gestural significance of Wagner's leitmotives, which also draw on topics.

7. For a thorough treatment of this conception of originality in Romantic music, see Meyer (1989). On the distinction between style growth and change, see Hatten (1982). For an example and an extended discussion of the processes of style-type generalization as a species of style growth, see Hatten (1994: 53–54 and 261–68, respectively).

8.   Mara Parker (2002) analyzes four kinds of what I term dialogical relationships
        in the string quartet from 1750–97: the "lecture," the "polite conversation," the
        "debate," and the "conversation." Illuminating observations on the play with
        closing gestures in Haydn may be found in Janet Levy (1981). Mark Evan Bonds
        (1991) offers a rhetorical interpretation of Haydn's Symphony No. 46 in B Major,
        and Michael Spitzer (1998) explores the "reversal" gesture in Haydn, using
        Eugene Narmour's (1990) approach to melodic analysis. William S. Newman
        (1986) offers an introduction to Haydn's innovative keyboard techniques, with
        relevance to Haydn's creativity in the realm of musical gesture.

9.   Owen Jander (1988) has explored aspects of dialogue between violin and piano
        in Beethoven's *Kreutzer* Sonata.

10.   Recall how even the dance-derived "Echo" that concludes Bach's Overture in
        B Minor tropes with concerto form and *concertato* style (see discussion in
        Chapter 4).

11.   Patrick McCreless is pursuing the study of rhetorical gesture along similar lines
        in a book in progress. His recent essay on music and rhetoric (2002) focuses on
        the German musical rhetorical tradition of roughly 1550 to 1800, during which
        time rhetoric encompassed many of the elements of structure that were eventu-
        ally treated less metaphorically and more analytically: formal functions and their
        sequence, and musical figures, many of which were merely labels for techniques
        of motivic development (although the more text-sensitive and declamatory style
        that develops in the early Baroque demanded an account of expressive figures
        that could achieve affects analogous to those of impassioned verbal expression,
        not merely oratory). As McCreless summarizes, with the development of specifi-
        cally musical theories of melody and form for instrumental music this applica-
        tion of rhetoric was subsumed under structure (876).
            However, in the Classical style the sense of a rhetorical gesture takes on fresh
        meaning, as reflected in the comments of Schindler and Czerny on Beethoven's
        rhetorical caesurae and dramatic pauses, and one could perhaps trace this ten-
        dency in discussions of performance and performance practice from the time of
        Koch. Indeed, McCreless notes the applicability of Scheibe's oratorical figures
        (interrogation, repetition, gradation, dubitation, exclamation, etc.) to our under-
        standing of the finale of Beethoven's Piano Sonata in D Major, Op. 10, no. 3.
        Mark Evan Bonds (1991) provides a broader historical overview that also ad-
        dresses the continuity of rhetoric in the first half of the nineteenth century
        (132–41), during the transition from a metaphor of the musical work as an ora-
        tion to that of a biological organism. Elaine Sisman has applied traditional rhe-
        torical concepts (along with a sensitive interpretation of gesture and topic) in her
        interpretations of Haydn's variations (1993), Mozart's *Prague* Symphony (1997),
        and Beethoven's *Pathétique* Sonata, Op. 13 (1994).

12.   Meyer (1973: 49) discusses the constraints on our interpretation of "conformant
        relationships" (thematic schemata that may include motives or entire melodies).
        His helpful formula for perceived conformance, expressed as an equation, pits
        regularity of pattern, individuality of profile, and similarity of patterning against
        variety of intervening events and temporal distance between events. Schoen-
        berg's important concept of developing variation (to be addressed below) may be
        refined for analytical purposes by consideration of these cognitive constraints.

13. Rosen (1972: 90–91) offers evidence from the slow movement of Haydn's String Quartet in E♭, Op. 33, no. 2, of the "hierarchy of weight" afforded each beat in a Classical meter. Haydn "echoes" the silent second and third beats of mm. 22 and 24 with offbeat chords marked *pp* and *p,* respectively.

14. This passage is not so easily dismissed as naive when we recall the concepts of "intersubjectivity" and "affect attunement" discussed in Chapter 5, although the latter are applied to the *developmental* origins of human musicality.

15. The passage is from Czerny's (1968 [1842]) reminiscence of his first lesson with Beethoven: "He then had me play through the studies given in the manual [C. P. E. Bach's *Versuch*] and pointed out especially the *legato,* which he himself had mastered to such an incomparable degree, and which all other pianists of that time considered to be impossible to execute on the fortepiano, as it was still the fashion (as in Mozart's time) to play in a detached [*gehackte*], abrupt [*kurz*] manner" (cited in MacClintock 1979: 384). Czerny also reports (in correspondence with Cocks in London) that "Beethoven, who had heard Mozart play, said afterwards that his playing was neat and clear, but rather empty, weak, and old-fashioned. The legato and cantabile on the piano were unknown at that time [?], and Beethoven was the first to discover [these?] new and grand effects on that instrument" (Thayer 1866–79, vol. 2: 363, cited in F. Kullak 1973 [1901]: 4–5). But a contemporary critic by the name of Mosel, who had heard both Mozart and Beethoven perform, offered the following comparison: "True, an important difference was apparent in the style of these two; the roundness, tranquility, and delicacy of Mozart's style were foreign to the new virtuoso; on the other hand, his enhanced vigor and fiery expression affected every listener" (*Wiener Musikzeitung,* October 18, 1843, cited in Thayer 1866–79, vol. 2: 39, and Kullak 1973 [1901]: 5).

16. Monelle (2000: 17) observes that the original label in the sixteenth century for the falling minor second was *pianto* (weeping), and that "during the eighteenth century the related idea of the sigh replaced that of weeping."

17. For more on the concept of markedness, see my Introduction to the present volume and Hatten (1994: 34–56).

18. Pierce's (1994) movement pedagogy is particularly successful in helping a performer balance the competing demands of gestural articulation and larger phrase contours (as well as their negotiation with the expressive flow of the meter). See discussion in Chapter 6.

19. This movement is also a good example of the troping of *concertato* and slow movement textures. Note the alternation in the opening theme between soft (solo) theme and loud (orchestral) chordal punctuation. I gratefully acknowledge my introduction to the subtleties of Mozart's keyboard style, in this same sonata, through the superb instruction of Prof. Roger Keyes, recently retired from the piano faculty at Baylor University.

20. See Selfridge-Field (1998: 13, 50–52) for a discussion of the prototype underlying Mozart's five variants of this melodic phrase throughout the movement. Selfridge-Field also presents Eugene Narmour's analyses of the variants, from their personal correspondence.

21. Beethoven's letter to Karl Holz (August 1825) on proofing the copy of his String

Quartet in A Minor, Op. 132, attests to the importance he attached to exact slur placement (although he could also be careless and inconsistent in his notation): "It is not all the same whether it is like this [a slur over three notes] or like this [a slur over the first two notes only]" (Anderson 1961: 1241–42, cited by Rosenblum 1988: 17). Barth (1992: 118) cites Türk's single example of slurs under an embracing slur (Türk 1982 [1789]: 344) and his recommendation for performance: all *legato*, but with each initial note of the interior two-note slurs "softly marked" (presumably dynamically, but the possibility of agogic marking exists). Türk (329–30) also warns the performer not to divide slurred subdivisions of a phrase even when only one level of slurring occurs; he gives clear examples of incorrect division by rests in which internal slurring is notated, and states that "a musical thought which has not been completed may never be divided by lifting the fingers from the keys at the wrong time (or by rests)." We have no evidence that Beethoven read Türk, but these examples suggest a change in preference from Mozart's non-*legato* articulation to Beethoven's *legato* with interior articulation.

22. Beethoven rarely uses the long slur for themes, however. In themes of movements specifically marked as singing, the themes are articulated by breaking up slurs, either with a *portato* (Op. 90, II, "sehr singbar vorzutragen") or by the use of shorter slurs (Op. 109, III, "Gesangsvoll"). The second theme from the first movement of the *Waldstein* is an exception with its longer slur; like the similarly slurred theme in the coda of the first movement of Op. 109, it is a chorale, and the *legato* may thus emulate the continuity of choral or organ sound (a "bound" effect without suspensions that echoes an older style). But the hymnlike slow movement of the *Hammerklavier* has at most shorter slurs; its *legato* is derived from the initial indication of *sostenuto,* and thus Beethoven can use shorter slurs to indicate interior inflections. A rhetorical articulation occurs in m. 5 with the inner qualm of a registrally displaced diminished-seventh chord. Longer slurs tend to occur over passage work, and thus themes built from scales or broken chords are likely to have longer slurs (e.g., the etude finales of Opp. 26 and 54). The finale from Op. 22 (see Example 7.5) is scalar, but hardly etude-like—one is tempted to view its melodic contour as outlining a spacious sigh/inhalation pair.

23. On Beethoven's *legato,* see note 15 in this chapter. Czerny contrasts Hummel's "pearly and brilliant style, so well adapted to the times [early 1800s]" with "Beethoven's playing of the Adagio and Legato in the strict style" which "exercised a wellnigh magic influence on every hearer, and has never, so far as I know, been surpassed by any one" (cited in Thayer 1866–79, vol. 2: 348, and Kullak 1973 [1901]: 10).

24. Gottfried Weber (1817–21) speaks of "internal weight" for metrical accents (see Clive Brown 1999: 15). That internal weight can be experienced even when, as in mm. 2, 5, and 7, there is no surface accentuation to underline it, because of the fieldlike properties of meter.

25. Hermann Keller (1965 [1955]: 98, 100) shows examples of slurring against the motivic groupings (the closing theme in the first movement of Beethoven's Symphony No. 4 in B♭ Major, Op. 60) and slurring over the phrase boundary (mm. 4–5 of the theme of the variation finale of Op. 109). For Keller, the latter slur "demonstrates an inner compulsion motivated by the crescendo in the fourth

measure—at the end of the sonata, where the theme enters once more quietly, transfigured, both the crescendo and the slur are missing" (100).

26. See Marston (1992: 179, n22; 186–89).

27. Compare the opening of Beethoven's *Ghost* Trio, analyzed in Chapter 1.

28. In an effective performance on a period instrument (Bilson et al. 1997), Malcolm Bilson heavily emphasizes the offbeat accent in the coda as a kind of gestural development of the potential only hinted at in the opening bar. The entire performance is gesturally conceived and illuminating, although in the coda the offbeat accentuation may strike some as too extreme, given the pastoral character of this passage. This accentuation, however, underscores the thematic opposition between anticipatory and contradictory upbeats, and thus brings out a vital rhythmic drama that is usually neglected.

29. As in the performance of Ursula Dütschler on fortepiano (Bilson et al. 1997).

30. Another stylistic gesture involves an upbeat detached from a subsequent longer note or slurred group. This may be metric (the theme of Op. 26, I) or syncopated (the middle section of Op. 2, no. 3, II, m. 19 ff.). This type is thematized in Beethoven (Op. 90, 101) and Schubert (D. 959); see Chapter 8.

31. Rosen uses the term *portamento* for dots under a slur. That term typically refers to the glide or slur used to link two separate pitches, although Clive Brown (1999: 558) notes that Brahms among others used the term *portamento* to mean *portato* in the context of keyboard instruments. I will adhere to the term *portato* to avoid confusion.

    Robert Taub (2002: 25) offers an example of the modulation of touch, here from *staccato* through *portato* to *legato*, in the soloist's transition to the second theme in the first movement (mm. 160–64) of the Piano Concerto in C Minor, Op. 37. Unlike Rosen's example, however, Taub's does not involve progressive transformation of a single motive but rather an articulatory transition to a *legato* theme. Taub also provides an enlightening discussion of the many uses of pedal, with bearing on gestural interpretation. For example, just before the *tutti* codetta at the end of the slow movement of Beethoven's Piano Concerto in G, Op. 58 (mm. 62–63), Beethoven notates eighth-note chords on the downbeats of two $\frac{2}{4}$ measures, but poetically sustains them with pedal markings that precisely extend their resonance to the last sixteenth in each measure. As Taub observes, the notation suggests a "lighter, more floating touch" (42). I would add that the chords are arpeggiated, and thus the effect is that of a harp allowed to resonate until the sixteenth rest between chords stops the sound—and here the deliberate articulation by rest suggests *empfindsamer* expressivity, not merely an augmented *portato* effect.

32. See Paul Badura-Skoda (1988: 84).

33. Compare the thematic and dramatized use of *portato* over the repeated three-eighth-note anacrusis in the second movement of Mozart's Piano Sonata in B♭ Major, K. 333, where the effect is initially consoling with the theme in m. 8. Consolation is then suffused with deeper feeling when the *portato* recurs in mm. 15 and 17, and 21 and 25. After the double bar, the thematized *portato* (m. 33) diverts the first theme in a way that echoes its second-theme and closing-

theme appearances, but now it spawns a mysterious transition that features the *portato* anacrusis ominously in the bass (as a threatening motto on the tympani?).

34. For confirmation of this distinction, see Christa Landon and Walther Dürr, *Neue Schubert Ausgabe* (1984: viii).

35. A fascinating theoretical application of dynamics may be found in Quantz (1985 [1752]). Evan Jones (2003) notes that in Quantz's composed example, labeled "Affettuoso di molto," Quantz uses indications of *mf, f,* and *ff* (against a *mp* background) to distinguish three levels of dissonant harmonies. Interestingly, Quantz dynamically marks only what Kirnberger would later call essential dissonances (those in which resolution requires a change of harmony) as opposed to dissonant suspensions that resolve over a bass (Kirnberger's inessential dissonances). C. P. E. Bach (1949 [1753]) rightly decries such attempted dynamic prescription, but as Jones observes, Quantz's theoretical use of dynamics is not intended to reform notational practice or codify a new practice of performance. Rather, Quantz's intent is "simply to reaffirm the traditional association between dynamics and dissonance in the context of the hierarchy of harmonic stability that he advances" (3). In terms of gesture, it is interesting to find such an attempt to generalize that association, even if the omission of striking suspensions and other nonharmonic dissonances runs counter to our intuitions by not bringing out such marked events.

36. See Richard Littlefield (2001: 58–73) for a fascinating treatment of the silence surrounding a work as a musical frame.

37. Even stylistically unmarked material can be marked as thematic if used in a thematically functional location (see Hatten 1994: 122; 126–32 for examples).

38. Elaine Sisman (1994) notes that these rhetorical devices are characteristic of the "pathétique," a style that has as its exemplary work Beethoven's Piano Sonata in C Minor, Op. 13, published as *Grande Sonate pathétique* in 1799. The "breaking off" on V_5^6 suggests the *aposiopesis* or *abruptio* in earlier Baroque rhetoric (97). Sisman discusses a text on rhetoric, Johann Christoph Adelung's *Über den Deutschen Styl* (1789–90; there were four editions between 1785 and 1800), and an essay by Schiller, "Über das Pathetische" (1984 [1793]), as evidence for the currency of these ideas around the time of Beethoven's *Pathétique.*

39. Mozart employs a similar strategy in the exposition of the first movement, although the sudden V^7 of E♭ appears just after a counterstatement of the opening gesture in *stretto.*

40. Such single-note sighs recall Kircher's *Suspiratio* figure, originating in early Baroque opera, in which frequent rests break up phrases and even words to suggest the sobbing of one overcome with grief (Ottavia's farewell to Rome, from act 3 of *L'incoronatione di Poppea*), or the last gasps of one who is dying (the Commendatore's death, from act 1 of *Don Giovanni*), as discussed by George Buelow (2001 [1980]: 269) and elaborated by Peter Burkholder (1995b: 376–77), respectively.

41. Compare the Cavatina of Op. 130, discussed in Hatten (1994: 203–23).

42. See Chapter 9 for Beethoven's use of a similar "lift" gesture in the opening of Op. 102, no. 1.

43. Bach's three-part Sinfonias were published by Hoffmeister in Vienna and Leipzig

in 1801, as "XV Symphonies Pour le Clavecin composées par J. S. Bach" (Zenck 1986: 188). One can reasonably conjecture that Beethoven was acquainted with them.

44. Warrant for dialogical interpretation in Beethoven comes from Schindler (1966 [1840, 1860]), an untrustworthy source, but worth considering with respect to the general concept of dialogue. Schindler claims that Beethoven informed him of his intent to represent a dialogue between a husband and wife, or lover and mistress, in both of his Op. 14 piano sonatas. The gestural dialogue is between "two *principles*, which he designated the *entreating* and the *resisting*" (cited in MacClintock 1979: 385). The opening of Op. 14, no. 2 is Schindler's first example: the overlapping melody in the right hand is the tender entreaty (see Example 7.8, where I characterized the gesture as "gracious"), and the left hand's triadic response is the resisting response. Although I find this interpretation unconvincing (Schindler may have confused weakly contrasting parts of one theme with contrasts between themes), the passage likely reflects something of Beethoven's own concern for poetic meaning as it might emerge from an imaginary gestural dialogue. The transitional theme sounds like a more insistent entreaty, and the progression appears to become more insistent until the codetta of the exposition, in which the two hands are in dialogical give and take, yet harmoniously "of one mind."

45. This dialogical relationship within a single hand is strongly marked registrally. Glenn Stanley (2000: 89–90) suggests a dialogue between the hands in the opening of Beethoven's Piano Sonata in E Major, Op. 109, based on their motivic exchange (textural inversion) later in the movement, but it is difficult, given the homogeneous texture of the opening, to hear the hands as two distinctly agential voices (their expressive and textural homogeneity is even greater than that found in the opening of Op. 14, no. 2, discussed in the previous note).

46. Note that rhetorical gestures are not always signs of the pathetic. Alfred Brendel (1992 [1990]: 15) analyzes what I would call rhetorical interpolations in the third movement of Haydn's Piano Sonata in C Major, Hob. XVI: 50, finding them to be the source of humor, or "the sublime in reverse" (21), "das umgekehrte Erhabene," in Jean Paul Richter's memorable phrase. Brendel discovers five generally comic traits in the movement, including "breaches of convention," "the appearance of ambiguity," "masquerades of professional incompetence," "veiled insults," and "nonsense" (21).

47. Schindler (1966 [1840, 1860]) speaks of Beethoven's rhetoric, giving as examples "the caesura which he often employed, and the rhetorical pause, both derived from Clementi" (!) (cited in Kullak 1973 [1901]: 25). His examples are from the Piano Sonata in C Minor, Op. 10, no. 1: the rhetorical pauses are in mm. 16, 18–19, and 20–21, and the caesura is marked at the cadence before the codetta of the exposition, enhanced by fermatas on either side of the tonic.
        Schindler and Czerny are in rare agreement on the Largo from the Piano Sonata in D Major, Op. 10, no. 3, when Schindler quotes from Czerny's *Von dem Vortrage:* "In this Largo, too, a well-calculated *ritardando* and *accelerando* must enhance the effect." But Schindler goes on to specify ten changes in the rate of motion. One might question whether Schindler meant distinct tempi or rather the kind of rhetorical underlining exemplified in his discussion of Op. 10, no. 1.

48. This concern is also raised in Rothstein (1995).

49. Frank Samarotto (1999) might interpret the Neapolitan expansion as another temporal plane, in his theory of temporal plasticity.

50. Debussy's piano prelude with the after-title "La fille aux cheveux de lin" (The Maid with the Flaxen Hair) opens with a pastoral-sounding arpeggiation of a mm^7 chord, and its poised, self-enclosed character and immediate repetition also foreground the gesture as a moment of reflection. I return to Beethoven's gesture in the Conclusion.

51. Examination of the sketches by William Kinderman (1995: 218) reveals that the opening theme was originally intended as a bagatelle.

52. It is this underlying coherence that is central to Schenker's (1971 [1913–20]: 6) overly demystifying interpretation of the events of these measures.

53. This is the rationalization of dissonance that Rosen (1972) credits Haydn as having contributed to the Classical style.

54. Note the cadential six-four appears, atypically, on the weaker second beat, but it is nevertheless strong relative to its resolution to five-three on the offbeat.

55. I would not support proportional tempo here, however, since the unmediated shock of difference is what is crucial to the expressive effect.

56. Based on a comparable use in Bruckner; see Hatten (2001).

57. See Chapter 11 for more on the issue of continuity.

58. Annette Richards (2001) has investigated the expressive potential of the free fantasia as a genre (beyond the mere topical designation in Ratner's catalog). She notes contemporaneous comparisons by Czerny (191), Amadeus Wendt (206), and E. T. A. Hoffmann (208) between the fantasia and the English landscape garden. Another bit of evidence is that Beethoven, who used long walks through the countryside to stimulate poetic inspiration, often referred to *Gartenkunst* in his conversations (213). These "natural" gardens were planned with walks that would gradually reveal the beauties of the landscape, and often included a labyrinthine grotto with Masonic inscriptions—"Choose, Wanderer, your way with judgment"—to symbolize a journey from darkness to enlightenment (218). Thus, a fantasia was viewed metaphorically as a similar voyage of discovery, wandering, and searching for insight "through a phantasmagoric, quasi-Masonic landscape" that "enacts the mythic quest of the apprentice at the temple of Isis, for whom bewilderment and amazement constitute climactic points on the journey of initiation into the secrets of nature" (219). Indeed, Richards notes that Beethoven copied out Schiller's inscription for "The Veiled Statue at Saïs" (from Schiller's 1795 ballad of that name), for this mystic and mythic deity of Nature: "I am all that is. / I am all that is, was and will be and no mortal has lifted my veil. / He originated by himself and to him all things owe their being" (219). Kant cited this inscription in his 1795 *Critique of Judgment* as the "touchstone of sublimity, the unknowable deity, identified with Nature itself, representing the profound limits of human reason" (221). From this perspective, the thematization of rhetorical gesture in the fantasia-like section of Op. 109 is fittingly coupled with a genre where "momentary disorientation" (206) and shifts in perspective are typical.

8. Thematic Gesture in Schubert

1. See Schoenberg, "New Music, Outmoded Music, Style and Idea" [1946] and "Brahms the Progressive" [1947] in *Style and Idea* (1975). A very helpful overview of Schoenberg's relevant concepts is found in Frisch (1984: 1–34).

2. The following interpretation is drawn from Hatten (1993).

3. This stylistic gesture plays a significant thematic role in Beethoven's Op. 101, as well—especially in the finale.

4. As Mendelssohn expressed it in a letter of 1842, "Words seem to me so ambiguous, so vague . . . in comparison to genuine music. . . . The thoughts which are expressed to me by music that I love are not too indefinite to be put into words, but on the contrary, too definite" (1945: 313).

5. Schubert's use of the theme from the finale in an earlier piano sonata is especially instructive with respect to gesture. The second movement (in E major) of his early Piano Sonata in A Minor, D. 537 (1817), features the same thematic contour in unbroken *"ligato"* above a staccato bass and offbeat chordal accompaniment (see Hatten 1993). This original version is less rhythmically interesting (it almost sounds like a reduction of the later theme) and lacks any of the articulatory breaks that make the later theme so gesturally expressive (whether as declamatory, tactile, or an intermodal synthesis of the two). The comparison supports an argument for Schubert's increasing attention to gesture in his late style.

6. The recital was one of several featured as part of "Schubert's Piano Music," an international symposium of performers, musicologists, and theorists, at the Smithsonian Collection of Musical Instruments, National Museum of American History, Washington, D.C., April 5–9, 1995.

7. As Sandra Rosenblum (1988: 38) observes, "fortepiano tone is silvery and rich in overtones."

8. For further arguments, see Hatten (1993).

9. For abstraction and sublimation, recall David Lidov's argument, critiqued in Chapter 6.

10. This is also the characteristic rhythmic pattern of the drum roll cadence used in a funeral cortège. I am grateful to my student Carl Kling for bringing this to my attention.

11. Schubert's early Piano Sonata in A Minor, D. 537 (mentioned in note 5 above) provides a precedent with its middle movement in E major.

12. I will pass over the development section, which may be analyzed in terms of its various thematic integrations. A dramatic integration of the tragic gesture with the heroic dotted figure suggests climactic struggle, echoed in the war between tragic D minor and illusory F major (mm. 114–24). Later a varied statement of the second theme is integratively enhanced with the dotted rhythms and the chromatic lower neighbor from the first theme group.

13. Although I tend to hear this transformative moment in spiritual terms, transcending the will in the sense of an *extrapersonal* agency, it is equally possible to interpret it purely psychologically, as a sudden integrative moment of insight: the "eureka" moment, which can be quite unexpected, but nevertheless reflects a *per-*

sonal agency (to the extent that we can be said to own our unconscious thought processes prior to their emergence in a conscious solution). However, we cannot consciously "will" such insights into being, and thus they appear transcendent. The dramatic opposition of means in these two transitions (willed vs. unwilled) and their expressive effect (heroic vs. transcendent) are the crucial interpretive issues with respect to their role in the unfolding expressive genre.

14. A more extreme example of a climactic outburst occurs in the middle section of the slow movement from Schubert's Piano Sonata in A Major, D. 959, but that movement already begins tragically in F♯ minor.

15. This release is difficult to achieve without a "bump" in performance; hence, the articulatory detail is typically ignored in overpedaled, Romantic interpretations.

16. There are no internal disruptions of the episode theme, as in the first movement's second theme, but each time the theme returns, the transition to the next idea is broken off more abruptly. Finally, with the third return the cadence to A major is immediately reversed by a shift to A minor.

9. Thematic Gesture in Beethoven

1. Bartók (1998 [1931]: 167) claims that Beethoven's theme is based on a Yugoslav melody.

2. This rising third, as a detachable gesture, plays a significant role in the development section, where it counterpoints an imitative treatment of the dotted rhythmic gesture (again, a mosaic development of gestural motives).

3. Formally this is a conflation of second theme and transitional functions, in that the lyrical contrast of G major suggests the dialectic of topic and theme found between first and second groups, whereas the larger tonal argument takes G major as the first step of a move to the dominant, E minor, the tragic tonal goal of the exposition. Thus, Beethoven achieves a moment of pastoral relief here, but ultimately maintains the tragic obsessiveness of minor. Another minor movement that provides dialectic contrast with the relative major in the main theme, but maintains the tragic in its move to the minor dominant, is the first movement of Op. 90, in E minor. The second movement of Op. 109, also in E minor, modulates to the dominant minor before offering a "yielding" moment of relief in C major (a parenthetical moment created by reiterated V_2^4-I^6 progressions), only to set up an even more wrenching return when the last reiteration of V_2^4 is reinterpreted as an inverted German augmented-sixth chord leading to the tragic arrival $_4^6$ in B minor. Thus, in these examples we see Beethoven experimenting with a range of solutions in this negotiation of expressive and functional tonal goals.

4. Huei-Ming Wang (1997: 70) discovers the finale's motive in the cello's punctuation of the closing theme of the second movement in A minor (exposition mm. 68–72 and recapitulation mm. 137–41). In these earlier locations the motive is not highly foregrounded, nor does its appearance meet one of Meyer's (1973) criteria for motivic conformance—there is too great a distance from its presumed source, the opening of the Andante. Although the rhythm is the same, the metric location is different—closing on the downbeat. Thus, I am inclined to interpret it as a less-than-motivic "riff" figure. The finale's theme, on the other hand, is in

close proximity to the quotation of the Andante and can thus be heard convincingly as a comically dismissive response to that visionary moment.

5. A truly grotesque moment would be hard to find in the Classical style, and I am using the term somewhat casually here. For an insightful treatment of the grotesque—as a trope on the ludicrous and the horrifying—see Sheinberg (2000: 207-309), who provides numerous examples from the work of Dmitri Shostakovich.

6. The first movement of Haydn's String Quartet in G Major, Op. 33, no. 5, has conspicuous similarities to Beethoven's finale. Haydn begins with a closing gesture, harmonized V^7-I, that features stepwise motion from $\hat{5}$ to $\hat{1}$ in the first violin. Unlike Beethoven's gesture, however, Haydn's is strongly closural, both harmonically and metrically, and serves initially as a frame, reappearing cadentially in the second phrase of the opening period. Another point of comparison is the rhetorical shift from V^7/G to E♭ with a reiterated open fifth in the cello, launching a coda. And finally, Haydn brings back the framing cadence at the end, echoing it with a unison statement of the gesture. I am grateful to Tamara Balter for pointing out these connections.

10. Gestural Troping and Agency

1. For more on the performative aspect of musical meaning see Cook and Dibben (2001), and for its relevance to musical gesture, Cook (2003b). For a performative approach to music theory and analysis, see Cook (1999).

2. The issue is not simple, of course. For a consideration of different kinds of evidence (and different kinds of relationships between the biographical and the compositional) see Hatten (2003a).

3. Beethoven employs a similar device in the *Diabelli* Variations, Op. 120, with the ironic or parodistic quotation of Mozart's "Notte e giorno faticar," from Leporello's aria in *Don Giovanni*. Since this variation is also number 22, and the riff motive is similar, perhaps Alkan is also troping (intertextually) on Beethoven. For an interesting account of the significance of Beethoven's parody of Mozart in the context of the entire variation set, see Kinderman (1995: 213).

4. It is in this sense that my use of the term "dialogical" comes closest to that of Bakhtin (1981 [1935]).

5. See Rink (1994, 1999) and Rothstein (1995) for more on the performer as narrator.

6. For the expressive interpretation of musical representation, see also Kivy (1984). Beethoven, in his famous comment on the Sixth Symphony, reveals his intent to move beyond simple pictorialism (representation) and instead express the feelings one would have upon encountering nature in a visit to the countryside. Clearly expression is wedded to agency in this claim.

7. Of course, if one claims that this level of narrativity is *not* implied by the music, then the performer would be enacting a Type 4 agency.

8. It is prefigured in the novels of Romantic contemporaries such as Jean Paul Richter and E. T. A. Hoffmann which were to have such an obvious impact on Schumann, and which may have influenced Beethoven as well. Solomon (2003: 42-70)

elaborates on various Romantic sources for the poetic images found in Beethoven's music; one can readily imagine that Romantics authors' shifts among different (levels of) agents might also have influenced Beethoven.

Conclusion to Part Two

1. The concepts of density, repleteness, and exemplification are drawn from Nelson Goodman (1968).

11. From Gestural Continuity to Continuity as Premise

1. One of the best accounts of the interaction of these aspects of Classical style is found in Rosen (1972: 53–98).

2. For more detailed explanation of markedness, style types, and style growth, see the examples in the Introduction (Mozart) and Chapter 1 (Beethoven), as well as Hatten (1994: 29–56).

3. For more on the distinction among these three types of material, see Hatten (1994: 115–19).

4. Beckerman (1992: 95–96) notes the use of pastoral idiom to create contrast and temporary relief after dramatically dark opening ideas, using this as one of his examples.

5. Schubert injects articulated textural contrast in his episodes, but like Mozart (whose K. 310 finale may well have been the inspiration for his own) he moves to A major in conjunction with perpetual-motion texture to launch the middle section's developmental integration of ideas. Other movements of Schubert sonatas find justification for their perpetual-motion thematic character (which is pervasive, if occasionally disrupted) through *genre:* the diminutional variations of the second movement of D. 845, or the topical tarantella used as the basis for the finale of D. 958.

6. Historical style change leading to the continuities of Schumann and Chopin may have been fueled not only by the breakdown of Classical formal hierarchies but by the urge to respond to inner expression in shorter character pieces (in turn, prefigured by the Classical character variation and bagatelle). Another possible influence is the virtuoso etude. The piano etudes of J. B. Cramer (1771–1858) may have influenced Beethoven in his perpetual-motion finales for the piano sonatas Opp. 26 and 54, as well as one or more of the variations in the *Diabelli* set (Kinderman 1995). Textural continuity as the substrate for single-affect emotional consistency in early Romantic character pieces may help explain the oft-noted parallel with Baroque textures, even when these works do not specifically reference Baroque style.

7. Further drama may be achieved by delaying or diverting that drive.

8. The *Satz* is a phrase design characteristic of many Classical themes (a prototype being the opening theme of Beethoven's Piano Sonata, Op. 2, no. 1). It features dynamic or propulsive phrase growth (by motivic fragmentation and acceleration) reconciled to a symmetrical outcome. The typical additive motivic pattern $(2) + (2) + (1 + 1) + (2)$ nevertheless results in $(4 + 4)$ periodicity. In the *Satz,*

additive and hierarchical phrase designs are yoked in perfect balance. Here Schubert's construction of his second theme tips the balance toward the additive, with its two-bar extension.

9.   I do not mean to imply that four-bar phrases cease to be the norm in Romantic music (Schumann's music would dispel that claim easily enough), but rather they cease to be constructed as hierarchically as in the Classical style. For an interesting account of early Romantic manipulation of the four-bar norm, see Rosen (1995: 258–78). For Schumann's extraordinary range of rhythmic and metric dissonances and displacements, see Krebs (1999).

10.   Interestingly, ritual performances also draw on the repetitive, often to generate a trancelike response, and some minimalist compositions reflect an awareness of the potential to generate a deeper expressive state or psychological mood by near-tantric repetition. One might also consider this state, in psychoanalytical terms drawn from Lacan, a re-creation of the bliss of the womb, or a presymbolic state, or the acoustic mirror of Kaja Silverman (1988). For an application of these concepts to music, see David Schwarz (1997).

11.   Beethoven's concept of *Kunstvereinigung* is drawn from his letter to Prince Rudolph dated July 29, 1819 (KK 900; BGA 4:1318) in which he speaks of a new synthesis of modern style and the best of Baroque style, referring specifically to the music of the "Deutsche Händel und Seb. Bach." For two complementary perspectives on this synthesis, through the direct influence of Bach and through the influence of Beethoven's contemporary Dusík, see Kinderman (2002) and Küthen (2002), respectively.

12.   Between the plenitude of *stretto* fragments in D major and the inversion entry section is a complete, normal entry in D major (m. 196)! This entry is preceded by an allusion to the slow movement in m. 195, by means of a chromatic collapse through diminished sevenths to a D root position triad, recalling the G♯–G♮–F♯ motive that has such resignational importance in the Adagio transition and second theme group (see Hatten 1994). Thus, the progressive amelioration of the extremities marked by the B minor retrograde section extends to other, motivic dimensions.

13.   That section had moved *up* a third from B minor; clearly, more than one tonal strategy is at play.

14.   The extra voices are rationalized by Beethoven's designation "con alcune licenze" at the beginning of the fugue. Recall as well the move toward homophonic texture at the end of the Op. 110 fugue.

15.   Kinderman (1995) notes the thematic link between the close of the *Diabelli* set and the Op. 111 piano sonata.

12. Discontinuity and Beyond

1.   Leonard B. Meyer had already treated the Romantic approach to stylistic convention quite extensively in his *Style in Music* (1989, see especially Chapter 7, "Convention Disguised—Nature Affirmed"), but McClary does not address Meyer's work where it is most relevant to her own.

2. See Gretchen Wheelock (1992).

3. I should mention here my three essays on this topic, "Tense and Music" (Hatten 1997), "Aspect and Music" (Hatten and Pearson, in press), and "The Troping of Temporality in Music" (Hatten 2002b). The latter two essays explore some fruitful analogies between linguistic aspect and musical means of cueing the temporal shape of events, actions, and processes. The principal difficulty with these linguistic analogies is that music does not predicate as language does, although there are clearly cues for temporal perspective.

4. Agawu's interpretation of the "march" highlights the absence of a downbeat, which makes for "a 'defective' march, whose 'ideal' form does not occur until the very end of the movement" (1991:114).

5. Compare their emblematic use in the slow movement of Op. 59, no. 2, as discussed in Hatten (1994: 192).

6. D minor is heard as vi of F major, not iv of A minor, as Kerman claims (1966: 245).

7. Or even between minuet and trio, as in Beethoven's String Quartet in C Minor, Op. 18, no. 4. In the third movement the Menuetto in C minor shifts to a Trio in A♭ major.

8. Except for the *Grosse Fuge,* Op. 133, which he found suitably modernist in its presumed abstraction.

9. Important interpretations of musical topics (or their Greimassian equivalents) may be found in Ratner (1980), Allanbrook (1983), Grabócz (1996 [1986]) Agawu (1991), Hatten (1994), Tarasti (1994), and Monelle (2000).

10. This strategy is more obviously the case for the finale of Op. 131, which emphasizes a permutation of the same four notes found in the head of the fugue subject from the first movement.

11. But recall the troping of march and minuet in Mozart's *Linz* Symphony (Example 4.8).

Conclusion

1. From a developmental perspective, gesture may appear immediate to the infant, but it is already being shaped by interactions with caregivers—indeed, it cannot develop without such interactions. We are innately primed to develop in this way, but gestural competency in the absence of an interactive environment is inconceivable. The qualitative Firstness of gesture is always presented in the dynamic context of various kinds of Secondness, from physical environmental forces to human affective intersubjective exchanges. But the condition of symbolic Thirdness remains the ultimate status of the sign, as fully developed.

2. It should be evident that Beethoven's strategy of reiterating a unique opening gesture—not only to articulate it as a segment, but also to foreground it as thematic, and in this case to allow reflection on its qualitative properties—is a signature procedure for Debussy, and for many of the same reasons. It allows us time to reflect on the "phenomenological" qualities of a functional sonority used nonfunctionally, or a pattern that might be unfamiliar as a syntactic unit.

3. For a virtuoso performance in this regard, see Kielian-Gilbert (1999).

4. A more productive analogy for an arabesque comes from its definition as a literary digression or *parabasis*. Schumann admired arabesques of this kind in Jean Paul Richter's novels, and according to Daverio (1993: 35) he incorporated the technique in the first movement of the *Fantasie*, Op. 17.

Bibliography

Abbate, Carolyn. 1991. *Unsung Voices: Opera and Musical Narrative in the Nineteenth Century.* Princeton, N.J.: Princeton University Press.

Adelung, Johann Christoph. 1789–90. *Über den Deutschen Styl.* 2 vols. Berlin: Voss.

Agawu, V. Kofi. 1991. *Playing with Signs: A Semiotic Interpretation of Classic Music.* Princeton, N.J.: Princeton University Press.

———. 1996. Review of Robert S. Hatten, *Musical Meaning in Beethoven: Markedness, Correlation, and Interpretation. Current Musicology* 60–61: 147–61.

Allanbrook, Wye J. 1983. *Rhythmic Gesture in Mozart:* Le Nozze di Figaro *and* Don Giovanni. Chicago: University of Chicago Press.

———. 1992. "Two Threads through the Labyrinth: Topic and Process in the First Movements of K. 332 and K. 333." In *Convention in Eighteenth- and Nineteenth-Century Music: Essays in Honor of Leonard G. Ratner,* ed. Wye J. Allanbrook, Janet M. Levy, and William P. Mahrt, 125–71. Stuyvesant, N.Y.: Pendragon Press, 1992.

Alpers, Paul. 1996. *What Is Pastoral?* Chicago: University of Chicago Press.

Anderson, Emily, ed. and trans. 1961. *The Letters of Beethoven.* 3 vols. London: Macmillan.

Armstrong, David F., William C. Stokoe, and Sherman E. Wilcox. 1995. *Gesture and the Nature of Language.* Cambridge: Cambridge University Press.

Austin, J. L. 1962. *How to Do Things with Words.* Cambridge, Mass.: Harvard University Press.

Auyang, Sunny Y. 2000. *Mind in Everyday Life and Cognitive Science.* Cambridge, Mass.: MIT Press.

Bach, Carl Philipp Emanuel. 1949 [1753]. *Essay on the True Art of Playing Keyboard Instruments.* Trans. William J. Mitchell (*Versuch über die wahre Art, das Clavier zu spielen,* vol. 1, Berlin, 1753). New York: W. W. Norton.

Badura-Skoda, Paul. 1988. "A Tie Is a Tie Is a Tie: Reflections on Beethoven's Pairs of Tied Notes" *Early Music* 16, no. 1: 84–88.

Baer, Eugen. 1987. "Thomas A. Sebeok's Doctrine of Signs." In *Classics of Semiotics,* ed. Martin Krampen, Klaus Oehler, Roland Posner, Thomas A. Sebeok, and Thure von Uexküll, 181–210. New York: Plenum Press.

Bakhtin, M. M. 1981 [1935]. *The Dialogic Imagination: Four Essays by M. M. Bakhtin.* Ed. Michael Holquist, trans. Caryl Emerson. Austin: University of Texas Press.

Barnett, David. 1972. *The Performance of Music: A Study in Terms of the Pianoforte.* New York: Universe Books.

Barnett, Dene. 1987. *The Art of Gesture: The Practices and Principles of 18th-Century Acting.* (With the assistance of Jeanette Massy-Westropp.) Heidelberg: C. Winter.

Barth, George. 1992. *The Pianist as Orator: Beethoven and the Transformation of Keyboard Style.* Ithaca, N.Y.: Cornell University Press.

Barthes, Roland. 1985 [1975]. "Rasch." In "Music's Body," Part II of *The Responsibility of Forms: Critical Essays on Music, Art, and Representation,* trans. Richard Howard, 299–312. Berkeley: University of California Press.

Bartók, Béla. 1998 [1931]. "The Influence of Peasant Music on Modern Music." In *Strunk's Source Readings in Music History,* vol. 7: *The Twentieth Century,* ed. Robert P. Morgan, 167–71. New York: W. W. Norton.

Beardsley, Monroe. 1982. "What Is an Aesthetic Quality?" In *The Aesthetic Point of View,* ed. M. Wreen and D. Callen, 93–110. Ithaca, N.Y.: Cornell University Press.

Beckerman, Michael. 1992. "Mozart's Pastoral." In *Mozart-Jahrbuch 1991* (Bericht über den Internationalen Mozart-Kongress Salzburg 1991), vol. 1, 93–99.

Becking, Gustav. 1928. *Der musikalische Rhythmus als Erkenntnisquelle.* Augsburg: Benno Filser.

Berry, Wallace. 1989. *Musical Structure and Performance.* New Haven, Conn.: Yale University Press.

Bilson, Malcolm, et al. 1997. *Ludwig van Beethoven: The Complete Piano Sonatas on Period Instruments.* Claves Records, CD 50-9707/10.

Bonds, Mark Evan. 1991. *Wordless Rhetoric: Musical Form and the Metaphor of the Oration.* Cambridge, Mass.: Harvard University Press.

Bregman, Albert S. 1990. *Auditory Scene Analysis: The Perceptual Organization of Sound.* Cambridge, Mass.: MIT Press.

Brendel, Alfred. 1992 [1990]. *Music Sounded Out.* New York: Noonday Press.

Brinkmann, Reinhold. 1995 [1990]. *Late Idyll: The Second Symphony of Johannes Brahms.* Trans. Peter Palmer. Cambridge, Mass.: Harvard University Press. (*Johannes Brahms: Die Zweite Symphonie: Späte Idylle* [Munich: Edition Text + Kritik, 1990].)

Brower, Candace. 2000. "A Cognitive Theory of Musical Meaning." *Journal of Music Theory* 44, no. 2: 323–79.

Brown, A. Peter. 1983. "Brahms's Third Symphony and the New German School." *Journal of Musicology* 2, no. 4: 434–52.

Brown, Clive. 1999. *Classical and Romantic Performing Practice, 1750–1900.* New York: Oxford University Press.

Brown, Lesley, ed. 1993. *The New Shorter Oxford English Dictionary.* Oxford: Clarendon Press.

Bruce, Vicki, and Andy Young. 1998. *In the Eye of the Beholder: The Science of Face Perception.* Oxford: Oxford University Press.

Buelow, George J. 2001 [1980]. "Rhetoric and Music." In *The New Grove Dictionary of Music and Musicians,* 2nd ed., ed. Stanley Sadie, vol. 21, 260–75. London: Macmillan.

Burkholder, J. Peter. 1995a. *All Made of Tunes: Charles Ives and the Uses of Musical Borrowing.* New Haven, Conn.: Yale University Press.

———. 1995b. "Rule-Breaking as a Rhetorical Sign." In *Festa Musicologica: Essays in Honor of George J. Buelow,* ed. Thomas J. Mathiesen and Benito V. Rivera, 369–89. Stuyvesant, N.Y.: Pendragon Press.

———. 2002. "A Simple Model of Musical Meaning." Paper delivered to the Musicology Colloquium Series, Indiana University.

Burnham, Scott. 1995. *Beethoven Hero.* Princeton, N.J.: Princeton University Press.

Campbell, Ruth. 1999. "Language from Faces: Uses of the Face in Speech and in Sign." In *Gesture, Speech, and Sign,* ed. Lynn S. Messing and Ruth Campbell, 57–73. Oxford: Oxford University Press.

Charlton, David, ed. 1989. *E. T. A. Hoffmann's Musical Writings: Kreisleriana, The Poet and the Composer, Music Criticism.* Cambridge: Cambridge University Press.

Christensen, Thomas, and Nancy K. Baker, eds. 1995. *Aesthetics and the Art of Musical*

Composition in the German Enlightenment: Selected Writings of Johann Georg Sulzer and Heinrich Christoph Koch (Sulzer, General Theory of the Fine Arts, selected articles, 1771-74). Cambridge: Cambridge University Press.

Churchland, Paul. 1995. The Engine of Reason, the Seat of the Soul: A Philosophical Journey into the Brain. Cambridge, Mass.: MIT Press.

Clark, Andy. 1997. Being There: Putting Brain, Body, and World Together. Cambridge, Mass.: MIT Press.

Clarke, Eric F. 1985. "Structure and Expression in Rhythmic Performance." In Musical Structure and Cognition, ed. Peter. Howell, Ian Cross, and Robert West, 209-36. London: Academic Press.

———. 1988. "Generative Principles in Music Performance." In Generative Processes in Music: The Psychology of Performance, Improvisation, and Composition, ed. John A. Sloboda, 1-26. Oxford: Clarendon Press.

Clynes, Manfred. 1977. Sentics: The Touch of Emotions. New York: Anchor Press.

———. 1995. "Microstructural Musical Linguistics: Composers' Pulses Are Liked Most by the Best Musicians." Cognition 55, no. 3: 269-310.

Clynes, Manfred, and Janice Walker. 1982. "Neurobiologic Functions of Rhythm, Time and Pulse in Music." In Music, Mind, and Brain: The Neuropsychology of Music, ed. Manfred Clynes, 171-216. New York: Plenum Press.

Coker, Wilson. 1972. Music and Meaning: A Theoretical Introduction to Musical Aesthetics. New York: Free Press.

Cone, Edward T. 1968. Musical Form and Musical Performance. New York: W. W. Norton.

Cook, Nicholas. 1999. "Analysing Performance, Performing Analysis." In Rethinking Music, ed. Nicholas Cook and Mark Everist, 239-61. Oxford: Oxford University Press.

———. 2003a. "Music as Performance." In The Cultural Study of Music: A Critical Introduction, ed. Martin Clayton, Trevor Herbert, and Richard Middleton, 204-14. New York: Routledge.

———. 2003b. "Embodying Performance: Sound, Sight and Gesture in the Improvisations of Jimi Hendrix." Keynote address, "Music and Gesture" international conference, University of East Anglia, Norwich.

Cook, Nicholas, and Nicola Dibben. 2001. "Musicological Approaches to Emotion." In Music and Emotion: Theory and Research, ed. Patrik N. Juslin and John A. Sloboda, 45-70. Oxford: Oxford University Press.

Cooke, Deryck. 1959. The Language of Music. Oxford: Oxford University Press.

Cooper, Barry. 1990. Beethoven and the Creative Process. Oxford: Clarendon Press.

Cross, Ian. 2001. "Music, Cognition, Culture, and Evolution." In The Biological Foundations of Music, ed. Robert J. Zatorre and Isabelle Peretz, 28-42. Annals of the NY Academy of Sciences, 930. New York: New York Academy of Sciences.

Cumming, Naomi. 2000. The Sonic Self: Musical Subjectivity and Signification. Bloomington: Indiana University Press.

Cusick, Suzanne G. 1994. "On a Lesbian Relation with Music: A Serious Effort Not to Think Straight." In Queering the Pitch: The New Gay and Lesbian Musicology, ed. Philip Brett, Elizabeth Wood, and Gary C. Thomas, 67-84. New York: Routledge.

Czerny, Carl. 1968 [1842]. Erinnerungen aus meinem Leben. Ed. Walter Kolneder. Strasbourg: Éditions P. H. Heitz.

———. 1970. On the Proper Performance of All Beethoven's Works for the Piano. Ed. Paul Badura-Skoda. Vienna: Universal Edition.

———. 1991 [1846]. Von dem Vortrage (Third Part of the Complete Theoretical-Practical

Pianoforte School, op. 500, facsimile of 1846 ed.). Intro. Ulrich Mahlert. Wiesbaden: Breitkopf und Härtel.

Damasio, Antonio R. 1994. *Descartes' Error: Emotion, Reason, and the Human Brain.* New York: G. P. Putnam's Sons.

———. 1999. *The Feeling of What Happens: Body and Emotion in the Making of Consciousness.* New York: Harcourt Brace & Company.

Daverio, John. 1993. *Nineteenth-Century Music and the German Romantic Ideology.* New York: Schirmer Books.

———. 2002. *Crossing Paths: Schubert, Schumann, and Brahms.* Oxford: Oxford University Press.

David, Hans T., and Arthur Mendel, eds. 1966 [1945]. *The Bach Reader: A Life of Johann Sebastian Bach in Letters and Documents.* Rev. ed. New York: W. W. Norton.

de Assis, Machado. 1952. *Epitaph of a Small Winner.* Trans. William L. Grossman. New York: Noonday.

Donald, Merlin. 2001. *A Mind So Rare: The Evolution of Human Consciousness.* New York: W. W. Norton.

Dreyfus, Laurence. 1996. *Bach and the Patterns of Invention.* Cambridge, Mass.: Harvard University Press.

Dunsby, Jonathan. 1995. *Performing Music: Shared Concerns.* Oxford: Clarendon Press.

Eckelmeyer, Judith A. 1986. "Structure as Hermeneutic Guide to *The Magic Flute.*" *Musical Quarterly* 72, no. 1: 51–73.

Edelman, Gerald M. 1992. *Bright Air, Brilliant Fire: On the Matter of the Mind.* New York: Basic Books.

Edelman, Gerald M., and Giulio Tononi. 2000. *A Universe of Consciousness: How Matter Becomes Imagination.* New York: Basic Books.

Efron, David. 1941. *Gesture and Environment: A Tentative Study of Some of the Spatio-temporal and "Linguistic" Aspects of the Gestural Behavior of Eastern Jews and Southern Italians in New York City, Living under Similar as Well as Different Environmental Conditions.* New York: King's Crown Press. (Ph.D. thesis, Columbia University.)

Ekman, Paul. 1972. "Universals and Cultural Differences in Facial Expressions of Emotion." In *Nebraska Symposium on Motivation, 1971,* ed. J. Cole, 207–83. Lincoln: University of Nebraska Press.

———. 1999. "Emotional and Conversational Nonverbal Signals." In *Gesture, Speech, and Sign,* ed. Lynn S. Messing and Ruth Campbell, 45–55. Oxford: Oxford University Press.

———. 2003. *Emotions Revealed: Recognizing Faces and Feelings to Improve Communication and Emotional Life.* New York: Times Books.

Emmorey, Karen. 1999. "Do Signers Gesture?" In *Gesture, Speech, and Sign,* ed. Lynn S. Messing and Ruth Campbell, 133–59. Oxford: Oxford University Press.

———. 2001. "Space on Hand: The Exploitation of Signing Space to Illustrate Abstract Thought." In *Spatial Schemas and Abstract Thought,* ed. Merideth Gattis, 147–74. Cambridge, Mass.: MIT Press.

Empson, William. 1960 [1935]. *Some Versions of Pastoral.* Norfolk, Conn.: New Directions Press.

Epstein, David. 1995. *Shaping Time: Music, the Brain, and Performance.* New York: Schirmer Books.

Fauconnier, Gilles, and Mark Turner. 2002. *The Way We Think: Conceptual Blending and the Mind's Hidden Complexities.* New York: Basic Books.

Fétis, F.-J. 1858. *Traité complet de la théorie et de la pratique de l'harmonie* [1844]. 6th ed. Paris: G. Brandus.

Floros, Constantin. 1980. *Brahms und Bruckner: Studien zur musikalischen Exegetik.* Wiesbaden: Breitkopf und Härtel.

———. 1993 [1985].*Gustav Mahler: The Symphonies.* Trans. Vernon Wicker. Portland, Ore.: Amadeus Press. (Gustav *Mahler III: Die Symphonien.* Wiesbaden: Breitkopf und Härtel, 1985.)

Forkel, Johann Nicolaus. 1802. *Über Johann Sebastian Bachs Leben, Kunst und Kunstwerke.* Leipzig: Hoffmeister und Kühnel.

Frisch, Walter. 1984. *Brahms and the Principle of Developing Variation.* Berkeley: University of California Press.

Frisch, Walter, ed. 1990. *Brahms and His World.* Princeton, N.J.: Princeton University Press.

Frykhold, G. 1983. *Action, Intention, Gender, and Identity, Perceived from Body Movement.* Uppsala, Sweden: Uppsala Universitet.

Gabrielsson, Alf. 1974. "Performance of Rhythm Patterns." *Scandinavian Journal of Psychology* 15: 63–72.

———. 1982. "Perception and Performance of Musical Rhythm." In *Music, Mind, and Brain: The Neuropsychology of Music,* ed. Manfred Clynes, 159–69. New York: Plenum Press.

———. 1988. "Timing in Music Performance and Its Relations to Music Experience." In *Generative Processes in Music: The Psychology of Performance, Improvisation, and Composition,* ed. John A. Sloboda, 27–51. Oxford: Clarendon Press.

Gabrielsson, Alf, ed. 1987. *Action and Perception in Rhythm and Music.* Stockholm: Royal Swedish Academy of Music.

Geertz, Clifford. 1973. *The Interpretation of Cultures.* New York: Basic Books.

Gibson, James J. 1966. *The Senses Considered as Perceptual Systems.* Boston: Houghton Mifflin.

Gjerdingen, Robert O. 1999. "Apparent Motion in Music?" In *Musical Networks: Parallel Distributed Perception and Performance,* ed. Niall Griffith and Peter M. Todd, 140–73. Cambridge, Mass.: MIT Press. (Revision of "Apparent Motion in Music." *Music Perception* 11 [1994]: 335–70.)

Godlovitch, Stan. 1998. *Musical Performance: A Philosophical Study.* London: Routledge.

Goodman, Nelson. 1968. *Languages of Art: An Approach to a Theory of Symbols.* Indianapolis: Bobbs-Merrill.

Grabócz, Márta. 1996 [1986]. *Morphologie des oeuvres pour piano de Liszt: Influence du programme sur l'évolution des formes instrumentals.* Paris: Éditions Kimé.

Graybill, Roger. 1994. "Prolongation, Gesture, and Tonal Motion." In *Musical Transformation and Musical Intuition: Eleven Essays in Honor of David Lewin,* ed. Raphael Atlas and Michael Cherlin, 199–224. Roxbury, Mass.: Ovenbird Press.

Greg, W. W. 1984 [1906]. *Pastoral Poetry and Pastoral Drama.* Excerpted in *The Pastoral Model: A Casebook,* ed. Brian Loughrey, 80. London: Macmillan.

HaCohen, Ruth, and Naphtali Wagner. Forthcoming. "The Gestural Power of the Wagnerian Leitmotifs: Self-promoting Jingles or Self-contained Expressions?" *Orbis Musicae.*

Hanslick, Eduard. 1974 [1854]. *The Beautiful in Music: A Contribution to the Revisal of Musical Aesthetics.* 7th ed. (*Vom musikalisch-Schönen,* Leipzig, 1885). Trans. Gustav Cohen. New York: Da Capo. (Reprint of London: Novello, 1891.)

Hasty, Christopher. 1997. *Meter as Rhythm.* New York: Oxford University Press.

Hatten, Robert S. 1982. "Toward a Semiotic Model of Style in Music: Epistemological and Methodological Bases." Ph.D. dissertation, Indiana University.

———. 1985. "The Place of Intertextuality in Music Studies." *American Journal of Semiotics* 3, no. 4: 69–82.

———. 1987. "Aspects of Dramatic Closure in Beethoven: A Semiotic Perspective on Music Analysis *via* Strategies of Dramatic Conflict." *Semiotica* 66, no. 1/3: 197–210.

———. 1992. "Interpreting Deception in Music." *In Theory Only* 12, no. 5/6: 31–50.

———. 1993. "Schubert the Progressive: The Role of Resonance and Gesture in the Piano Sonata in A, D. 959." *Intégral* 7: 38–81.

———. 1994. *Musical Meaning in Beethoven: Markedness, Correlation, and Interpretation.* Bloomington: Indiana University Press.

———. 1996. Review-article, *The Practice of Performance: Studies in Musical Interpretation,* ed. John Rink (Cambridge: Cambridge University Press, 1995). *Indiana Theory Review* 17, no. 1: 87–117.

———. 1996 [1998]. "Grounding Interpretation: A Semiotic Framework for Musical Hermeneutics." *American Journal of Semiotics* 24, no. 1–4: 25–42 (special issue on "Signs in Musical Hermeneutics," guest-edited by Siglind Bruhn).

———. 1997. "Music and Tense." In *Semiotics around the World: Synthesis in Diversity,* ed. Irmengard Rauch and Gerald F. Carr, 627–30. Berlin: Mouton de Gruyter.

———. 1997–99. "Musical Gesture." Eight lectures for the Cybersemiotic Institute (created by Prof. Paul Bouissac, University of Toronto), http://www.chass.utoronto.ca/epc/srb/cyber/hatout.html.

———. 1998. "Gestural Troping in Music and Its Consequences for Semiotic Theory." In *Musical Signification: Between Rhetoric and Pragmatics* (Proceedings of the Fifth International Congress on Musical Signification, Bologna, Italy, November 14–16, 1996), ed. Gino Stefani, Luca Marconi, and Eero Tarasti, 193–99. Bologna: Clueb.

———. 2001. "The Expressive Role of Disjunction: A Semiotic Approach to Form and Meaning in Bruckner's Fourth and Fifth Symphonies." In *Perspectives on Anton Bruckner,* ed. Paul Hawkshaw, Crawford Howie, and Timothy L. Jackson, 145–84. Aldershot, U.K.: Ashgate.

———. 2002a. Review of Harald Krebs, *Fantasy Pieces: Metrical Dissonance in the Music of Robert Schumann* (New York: Oxford University Press, 1999). *Music Theory Spectrum* 24, no. 2: 273–82.

———. 2002b. "The Troping of Temporality." Paper presented to the International Musicological Society, Leuven, Belgium.

———. 2003a. "Interpreting Personal Motivations: Responses to Life Crises in the Later Works of Beethoven, Schubert, and Chopin." In *Beethoven 2: Studien und Interpretationen,* ed. Mieczysław Tomaszewski and Magdalena Chrenkoff, 203–20. Kraków: Akademia Muzyczna.

———. 2003b. "Schubert's *Pastoral*: The Piano Sonata in G Major, D894." In *Schubert the Progressive: History, Performance Practice, Analysis,* ed. Brian Newbould, 151–68. Aldershot, U.K.: Ashgate.

———. Forthcoming. "Plenitude as Fulfillment: The Third Movement of Beethoven's String Quartet, Op. 130." In *The String Quartets of Beethoven,* ed. William Kinderman. University of Illinois Press.

Hatten, Robert S., and Charles Pearson. Forthcoming. "Aspect in Music." In *Proceedings of the 7th International Congress on Musical Signification,* Imatra, Finland, June 2001.

Hemingway, Ernest. 1999 [1953–54]. *True at First Light: A Fictional Memoir*. Ed. Patrick Hemingway. New York: Scribner.

Hobson, R. Peter. 1993. *Autism and the Development of Mind*. Hove, U.K.: Lawrence Erlbaum Associates.

Hoffmann, E. T. A. 1972 [1809]. "Ritter Gluck." In *Tales of E. T. A. Hoffmann*, ed. and trans. Leonard J. Kent and Elizabeth C. Knight, 3–13. Chicago: University of Chicago Press.

Imberty, Michel. 2000. "The Question of Innate Competencies in Musical Communication." In *The Origins of Music*, ed. Nils L. Wallin, Björn Merker, and Steven Brown, 449–62. Cambridge, Mass.: MIT Press.

Jakobson, Roman. 1963. *Essais de linguistique générale*. Paris: Minuit.

Jander, Owen. 1988. "The 'Kreutzer' Sonata as Dialogue." *Early Music* 16, no. 1: 34–49.

Johnson, Mark. 1987. *The Body in the Mind: The Bodily Basis of Reason and Imagination*. Chicago: University of Chicago Press.

Jones, Evan. 1993. "Dynamics and Dissonance: The Implied Harmonic Theory of J. J. Quantz." Paper presented to Music Theory Midwest, Indiana University.

Keijzer, Fred. 2001. *Representation and Behavior*. Cambridge, Mass.: MIT Press.

Keil, Charles, and Steven Feld. 1994. *Music Grooves*. Chicago: University of Chicago Press.

Keller, Hermann. 1965 [1955]. *Phrasing and Articulation: A Contribution to a Rhetoric of Music*. Trans. Leigh Gerdine. New York: W. W. Norton. (*Phrasierung und Artikulation*, Kassel: Bärenreiter-Verlag, 1955.)

Kendon, Adam. 1981. "Introduction: Current Issues in the Study of Nonverbal Communication." In *Nonverbal Communication, Interaction, and Gesture: Selections from Semiotica*, ed. Adam Kendon, 1–53. The Hague: Mouton.

———. 1986. "Current Issues in the Study of Gesture." In *The Biological Foundations of Gestures: Motor and Semiotic Aspects*, ed. Jean-Luc Nespoulous, Paul Perron, and André Roch Lecours, 23–47. Hillsdale, N.J.: Lawrence Erlbaum Associates.

———. 1988. "How Gestures Can Become like Words." In *Cross-cultural Perspectives in Nonverbal Communication*, ed. F. Poyatos, 131–41. Toronto: Hogrefe.

Kerman, Joseph. 1965. "A Profile for American Musicology." *Journal of the American Musicological Society* 18: 61–69. Reprinted in *Write All These Down: Essays on Music*, 3–11. Berkeley: University of California Press, 1994.

———. 1966. *The Beethoven Quartets*. New York: W. W. Norton.

———. 1985. *Contemplating Music: Challenges to Musicology*. Cambridge, Mass.: Harvard University Press.

Kielian-Gilbert, Marianne. 1999. "On Rebecca Clarke's *Sonata for Viola and Piano*: Feminist Spaces and Metaphors of Reading." In *Audible Traces: Gender, Identity, and Music*, ed. Elaine Barkin and Lydia Hamessley, 71–114. Zurich: Carciofoli Verlaghaus.

Kinderman, William. 1986. "Schubert's Tragic Perspective." In *Schubert: Critical and Analytical Studies*, ed. Walter Frisch, 65–83. Lincoln: University of Nebraska Press.

———. *1995. Beethoven*. Berkeley: University of California Press.

———. 1997. "Schubert's Piano Music: Probing the Human Condition." In *The Cambridge Companion to Schubert*, ed. Christopher H. Gibbs, 155–73. Cambridge: Cambridge University Press.

———. 2002. "Rückblick nach vorn: Beethovens 'Kunstvereinigung' und das Erbe Bachs." In *Beethoven und die Rezeption der Alten Musik: Die hohe Schule der Überlieferung*, ed. Hans-Werner Küthen, 121–45. Bonn: Beethoven-Haus.

Kirkland, Gelsey, with Greg Lawrence. 1987. *Dancing on My Grave.* New York: Jove Books.

Kivy, Peter. 1984. *Sound and Semblance.* Princeton, N.J.: Princeton University Press.

———. 1990. *Music Alone: Philosophical Reflections on the Purely Musical Experience.* Ithaca, N.Y.: Cornell University Press.

Koch, Heinrich Christoph. 1969 [1782]. *Versuch einer Anleitung zur Composition.* Vol. I. Rudolstadt: Löwe Erben und Schirach. Facsimile, Hildesheim: Olms.

Koffka, Kurt. 1935. *Principles of Gestalt Psychology.* London: Routledge and Kegan Paul.

Kramer, Jonathan D. 1988. *The Time of Music: New Meanings, New Temporalities, New Listening Strategies.* New York: Schirmer Books.

Kramer, Lawrence. 1990. *Music as Cultural Practice, 1800–1900.* Berkeley: University of California Press.

———. 1995. *Classical Music and Postmodern Knowledge.* Berkeley: University of California Press.

———. 2002. *Musical Meaning: Toward a Critical History.* Berkeley: University of California Press.

Kramer, Richard. 1992. "Between Cavatina and Ouverture: Opus 130 and the Voices of Narrative." *Beethoven Forum* 1, 178–84. Lincoln: University of Nebraska Press.

Krause, Andreas. 1996. *Die Klaviersonaten Franz Schuberts: Form, Gattung, Ästhetik.* Kassel: Bärenreiter.

Krebs, Harald. 1999. *Fantasy Pieces: Metrical Dissonance in the Music of Robert Schumann.* New York: Oxford University Press.

Krims, Adam, ed. 1998. *Music/Ideology: Resisting the Aesthetic.* Amsterdam: G + B Arts International.

Kropfinger, Klaus. 1987. "Das gespaltene Werk Beethovens Streichquartett Op. 130/133." In *Beiträge zu Beethovens Kammermusik* (Symposium Bonn 1983), ed. Sieghard Brandenburg and Helmut Loos, 296–335. Munich: G. Henle Verlag.

———. 1994. "Streichquartett B-Dur op. 130." In *Beethoven: Interpretationen seiner Werke,* vol. 2, ed. Albrecht Riethmüller, Carl Dahlhaus, and Alexander L. Ringer, 299–316. Laaber: Laaber-Verlag.

Kugler, Peter Noble, and Michael T. Turvey. 1987. *Information, Natural Law, and the Self-assembly of Rhythmic Movement.* Hillsdale, N.J.: Lawrence Erlbaum Associates.

Kuhl, P. K., and A. N. Meltzoff. 1982. "The Bimodal Perception of Speech in Infancy." *Science* 218: 1138–41.

Kullak, Franz. 1973 [1901]. *Beethoven's Piano-Playing.* Trans. Theodore Baker. New York: G. Schirmer. (Reprint, New York: Da Capo Press, 1973.)

Kurth, Ernst. 1917a. "Zur Motivbildung Bachs: Ein Beitrag zur Stilpsychologie." *Bach-Jahrbuch:* 80–136.

———. 1956 [1917b]. *Grundlagen des linearen Kontrapunkts: Bachs melodische Polyphonie.* 5th ed. Bern: Krompholz.

Küthen, Hans-Werner. 2002. "'Szene am Bach' oder Der Einfluss durch die Hintertür: Die Bach-Rezeption der anderen als Impuls für Beethoven." In *Beethoven und die Rezeption der alten Musik: Die hohe Schule der Überlieferung,* ed. Hans-Werner Küthen, 243–280. Bonn: Beethoven-Haus.

Laban, Rudolf. 1971. *The Mastery of Movement.* Rev. and ed. Lisa Ullmann. London: Macdonald and Evans.

Lakoff, George. 1987. *Women, Fire, and Dangerous Things: What Categories Reveal about the Mind.* Chicago: University of Chicago Press.

Lakoff, George, and Mark Johnson. 1979. *Metaphors We Live By.* Chicago: University of Chicago Press.

——. 1999. *Philosophy in the Flesh: The Embodied Mind and Its Challenge to Western Thought.* New York: Basic Books.

Landon, Christa, and Walther Dürr. 1984. *Neue Schubert Ausgabe.* Ser. VII, 2, vol. 5 Kassel: Bärenreiter.

Larson, Steve. 1993. "Scale Degree Function: A Theory of Expressive Meaning and Its Application to Aural-Skills Pedagogy." *Journal of Music Theory Pedagogy* 7: 69–84.

——. 1994. "Musical Forces, Step Collections, Tonal Pitch Space, and Melodic Expectation." *Proceedings of the Third International Conference on Music Perception and Cognition,* 227–29.

——. 1997. "The Problem of Prolongation in Tonal Music: Terminology, Perception, and Expressive Meaning." *Journal of Music Theory* 41: 101–36.

——. 1997–98. "Musical Forces and Melodic Patterns." *Theory and Practice* 22/23: 55–71.

——. 2003. "Musical Gestures and Musical Forces." Paper presented to the "Music and Gesture" international conference, University of East Anglia, Norwich.

Lerdahl, Fred. 2002. *Tonal Pitch Space.* New York: Oxford University Press.

Lerdahl, Fred, and Ray Jackendoff. 1983. *A Generative Theory of Tonal Music.* Cambridge, Mass.: MIT Press.

Levenson, R. W., P. Ekman, and W. V. Friesen. 1990. "Voluntary Facial Action Generates Emotion-Specific Autonomic Nervous System Activity." *Psychophysiology* 27: 363–84.

Levinson, Jerrold. 2002a. "Sound, Gesture, Spatial Imagination and the Expression of Emotion in Music." In *European Review of Philosophy,* vol. 5: *Emotion and Action,* ed. Élisabeth Pacherie, 137–50. Stanford University, Palo Alto, Calif.: CSLI Publications.

——. 2002b. "Musical Thinking." Paper delivered to the Danish Network for the Interdisciplinary Study of Music and Meaning, University of Southern Denmark, August 2002.

Levy, Janet. 1981. "Gesture, Form, and Syntax in Haydn's Music." In *Haydn Studies: Proceedings of the International Haydn Conference, Washington, D.C., 1975,* ed. Jens Peter Larsen, Howard Serwer, and James Webster, 355–62. New York: W. W. Norton.

Lidov, David. 1987. "Mind and Body in Music." *Semiotica* 66, no. 1/3: 69–97.

——. 1993. "The Discourse of Gesture." Paper delivered to the Semiotic Society of America, St. Louis, October 1993.

——. 1999. *Elements of Semiotics.* New York: St. Martin's Press.

Litschauer, Walburga, and Walter Deutsch. 1997. *Schubert und das Tanzvergnügen.* Vienna: Holzhausen.

Little, Meredith, and Natalie Jenne. 1991. *Dance and the Music of J. S. Bach.* Bloomington: Indiana University Press.

Littlefield, Richard. 2001. *Frames and Framing: The Margins of Music Analysis.* Acta Semiotica Fennica 12, Approaches to Musical Semiotics 2. Imatra: International Semiotics Institute and the Semiotic Society of Finland.

MacClintock, Carol, ed. and trans. 1979. *Readings in the History of Music in Performance.* Bloomington: Indiana University Press.

Margolis, Joseph. 1974. "Works of Art as Physically Embodied and Culturally Emergent Entities." *British Journal of Aesthetics* 14, no. 3: 187–96.

Marinelli, Peter V. 1971. *Pastoral.* London: Methuen.

Marston, Nicholas. 1992. "Beethoven's 'Anti-organicism'? The Origins of the Slow Movement of the Ninth Symphony." In *The Creative Process* 3, 169–200. New York: Broude.

Massaro, Dominic W. 1998. *Perceiving Talking Faces: From Speech Perception to a Behavioral Principle.* Cambridge, Mass.: MIT Press.

McCabe, Viki. 1986. "Introduction: Event Cognition and the Conditions of Existence." In *Event Cognition: An Ecological Perspective,* ed. Viki McCabe and Gerald J. Balzano, 3–23. Hillsdale, N.J.: Lawrence Erlbaum Associates.

McCabe, Viki, and Gerald J. Balzano, eds. 1986. *Event Cognition: An Ecological Perspective.* Hillsdale, N.J.: Lawrence Erlbaum Associates.

McClary, Susan. 1986. "A Musical Dialectic from the Enlightenment: Mozart's Piano Concerto in G Major, K 453, Movement 2." *Cultural Critique* 4: 129–69.

———. 1991. *Feminine Endings: Music, Gender, and Sexuality.* Minneapolis: University of Minnesota Press.

———. 2000. *Conventional Wisdom: The Content of Musical Form.* Berkeley: University of California Press.

———. 2002. "*Feminine Endings* in Retrospect." New introduction to a reprint of *Feminine Endings: Music, Gender, and Sexuality,* ix–xx. Minneapolis: University of Minnesota Press.

McCreless, Patrick. 2002. "Music and Rhetoric." In *The Cambridge History of Western Music Theory,* ed. Thomas Christensen, 847–79. Cambridge: Cambridge University Press.

McNeill, David. 1992. *Hand and Mind: What Gestures Reveal about Thought.* Chicago: University of Chicago Press.

———. 1999. "Triangulating the Growth Point—Arriving at Consciousness." In *Gesture, Speech, and Sign,* ed. Lynn S. Messing and Ruth Campbell, 77–92. Oxford: Oxford University Press.

McNeill, David, and Susan D. Duncan. 2000. "Growth Points in Thinking-for-Speaking." In *Language and Gesture,* ed. David McNeill, 141–61. Cambridge: Cambridge University Press.

Mead, Andrew. 1999. "Bodily Hearing: Physiological Metaphors and Musical Understanding." *Journal of Music Theory* 43: 1–19.

Mendelssohn, Felix. 1945. *Letters.* Ed. G. Selden-Goth. New York: Pantheon.

Meyer, Leonard B. 1956. *Emotion and Meaning in Music.* Chicago: University of Chicago Press.

———. 1973. *Explaining Music: Essays and Explorations.* Chicago: University of Chicago Press.

———. 1989. *Style and Music: Theory, History, and Ideology.* Philadelphia: University of Pennsylvania Press.

Mirka, Danuta. 1997. *The Sonoristic Structuralism of Krzysztof Penderecki.* Katowice: Music Academy of Katowice.

Monelle, Raymond. 1992. *Linguistics and Semiotics in Music. Contemporary Music Studies,* 5. Chur, Switzerland: Harwood.

———. 2000. *The Sense of Music: Semiotic Essays.* Princeton, N.J.: Princeton University Press.

Moore, Stephen. 1992. "The Writings of Émile Jaques-Dalcroze: Toward a Theory for the Performance of Musical Rhythm." Ph.D. dissertation, Indiana University.

Mozart, Leopold. 1951 [1756]. *A Treatise on the Fundamental Principles of Violin Playing.* 2nd ed., trans. Editha Knocker. London: Oxford University Press. (*Versuch einer gründlichen Violinschule*. Augsburg: Verlag des Verfassers, 1756; 3rd ed. Augsburg: Lotter und Sohn, 1787.)

Narmour, Eugene. 1977. *Beyond Schenkerism*. Chicago: University of Chicago Press.

———. 1990. *The Analysis and Cognition of Basic Melodic Structures: The Implication-Realization Model*. Chicago: University of Chicago Press.

Nespoulous, Jean-Luc, and André Roch Lecours. 1986. "Gestures: Nature and Function." In *The Biological Foundations of Gestures: Motor and Semiotic Aspects*, ed. Jean-Luc Nespoulous, Paul Perron, and André Roch Lecours, 49–62. Hillsdale, N.J.: Lawrence Erlbaum Associates.

Newcomb, Anthony. 1997. "Action and Agency in Mahler's Ninth Symphony, Second Movement." In *Music and Meaning*, ed. Jenefer Robinson, 131–53. Ithaca, N.Y.: Cornell University Press.

Newman, William S. 1986. "Haydn as Ingenious Exploiter of the Keyboard." In *Joseph Haydn: Bericht über den Internationalen Joseph Haydn Kongress, Wien 1982*, ed. Eva Badura-Skoda, 43–53. Munich: G. Henle Verlag.

———. 1988. *Beethoven on Beethoven: Playing His Piano Music His Way*. New York: W. W. Norton.

O'Brian, Patrick. 1989. *The Thirteen Gun Salute*. New York: W. W. Norton.

Papousek, Hanus. 1996. "Musicality in Infancy Research: Biological and Cultural Origins of Early Musicality." In *Musical Beginnings*, ed. Irène Deliège and John Sloboda, 37–55. Oxford: Oxford University Press.

Parker, Mara. 2002. *The String Quartet, 1750–1797: Four Types of Musical Conversation*. Brookfield, Vt.: Ashgate.

Patel, Aniruddh D., and Isabelle Peretz. 1997. "Is Music Autonomous from Language? A Neuropsychological Appraisal." In *Perception and Cognition of Music*, ed. Irène Deliège and John Sloboda, 191–215. Hove, U.K.: Psychology Press.

Peirce, Charles Sanders. 1931, 1960. *Collected Papers of Charles Sanders Peirce*. Vols. 1–6, ed. Charles Hartshorne and Paul Weiss; vols. 7–8, ed. Arthur W. Burks. Cambridge, Mass.: Harvard University Press.

———. 1982–2000. *Writings of Charles S. Peirce: A Chronological Edition*. General ed., Max H. Fisch, succeeded by Nathan Houser, general editor and director of the Peirce Edition Project. (Six volumes have appeared, chronologically through 1890; thirty volumes are projected.) Bloomington: Indiana University Press.

———. 1992. *The Essential Peirce: Selected Philosophical Writings*. Ed. Nathan Houser and Christian Kloesel. Bloomington: Indiana University Press.

Pierce, Alexandra. 1994. "Developing Schenkerian Hearing and Performing." *Intégral* 8: 51–123.

Pierce, Alexandra, and Roger Pierce. 1989. *Expressive Movement: Posture and Action in Daily Life, Sports, and the Performing Arts*. New York: Plenum Press.

———. 1991. *Generous Movement: A Practical Guide to Balance in Action*. Redlands, Calif.: Center of Balance Press.

Poggioli, Renato. 1969 [1959]. "The Pastoral of the Self." *Daedalus* 88 (1959): 686–99. Reprinted in *Pastoral and Romance: Modern Essays in Criticism*, ed. Eleanor Terry Lincoln, 47–60. Englewood Cliffs, N.J.: Prentice-Hall, 1969.

———. 1975 [1957]. "Pastorals of Innocence and Happiness." Reprinted in Poggioli, *The Oaten Flute: Essays on Pastoral Poetry and the Pastoral Ideal*, 1–16. Cambridge, Mass.: Harvard University Press.

Pribram, Karl H. 1976. "Problems concerning the Structure of Consciousness." In *Con-*

sciousness and the Brain: A Scientific and Philosophical Inquiry, ed. Gordon G. Globus, Grower Maxwell, and Irwin Savodnik, 297–313. New York: Plenum Press.

Quantz, Johann Joachim. 1985 [1752]. *On Playing the Flute.* Trans. and ed. Edward R. Reilly. 2nd ed. New York: Schirmer. (*Versuch einer Anweisung die Flöte traversiere zu spielen.* Berlin: Voss, 1752; 3rd ed., Breslau: J. F. Korn, the elder, 1789.)

Rameau, Jean Philippe. 1737. *Génération harmonique, ou Traité de musique théorique et pratique.* Paris: Praoult fils.

Ratner, Leonard G. 1980. *Classic Music: Expression, Form, and Style.* New York: Schirmer Books.

Repp, Bruno H. 1998. "Musical Motion in Perception and Performance." In *Timing of Behavior: Neural, Psychological, and Computational Perspectives,* ed. David A. Rosenbaum and Charles E. Collyer, 125–44. Cambridge, Mass.: MIT Press.

Réti, Rudolph. *The Thematic Process in Music.* New York: Macmillan, 1951.

Richards, Annette. 2001. *The Free Fantasia and the Musical Picturesque.* Cambridge: Cambridge University Press.

Riemann, Hugo. 1884. *Musikalische Dynamik und Agogik.* Hamburg: D. Rahter.

Rink, John. 1994. "Chopin's Ballades and the Dialectic: Analysis in Historical Perspective." *Music Analysis* 13, no. 1: 112.

———. 1999. "Translating Musical Meaning: The Nineteenth-Century Performer as Narrator." In *Rethinking Music,* ed. Nicholas Cook and Mark Everist, 217–38. Oxford: Oxford University Press.

Rink, John, ed. 1995. *The Practice of Performance: Studies in Musical Interpretation.* Cambridge: Cambridge University Press.

———. 2002. *Musical Performance: A Guide to Understanding.* Cambridge: Cambridge University Press.

Robinson, Paul. 1985. *Opera and Ideas: From Mozart to Strauss.* Ithaca, N.Y.: Cornell University Press.

Rosch, Eleanor. 1978. "Principles of Categorization." In *Cognition and Categorization,* ed. E. Rosch and B. Lloyd, 27–48. Hillsdale, N.J.: Lawrence Erlbaum Associates.

Rosch, Eleanor, Carolyn B. Mervis, Wayne D. Gray, David M. Johnson, and Penny Boyes-Braem. 1976. "Basic Objects in Natural Categories." *Cognitive Psychology* 8: 382–439.

Rosen, Charles. 1972. *The Classical Style: Haydn, Mozart, Beethoven.* New York: W. W. Norton.

———. 1995. *The Romantic Generation.* Cambridge, Mass.: Harvard University Press.

———. 2002a. *Beethoven's Piano Sonatas: A Short Companion.* New Haven, Conn.: Yale University Press.

———. 2002b. *Piano Notes: The World of the Pianist.* New York: The Free Press.

Rosenblum, Sandra. 1988. *Performance Practices in Classic Piano Music: Their Principles and Applications.* Bloomington: Indiana University Press.

Rothfarb, Lee. 1988. *Ernst Kurth as Theorist and Analyst.* Philadelphia: University of Pennsylvania Press.

———. 2002. "Energetics." In *The Cambridge History of Western Music Theory,* ed. Thomas Christensen, 927–55. Cambridge: Cambridge University Press.

Rothfarb, Lee, trans. and intro. 1991. *Ernst Kurth: Selected Writings.* Cambridge: Cambridge University Press.

Rothstein, William S. 1989. *Phrase Rhythm in Tonal Music.* New York: Schirmer Books.

———. 1995. "Analysis and the Act of Performance." In *The Practice of Performance:*

Studies in Musical Interpretation, ed. John Rink, 217–40. Cambridge: Cambridge University Press.

Sacks, Oliver. 1974 [1973]. *Awakenings.* Garden City, N.Y.: Doubleday.

———. 1985. *The Man Who Mistook His Wife for a Hat, and Other Clinical Tales.* New York: Simon and Schuster.

———. 1996. *An Anthropologist from Mars: Seven Paradoxical Tales.* New York: Vintage Books.

Samarotto, Frank. 1999. "A Theory of Temporal Plasticity in Tonal Music: An Extension of the Schenkerian Approach to Rhythm with Special Reference to Beethoven's Late Music." Ph.D. dissertation, City University of New York.

Samuels, Robert. 1995. *Mahler's Sixth Symphony: A Study in Musical Semiotics.* Cambridge: Cambridge University Press.

Schachter, Carl. 1976. "Rhythm and Linear Analysis: A Preliminary Study." *Music Forum* 4: 281–334.

———. 2000. "Playing What the Composer Didn't Write: Analysis and Rhythmic Aspects of Performance." In *Pianist, Scholar, Connoisseur: Essays in Honor of Jacob Lateiner,* ed. Bruce Brubaker and Jane Gottlieb, 47–68. Stuyvesant, N.Y.: Pendragon Press.

Schenker, Heinrich. 1921 *Der Tonwille,* Bd. 1. Vienna: A. Gutmann Verlag.

———. 1930. *Das Meisterwerk in der Musik.* Jahrbuch III. Munich: Drei Masken.

———. 1954 [1906]. *Harmony.* Trans. E. M. Borgese, ed. Oswald Jonas. Chicago: University of Chicago Press.

———. 1971 [1913-20]. *Die letzten Sonaten: Sonate E Dur Op. 109: Kritische Einführung und Erläuterung.* New edition, ed. Oswald Jonas. Vienna: Universal Edition.

———. 1979 [1935]. *Free Composition.* Trans. and ed. E. Oster. New York: Longman.

———. 2000 [ca. 1911]. *The Art of Performance (Die Kunst des Vortrags).* Trans. Irene Schreier Scott, ed. Heribert Esser. Oxford: Oxford University Press.

Schiller, Johann Christoph Friedrich. 1958 [1794]. "Über Matthissons Gedichte." In *Schillers Werke,* vol. 22, ed. Herbert Meyer, 265–83. Weimar: Hermann Böhlaus Nachfolger.

———. 1984 [1793]. Über das Pathetische." In *Über das Schöne und die Kunst: Schriften zur Ästhetik.* Ed. Gerhard Fricke and Herbert G. Göpfert, 115–38. Munich: Deutscher Taschenbuch Verlag.

Schindler, Anton F. 1966 [1840, 1860]. *Beethoven as I Knew Him.* Trans. Constance Jolly, ed. Donald W. MacArdle. Chapel Hill: University of North Carolina Press. (*Biographie von Ludwig van Beethoven.* 3rd ed. Munster: Aschendorff, 1860 [1st ed. 1840].)

Schmalfeldt, Janet. 1985. "On the Relation of Analysis to Performance: Beethoven's Bagatelles, Op. 126, Nos. 2 and 5." *Journal of Music Theory* 29, no. 1: 1–31.

Schoenberg, Arnold. 1975 [1946-47]. "New Music, Outmoded Music, Style and Idea" [1946] and "Brahms the Progressive" [1947]. In *Style and Idea,* trans. Leo Black, ed. Leonard Stein, 113–23 and 398–441. Berkeley: University of California Press.

Schubart, Christian Friedrich Daniel. 1972 [1806]. *Ideen zu einer Ästhetik der Tonkunst.* Wien. Reprinted in Schubart, *Gesammelte Schriften und Schicksale* V/VI, Hildesheim/New York (Stuttgart: J. Scheible, 1839–40).

Schwarz, David. 1997. *Listening Subjects: Music, Psychoanalysis, Culture.* Durham, N.C.: Duke University Press.

Scruton, Roger. 1997. *The Aesthetics of Music.* Oxford: Oxford University Press.

Searle, John R. 1970. *Speech Acts*. Cambridge: Cambridge University Press.

Sebeok, Thomas A. 1963 "Communication among Social Bees; Porpoises and Sonar; Man and Dolphin." Review article. *Language* 39: 448–66.

———. 1972. *Perspectives in Zoosemiotics*. The Hague: Mouton.

———. 1976. *Contributions to the Doctrine of Signs*. Lanham, Md.: University Press of America.

Sebeok, Thomas A., ed. 1977. *How Animals Communicate*. Bloomington: Indiana University Press.

Selfridge-Field, Eleanor. 1998. "Conceptual and Representational Issues in Melodic Comparison." In *Melodic Similarity: Concepts, Procedures, and Applications*, ed. Walter B. Hewlett and Eleanor Selfridge-Field, 3–64. *Computing in Musicology*, 11. Cambridge, Mass.: MIT Press.

Sheinberg, Esti. 2000. *Irony, Satire, Parody and the Grotesque in the Music of Shostakovich: A Theory of Musical Incongruities*. Aldershot, U.K.: Ashgate.

Shove, Patrick, and Bruno H. Repp. 1995. "Musical Motion and Performance: Theoretical and Empirical Perspectives." In *The Practice of Performance: Studies in Musical Interpretation*, ed. John Rink, 55–83. Cambridge: Cambridge University Press.

Shuring, D. J. 1978. *Scale Models in Engineering*. New York: Pergamon Press.

Sievers, Eduard. 1924. *Ziele und Wege der Schallanalyse*. Heidelberg: Carl Winters Universitätsbuchhandlung.

Silverman, Kaja. 1988. *The Acoustic Mirror: The Female Voice in Psychoanalysis and Cinema*. Bloomington: Indiana University Press.

Sisman, Elaine. 1993. *Haydn and the Classical Variation*. Cambridge, Mass.: Harvard University Press.

———. 1994. "Pathos and the *Pathétique*: Rhetorical Stance in Beethoven's C-minor Sonata, Op. 13." *Beethoven Forum* 3: 81–106.

———. 1997. "Genre, Gesture, and Meaning in Mozart's 'Prague' Symphony." In *Mozart Studies II*, ed. Cliff Eisen, 27–84. Oxford: Clarendon Press.

———. 2000. "Memory and Invention at the Threshold of Beethoven's Late Style." In *Beethoven and His World*, ed. Scott Burnham and Michael P. Steinberg, 51–87. Princeton, N.J.: Princeton University Press.

Solomon, Maynard. 2003. *Late Beethoven: Music, Thought, Imagination*. Berkeley: University of California Press.

Sonneck, Oscar G. T., ed. 1926. *Beethoven: Impressions of Contemporaries*. New York: G. Schirmer. (Reprint, New York: Dover, 1967.)

Spitzer, Michael. 1998. "Haydn's Reversals: Style Change, Gesture, and the Implication-Realization Model." In *Haydn Studies*, ed. W. Dean Sutcliffe, 177–217. Cambridge: Cambridge University Press.

Staiger, Emil. 1991 [1946]. *Basic Concepts of Poetics* (*Grundbegriffe der Poetik*). Trans. J. C. Hudson and L. T. Frank, ed. M. Burkhard and L. T. Frank. University Park: Pennsylvania State University Press.

Stanley, Glenn. 2000. "Voices and Their Rhythms in the First Movement of Beethoven's Piano Sonata Op. 109: Some Thoughts on the Performance and Analysis of a Late-Style Work." In *Beethoven and His World*, ed. Scott Burnham and Michael P. Steinberg, 88–123. Princeton, N.J.: Princeton University Press.

Stebbins, Genevieve. 1894. *Delsarte System of Expression*. 5th ed. New York: E. S. Werner.

Stern, Daniel N. 1985. *The Interpersonal World of the Infant: A View from Psychoanalysis and Developmental Psychology*. New York: Basic Books.

Sudnow, David. 1978. *Ways of the Hand: The Organization of Improvised Conduct.* Cambridge, Mass.: Harvard University Press.

Tarasti, Eero. 1994. *A Theory of Musical Semiotics.* Bloomington: Indiana University Press.

———. 2002. *Signs of Music: A Guide to Musical Semiotics.* Approaches to Applied Semiotics, ed. Jean Umiker-Sebeok. Berlin: Mouton de Gruyter.

Taruskin, Richard. 1997. *Defining Russia Musically.* Princeton, N.J.: Princeton University Press.

Taub, Robert. 2002. *Playing the Beethoven Piano Sonatas.* Portland, Ore.: Amadeus Press.

Thayer, Von Alexander Wheelock. 1866–79. *Ludwig van Beethoven's Leben.* 3 vols. Berlin: F. Schneider.

Thelen, Esther, and Linda B. Smith. 1994. *A Dynamic Systems Approach to the Development of Cognition and Action.* Cambridge, Mass.: MIT Press.

Tootell, R. B. H., E. Switkes, M. S. Silverman, and S. L. Hamilton. 1988. "Functional Anatomy of Macaque Striate Cortex. II. Retinotopic Organization." *Journal of Neuroscience* 8: 1531-68.

Trehub, S., G. Schellenberg, and D. Hill. 1997. "The Origins of Music Perception and Cognition: A Developmental Perspective." In *Perception and Cognition of Music,* ed. Irène Deliège and John Sloboda, 103–28. Hove, U.K.: Psychology Press.

Treitler, Leo. 1989. *Music and the Historical Imagination.* Cambridge, Mass.: Harvard University Press.

Trevarthen, Colwyn. 1986a. "Development of Intersubjective Motor Control in Infants." In *Motor Development in Children: Aspects of Coordination and Control,* ed. M. G. Wade and H. T. A. Whiting, 209–61. Proceedings of the NATO Advanced Study Institute on "Motor Skill Acquisition in Children," Maastricht, Netherlands, 1985. Dordrecht: Martinus Nijhoff.

———. 1986b. "Form, Significance and Psychological Potential of Hand Gestures of Infants." In *The Biological Foundations of Gestures: Motor and Semiotic Aspects,* ed. Jean-Luc Nespoulous, Paul Perron, and André Roch Lecours, 149–202. Hillsdale, N.J.: Lawrence Erlbaum Associates.

———. 1989. "Les Relations entre autisme et développement socioculturel normal: Arguments en faveur d'un trouble primaire de la régulation du développement cognitive par les émotions." In *Autisme et troubles du développement global de l'enfant,* ed. G. Lelord, J. P. Muk, M. Petit, and D. Sauvage. Paris: Expansion Scientifique Français.

———. 1999. "Musicality and the Intrinsic Motive Pulse: Evidence from Human Psychobiology and Infant Communication." *Musicae Scientiae,* Special Issue: 155–215.

Truslit, Alesander. 1938. *Gestaltung und Bewegung in der Musik.* Berlin-Lichterfelde: Chr. Friedrich Vieweg.

Türk, Daniel Gottlob. 1982 [1789]. *School of Clavier Playing.* Trans. Raymond H. Haggh. Lincoln: University of Nebraska Press. (*Klavierschule,* Leipzig.)

Turvey, Michael T., and Claudia Carello. 1995. "Dynamic Touch." In *Perception of Space and Motion,* ed. William Epstein and Sheena Rogers, 401–90. New York: Academic Press.

Tye, Michael. 1995. *Ten Problems of Consciousness: A Representational Theory of the Phenomenal Mind.* Cambridge, Mass.: MIT Press.

Uexküll, Jakob von. 1928. *Theoretische Biologie.* Frankfurt: Suhrkamp.

Uexküll, Thure von. 1987. "The Sign Theory of Jakob von Uexküll." In *Classics of Semi-*

otics, ed. Martin Krampen, Klaus Oehler, Roland Posner, Thomas A. Sebeok, and Thure von Uexküll, 147–79. New York: Plenum Press.

van Gelder, Timothy, and Robert F. Port. 1995. "It's about Time: An Overview of the Dynamical Approach to Cognition." In *Mind as Motion: Explorations in the Dynamics of Cognition,* ed. Robert F. Port and Timothy van Gelder, 1–43. Cambridge, Mass.: MIT Press.

Viereck, Peter. 1987. *Archer in the Marrow: The Applewood Cycles of 1967–1987.* New York: W. W. Norton.

Wang, Huei-Ming. 1997. *Beethovens Violoncell-und Violinsonaten.* Kassel: Gustav Bosse Verlag.

Weber, Gottfried. 1818–21. *Versuch einer geordneten Theorie der Tonsetzkunst.* 2nd ed. Mainz: B. Schott.

Weiskrantz, Lawrence. 1986. *Blindsight: A Case Study and Its Implications.* New York: Oxford University Press.

Wellbery, David E. 1996. *The Specular Moment: Goethe's Early Lyric and the Beginnings of Romanticism.* Stanford, Calif.: Stanford University Press.

Wheelock, Gretchen. 1992. *Haydn's Ingenious Jesting with Art: Contexts of Musical Wit and Humor.* New York: Schirmer Books.

Will, Richard. 1994. "Programmatic Symphonies of the Classical Period." Ph.D. dissertation, Cornell University.

Williams, C. 1981. *Origins of Form.* New York: Architectural Books.

Williams, Peter. 1997. *The Chromatic Fourth during Four Centuries of Music.* Oxford: Clarendon Press.

Wolff, Konrad. 1990. *Masters of the Keyboard: Individual Style Elements in the Piano Music of Bach, Haydn, Mozart, Beethoven, Schubert, Chopin, and Brahms.* Bloomington: Indiana University Press.

Zbikowski, Lawrence M. 2002. *Conceptualizing Music: Cognitive Structure, Theory, and Analysis.* AMS Studies in Music. Chicago: University of Chicago Press.

Zenck, Martin. 1986. *Die Bach-Rezeption des späten Beethoven: Zum Verhältnis von Musikhistoriographie und Rezeptionsgeschichtsschreibung der 'Klassik.'* Stuttgart: Steiner Verlag Wiesbaden.

Zuckerkandl, Victor. 1956. *Sound and Symbol.* 2 vols. Trans. W. R. Trask. New York: Pantheon Books.

Index of Names and Works

Page numbers in bold indicate musical examples and/or extensive analytical discussion.

Abbate, Carolyn, 29
Adams, John, 120
Adelung, Johann Christoph, 312n38
Adorno, Theodor W., 278
Agawu, V. Kofi, 125, 267–68, 270, 272–73, 275, 277, 292n8, 320nn4,9
Alice in Wonderland, 53
Alkan (Charles Valentin Morhange)
   Le Festin d'Ésope or "Aesop's Banquet,"
     Op. 39 (1857), **225–26,** 232, 317n3
Allanbrook, Wye J., 8, 71, 94, 119, 125, 295n3.1, 307n6, 320n9
Alpers, Paul, 67
Anderson, Emily, 310n21
Armstrong, David F., 300n14
Artaria, Matthias, 36
Austin, J. L., 13, 224
Auyang, Sunny Y., 299n7

Bach, Carl Philipp Emanuel, 140, 307n5, 309n15, 312n35
Bach, Johann Sebastian, 266, 297n2, 319n11
   Fugue in A♭ Major, WTC II, **68–69,** 164
   French Suite No. 1 in D Minor, Gigue, **68–70**
   French Suite No. 2 in C Minor, Gigue, 69
   French Suite No. 3 in B Minor, Gigue, 69
   Goldberg Variations, 262
   Italian Concerto (*Clavier-Übung,* Part II), 69
   Overture in B Minor (*Clavier-Übung,* Part II), Echo, 69–70
   Partita No. 1 in B♭, Gigue, 71
   Prelude in E♭ Minor, WTC I, (Czerny's edition), **227–28**
   Sinfonias, 312n43
     G Major, BWV 796, 252
     G Minor, BWV 797, **162,** 202, 203
     B♭ Major, BWV 800, 252
Badura-Skoda, Paul, 311n32
Baer, Eugen, 298n1
Baker, Nancy K., 138, 139
Bakhtin, M. M., 317n4

Balanchine, George, 305n26
Balter, Tamara, 317n9.6
Balzano, Gerald J., 99
Barnett, David, 307n2
Barnett, Dene, 119
Barth, George, 165, 301n8, 310n21
Barthes, Roland, 121–122, 124, 186
Bartók, Béla, 316n1
Beardsley, Monroe, 305–306n30
Beckerman, Michael, 296n5, 318n4
Becking, Gustav, 128
Beethoven, Ludwig van, 140, 143, 145, 183, 249, 308n11, 309nn15,21, 310nn21,23, 314n58, 317nn9.6,10.8, 320nC.2
   33 Variations on a Waltz by Diabelli,
     Op. 120, 317n3, 318n6, 319n15
     Variation 32 (Fugue), 252, **261–65**
   Bagatelle in G Major, Op. 126, no. 5, 115
   Missa solemnis in D Major, Op. 123
     Credo, "Et vitam venturi saeculi, amen," 250
     Sanctus, "Pleni sunt coeli," **250, 252**
   Piano Concerto No. 3 in C Minor, Op. 37, first movement, 311n31
   Piano Concerto No. 4 in G Major, Op. 58
     first movement, 56
     second movement, 311n31
   Piano Sonata in F Minor, Op. 2, no. 1, first movement, 24, 180, 318n8
   Piano Sonata in A Major, Op. 2, no. 2
     second movement, **37**
     fourth movement (finale), **163,** 167, 202
   Piano Sonata in C Major, Op. 2, no. 3, second movement, **157–59,** 311n30
   Piano Sonata in E♭ Major, Op. 7, finale, **142,** 143, 167–68
   Piano Sonata Op. 10, no. 1
     first movement, 313n47
     third movement (finale), 167
   Piano Sonata in D Major, Op. 10, no. 3
     first movement, 21, **147–48**
     second movement, 313n47
     fourth movement (finale), 308n11

Piano Sonata in C Minor (*Pathétique*),
  Op. 13, 308n11, 312n38
  second movement, **145–47,** 275
  third movement (finale), **149–50**
Piano Sonata in E Major, Op. 14, no. 1,
  313n44
Piano Sonata in G Major, Op. 14, no. 2, first
  movement, **147–48,** 313nn44,45
Piano Sonata in B♭ Major, Op. 22, finale,
  opening theme, **143, 145,** 310n22
Piano Sonata in A♭ Major, Op. 26
  first movement, 311n30
  fourth movement (finale), 310n22, 318n6
Piano Sonata in D Major (*Pastoral*),
  Op. 28, 58
Piano Sonata in D Minor (*Tempest*), Op. 31,
  no. 2
  first movement, 24, 192
  second movement, 275
  third movement (finale), 192, 244
Piano Sonata in E♭ Major, Op. 31, no. 3
  first movement, 16, 56, 62, **167, 168–69,**
    287–89
  second movement, **37**
Piano Sonata in C Major, Op. 53
  first movement, **230–31,** 305n29, 310n22
Piano Sonata in F Major, Op. 54
  second movement (finale) 39, 310n22,
    318n6
Piano Sonata in F Minor (*Appassionata*),
  Op. 57
  second movement, 275
  third movement (finale), 192, **244–45,**
    305n29
Piano Sonata in F♯ Major, Op. 78, 39
Piano Sonata in G Major, Op. 79
  finale, **173–74**
Piano Sonata in E♭ Major (*Les adieux*),
  Op. 81a, 56, 65
Piano Sonata in E Minor, Op. 90, 39, 239
  first movement, **178–80,** 217, 311n30,
    316n3
  second movement (finale), 58, 310n22
Piano Sonata in A Major, Op. 101, 53, 56,
  59, 66–67, 201, 239, 296n2, 311n30
  first movement, 24, **143, 145,** 217
  second movement, 58, **217, 219**
  third movement, **217, 219**
  fourth movement (finale), **165–66,**
    210, **217–18, 220,** 224, 227, 268,
    315n3
Piano Sonata in B♭ major (*Hammerklavier*),
  Op. 106
  first movement, 180

third movement, 24, 167, 261, 310n22,
  319n12
slow introduction to the finale, 270
fourth movement (finale), 252, **254–55,**
  257–61, 263, 319nn12–14
Piano Sonata in E Major, Op. 109
  first movement, **169–76,** 177, 289,
    310n22, 313n45
  second movement, 316n3
  third movement (finale), 310nn22,25
Piano Sonata in A♭ major, Op. 110
  third movement (finale), **254–56,** 261,
    319n14
Piano Sonata in C Minor, Op. 111, 39
  first movement, **26–27, 149**
  second movement (finale), 26, 111, 249,
    319n15
Piano Trio in E♭ Major, Op. 1, no. 1, 167
Piano Trio in D Major (*Ghost*), Op. 70,
  no. 1
  first movement, **21–25, 28–32,** 311n27
Piano Trio in B♭ Major (*Archduke*), Op. 97
  third movement, 249
Sonata for Piano and Cello in G minor,
  Op. 5, no. 2, 202
  second movement (finale), **249–51**
Sonata for Piano and Cello in A Major,
  Op. 69, 202
  fourth movement (finale), **26–27**
Sonata for Piano and Cello in C Major,
  Op. 102, no. 1, **201–216,** 239, 296n2
  first movement, **202–204**
  second movement, **204–208**
  third movement, **208–210**
  fourth movement (finale), 167, **210–16,**
    225, 231–32, 268, 289, 317n9.6
Sonata for Piano and Cello in D Major,
  Op. 102, no. 2, 202
  first movement, **26, 28,** 167
  third movement (finale), 261
Sonata for Violin and Piano in A Minor
  (*Kreutzer*), Op. 47, 308n9
Sonata for Violin and Piano in G Major,
  Op. 96, 295n3.2
String Quartet in C Minor, Op. 18, no. 4
  third movement, 320n7
String Quartet in E Minor, Op. 59, no. 2
  second movement, 320n5
  third movement, 58
String Quartet in F Minor, Op. 95
  fourth movement (finale), 285
String Quartet in B♭ Major, Op. 130
  first movement, 16, **38,** 51, 232, 240,
    292n2.3

second movement (Presto), 36, **38**, 39, **40**, 40–41, 43, 51
third movement (Andante), **35–52,** 135, 204
fourth movement (Alla danza tedesca), 35, 36, 39, **41–42,** 51, 223, 268
fifth movement (Cavatina), 32, 35, 36, 39–40, **41, 43,** 51, 111, 157, 292n8, 295n2.2, 312n41
sixth movement (Grosse Fuge), 35, 39, 320n8
String Quartet in C♯ Minor, Op. 131
first movement, 250
seventh movement (finale), 320n10
String Quartet in A Minor, Op. 132, 310n21
first movement, 232, **267–78**
fifth movement (finale), 270, **278–86**
String Quartet in F Major, Op. 135
first movement, 268
fourth movement (finale), 166
Symphony No. 2 in D Major, Op. 36
fourth movement (finale), 125, **151–52**
Symphony No. 3 in E♭ Major (*Eroica*), Op. 55, 89
Symphony No. 4 in B♭ Major, Op. 60
first movement, 310n25
Symphony No. 5 in C Minor, Op. 67, 23
Symphony No. 6 in F Major, Op. 68, 53, 59, 317n6
first movement, **202–203**
Symphony No. 7 in A Major, Op. 92, 59
Symphony No. 9 in D Minor, Op. 125
third movement, 43, **146–47,** 249–50
fourth movement (finale), 71
Berlioz, Hector
Harold in Italy, second movement, 74
Lélio, "Les derniers soupirs de la harpe," 297n10
Les Troyens, 54
Berry, Wallace, 307n2
Bilson, Malcolm, 183, 186, 311n28
Blake, William, 196
Bonds, Mark Evan, 308n8, 11
Boulez, Pierre
Structures, 186
Brahms, Johannes, 25, 177–178, 227
Capriccio, Op. 116, no. 3, 79
Edward Ballade, Op. 10, no. 1, **58–59**
Symphony No. 3 in F Major, **75–89**
first movement, **75–80**
second movement, **77, 79, 81–82**
third movement, **79, 82, 84,** 117
fourth movement (finale), **82–89**

Variations on a Theme of Haydn, Op. 56a, 58
Brecht, Bertolt, 131
Bregman, Albert S., 298n4
Brendel, Alfred, 313n46
Brinkmann, Reinhold, 296n2
Brower, Candace, 302n9
Brown, A. Peter, 297n4.3
Brown, Clive, 115, 136, 137–38, 307n5, 310n24, 311n31
Bruce, Vicki, 101
Bruckner, Anton, 314n56
Symphony No. 3 in D Minor, finale, **71, 74**
Symphony No. 4 in E♭ Major, 292n7
second movement, **74–75**
fourth movement (finale), **74–75,** 79
Symphony No 5 in B♭ Major, 292n7
Buelow, George J., 312n40
Burkholder, J. Peter, 305n27; 312n40
Burnham, Scott, 29, 231

Campbell, Ruth, 101
Carello, Claudia, 98
Cervantes, Miguel de
Don Quixote, 54
Charlton, David, 23
Chopin, Frédéric, 130, 247, 318n6
Ballade in A♭ Major, 122
Nocturne in F Minor, Op. 55, no. 1, 151
Nocturne in B Major, Op. 62, no. 1, 151
Prelude in F Major, Op. 28, no. 23, 297n10
Christensen, Thomas, 138, 139
Churchland, Paul, 98, 123
Clarke, Erik F., 305n24
Clementi, Muzio, 313n47
Clynes, Manfred, 109, 119, 123, 124, 126, 128, 305n24, 306n33
Cohn, Richard, 25
Coker, Wilson, 305n28
Collin, Heinrich von, 21
Cone, Edward T., 118, 307n2
Cook, Nicholas, 9, 292n8, 292–93n9, 305n28, 317n1
Cooke, Deryck, 150, 282
Cooper, Barry, 35–36
Cramer, Johann Baptist, 318n6
Cross, Ian, 299n13
Cumming, Naomi, 1, 305–306n30
Cusick, Suzanne G., 7
Czerny, Carl, 21, **227–28,** 301n7, 308n11, 309n15, 313n47, 314n58

Dahlhaus, Carl, 5
Dalcroze, Émile Jaques-, 130, 306n35

Damasio, Antonio R., 98, 300n18
Daverio, John, 296n4, 321n4
David, Hans T., 297n2
da Vinci, Leonardo, 223
de Assis, Machado
    Epitaph of a Small Winner, 221
Debussy, Claude, 320nC.2
    Préludes, Book I
        no. 6, "Des pas sur la neige," **228–29**
        no. 8, "La fille aux cheveux de lin," 56,
            314n50
Derrida, Jacques, 9
Deutsch, Walter, 296n7
Dibben, Nicola, 292n8, 317n1
Dietrich, Albert
    FAE Sonata for Violin and Piano, first move-
        ment, 25
Donald, Merlin, 299n12
Dreyfus, Laurence, 69–70
Duncan, Susan D., 171
Dunsby, Jonathan, 307n2
Dürr, Walther, 312n34
Dusík (Dussek), Johann Ladislaus, 319n11
Dütschler, Ursula, 311n29

Eckelmeyer, Judith A., 29
Edelman, Gerald M., 98, 298n2, 299n11
Eggebrecht, Hans H., 5
Ekman, Paul, 104–106, 109, 299n8
Emmorey, Karen, 300n14
Empson, William, 53
Epstein, David, 300n2

Fauconnier, Gilles, 97, 297n1
Feld, Stephen, 120, 126, 304n21
Fétis, F.-J., 114
Fisch, Max, 293n10
Floros, Constantin, 5, 74–75
Forkel, Johann Nicolaus, 297n2
Friesen, W. V., 105
Frisch, Walter, 25, 297n4.3, 315n1
Frost, Robert, 131
Frykhold, G., 299n9

Gabrielsson, Alf, 305n24
Geertz, Clifford, 5
Gibson, James J., 99
Gjerdingen, Robert O., 299n6
Gluck, Christoph Willibald
    Orfeo ed Euridice, act 2, ballet, "Dance of
        the Blessed Spirits," **157, 160–62,** 202
Godlovitch, Stan, 307n2
Goethe, Johann Wolfgang von, 54
Goodman, Nelson, 318nC.1

Grabócz, Márta, 320n9
Grandin, Temple, 104
Graybill, Roger, 302n9
Greg, W. W., 54
Greimas, A. J., 225, 320n9

HaCohen, Ruth, 307n6
Handel, George Friedrich, 319n11
Hanslick, Eduard, 9, 203, 224, 290
Haslinger, Tobias, 65
Hasty, Christopher, 304n20
Hatten, Robert S.
    Musical Meaning in Beethoven (1994), 1, 2,
        6, 8, 9, 10, 16, 24, 25, 30, 32, 47, 48, 51,
        56, 58, 67, 68, 89, 95, 111, 120, 143, 146,
        150, 156, 157, 167, 169, 171, 194, 217,
        226, 231, 240, 248, 269, 270, 280, 287,
        291n4, 292n8, 293n10, 294nn12–
        13,15,1.3, 295nn2–3, 296n8, 304n16,
        306n1, 307nn3,7, 309n17, 312nn37,41,
        320n9
Haydn, Franz Joseph, 125, 135, 164, 194, 249,
    308n11, 314n53, 318n2, 319n12
    Piano Sonata in C Major, Hob. XVI: 50,
        313n46
    String Quartet in E♭ Major, Op. 33, no. 2,
        309n13
    String Quartet in G Major, Op. 33, no. 5,
        317n9.6
    Symphony No. 46 in B Major, 308n8
Hemingway, Ernest, 107
Hill, D., 299n13
Hobson, R. Peter, 104
Hoffmann, E. T. A., 23, 29–30, 314n58, 317n8
Holz, Karl, 35, 309n21
Houser, Nathan, 293n10

Imberty, Michel, 103
Ives, Charles, 305n27

Jackendoff, Ray, 3, 138, 302n9
Jakobson, Roman, 106
Janáček, Leoš, 131
Jander, Owen, 308n9
Jenne, Natalie, 119, 297n2, 304n19
Jenner, Gustav, 25
Johnson, Mark, 97, 101, 297n1, 299n7, 302n9
Jones, Evan, 312n35

Kant, Immanuel, 314n58
Keijzer, Fred, 303n10
Keil, Charles, 120, 126, 304n21
Keller, Hermann, 310n25
Kendon, Adam, 105, 109, 112

Kerman, Joseph, 4–5, 51, 267–68, 270, 272, 277, 320n6
Keyes, Roger, 309n19
Kielian-Gilbert, Marianne, 321n3
Kinderman, William, 21, 55, 58, 173, 265, 269, 295n5, 314n51, 317n3, 318n6, 319n11
Kircher, Athanasius, 312n40
Kirkland, Gelsey, 305n26
Kirnberger, Johann Philipp, 312n35
Kivy, Peter, 186, 304n18, 317n10.6
Kling, Carl, 315n10
Koch, Heinrich Christoph, 137–38, 308n11
Koffka, Kurt, 301n6
Kontarsky, Alfons, 186
Kontarsky, Aloys, 186
Kramer, Jonathan D., 125, 268–69
Kramer, Lawrence, 4–5, 13, 15, 32–33, 39, 82, 201
Kramer, Richard, 295n2
Krause, Andreas, 65–66
Krebs, Harald, 304n20, 319n9
Krims, Adam, 291n4
Kropfinger, Klaus, 36
Kugler, Peter Noble, 99, 107, 171
Kuhl, P. K., 103
Kullak, Franz, 309n15, 313n47
Kurth, Ernst, 114, 128, 301nn5,6
Küthen, Hans-Werner, 319n11

Laban, Rudolf, 306n35
Lacan, Jacques, 319n10
Lakoff, George, 97, 101, 297n1, 299n7
Landon, Christa, 312n34
Larson, Steve, 115–116, 303n12
Lecours, André Roch, 106, 109, 300n15
Lenz, Wilhelm von, 295n3.2
Lerdahl, Fred, 3, 138, 302n9
Levenson, R. W., 105
Levinson, Jerrold, 303n15, 306n36
Levy, Janet, 291n1, 308n8
Lewin, David, 138
Lidov, David, 1, 106, 112, 122, 124, 125, 306n32, 315n9
Liszt, Franz, 25–26, 71, 224, 227
Litschauer, Walburga, 296n7
Little, Meredith, 119, 297n2, 304n19
Littlefield, Richard, 312n36

MacClintock, Carol, 309n15, 313n44
Mahler, Gustav
    Symphony No. 6 in A Minor, 84
        second movement, **74–75**
    Symphony No. 9
        second movement, 297n11

Malin, Yonatan, 295n1, 296n3
Margolis, Joseph, 306n30
Marinelli, Peter V., 53
Marston, Nicholas, 311n26
Massaro, Dominic, 101
Matthisson, Friedrich, 55
McCabe, Viki, 99, 102, 298n5, 299n9
McClary, Susan, 4–5, 29, 267–68, 270, 272–73, 277, 292n5, 319n1
    Feminine Endings, 291n3
McCreless, Patrick, 308n11
McNeill, David, 95, 105–109, 171, 227
Mead, Andrew, 7
Meltzoff, A. N., 103
Mendel, Arthur, 297n2
Mendelssohn, Felix, 182, 315n4
Meyer, Leonard B., 4, 6, 10, 23, 115, 116, 117, 239, 282, 291n5, 303n11, 304n16, 306n30, 307nn3,7, 308n12, 316n4, 319n1
Mirka, Danuta, 12
Momigny, Jérôme-Joseph de, 23
Monelle, Raymond, 9, 68, 164, 230, 309n16, 320n9
Monteverdi, Claudio
    L'incoronatione di Poppea, 312n40
Moore, Stephen, 306n35
Mozart, Leopold, 140, 295n3.1
Mozart, Wolfgang Amadeus, 140, 145, 178, 249, 309n15, 310n21
    Don Giovanni, 312n40, 317n3
    Fantasy and Fugue in C major, K. 394, **252–53**
    The Magic Flute, **13–15**
    The Marriage of Figaro, 295n3.1
    Piano Sonata in D Major, K. 284
        third movement (finale), **70–72**
    Piano Sonata in A Minor, K. 310
        first movement, **241–42,** 307n5
        third movement (finale), 187, **241, 243–44,** 318n5
    Piano Sonata in D Major, K. 311
        second movement, **142–44**
    Piano Sonata in B♭ Major, K. 333
        second movement, 311n33
    Piano Sonata in C Minor, K. 457, **152–56, 164–65**
        first movement, 135, 164, 312n39
        third movement (finale), **152–56, 164–65,** 177, 216, 239
    Symphony No. 36 in C Major (*Linz*), K. 425
        third movement, **75–76,** 223, 320n11
    Symphony No. 38 in D Major (*Prague*), K. 504
        first movement, 305n29, 308n11

Symphony No. 41 in C Major (*Jupiter*),
K. 551
first movement, 135, 164, 225

Narmour, Eugene, 239, 307n3, 308n8, 309n20
Nespoulous, Jean-Luc, 106, 109, 300n15
Neumeyer, David, 296n7
Newcomb, Anthony, 297n11
Newman, William S., 301n3, 308n8

O'Brian, Patrick, 300n17

Papousek, Hanus, 299n13
Parker, Mara, 308n8
Patel, Aniruddh D., 300n16
Pearson, Charles, 320n3
Peirce, Charles Sanders, 10, 12, 14, 15, 102,
105, 110, 122, 125, 293n10
Penderecki, Krzysztof, 12
Peretz, Isabelle, 300n16
Pierce, Alexandra, 1, 7, 118, 126–31, 186, 202,
288, 306nn32,37, 307n2
Pierce, Roger, 124, 306n37, 309n18
Poggioli, Renato, 54
Port, Robert F., 100
Pressler, Menachem, 300n1
Pribram, Karl H., 99
Proust, Marcel, *Remembrance of Things
Past*, 98

Quantz, Johann Joachim, 140, 301n7, 312n35

Rameau, Jean Philippe, 114
Ratner, Leonard G., 43, 94, 173, 282, 314n58,
320n9
Reich, Steve
Different Trains, 131
Repp, Bruno H., 119, 128, 306n33
Réti, Rudolph, 23
Richards, Annette, 314n58
Richter, Jean Paul, 313n 46, 317n8, 321n4
Riemann, Hugo, 114
Ries, Ferdinand, 133
Rink, John, 307n2, 317n10.5
Robinson, Paul, 54
Rosch, Eleanor, 298n5, 304n22
Rosen, Charles, 55, 56, 140, 149, 172, 203, 259,
265, 278, 296n8, 307n2, 309n13, 311n31,
314n53, 318n11.1, 319n9
Rosenblum, Sandra, 115, 133, 137, 310n21,
315n7
Rothfarb, Lee, 114, 301nn4,6
Rothstein, William S., 118, 129, 314n48, 317n5
Rudolph, Prince, 319n11

Sacks, Oliver, 101, 102, 104
Samarotto, Frank, 314n49
Samuels, Robert, 75
Saussure, Ferdinand de, 11
Schachter, Carl, 117, 307n5
Scheibe, Johann Adolf, 308n11
Schenker, Heinrich, 23, 93, 116, 118, 124, 127–
30, 172, 277, 292n7, 314n52
The Art of Performance, 294nn1,4,
305n23
Schiller, Johann Christoph Friedrich, 55,
312n38, 314n58
Schindler, Anton F., 308n11, 313nn44,47
Schlegel, Friedrich, 54
Schmalfeldt, Janet, 307n2
Schnittke, Alfred, 278
Schoenberg, Arnold, 3, 23, 177–78, 308n12,
315n1
Schubart, Christian Friedrich Daniel, 65–66
Schubert, Franz, 249, 296nn4,6,7, 297n9
Adagio and Rondo in E Major, D. 505/6, 151
Fierrabras, finale of act 1, Fierrabras's recita-
tive and aria (scene 9), **190–91**
Impromptus, D. 935, 296n4
Piano Sonata in A Minor, D. 537
first movement, **58–59**
second movement, 315nn5,11
Piano Sonata in E♭, D. 567 [rev. 1826], first
movement, **16–18**
Piano Sonata in A Major, D. 664, second
movement, **140–41**
Piano Sonata in A Minor, D. 784, **187–200,**
201, 208, 212, 223, 287, 289
first movement, 58, **187–194,** 221
second movement, **194–98**
third movement (finale), **198–200,
222–23**
Piano Sonata in C Major (*Reliquie*), D. 840,
65–66
Piano Sonata in A Minor, D. 845, 65–66
second movement, **111–12,** 318n5
fourth movement (finale), 187, **245–47**
Piano Sonata in D Major, D. 850, 65–66
Piano Sonata in G Major, D. 894, **53–67,** 247
first movement, **56–61**
second movement, **62–63**
third movement, **62–64**
fourth movement (finale), **64–66**
Piano Sonata in C Minor, D. 958
fourth movement (finale), 318n5
Piano Sonata in A Major, D. 959, 62, 217,
223, 239, 311n30
continuity draft for the first movement,
180, 182

first movement, **150–51,** 164, 178, **180–84, 185,** 289, 296n8

second movement, **183–185,** 223, 316n14

third movement, **185**

fourth movement (finale), **26, 28, 183–84**

Piano Trio in E♭ Major, D. 929, 296n4

Waltz in E Major, D. 145, no. 12, **71, 73,** 223, 297n12

Winterreise, 151, 220–21, 225

"Der Lindenbaum," 56

Schultz, J. A. P., 139

Schumann, Robert, 25, 186, 247, 317n8, 318n6, 319n9

Carnaval, Op. 9, finale, **71, 73,** 297n12

Davidsbündlertänze, Op. 6, 55

Fantasie, Op. 17, 321n4

Kreisleriana, Op. 16, 121–22

Papillons, Op. 2, 297n12

Schwarz, David, 319n10

Scruton, Roger, 305n30

Searle, John R., 13, 224

Sebeok, Thomas A., 298n1

Selfridge-Field, Eleanor, 309n20

Shakespeare, William, 54

Hamlet and *Macbeth,* 21

Sheinberg, Esti, 317n9.5

Shellenberg, G., 299n13

Shostakovich, Dmitri, 317n9.5

Shove, Patrick, 128

Shuring, D. J., 99

Sibelius, Jean, 296n6

Sievers, Eduard, 128

Silverman, Kaja, 319n10

Sisman, Elaine, 296n2, 308n11, 312n38

Smith, Linda, 100–101, 102, 107

Solomon, Maynard, 295n3.2, 317n8

Sonneck, Oscar G. T., 133

Spitzer, Michael, 308n8

Staiger, Emil, 296n4

Stamitz, Johann, 295n3.1

Stanley, Glenn, 313n45

Stebbins, Genevieve, 105

Stern, Daniel N., 103, 107

Stokoe, William C., 300n14

Strauss, Richard

Salome, 222

Stravinsky, Igor, 120, 278

The Rite of Spring, 13

Sudnow, David, 120

Sulzer, Johann Georg, 138–39

Tarasti, Eero, 95, 225, 229–30, 296n6, 298n1, 320n9

Taruskin, Richard, 13

Taub, Robert, 311n31

Thayer, Von Alexander Wheelock, 309n15

Thelen, Esther, 100–101, 102, 107

Theocritus

Idylls, 54

Tononi, Giulio, 299n11

Tootell, R. B. H., 300n18

Trehub, S., 299n13

Treitler, Leo, 4

Trevarthen, Colwyn, 97, 103–104, 299n13

Truslit, Alesander, 128

Türk, Daniel Gottlob, 138, 155, 307n5, 310n21

Turner, Mark, 97, 297n1

Turvey, Michael T., 98, 99, 107, 171

Tye, Michael, 98, 298n3

Uexküll, Jakob von, 298n1

Uexküll, Thure von, 298n1

Ullmann, Lisa, 306n35

van Gelder, Timothy, 100

Viereck, Peter, 94

Wagner, Naphtali, 307n6

Walker, Janice, 305n24

Wang, Huei-Ming, 316n4

Weber, Gottfried, 310n24

Weill, Kurt, 131

Weiskrantz, Lawrence, 298n3

Wellbery, David E., 54

Wendt, Amadeus, 314n58

Wheelock, Gretchen, 320n12.2

Wilcox, Sherman E., 300n14

Wilde, Oscar, 222

Will, Richard, 295n3.1

Williams, C., 99

Williams, Peter, 68

Wolff, Konrad, 307n4

Young, Andy, 101

Zbikowski, Lawrence M., 97, 297n1, 304n22

Zenck, Martin, 313n43

Zuckerkandl, Victor, 114, 202

Index of Concepts

Abnegation, 31, 143, 261, 294n3
Abstract pointing (D. McNeill), 106, 227
Abstraction, abstract types (D. Lidov)
  vs. generalization, 122
  vs. immediacy of gesture, 122
Accent, accentuation, 114, 137–38
  initiating a slur, 137, 140
  Koch's categories of, 137–38
  offbeat, gestural development of, 311n28
  Türk's hierarchy of, 138
Aesthetic, 6
  vs. critical, 8
  and ideological, 13
  "resisting," 291n4
  Sulzer on expression, 138–39
Affect, affective, 93
  associations, 97
  attunement (D. Stern), 102–103, 107
  categorical (D. Stern), 103
  precision of, for music, 182
  vitality (D. Stern), 103
Affektenlehre, 196
Agent, agency in music, 16. *See also* Dialogue;
  Intention; Musical forces
  actant and negactant (E. Tarasti, from
    A. J. Greimas), 225
  biographical evidence, 224–25
  coherent subjectivity, 270
  "deactorializing" process (E. Tarasti), 296n6
  emerging individual subjectivity, 290
  external, 30, 47, 172, 271, 315n13
  fragmented/shattered subjectivity
    (S. McClary), 237, 267, 277
  fusion vs. separation, 225
  gestural, 125, 224–32
  implied, 29, 139, 233
  interaction with virtual environmental con-
    straints, 115–16, 303nn10–13
  interchangeable, 232
  internal vs. external, 230–31, 315–16n13
  modern subjectivity, 33
  multiple, 228
  narrative, 165, 216, 230–32, 317nn5,7
  negative, 194
  as orator (G. Barth), 165, 301n8

  persona (E. T. Cone), 180, 184, 230
  reversal of roles, 232
  "schizophrenic postmodern subject"
    (S. McClary), 267, 277
  Self, as construction, 291n4
  self-willed, 146, 172, 192, 230
  shifts among levels of, 318n10.8
  singular, protagonist, 30, 47
  split between two gestural fields, 228–29
  subject, 182
  super-subjectivity, 231–32
  types of, 225–26
  willed vs. unwilled, 316n13
Allegory, 89, 164
  spiritual, 254
Alteroception (C. Trevarthen), 103
Amelioration
  gestural, 193
  motivic, 222–23, 255
  tonal, 198, 258, 319n12
Analog, 113, 124. *See also* Continuity
Analogy, 9, 117, 240, 299n11, 303nn10,13,
  321n4
Apex, 248
Apotheosis, 254, 284
Arabesque (E. Hanslick), 224, 290, 321n4
  bodily, 203
Arbitrary, arbitrariness of association, 15, 106
Arrival six-four, 24–28, 169, 192
  as initiation, 24
  pedestal effect, 24, 26
  tragic, 316n3
Arrival six-three, 26, 28
Ars combinatoria, 71, 203, 268
Articulation, musical, 115. *See also* Accent; Slur
  abrupt/choked off release, 156, 198
  bowing, 142
  gestural, 142–50
  illusion of *legato,* 121
  incises, 145
  inner articulation of legato melody, 145
  legato, 140, 142–45, 147–50, 222, 309n15,
    310n23, 311n31, 315n5
  levels of, 94
  "natural," 142

non *legato,* 140, 147–50
portamento, 311n31
portato, 147–50, 156, 191, 221, 311n31
rhetorical, 310n22
staccato, 140, 147–50, 311n31
transition (modulation) from detached to connected, 149, 311n31
Articulation of types into subtypes, 16
Association, 7, 12–13
Auditory scene analysis (A. Bregman), 298n4
Ausbruck (vs. *Ausdruck*), 10
Autism as intersubjective disorder (C. Trevarthen), 104
Autonomy, autonomous work, 34, 291n4
Avant-garde music, 120, 186

Background, backgrounding, 9, 113, 127, 215, 245, 305n29
Basic-level categories (E. Rosch, L. Zbikowski), 118, 302n22
Binary opposition, binarism, 9–10, 32
flexible approach, 14–16
logic of alterity, 32
mechanistic approach, 12–13
Biographical evidence, 224–25, 317n2
Blindsight (L. Weiskrantz), 298n3
Bricolage, 71

Canon, 291n3
Category, categorization
alternative to, 99
basic level (music), 304n22
perception-action (E. Thelen and L. Smith), 100
perceptual, 32
prelinguistic and embodied, 97
topical (music), 151
Cause-and-effect, 12, 108, 109, 294n11
Cognition, cognitive, 11, 99, 292n6. *See also* Concept; Embodiment, embodied image schemata
Coherence, coherent
of dramatic trajectory, 270, 277
of dynamic/dramatic oppositions, 240
gestural, 89
higher-level, 239
perceptual, 239
thematic, 178
structural, 117
subjectivity, 270
systematic, 287
of systematic oppositions, 24
Communicative economy (L. Kramer), 33
Comparative analysis, 5

Compensation, 194, 240, 304n16
Competent, competency
biological, 95
defined for musical style, 306n1
perceptual, cognitive, 95
prelinguistic, 97
social, 95
stylistic, 6, 8, 33
Composers' pulses (M. Clynes), 119, 123–24, 126
Concept
alternative to concepts, 99
cognitive, 32
Congruence of musical elements (L. B. Meyer), 23. *See also* Noncongruence
Consciousness, characteristics of, 299n11
Constraints
on choices within a style (L. B. Meyer), 6, 292n5
on gestural troping, 136
Content, musical (H. Schenker), 23
Context, contextual, contextualization
of culture, 8
of gesture, 124
of music history, 4
of musical meaning, 5
Contiguity, 12, 294n11
Continuity, 3, 47, 51, 94, 282
across breaks in sound, 124, 239
defined for musical texture, 248
dramatic, 4, 240
of events as flow patterns, 102
expressive crux diffused by, 248
of gesture, 30, 112, 123, 187, 233–34
"hierarchy of continuities," 239
leading to trance, 249, 319n10
legato, 145, 223
of level composed of regularly patterned, discrete units (as "grain"), 239
of plenitude, 249–66
of texture, 39, 173, 237, 240–49
timelessness, 47
Convention, conventional, 12, 292n5
cadences, 140
"counterconventions" (McClary), 268
originality as adaptation of, 134, 307n7
Romantic approach to (L. B. Meyer), 319n1
ritualized, 106
self-awareness of, 278
as transformed by Beethoven, 277
Correlation, correlational, 2, 12–14, 24, 136, 224
Criticism, critical
(J. Kerman), 4

vs. aesthetic, 8
   poetic (R. Schumann), 277
Cross-domain mapping, 101. *See also* Embodied, image schemata; Metaphor
Crux. *See* Expressive crux
Cultural meaning, 6
Cultural practice (L. Kramer), 4, 12
   historical sense, 33
Culture, cultural, 9, 12
   communicative competencies, 103
   evolution in brain, 299n12

Dance meters, 106
Dance types and topics
   in Bach fugues, 297n2
   Baroque, classical, 119, 304n19
   Deutcher Tanz, 39, 223, 296n7
   gavotte, 70–72
   gigue, 58, 63, 68–70, 71–72
   Ländler, 39, 56, 62, 74–75, 111, 199, 268, 296n7, 297n11
   minuet, 75–76, 223, 265, 268, 320n7
   musette, 62, 64–65, 183, 217, 220
   rhythmic gestures of (W. Allanbrook), 119
   rustic/folk, 183, 220
   siciliano, 56, 58–59, 162, 204, 296n7
   tarantella, 318n5
   waltz, 58–59, 62–63, 223, 248, 296n7, 297n11
Deception in music, 95
Deconstruction, 4–5, 32, 164
   of structure-expression opposition, 9–11
Deictic, deixis, 104–6, 227, 294n11
Developing variation (A. Schoenberg), 2, 3, 308n12
   gestural, 177–216
   identity of idea across variation, 180
Diachronic, 106
Diagrammatic (C. S. Peirce), 12
Dialectic, dialectical opposition of. *See also* Methodological dialectic
   gestures, 204
   inversion of thematic gesture, 143
   movements in a work 201, 208 (*see also* Expressive doubling)
   themes, 18, 29, 51, 180
   topic and theme, 316n3
Dialogical (M. M. Bakhtin), 317n4
Dialogue, dialogical, for music. *See also* Gesture (musical), dialogical
   climax, 275
   of different agencies or voices, 139, 164, 210–12, 270, 308n9, 313n44
   dissonance vs. consonance, 172

four kinds of, in Classical string quartet (M. Parker), 308n8
   by imitation, 143
   leading to (or from) integration, 164
   loud vs. soft, 172
   pairing of themes, 16, 164, 180
   play of agencies, 225, 231–32
   registrally marked, 313n45
   topical, 71, 210
Discontinuity, 3, 47, 51, 223
   digital, discrete (vs. analog), 113
   in musical discourse, 237, 267–78, 292n7 (*see also* Reversal; Rhetoric; Shift in level of discourse)
   of temporality, 268
   in verbal discourse, 106
Discourse, musical, 139
   dramatic, 16, 29
   thematic gesture as subject of, 135
   unfolding motivic, 203
   unmarked, 269
Discrete, 113, 124
   alternation with continuous in perceptual hierarchy, 239
   mechanism of piano keys, 121
Dissociation, 39, 42, 228
   and integration (J. Kerman), 51
Doubling (chordal), 193–94
Drama, dramatic
   enacted, 29
   trajectory in opening theme, 168
Dynamic systems theory, 99–100
   movement as perceptual system, 101
Dynamic vectors, music (M. Imberty), 103
Dynamics, music, 115
   calando, 151
   cross-currents as rhetorical, 146
   decrescendo vs. *diminuendo*, 119, 151
   dialogical play of loud vs. soft, 172
   morendo, 151
   rhetorical role of, 215–16, 227–28
   theoretical application (J. J. Quantz), 312n35
   smorzando, 151
Dynamics of event, 97–98

Ecological perception, 99
Elliptical structure, 23
Embodiment, embodied
   experience, 121
   expressiveness, 290
   embodied image schemata (G. Lakoff, M. Johnson), 101
   meaning/interpretation, 1, 6–7, 116

motion/movement, 117, 124, 202
  performance, 186, 227
  vs. rigid notion of, 299n7
  vs. situatedness, 303n10
Emergence, emergent, 1, 2, 3, 4, 7, 16, 94, 117,
  125, 139, 305n30
  affect, 150, 287
  coherent sentiment, 301n7
  expressivity, 112
  of gestural character from performance of
    abstract composition, 186
  of gesture into thematized gesture, 122
  illusion of, 15
  of laminated motive, 245
  of meanings from sensations, 108
  of musical process or theme (L. B. Meyer),
    306n30
  of perceptual-motor pattern, 100
  three kinds (for aesthetics of music),
    305n30
  of tropological meaning, 220–21, 297n1
Emotion
  basic types, 299n8
  as interpretation of motion, 123
Empfindsamkeit, empfindsamer, 39–40, 70,
  152, 156, 200, 239, 311n31
Energetics (E. Kurth, L. Rothfarb), 113–14
Envelope, 124
Event cognition, 99–100, 102, 298n5
  events as integral wholes, 102
Exemplification (N. Goodman), 233, 318nC.1
Expectation. See Implication
Expression
  as opposed to structure, 9–11, 292n8
  and structure, 23, 136
  as translation of structure, 9
Expressive crux, 30–31, 47–49, 157
  diffused, 248
Expressive doubling (L. Kramer), 39–43, 51,
  82, 201, 206
  as Derridean supplement, 82
Expressive genre, 25, 51, 177, 194, 292n7,
  294n3
  comic, 210–12, 231–32
  fantasia as Masonic journey (A. Richards),
    314n58
  pastoral, 67, 220
  non-tragic, 25
  tragic, 156, 187–200, 270–77, 280
  tragic-to-transcendent, 280–86
  tragic-to-triumphant, 254
  trajectory of, 290
  transcendent goal, 31
  undercutting of transcendence, 208

Expressive resolution, 194
Expressive timing, 119, 305n24
Extramusical meaning (as intrinsic), 33

Fantasia, fantasie, 65, 314n58. See also
  Phantasie
Feminist approaches to music, 4, 11
Figures of the body (R. Barthes), 121, 124
Fingering, 305n23
Firstness, Secondness, Thirdness (C. S. Peirce),
  102, 105, 125, 224, 305n30, 320n1
Foreground, foregrounding, 9, 15, 113, 116,
  124, 127, 129, 215, 305n29, 320nC.2
  of gesture as thematic, 123, 135
  of unmarked cadence as thematic (strategi-
    cally marked), 140–41
Formalist, 28
Framing, 152, 312n36, 317n6
Fugue, plenitude as fulfillment in, 249–66
Functional coherence, 97–98, 102, 171
Fuzzy set, 150

Galant style, 64, 68, 164, 241, 265, 282
  sigh as galant gesture, 141–42
  weak-beat cadence, 140
Generalization, 7
Generative code, 9
Generous movement (A. and R. Pierce), 124
Genre, 1, 314n58, 318n5. See also Expressive
  genre
Gestalt. See also Synthesis
  dynamic wholes, 301n6, 304n22
  identity, 233
  law of good continuation, 116, 303n13
  temporal, 101–102
Gesture, gestural (human), 1, 119
  accompanying speech (paralinguistic),
    104–107, 109
  biological aspects, 97–98, 234, 290
  cognitive aspects, 98–104, 234
  foundational principles, 97–110
    summarized, 109–110
  sign language, 105, 299n14
  vocal (intonational curves in language),
    106–107, 109, 118, 300n17
Gesture, gestural (musical), 1, 2, 3, 7, 18, 30,
  32, 93–234, 294n14, 295nn4,5. See also
  Agent; Developing variation, gestural;
  Intonation curves; Performance; Trope;
  Reversal
  amelioration of, 194
  "articulated" gesture, 178–84, 217–20, 223,
    289, 311n30
  beginning with closing, 317n6

characterized as, 124

choked-off, 156–57, 212

comic, 210, 232, 289

competency, aspects of, 124, 233, 320n1

competency, sources of, 234

continuity, 30, 112, 123, 305n23

dance, 8, 16

vs. default level of interpretation, 290

definitions, 93, 95, 100, 108, 112, 125, 301n2

derived from poetic or speech intonations, 131–32

dialogical, 125, 135–36, 157, 164, 210–11, 305n8

discrete vs. continuous, 115

embodied, 131–32, 226, 234

expressiveness as motivation for form/ structure, 123

"gestural time" (J. Kramer), 268

grieving, 187, 192, 289

harmonic (see Gesture [musical], rhetorical)

illusion of continuity for pianist, 113

interaction with musical syntax, 107

intentionality of, 112, 116, 300n2

"lift" gesture, 157, 162–63, 202, 204, 210–16

marked for significance (D. Lidov), 112, 125

meaning of, 288

motivation for form, 178

vs. movement, 301n2

opposition, 124 (see also Dialectic)

outline of music-gestural characteristics, 93–95

overlapping classes of gestural functions, 136–37, 175

pedagogy of movement, 126–31

performance, 111–12

pose, 288

posture, "under fermata," 126

prototypical, 101

qualitative character, 233–34

reverberant, 149–50, 194

rhetorical, 113, 125, 135, 155–57, 164–76, 212, 216, 227, 289, 308n11

significance of leitmotive, 307n6

spontaneous, 125, 135–36, 152, 157, 202, 210

strategic functions, 125, 134–36

"stretching," 82, 84–85, 89

stylistic types of, 125, 133–34, 136–38, 140–51, 176, 178, 202

syntactic function (opening vs. closing), 291n1

tactile, 149

thematic, 113, 122–23, 125, 132, 135–36, 157, 177–216

vs. "tonally sounding form" (E. Hanslick), 290

top-down integration, 118

topic as, 125, 307n6

topical development of, 216

trope, 142, 143, 217–24

tropological, 125, 135–37

tropological development of, 216

typology, 8

unconscious, 300n2

Grain (not R. Barthes), 102, 239, 248

Gravity. See Musical forces

Groove (C. Keil and S. Feld), 119–120, 126, 304n21

swing (jazz), 227

Grotesque, 317n5

Grounding interpretation, 21–34

in analytical evidence, 7, 22–24, 30–32

in historical context, 34

in intensity and shape, 132

intertextually, 120

in markedness, 24–25

in musical style, 6, 7–8, 24–29

Growth point (D. McNeill), 107–108, 171

Grundgestalt (A. Schoenberg), 3, 23, 178, 214, 289–90

Hermeneutic

approach to music interpretation, 2, 5, 12, 21, 267

component of music semiotics, 32

window (L. Kramer), 4, 15

Heroic, 169, 180, 192, 194, 197–98, 217, 220, 252, 316n13. See also Tragic, stoic-heroic response to

Heuristic, 7, 287

approach to performance, 120, 123, 130, 187

Hierarchy, hierarchical

alternation of closed units and open processive levels (L. B. Meyer), 239

of closures (L. B. Meyer), 115, 239

of continuities, 239

organization of gestures, 94, 124

and processive (L. B. Meyer), 10

tree, 3, 10

Hypermeasure (for waltz), 75

Icon, iconic, iconism (C. S. Peirce), 12, 106, 110, 122, 124, 177, 188, 287, 293n11

Iconographic representation of Satan as serpent, 196

Ideolect (L. B. Meyer), 282

Ideology, ideological

interpretation, 4–5, 7, 12

loaded oppositions, 32

Imagistic perception, 101
Immediacy, 102
Implication (L. B. Meyer), 116
    contradicting without contravening
        (meter), 117
    deferral or delayed realization of, 23, 126
    violation of, 117
Improvisation, improvisatory, 120, 201, 248
Index, indexical, indexicality (C. S. Peirce), 12,
    106, 110, 122, 124, 177, 188, 287, 293n11
Integration
    of disparate materials, 277–78
    dissociation and (J. Kerman), 268
    of gesture and speech, 105
    of motor activity and perception, 99
    perceptual, 97
    property of consciousness, 299n11
Integration, musical, 3, 139
    derivation of countersubject(s) from sub-
        ject, 250
    of musical gesture, 118
    of notated elements, 138
    textural (mirror inversion, *stretto*), 249–51
    thematic, 29, 89, 180, 199, 212, 252, 261,
        275, 315n12
    thematic, as dramatic resolution, 240
    topical (*see* Trope)
Intention, intentional, intentionality, 5, 7, 112–
    113, 293n9
    action, 99
    of gesture, 116, 117
    requiring semantic and pragmatic con-
        text, 130
Intermodality, 97, 100–101, 107–108, 127, 130–
    31, 142, 187, 288, 299n6, 315n5
    amodality, 100
    cross-modality, 100
    hypotheses, 107–108
Inter-movement relationships, 35–43, 82, 83,
    89, 217, 261, 319n12
Interpret, interpretation, 3, 4, 7, 12, 15–16, 24,
    30, 34, 290
    ideological, 13
Interpretant (C. S. Peirce), chain of, 10
Intersubjectivity (for music interpretation),
    intersubjective, 6, 97, 288–89
Intersubjectivity in human development
    (C. Trevarthen), 102–104, 309n14
    alteroception, 103
    perception and enactment of rhythm and
        contour, 104
Intertextuality, intertextual, 62, 120, 190, 202,
    241–42, 270, 305n27, 317n3. *See also* Inter-

movement relationships; Inter-work rela-
    tionships
Inter-work relationships, 35, 37, 201–202
Intonation curves, 106–107, 131–32, 300n16
Irony, ironic, 294n15. *See also* Romantic irony;
    Trope
    comic deflating, 201, 210, 225
    contradiction of text by music, 294n13
    dramatic, 222
    objectivity in Stravinsky, 120
    parodistic quotation, 317n3
Isomorphism, isomorphic, 293n11

Kinematic interpretation (A. Truslit), 128
Kinesthetic, 7, 122, 127, 187
Kinetic energy
    (E. Kurth), 114
    (A. Pierce), 129–30
Kunstvereinigung, 254, 319 n11

Language, developmental interactions preced-
    ing, 103
Language and music, prelinguistic competen-
    cies, 97, 299n13
Level of discourse. *See* Shift in level of dis-
    course
Liquidation (A. Schoenberg)
    "congealed" reduction to sustained val-
        ues, 263
    diminutional, 172, 254
    motivic, 50, 269, 272, 277
    motivic and accentual, 147
    topical (march into waltz), 76
Local knowledge (C. Geertz), 5

Markedness
    asymmetry, 11
    contrasts, 231
    definition of gesture as marked movement,
        112, 125, 186
    of events implying "new" meanings, 127
    as implied by accent, 138
    music examples of, 13–16, 24–25, 143, 150,
        155–56, 166, 171, 261, 265, 280
    oppositions, 8, 11–16, 110 (*See also* Opposi-
        tions)
    by reiteration/use, 152
    reversal, 143
    rhetorical, 165, 270
    strategic or thematic, 10, 15, 29, 152, 186
    stylistic, 166
    texture (perpetual motion), 240–49
    theory of, 11–16

unmarked continuity, 15
unmarked discourse, 269
unmarked flow of temporality, 239
unmarked metric flow, 146
(stylistically) unmarked raised (strategically) to marked, 140, 164, 216, 305n29, 312n37
unmarked slur, 137
unmarked syntactic progression, 289
unmarked texture, 172
unmarked theme, 169
McGurk illusion, 101
Mediacy
    temporal, 102
Melody
    energetic continuity, 301n6
    kinetic energy of
        (E. Kurth), 114
        (A. Pierce), 129
    as movement through pitch space, 239
    as prototypical temporal gestalt, 101–102
Memory, 98
    working, 101
Metaphor
    in language, 101
    vs. literal, 101
    in music, 16 (see also Trope)
    vs. musical troping, 297n1
Meter, metric
    accentual hierarchy, 147
    Classical hierarchy of weight, 309n13
    conflicting metrical expectations, 74–76
    critiques of meter as grid, 304n20
    dance-derived, 278
    dissonance, 319n9
    hypermeter, 127, 138
    hypermetric downbeat, 173
    internal weight for accent (G. Weber), 310
    kinematic implications (B. Repp), 119
    overlapping with grouping, 147
    potential metric closure as premise, 210
    space as grid (F. Lerdahl), 302n9
    vs. up-down orientation in dance, 304n19
    vectoral field, 119
    as virtual gravitational field, 115, 117, 125, 146, 202, 290
    warpings of metric timing and accent, 118–19, 227
    wave (V. Zuckerkandl), 202
Methodological dialectic
    between reconstructing a style and interpreting a work, 8
    between stylistic and strategic functions, 34

Microstructure, microstructural
    composers' pulses (M. Clynes), 119
    variations in performance, 118–19, 305n24
Modalities (A. J. Greimas, E. Tarasti), 95
    of action, 203
Motivation
    expressive, 28
    formalist, 28
    of gesture, 116
    iconic, indexical, symbolic, 287
    personal, 103
    of rhetorical by thematic gestures, 216
    of sequence of fugal techniques, 254–55
    strategic, 34
    stylistic, 34
    systematic, 12
    topical, 183
    for unusual tonal design, 192
Motive. See also Gesture (musical), thematic
    conformant relationships (L. B. Meyer), 308n12, 316n4
    detachable from a theme, 189, 203, 316n2
    scale-degree, 150
Musical forces
    beat attractions within metric grid (F. Lerdahl), 302n9
    biological urges (H. Schenker), 114
    dynamic (force) field (F.-J. Fétis, V. Zuckerkandl), 114
    "friction," 116
    gravity (J. P. Rameau, S. Larson), 114, 303n12
    implied/embodied/freely willing musical agent, 115–16
    inertia (S. Larson), 115–16, 303n13
    life force (H. Riemann), 114
    magnetism (S. Larson), 115–16, 303n12
    momentum, 116
    tonal environmental field, 116
    tonal pitch space (C. Brower, F. Lerdahl), 302n9
    vectoral space, 117
    virtual dynamics, 117
    virtual field forces, 103, 133, 301n6
    weighting of, 116
Musical meaning
    as defined in Hatten (1994), 287
    denotative and connotative, 130
    as essentialized, 5
    how vs. what, 21
    as mobile, contingent, 4
    multileveled, 278

Narrative, narrativity, 269. *See also* Agent
  master narrative of history, 5
  narratizing by gestural highlighting, 227
  performer as narrator, 317n5
  role of gesture, 95
Negative climax, 204
Neural networks, 98
New Musicology, 7, 33
Noncongruence (L. B. Meyer), 268, 272
Notation, musical
  exact placement of slurs, 310n21
  of gesture, 94–95, 113, 124
  implying gestures, 131, 133, 301n3
  as script (N. Cook), 131, 292n9

Objective historical meanings, 6. *See also* Intersubjectivity (for music interpretation)
Oppositions, 11–18. *See also* Binary opposition; Markedness
  vs. fixed meaning of each term, 15
  major vs. minor, 13–14, 55
  in structure and (correlated) affect, 240
  thematic, 29
Ostention, 294n11
Ostinato, 187, 208, 279, 282
Overtone effects, 62, 183
  Aeolian harp effect, 297n10
  on fortepiano, 315n7
  as gesture, 183–84

Parenthetical, 39, 65, 173, 194, 316n3
  Neapolitan expansion (in coda), 167–68,
    208, 212
  parenthetical enclosure (W. Kinderman), 269
  rhetorical, 230–31
Parkinson's disease, 102
Passus duriusculus, 68
Pastoral. *See also* Dance types and topics;
  Expressive genre; Trope
  arcadia, 273
  as expressive genre, 53–67, 201
  idealized space and time, 53
  idyll, 54, 296n2
  idyllic time, 111
  inner temporality and reflection, 54
  landscape, 55
  lost happiness or innocence, 54, 296n4
  lyric, 54
  as mode, 25, 53–67, 111, 273, 282
  musical features, 56, 64, 202, 250, 296n5
  oasis, 63, 206, 273, 282, 316n3, 318n4
  organic (E. Tarasti), 296n6
  past-orientation, 296nn2,4
  pastoral of the self, 54

programmatic symphonies, 295n3.1
simplicity, 53
sonority, 56, 314n50
stasis, 62, 77
  as style, 295n3.2
summary of features, 55–56
  as topic, 28, 111, 166, 168–69, 190, 295n3.1
undercuttings, 202
"visions" (E. Sisman), 296n2
Pedagogy of movement and gesture (A.
  Pierce), 7, 118, 124–31, 186
  arcing, 129
  arm swings (metric), 128
  climax, 129
  coalescence, 128
  contouring, 127–28
  middleground vitality, 128
  performance phrases, 129
  as Schenkerian, 126–30
  spanning, 129
  stepping, 128
  tone of voice, 129, 130, 288
Pedaling, 305n23, 311n31
  moderator, 194
  over-Romantic, 183, 316n15
Perception, perceptual. *See also* Category;
  Synthesis
  alteroception (C. Trevarthen), 103
  categorical, 98
  ecological, 99
  exteroception, 98, 103
  imagistic and temporal, 101–102, 108
  integration, 97
  movement as perceptual system, 101
  proprioception, 98, 103
Performance, performer, 7. *See also* Heuristic;
  Pedagogy of movement and gesture
  approach, 292n9
  bias for pitch-oriented development of ges-
    ture, 183
  bias for Romantic School legato and
    pedal, 183
  discipline of performance studies
    (J. Dunsby), 307n2
  embodied, 124, 186
  expressive nuances, 3, 130
  influence of large-scale motivic connection
    on gestural interpretation, 307n5
  not prescribed, 118, 187
  overly didactic, 167
  Schenker, treatise on, 294n1, 294–95n4,
    305n23
Performance practice, 115, 119, 134, 186
  conventions of, 155

Performative approach (W. Coker, N. Cook), 224, 293n9, 305n28, 317n1

Perpetual motion. *See* Texture, perpetual motion

Persona. *See* Agent

Phantasie (for Beethoven), 65, 270, 295n2.2

Phenomelogy, phenomenological, 114, 320nC.2
  vs. semiotic, 121
  vs. systematic, 287

Phrase, phrase structure, 29, 39, 42, 59, 61, 62, 302n9
  additive/paratactic, 246, 248
  definition of phrase (W. Rothstein), 129
  effect of thematic labyrinth, 247
  expansion, 82, 111, 172–73, 241
  interpolation enhancing continuity, 241
  less-hierarchical four-bar construction, 319n9
  out of phase with meter, 302n9
  recycling, 241, 246
  Schenkerian interpretation, 118

Pilgrim's processional. *See* Topic/style; Trope

Plenitude, 1, 4, 35, 43–52, 59–60, 62, 67, 172, 201, 204, 210, 212, 237, 247, 319n12
  as premise, 249–66

Pluralism, 33

Poetry, 131, 196

Popular music, 118, 120

Positivist musicology, 5

Postmodernism, postmodernist
  as critical approach (L. Kramer), 4–6, 32–33
  fragmentation of subject, 237
  vs. modernism, 278
  musical style (J. Adams), 120

Premise for musical work (D. Epstein)
  expressive, 4
  plenitude, 35, 43–52
  tragic, 198

Presence (S. Burnham), 29

Processive strands vs. structural segments of music, 114–15

Program, programmatic meaning, 21

Proportional tempo, 314

Prototype, prototypical
  gesture, 101, 157
  melody as prototypical temporal gestalt, 101
  non-prototypical topics, 278–86
  underlying variants of melody, 309n20

Psychoanalytical approach to music, 33, 319n10

Quotation. *See* Inter-movement relationships; Intertextuality

Recitative chord, 48, 231

Reconstruction
  of historical gestural language, 120
  of ideological stance, 7
  of meaning, 5, 6
  of relation of classical music to modern subjectivity, 33
  of style, 6–7
  of style growth and change, 290
  of stylistic competency, 33, 290, 293n9

Reference, referents
  vs. referential precision in music, 182

Reflection (Romantic), 183

Reflexivity
  self-reflexive agency, 47, 51–52

Representation
  and expression, 229, 304n18, 317n6
  musical, 186
  near-immediate, 98
  topographic, 98

Resignation, 31, 206, 208, 261, 319n12. *See also* Abnegation

Resonance, 184. *See also* Overtone effects
  spiritual association of, 186

Reverberant effect, 62, 193, 288. *See also* Overtone effects

Reversal, 47, 49, 136, 169–76, 192–93. *See also* Abnegation; Implication; Shift in level of discourse
  chromatic, 30, 143
  climactic, 111
  comic (deflation), 168–69, 263, 268
  dynamic, 215–16
  gesture of radical annihilation, 169
  intervallic (inversion), 180
  melodic (E. Narmour), 308n8
  modal, 316n16
  of Phrygian half cadence, 182
  registral, 180
  rhetorical tonal, 208
  syntactic/scale-degree, 168, 169, 171–72, 192, 282, 289, 294n2
  tonal (key), 192
  topical, 173, 194, 221
  tragic, 32
  undercutting, 31, 169, 207, 263, 265, 268
  yielding, 31

Rhetoric, rhetorical. *See also* Gesture (musical), rhetorical; Reversal; Shift in level of discourse
  accent, 136, 138–39
  culminating thematic integrative techniques, 250, 252
  Classical style, 308n11

comic interpolations in Haydn, 313n46
doubling, 295n2.2
dynamic cross-currents, 146
dynamic highlighting, 227–28
German tradition (1550 to 1800), 308n11
gesture, 95, 125, 135, 164–76
harmony, harmonic, 26, 165–66, 227–28,
   260, 263, 265
in *pathétique* style, 312n38
rest or pause, 26, 173, 227, 260, 288,
   308n11, 313n47
rhythmic, 295n4
stylistically encoded, 227
tonal shift, 167–68, 212, 230–31, 317n6
topical shift, 168
underlining, 313n47
Romantic irony, 137, 171, 216, 270, 285
Rubato, 114, 123, 165, 227, 294nn1,4, 313n47
Rule as regularity or generalization, 304n16

Satz ("sentence" phrase structure), 29, 59, 248
   defined, 318n8
Scheme, schemata (M. Johnson), 97
   vs. event cognition, 99, 298n5
Science, scientific
   illusion of scientific objectivity, 5
   interdisciplinary insights from, 97–110
Semiology. *See also* Semiosis; Semiotics of music
   embodied gesture vs. discrete semiology
      (R. Barthes), 121
   meaning as difference (F. de Saussure), 11
Semiosis (C. S. Peirce), 10, 12, 15, 293n10,
   305n28
   chain of interpretants, 10, 15, 229, 293n10
   diagrammatic, 12, 293n11
   Firstness, Secondness, Thirdness, 102, 105,
      224, 305n30, 320n1
   icon, index, symbol, 12, 106, 110, 122, 124,
      177, 188, 287, 293n11
   interpretant, 293n10
   type, token, 12, 21, 24, 34, 108, 133–34
Semiotics of music, 7
   illustration of semiotic approach, 21–34
Sensorimotor system, 97
   perceptual-motor reactive loops, 98
Sentic forms/shapes (M. Clynes), 105, 123, 184
Sequence type (musical), 169
   deceptive, 173, 197
   elevation or transfiguration, 173
Shift in level of discourse, 35, 47–48, 51–52,
   137, 169, 216, 231, 269, 272, 295n1
   lateral, 171
   parabasis, 321n4
Shifters (R. Jakobson), 106

Sigh, 140–42, 152, 200, 272, 279, 288
   origin as *pianto,* 309n16
   single-note (*Suspiratio*), 156, 228, 312n40
Signifying, field of (R. Barthes), 121–22
Similarity, 12. *See also* Icon
Sketch history
   for Beethoven (Op. 130), 35–36
   for Schubert (continuity draft, D. 959, I),
      180, 182
Slur, 137, 140–47
   against motivic grouping or phrase bound-
      ary, 310n25
   exact placement, 310n21
   from an upbeat, 147
   hierarchy of gestural nuances, 142–45
   interior articulation of longer slur,
      310nn21,22
   two-note (two-event), 140–42
Somasthemes (R. Barthes), 121. *See also*
   Figures of the body
Sonata form
   alternative sites of drama, 51
   boundaries of second theme, Op. 109, I, 172
   compensatory strategy, 194
   with "Fantasie" title, 247
   pre-development in exposition, D. 959, I, 183
   as problematic interpretation of form,
      Op. 130, III, 50
Sound, four fundamental properties, 102
Spatial imagination (J. Levinson), 303n15
Strategic interpretation
   as token of a stylistic type, 24, 133
Strategy, strategic (L. B. Meyer), 10
   functions of musical gesture, 134–36
   of tonal motion, 127
   type, 278
Structuralism, structuralist, 2, 21, 267
   component of music semiotics, 32
   linguistics as model, 121
Structure, structural
   and expression, 3, 136
   and ideological, 13
   as generative code, 9
   as opposed to expression, 9–11, 292n8
Style, stylistic, 6, 7. *See also* Markedness,
   stylistic
   change, 6, 25–28, 241, 247, 291n5, 318n6
   choice (L. B. Meyer), 292n5
   competency (defined), 6, 306n1
   constraint, 6, 8, 291n4
   correlation, 24
   growth, 2, 6, 8, 16, 25–28, 134, 291n5
   high (register), 173
   principle, 291n4

reconstruction of, 6
topic, 1
type, 1, 21–34, 108, 133–34, 142, 167, 173,
    240, 249, 307n3
Subjective bodily responses, 7
Subjectivity. *See* Agent
Sublimation of gesture into motive
    (D. Lidov), 122
Sublime, 32, 55, 67, 314n58
    in reverse (J. P. Richter), 313n46
Supplement (J. Derrida), 13, 82
Surface (musical), 15
Symbol (C. S. Peirce), 106, 110, 122, 125,
    177, 188
    symbolic level, 12
Synecdoche, 294n11
System (for music). *See also* Dynamic systems
    theory; Sensorimotor system
    analysis, 5
    vs. body, 122
    growth in a style, 8
    motivation for association, 12
Syntax, music-stylistic
    play with regulative syntax, 118
    reversal, 169, 171
Synthesis, synthetic, 1–4, 102, 112, 216, 287–
    88. *See also* Integration
    gestalts, 94, 304n22
    gestural, 134
    intermodal, 108
    of microstructural variations in perfor-
        mance, 118
    of separately notated elements in perfor-
        mance, 134, 138, 301n7
    topics as prefabricated, 134, 233

Taxonomy, 5
Temporality, shift in, 268
    temporal plane, 314n49
    troping of, 320n3
Text (musical work as), 4, 6
    situated culturally, 4
Texture. *See also* Plenitude
    articulation of, 240
    continuity as marked, 240–49, 266
    continuity as thematic premise, 240–244
    lamination, 244
    monolithic, 230
    motet-style, 268
    perpetual motion, 187, 198–99, 210, 237,
        240–49, 282, 318nn5,6
    stretto, 249–51, 254, 258–62, 312n39
    thematization of move from discrete to con-
        tinuous, 247

undercutting, 136
Thematic, 95, 188. *See also* Gesture (musical),
    thematic; Strategy; Markedness, strategic or
    thematic
Thematic transformation, 71
Thematization, 117, 123, 247
Thick description, 5
Timbre, 102
    sequence of (*Klangfarbenmelodie*), 102
Token (C. S. Peirce), 12, 21, 24, 34, 108, 122,
    133–34, 157
Tonal rhythm (C. Schachter), 117
Tonal space
    vectoral field, 119
    virtual environmental forces in, 115
Topic/style (L. Ratner) 2, 3, 8, 287, 290, 292n7,
    294n17, 320n9. *See also* Dance types and
    topics; *Empfindsamkeit*; Galant style; Pas-
    toral; Plenitude; Trope
    aria, 272
    bagatelle, 173, 314n51
    bound, 241
    brilliant, 70, 272
    buffa or comic, 70, 151, 168–69, 268
    clockwork, 43, 48–49, 282
    dance of death, 75
    Empfindsamer, 70
    epic/balladic, 60
    etude, 318n6
    fanfare, 71, 192, 297n12
    fantasia, 169, 173, 208, 314
    French overture, 68–70
    funeral march (cortège), 187, 287, 315n10
    gavotte, 272
    as gestures, 307n6
    horn fifth, 220, 268
    hunting horn fanfare, 225–26
    hurdy-gurdy accompaniment, 278
    hymn, 71, 175, 190, 192
    lament bass, 38, 156, 272
    learned style, 70, 198, 224, 241, 280, 284
    march, 71, 76, 77, 82, 223, 272, 279–280,
        297n12, 320n4
    martial, 190
    motet, 271
    musette, 62, 64–65, 76, 224, 244
    noble/ceremonial march, 82, 84
    ombra, 168–69, 173
    pastoral, 28, 111, 168, 190, 192, 198, 224
    "pilgrims' processional," 71, 74, 77, 79, 81–
        82, 89
    recitative, 39, 272, 279
    rhetorical use of, 168
    riff (drumroll), 225, 232

singing style, 70, 278

Sturm und Drang, 155

transformation (imitative to homophonic), 254

Turkish march, 270

unclear identification, 278

unrelated topoi, 267

Topographic representation (neural), 98, 108, 298n2, 300n18

Tragic, 204, 206–208, 244, 316n3. *See also* Expressive genre

closure, 275–76

Fate, 271

and heroic, 204

peroration, 200

stoic-heroic response to, 157, 180, 184, 190

Transcendence, transcendent, 31, 111, 194, 206, 208, 248, 252, 284. *See also* Expressive genre

as emanating from beyond the body, 184

Triumphant. *See* Heroic

Trope, troping, tropological, 2, 3, 8, 15, 51, 125, 287, 290, 292n7. *See also* Gesture (musical), trope; Irony; Metaphor

constraints on gestural, 221

constraints on topical, 217, 220

creative, 16, 221, 297n1

cultural (L. Kramer), 4

as fusion of emotions, 222

as fusion of gestures, 222

at level of the discourse, 225

in nineteenth-century symphonies, 71–89

in operatic characterizations, 71

of repressed feeling and negated hope, 228–29

triggered by extreme juxtapositions, 270

Troping of expressive genres, 89

Troping of genres, 35, 51–52

Troping of topics

binary dance and concerto, 69–70

classical material functions, 156

classical materials with functional locations, 16

concertato and slow-movement textures, 309n19

dance and developmental styles, 16–18

expressive doubling (Beethoven), 39

fanfare and waltz, 71, 73, 223

fanfare, learned, and pastoral, 217

French overture, fugue, and gigue, 68–70

galant and lament-based themes, 68–69

galant and pastoral styles, 280

hymn, gigue, double-fugue, and chorale prelude, 71

influence of classical character variation on, 70–71

march and aria, 272

march and chorale, 71, 74 (*see also* Topic/style, "pilgrim's processional")

march and *Ländler,* 74–75

march and minuet, 75–76

march and pastoral, 217

march and scherzo, 74–75

march and waltz, 71, 73, 75

monumental/religioso march, 84

music box musette and *Ländler,* 62

pastoral and balladic, 58

pastoral and *buffa,* 210

pastoral and fanfare, 58

pastoral and hymn, 58, 192, 221

pastoral and learned, 58

pastoral/hymn and grieving gesture, 192

pastoral and waltz, 58–59, 62, 248

polka and chorale, 71, 74

singing and learned, 211

subject and countersubject, 68–69, 164

temporality, 320n3

three march-inflected ideas, 89

three reductive and rhythmic layers, 250

yielding harmonic progression and upward melodic leap, 147

Troping of topic(s) and genre(s), 1, 68–89

gestural vs. topical, 220

Type (C. S. Peirce), 12, 21, 24, 34, 108, 122. *See also* Style, type

generation, generalization, 12, 122, 134

vs. lexical status for music, 150

strategic, 278

Typology

of gestures, 8

Umwelt (J. von Uexküll), 298n1

Virtual field forces. *See* Meter; Musical forces

Voice (C. Abbate), 29. *See also* Agent; Dialogical; Dialogue

authoritative, 291n3

Work (musical). *See also* Text

vs. intersection of codes, 291n4

regulative concept of, 292n9

Yearning, 89, 228

Yielding, 31

yielding harmonic progression, 146–47, 206, 280, 316n3

Zen approaches, 98

Zoosemiotics (T. Sebeok), 298n1

ROBERT S. HATTEN is Professor of Music Theory in the Indiana University School of Music. He is the editor of the series Musical Meaning and Interpretation, and author of *Musical Meaning in Beethoven* (Indiana University Press, 1994), which was co-recipient of the Wallace Berry Book Award from the Society for Music Theory in 1997.

CPSIA information can be obtained
at www.ICGtesting.com
Printed in the USA
BVHW021532040619
549984BV00024B/458/P